Feminism and Psychoanalytic Theory

NANCY J. CHODOROW

Yale University Press
New Haven and London

First published 1989 in the United Kingdom by Polity Press
in association with Basil Blackwell.

Published 1989 in the United States by Yale University Press.

Library of Congress catalog card number: 89-51037

International standard book number: 0–300–04417–8 (cloth)
0–300–05116–6 (pbk.)

Printed in the United States of America

6   8   10   9   7

Contents

For Rachel and Gabriel

Preface

I have been privileged over the years to be supported by many friends and colleagues. The chapters in this work acknowledge some of these people, but such individual acknowledgment does not fully indicate the extent of my overarching personal gratitude and intellectual debts. Susan Contratto, my co-author in chapter 4, has been a close friend and intellectual colleague and critic since our undergraduate years, as was the late Michelle Z. Rosaldo. I also received sustained personal support and intellectual engagement as I developed these essays from Elizabeth Abel, Rose Laub Coser, Barbara Laslett, Sherry Ortner, Barrie Thorne and Abby Wolfson. It has been important that several people read, listened, and simply believed in my work, and I think especially of Janet Adelman, Nathan Hale, Ravenna Helson, Arlie Hochschild, Neil Smelser and Robert Wallerstein. My husband, Michael Reich, has seen me through this work intellectually and emotionally, and I have not made it easy to do so.

Individual chapters also acknowledge institutional support. Here, I note that the Institute of Personality Assessment and Research, University of California, Berkeley, provided a welcoming institutional home at a time when I felt very much in institutional limbo, although its members meant to be providing a home for a different endeavor than the one in these pages.

Anthony Giddens at Polity Press thought to suggest that I collect and publish these essays and supported their publication enthusiastically. Gladys Topkis of Yale University Press was equally enthusiastic in undertaking their publication.

With the exception of chapter 1, the previously published essays in this volume have not been revised or updated except to correct minor errors. I must therefore make the usual apologies about unavoidable repetitions.

Acknowledgments

A number of the essays in the present collection were originally published elsewhere. The author and publishers are grateful for permission to use the following:

Being and Doing: A Cross-Cultural Examination of the Socialization of Males and Females
adapted from Vivian Gornick and Barbara K. Moran (eds), *Woman in Sexist Society: Studies in Power and Powerlessness* (New York, Basic Books). © 1971 by Basic Books, Inc.

Family Structure and Feminine Personality
originally in Michelle Zimbalist Rosaldo and Louise Lamphere (eds), *Woman, Culture and Society*, (Stanford, Stanford University Press). © 1974 by the Board of Trustees of the Leland Stanford Junior University;

Oedipal Asymmetries and Heterosexual Knots
originally in *Social Problems*, vol. 23, no. 4, 1976. © 1976 by the Society for the Study of Social Problems, Inc.;

The Fantasy of the Perfect Mother (with Susan Contratto)
originally in Barrie Thorne (ed.), with Marilyn Yalom, *Rethinking the Family: Some Feminist Questions* (New York, Longman, 1982). © 1980 by Nancy Chodorow and Susan Contratto;

Gender, Relation, and Difference in Psychoanalytic Perspective
originally in *Socialist Review*, no. 46 (1979).

Beyond Drive Theory: Object-Relations and the Limits of Radical Individualism
originally in *Theory and Society*, vol. 14, no. 3, 1985. © 1985 by Elsevier Science Publishers B.V.;
Toward a Relational Individualism: The Mediation of Self Through Psychoanalysis
originally in Thomas C. Heller, Morton Sosna, and David E. Wellbery (eds), *Reconstructing Individualism: Autonomy, Individuality, and the Self in Western Thought* (Stanford, Stanford University Press). © 1986 by the Board of Trustees of the Leland Stanford Junior University;
Feminism, Femininity, and Freud
originally in Jerome Rabow, Gerald M. Platt and Marion S. Goldman (eds), *Advances in Psychoanalytic Sociology* (Malabar, Fla., Robert E. Krieger Publishing Company).

Introduction: Feminism and Psychoanalytic Theory

In the early period of the contemporary feminist movement, feminists searched for a grand theory. This single cause, or dominant factor, theory would explain a sexual inequality, hierarchy, and domination that were omnipresent and that defined and circumscribed entirely the experience and organization of gender and sexuality. For some theorists, gender oppression inhered in capitalist relations of work and exploitation, in the state or the family, in divisions among women or alliances among men, or in male violence and control of women's reproductive and sexual capacities. For others, women were entrapped through their own reproductive anatomy, the objectification of their bodies, the mothering relation or the marriage relation, compulsory heterosexuality, the cultural or ideological construction of "woman," location in the domestic sphere, or association with nature.

For members of the feminist subculture that developed out of the New Left, Marxism presented the hegemonic theoretical claim to explain oppression. Yet as I reflected during the late 1960s upon the historical and cross-cultural record, it seemed clear that women's oppression well preceded class society and that its dynamics did not inhere exclusively or dominantly in material relations of work. I turned to psychological anthropology for an alternative to the Marxist account of women's oppression that would still privilege actual social relations as an explanatory underpinning. I concluded, as I argue in chapter 1, that women's mothering generated, more or less universally, a defensive masculine identity in men and a compensatory psychology and ideology of masculine superiority. This psychology and ideology sustained male dominance.

Following out this psychological focus, and supported by the early feminist claim that the personal is political, I turned to psychoanalysis as a basis for feminist theory. This choice of theoretical focus was an expectable outcome of my disciplinary origins and training throughout the 1960s and early 1970s. I was first trained as an undergraduate anthropology student at Radcliffe College by Beatrice and John W. M. Whiting in a culture and personality anthropology that might be considered prefeminist but that was certainly gender and generation sensitive.[1] I was later influenced as a graduate student in sociology at Brandeis University by the protofeminist psychoanalytic sociology of Philip Slater, who told me quite forcefully after reading the original version of chapter 1 that I would never understand personality if I focussed only on conscious phenomena. Slater's *The Glory of Hera*, itself influenced by Whiting and Whiting, remains one of the most powerful accounts we have of the psychodynamics of male fear of women and its cultural institutionalization.[2] These approaches indicated a psychological depth to cultural attitudes, implying that we must always investigate the conflictual emotional components in cultural categories and practices.

The advantages of a psychoanalytic feminist approach were substantial. In psychoanalytic theory, as in psychological anthropology and anthropological kinship theory, explicit attention to sex and gender, though not approached from a feminist perspective, has been central and basic to both theory and practice. It would be difficult for a psychoanalyst to ignore completely an analysand's sexuality or gender or to argue that a theory of sexuality or gender was irrelevant to the field. In other disciplines that feminists have tried to reshape, the argument for gender neutrality or irrelevance has been more easily sustained by traditionalists.

I argued that this centrality of sex and gender in the categories of psychoanalysis, coupled with the tenacity, emotional centrality, and sweeping power in our lives of our sense of gendered self, made psychoanalysis a particularly apposite source of feminist theorizing.[3] I suggested that our experiences as men and women come from deep within, both within our pasts and, relatedly, within the deepest structures of unconscious meaning and the most emotionally moving relationships that help constitute our daily lives. I showed that the selves of women and men tend to be constructed differently – women's self more in relation and involved with boundary negotiations, separation and connection, men's self more distanced and based on defensively firm boundaries and denials of self–other connection. This emotional meaningfulness has something to do more generally with the continuing theoretical appeal of psychoanalytic feminism and with the emotional–intellectual engrossment of psychoanalytic feminists.

Psychoanalytic feminism has a rather complex and sometimes underground prehistory, a prehistory which recent work on early women psychoanalysts helps us to excavate. I locate its political and theoretical origins with Karen Horney, a second-generation analyst whose early essays on femininity forcefully challenge Freud. Horney asserts a model of women with positive primary feminine qualities and self-valuation, against Freud's model of woman as defective and forever limited, and she ties her critique of both psychoanalytic theory and women's psychology to her recognition of a male-dominant society and culture. Horney's theories, and indeed the early psychoanalytic debates about femininity, do not seem to have made a major impact on mainstream psychoanalysis for many years, indeed, until the current revival of interest in female psychology sparked by the feminist movement and challenge. However, her theories form the basis, acknowledged or unacknowledged, for most of the recent revisions of psychoanalytic understandings of gender and for most psychoanalytic dissidence on the question of gender in the early period as well.[4]

The work of Melanie Klein is another, more theoretical than political, early source of psychoanalytic feminism, although one not much drawn upon by feminists in the contemporary period except in its object-relational transformation.[5] Klein turned psychoanalysis from a psychology of the boy's relation to the father to a psychology of the relation to the mother in children (people) of both sexes. For Klein, children's intense reactions to and infantile fears of their mother, her breast, her insides, and her powers shape subsequent emotional life, leading to the construction of self and other and to moral (guilty, reparative) concern for the other. The Kleinian contribution, as feminism, is even less explicit than the buried 1920s and 1930s debates on femininity, but it introduces, both in its content and in the debate it generated, a passion-laden, even painful, rawness and immediacy to psychoanalytic discourse about gender, and more specifically, about mothers.[6] Kleinian theory in itself, and as it has been translated by object-relations theorists, offers a reading of the psyche not so directly tied to cultural gender as Freudian theory. But it is more attentive, in an unmediated way, to the emotions and conflicts that relations rooted in gender evoke in the child and in the child within the adult.

Contemporary psychoanalytic feminism begins with its opposite, a history of feminist challenge, dismissal, and excoriation. Many feminists saw Freudian psychoanalysis as a great enemy, and, consequently, most early psychoanalytic feminist writings, whatever their specific argument, spend some time simply arguing directly for the usefulness of psychoanalytic insights to feminism.

Like all theoretical approaches within the feminist project, psychoanalytic feminism does specific things and not others. First, like the theory from which it derives, it is not easily or often historically, socially, or culturally specific. It tends toward universalism and can be read, even if it avoids the essentialism of psychoanalysis itself, to imply that there is a psychological commonality among all women and among all men. Psychoanalytic feminism has not tried enough to capture the varied, particular organizations of gender and sexuality in different times and places, nor has it made the dynamics of change central. The dominant theoretical lexicon of psychoanalysis includes gender but not class, race, or ethnicity. Accordingly, psychoanalytic feminism has not been especially attuned to differences among women – to class, racial, and ethnic variations in experience, identity, or location in social practices and relations. Feminist theory and practice, of course, need to be culturally and historically specific, and it would be useful if psychoanalysis had the data and theory to differentiate genders and sexualities finely across history and culture. Psychoanalytic feminism would also be considerably enriched by clinical, theoretical, or psychoanalytically informed phenomenological and experiential accounts of gender identity, self, and relation among women and men of color and of non-dominant classes.

It is a serious mistake, however, to conflate this delimitation of the contribution of psychoanalysis to feminism with a dismissal of its importance. People everywhere have emotions that they care about, connections to others, sexual feelings, and senses of self, self-esteem, and gender. People everywhere form a psyche, self, and identity. These are everywhere profoundly affected by unconscious fantasies as well as by conscious perceptions that begin as early as infancy. Psychoanalysis is the method and theory directed toward the investigation and understanding of how we develop and experience these unconscious fantasies and of how we construct and reconstruct our felt past in the present. Historically, this method and theory have not often been applied in a socially or culturally specific manner, but there is not a basic antagonism between psychoanalytic thinking and social specificity. Psychoanalysis uses universal theoretical categories – distinguishing conscious from unconscious mental processes, labelling and analyzing defenses, arguing that basic ego or self feelings are a product of and constructed by early experienced object relations – but it need not (though it may in some versions) prescribe the content of unconscious fantasy, the inevitable invocation of particular defenses, or particular developmental or self stories. As factors of race, class, culture, or history enter either into a labelled (conscious or unconscious) identity, or as they shape particular early object-relational and family patterns and forms of subjectivity, psychoanalytic tools should be able to analyze these. Until we have another theory which can tell us about unconscious mental processes, conflict, and relations of gender, sexuality, and self, we had best take psychoanalysis for what it does include and can tell us rather than dismissing it out of hand. We might also bear in mind that on some kinds of differences among women, psychoanalysis already has great interpretive potential experientially and clinically on the individual case level, if not theoretically – that is, as a general developmental theory. I think here of differences of sexual orientation and identity, of sexual victimization and its sequelae, of married and single, of mother and not-mother.

My own project, represented in this book, continues to be a project in psychoanalytic feminism, to engage and weave together strands of feminism and of psychoanalysis, but it has changed in both these terrains. During the early period of single-cause feminism, I probably would have continued to develop as a Marxist feminist if I had thought that gender inequality inhered primarily in capitalist or capitalist–patriarchal work relations. I would have learned political theory if I had thought that the state was the primary locus of women's oppression or become a cultural critic or philosopher if I thought woman's oppression was located in her otherness. I might have tried to become an expert on aggression and testosterone or female hormonal cycles if biology seemed the key. My drawing upon psychoanalysis, in some sense the creation of a single individual, during that period was itself in the context of, and remains a sort of carryover from, feminist grand theory days.

Now, however, when I speak of feminist theory, I mean something more holistic and pluralistic – encompassing a number of organizational axes – and at the same time not absolute. In my current view, feminist understanding requires a multiplex account – perhaps not as acausal as thick description, but yet not necessarily claiming causal explanatory status – of the dynamics of gender, sexuality, sexual inequality, and domination. It is the focus on relations among elements, or dynamics, along with an analysis and critique of male dominance, which define an understanding of sex and gender as feminist, and not just the exclusive focus on male dominance itself. I no longer think that one factor, or one dynamic, can explain male dominance (even if I still have my own predilections for particular theoretical contenders). An open web of social, psychological, and cultural relations, dynamics, practices, identities, beliefs, in which I would privilege neither society, psyche, nor culture, comes to constitute gender as a social, cultural, and psychological phenomenon. This multiplex web composes sexual inequality, but, at the same time, feminist understanding encompasses relations of gender and sexuality not immediately comprehended in terms of hierarchy, domination, or inequality or by concepts like patriarchy, male dominance, or the law of the father. Gender and sexuality are more fragmentary, so that some differences are not implicated in dominance, and the complex of gender may include benefits to women as well as liabilities. This complex is manifold, constituted by multiple, often contradictory, locations and identities. There are times when gender itself as well as sexual inequality are more or less relevant to our experiences or the conclusions of our investigations. Such complexity is among other things a necessary correlate to the multiple social, psychological, and cultural identities of different women and to the polyvocality we find in women's accounts of their lives and situations. These accounts show that psychological, cultural, and social constructions of gender vary and that gender varies in its link to the self and in how and when it is invoked. Chapters 9 and 10 begin to address these issues.

This global shift in my general view of feminist theory has substantive import for my psychoanalytic feminist analysis. My early writing, in articles represented in this volume and in my book, *The Reproduction of Mothering*, implied that women's mothering was *the* cause or prime mover of male dominance.[7] I would now argue that these writings document and delineate one extremely important, and previously largely unexamined, aspect of the relations of gender and the psychology of gender. My focus on the mother and the pre-Oedipal period must also be understood historically and contextually, as a reaction to and dialogue with the nearly exclusive Freudian focus on the father and the Oedipus complex. That we are mothered by women, that in all societies women rather than men have primary parenting responsibilities, is an important social and cultural fact that still bears remarking and analyzing. In those individual and cultural cases where we have some insight into human emotions and psychodynamics, this fact also seems to have significant import for people's constructions of self and interpersonal relations, for their emotions, their fantasies, and their psychological apprehensions of gender. Women's inequality may be multiply caused and situated, but I have yet to find a convincing explanation for the virulence of masculine anger, fear, and resentment of women, or of aggression toward them, that bypasses – even if it does not rest with – the psychoanalytic account, first suggested by Horney, that men resent and fear women because they experience them as powerful mothers.

To emphasize the emotional (and even social, cultural, or political) power of the mother, which I have done, following psychoanalytic object-relations theory, does not preclude a recognition of the father's social, cultural, and political (and even emotional) power. However, although such a position is not incompatible with a view that locates power in the father, it is incompatible with arguments that the father, either as actual or symbolic presence, controls the mother–child relation entirely, or that motherhood is solely an institution that sustains women's powerlessness, or that we can only understand the mother–daughter relation as it is experienced in the domain of the father. Fathers are not only socially and culturally dominant; they can be personally domineering, seductive, and exciting, often as an alternative to the taken-for-granted mother. Mothers can, in contrast to such fathers, be perceived as submissive, self-effacing, and powerless.[8]

My position here is consonant with modern, more decentered, views of theory in general and feminist theory in particular – views of the multiplicities of gender(ed) experience which include varied axes of power and powerlessness and dimensions of gender which do not encode power. The complexity of the emotional and personal is best captured by decentered views, such that attempts to polarize personal and emotional experiences as all bad, or to valorize them as all good, are often insufficient. Such a perspective enables us to understand that one can both valorize feminine qualities like women's self in relation and see them as products of inequality. As a result of investigating how the relational development of self differs for women and men, I have criticized men's denial of relatedness and individualism in social and psychoanalytic theory. I have implied that women's self in relation is a potential strength. But such critique does not mean that I do not acknowledge many women's very difficult problems with establishing differentiated selfhood, autonomy, and an agentic subjectivity.

There is a second change in my project from the period when I wrote *The Reproduction of Mothering*, and that is a greater interest in writing about psychoanalysis for its own sake. As I now see feminist theory as a more multiplex account of relations in many domains, I care less to justify my interests by arguing that psychoanalysis is *the* feminist theory. I am more convinced even than I was during an earlier period that psychoanalysis describes a significant level of reality that is not reducible to, or in the last instance caused by, social or cultural organization. I would not, as I believe I do in *Reproduction*, give determinist primacy to social relations that generate certain psychological patterns or processes but would argue that psychology itself is equally important to, constitutive and determinative of, human life. If I were to discover that the "central dynamic" or "cause" of women's oppression were located outside of the personal, interiorized, subjective, and intersubjective realm of psychic life and primary relationships that psychoanalysis describes, I would still be concerned with this realm and its relation to gender, sexuality, and self.

Part of the explanation for this shift may lie in the particular psychoanalytic feminist approach that I chose. Object-relations theory is originally a set of accounts about the constitution of self in the context of primary emotional relationships.[9] It is not primarily a theory of gender. This branch of psychoanalytic feminism in some sense imposed a non-explicitly gendered object-relational account on gender and the gender-infused relations of parenting and heterosexual intimacy. As a result, some of my writings more easily grew to encompass an independent interest in self or subjectivity, as these experiences are and are not so gender-related. Part II exemplifies these interests.

For some readers and colleagues, this direct fascination with – what I sometimes consider this experience of being passionately "hooked on" – psychoanalytic theory may make my more recent writing less powerful as feminist theory, which should in their opinion focus unswervingly on gender domination.[10] My own view, of course, is that such a position is wrong. I continue to locate important experiences and oppressions of gender in emotional and intrapsychic life and in the arena of primary relations. This personal sphere is psychologically, culturally, and socially meaningful, even if we now understand that our cultural legacy conceptualizing such a sphere as separate is historically and structurally inaccurate. I certainly recognize relations of gender and male dominance in the community, the economy, and the state, and I think that feminist politics and analysis in these arenas are extremely important. But I do not agree with the strand of feminist theory that argues that the central arena of gender oppression in the modern period has moved from the family and the personal to the public and social realm.[11] Moreover, it does seem to me that the most heatedly contested gender politics concern what we conceptualize and experience as the personal and familial – abortion, marriage, divorce, the regulation of sexuality, parenting.

I would stress, probably more now than in my earliest writings, the extent to which concerns in the emotional realm, gender related or not, are tied up with (at least our own society's) notions of human fulfillment – selfhood, agency, meaningful relationship, depth and richness of experience, a comfortable centering in our bodies and in our sexuality. Psychoanalysis enables us to understand such experiences particularly well, to recognize their acute intensity and yet to analyze them in their full multilayered complexity. Such concerns are a natural extension of my interests in object-relations theory.

I believe that this concern for psychoanalysis-in-itself infuses, and explains, the writings in this volume. I have begun to delineate the origins of such concerns. Writers like myself who draw upon psychoanalysis seem to do so for reasons that go beyond its aptness for their/our intellectual project. We are hooked, have fallen intellectually in love. This passionate attachment (and psychoanalysis tells us that all passionate attachments are ambivalent) seems to come first from Freud. The intensity in his own writing, the tortured conflict as well as the often sweeping brilliance that both his texts and his subtexts exhibit, seem to draw (at least some) readers in emotionally. Freud challenges us to maintain that precarious balance between objective assessment and subjective involvement which may be the mark of our most profound intellectual insights and which is certainly the mark of our most emotion-laden intellectual experiences.

In psychoanalytic terms, we have transferences to Freud and to other analytic writers. These are based on our own intellectual prehistories (our intellectual infancies and childhoods), on our feelings about authoritative (and authoritarian) parents, teachers, and writers, and, I believe, on our unavoidable entanglement, or entrapment, in the history of controversy within psychoanalysis. These transferences mean that we always bring something active and involved to our reading of psychoanalysis. We also have countertransferences to Freud's own transferences, that is, to those many parts of his (and other psychoanalysts') writings that are themselves emotion-laden and driven by unconscious conflict and desires.[12]

Many of us, also, are gripped by the grand humanistic claims of psychoanalysis. Freud, and others who follow him, give us standards for human fulfillment in both the emotional and interpersonal spheres. My own involvement in this theory has led me away from the social determinism prevalent in sociology and in political movements and from an exclusive reliance on social standards as measures of human life. I do not mean to deny or pass over the important recognition that social conditions can be life-draining and debilitating, and psychoanalysis should certainly explore more fully just how much difficult social conditions shape and constrain subjectivity and psychic life. But I have learned from psychoanalysis that we cannot measure human life solely in socially determinist terms. In the integration of their conscious and unconscious lives, in the quality of their primary emotional relationships with others, as in social organization and politics, people can help to create for themselves a more meaningful life.

The intellectual trajectory described by this volume began with a concern for the structure of male dominance, and shortly thereafter, for the dynamics of the mother–daughter relationship. This latter interest led me directly to issues of separation and connection, as these are discussed by psychoanalytic writers, and indirectly to a broader set of concerns that these writers also address. These concerns, like those of psychoanalytic theorists in other traditions, tie psychoanalysis to claims about the nature and meaning of life. As with much feminist theory, a focus on gender-related issues and a feminist theoretical critique turned back upon the original theory itself and pointed toward transformative concerns for theory in general. My originally neatly contained project in feminist theory and the psychology of gender has spilled over to other (I emphatically do not mean "larger") theoretical questions. I wanted a method to understand what seemed to me the prevalent intertwining of conscious and unconscious feeling and emotion in interpersonal and intrapsychic life. Freud's insistently individualist drive psychology and structural theory do not tie issues of self and feeling closely enough to questions of gender; Lacanian theory does not have categories for self and relation as I conceive these at all. Because object-relations theorists make such concerns central and discuss them most extensively, these theorists form the dominant psychoanalytic theoretical basis of my work.

Object-relations theorists, emerging from and reacting to the work of Melanie Klein, image a course of transactions between self and other(s) that help form our first subjectivity and sense of self, and that throughout life are renegotiated to recreate the sense of self and other in terms of connection, separation, and in between. These transactions give depth and richness of meaning to experience, by resonating with the past and with constructions of the past.[13]

Winnicott, currently seen as the pre-eminent British object-relations theorist, elaborates the social and cultural import of issues of connection and separation more than any other psychoanalyst, as he points us to the transitional space between mother and infant that is neither me nor not-me and that becomes the creative arena of play and culture. Chapters 5, 6, and 7 contain some discussion of Winnicott.

Others also speak to the continual preoccupation with establishing and maintaining such intrapsychic and interpersonal space, claiming it as the individual's life project. According to infant researcher and theorist of separation–individuation Margaret Mahler:

For the more or less normal adult, the experience of being both fully "in" and at the same time basically separate from the "world out there" is among the givens of life that are taken for granted. Consciousness of self and absorption without awareness of self are the two polarities between which we move, with varying ease and with varying degrees of alternation or simultaneity . . . *As is the case with any intrapsychic process, this one reverberates throughout the life cycle.* . . Here, in the rapprochement subphase, we feel is the mainspring of man's eternal struggle against both fusion and isolation.

One could regard the entire life cycle as constituting a more or less successful process of distancing from and introjection of the lost symbiotic mother, an eternal longing for the actual or fantasied "ideal state of self," with the latter standing for a symbiotic fusion with the "all good" symbiotic mother, who was at one time part of the self in a blissful state of well-being.[14]

Mahler here captures the essence of oscillation between connection and separation, though, in the end, she does indicate a tendency – perhaps partially in reaction to the individualist biases of traditional theory – to see the tension more in terms of the attractions of connection and the collapse of boundaries, with separateness and distance more residual.[15]

Among psychoanalysts, Hans Loewald perhaps best expresses an evenhanded ability to see fully the promises and limitations of what we conventionally think of as early developmental and later developmental stances like connection and separation. He wants us to rethink these stances and to move beyond associating them with regressive and progressive moments in human development and human psychological life. He also ties these more directly than either Mahler or the object-relations theorists not only to powerful affects but also to drive derivatives. In a relatively early paper, he writes:

As we explore these various modes of separation and union, it becomes more and more apparent that the ambivalence of love–hate and of aggression–submission (sadism–masochism) enters into all of them and that neither separation nor union can ever be entirely unambivalent. The deepest root of the ambivalence that appears to pervade all relationships, external as well as internal, seems to be the polarity inherent in individual existence of individuation and "primary narcissistic" union.[16]

Such a reading of development and psychic life enables Loewald to resolve a number of theoretical and clinical problems. He can move beyond the traditional privileging of Oedipal development as a more advanced stage without reverting to the sometime anti-Oedipal tendency of cultural critics and feminists who tend to see only pre-Oedipal modes of connectedness as a model for a desirable human life. He overcomes the tendency in object-relations thinkers and other theorists of early development like Mahler and Kohut to be unable to integrate their approach into Oedipal theory. These theorists tend simply to add on classical assumptions about Oedipal drive, ego, and superego development to their broadly object-relational theories, based on different metapsychological premises, of early development, and to hold an implicit developmental model that the analysis of pre-Oedipal issues in adults is a residual necessity for those patients who need to be brought up to the Oedipal stage. For Loewald, "Oedipal" projects of individuation and morality and "pre-Oedipal" concerns with boundaries, separation, connection, and the transitional space continue throughout life:

[psychoanalysis] seems to stand and fall with the proposition that the emergence of a relatively autonomous individual is the culmination of human development. How this may come about, and what interferes with such an outcome, resulting in psychopathology, is a most important aspect of psychoanalytic research, reconstruction, and treatment.

On the other hand, owing in part to analytic research, there is a growing awareness of the force and validity of another striving, that for unity, symbiosis, fusion, merging, or identification – whatever name we wish to give to this sense of and longing for nonseparateness and undifferentiation. . .

The Oedipus complex is a constituent of normal psychic life of the adult, and as such is active again and again. A psychotic core, related to the earliest vicissitudes of the ambivalent search for primary narcissistic unity and individuation, also is an active constituent of normal psychic life.[17]

Echoing both Freud, in his invocation of the Oedipal killing of the father and subsequent instigation of guilt, and Klein, in his focus on the desire to repair or atone toward the other rather than simply to criticize and undermine the self, Loewald describes the psychoanalytic contribution to our understanding of morality:

If without the guilty deed of parricide there is no individual self worthy of that name, no advanced internal organization of psychic life, then guilt and atonement are crucial motivational elements of the self.[18]

My own recent thinking about the psychoanalytic contribution to our understanding of self, meaning, and experience is indebted to Loewald. This growing appreciation of his writing may be partly a result of my psychoanalytic clinical training, which has focussed me more on the psychoanalytic dialogue and less on the psychoanalytic story of development and the early dialogue of mother and child. Loewald's writing bridges and sees as parallel these two sometimes disparate dialogues. He indicates for us the often missing connection between psychoanalytic practice, psycho-analytic theory, and the potential uses and applications of that theory in other fields.

Loewald is certainly familiar to psychoanalysts, as he has been a consistently productive and wide-ranging psychoanalytic writer for several decades. He is highly respected within the profession but until recently has not been particularly lionized, adulated, or seen as a theoretical leader.[19] He is not associated with a specific theoretical tradition and is not seen as an independent innovator, maverick, or rebel. There are no (at least not yet) "Loewaldians," as there are Winnicottians, Kohutians, or Mahlerians. Indeed, he himself seems to be an insistent synthesizer rather than polarizer within psychoanalytic discourse, committed to and able to maintain himself as a drive theorist, ego psychologist, and object-relations theorist who respects self psychology, while also remaining fully enmeshed in the clinical situation that ultimately provides psychoanalysis its truths.[20] Psychoanalytic feminists and other psychoanalytic social or cultural critics have not drawn much upon his work. Here, I cannot do justice to the Loewaldian *œuvre*, but I indicate some of those directions in his thinking that I think show most promise for an expanded psychoanalytic sociology and psychoanalytic understanding of the life course, and, thereby, an expanded psychoanalytic feminism as well.

Loewald seems particularly able to capture the ways that unconscious processes resonate with conscious and thus give conscious life depth and richness of meaning. As he does so, he gives us a vision of intersubjectivity deeply imbued with multiply tiered ways to understand and experience self and other. Against those who would maintain a negative view of transference as something that interferes with the reality of daily life, as well as those who would idealize the unconscious, he argues:

far from being . . . "the enduring monument of man's profound rebellion against reality and his stubborn persistence in the ways of immaturity," transference is the "dynamism" by which the instinctual life of man, the id, becomes ego and by which reality becomes integrated and maturity is achieved. Without such transference – of the intensity of the unconscious, of the infantile ways of experiencing life that have no language and little organization, but the indestructibility and power of the origins of life – to the preconscious and to present-day life and contemporary objects – without such transference, or to the extent to which such transference miscarries, human life becomes sterile and an empty shell. On the other hand, the unconscious needs present-day external reality (objects) and present-day psychic reality (the preconscious) for its own continuity, lest it be condemned to live the shadow life of ghosts or to destroy life.[21]

Similarly, he links, rather than opposes, fantasy and reality, and claims that these give meaning one to the other:

But fantasy is unreal only insofar as its communication with present actuality is inhibited or severed. To that extent, however, present actuality is unreal too. Perhaps a better word than "unreal" is "meaningless." In the analytic process the infantile fantasies and memories, by being linked up with the present actuality of the analytic situation and the analyst, regain meaning and may be reinserted within the stream of total mental life. Thereby they may resume that growth process (an element of which we call sublimation) which was interrupted or interfered with at an earlier time, leading to neurosis. At the same time, as the present actuality of the analytic situation is being linked up with infantile fantasies, this present gains or regains meaning, i.e., that depth of experience which comes about by its live communication with the infantile roots of experience. The disruption of that communication is the most important aspect of the problem of defense, of repression, isolation, etc.[22]

This connection of transference and current relationship, of fantasy and reality, of rational and irrational, itself turns back upon the psychoanalytic enterprise (and upon any enterprise, like that of psychoanalytic feminism, that draws upon psychoanalysis):

While it has been [psychoanalysis's] intent to penetrate unconscious mentality with the light of rational understanding, it also has been and is its intent to uncover the irrational unconscious sources and forces motivating and organizing conscious and rational mental processes . . . unconscious processes became accessible to rational understanding, and at the same time rational thought itself and our rational experience of the world as an "object world" became problematic.[23]

This volume traces my thoughts about the relations between feminism and psychoanalytic theory over the past twenty years, since the beginning of the contemporary feminist movement. The essays argue for the necessity to include psychoanalytic understanding, broadly construed, in feminist theory and also feminist understanding, broadly construed, in psychoanalysis. Both the feminism and psychoanalytic theory in the essays are to some extent matricentric and woman-related. They begin from my argument for the importance of women's mothering for the constitution of psychic life and of experiences of self and other. They focus on the relations and psychologies of gender and sexuality. Even as they see some need to move beyond such a polarization, they privilege psychoanalytic theories that stress the mother-dominated pre-Oedipal period over the father-dominated Oedipal period.

Part I provides an overview of the development of my thought about the significance of women's mothering. I describe the developmental unfolding of mother–daughter and mother–son relationships and delineate the impact of mothering on feelings about women in men and about mothers in women and men. I suggest that this relation to the mother will be especially implicated in those transferences and fantasies discussed by Loewald that imbue the relations and interactions of daily life with meaning and a vibrant, or problematic, reality. If my work in general can be seen as a series of investigations about the intertwining of female and male personality development with the psychological underpinnings of male dominance, it might be said that *The Reproduction of Mothering* focusses more on the former, while the essays in Part I and throughout the book, as they examine male fear and objectification of women, the casting of woman as other, and the refusal to accord subjectivity to mothers, focus more on the latter.

I do not address an issue that recent psychoanalytic theorizing points to, that is, the extent to which these transferences and fantasies reproduce actual early experiences – whether they are constructions or reconstructions.[24] I note only that whatever their original status, we do seem regularly to construct unconscious senses of self in relation to our mothers, including relational stories and self-images which have some of those qualities that we currently believe to characterize our earliest relationship and earliest sense of self. As Susan Contratto and I argue in chapter 4, we also bring these (constructed or reconstructed) infantile expectations and experiences to our relations with our mothers and our adult senses of self as mother or mothered, and we inscribe them in our cultural ideology about mothers.

Chapter 1, "Being and doing: a cross-cultural examination of the socialization of males and females," is included because it incorporates my first explorations into the psychological and cultural import for male dominance of the fact that women mother and puts forth my first insights into the greater continuities in female than in male development.[25] It casts its quest universally, reflecting the early feminist search for universals and single-cause theories of male dominance. The essay is predominantly pre-psychoanalytic. It makes some reference to psychoanalytic writers and uses the notion of defense as a central explanatory category, but its argument is put forth in the terms of a psychological anthropology of role training and identity formation. The essay reflects my early training as a culture and personality anthropologist.

Chapter 2, "Family structure and feminine personality," previews the psychoanalytic argument I develop in *The Reproduction of Mothering*, that, through relation to their mother, women develop a self-in-relation, men a self that denies relatedness. It presages themes in my subsequent writing, differentiating gender identity from gender personality and arguing that there may be qualities that tend to characterize each gender that are not a consequence or cause of consciousness of self as male or female. It also argues, implicitly against anthropological and sociological colleagues, for the independent reality of the object-relational level of analysis, asserting that we should investigate the mother–daughter relationship whether or not it is of structural (I would now add cultural) importance in the society under consideration. This essay bridges culture and personality anthropology and psychoanalytic sociology, as it argues for a more psychoanalytic understanding of personality than culture and personality studies have heretofore provided.

Both these chapters exhibit the limitations one would expect in any scholar's early work, and any work that bears the mark of a field's earliest investigations. The data we now have on gender cross-culturally far surpasses anything I could draw on, and the essays, as many essays in the early period of feminist anthropology, probably read some Western differences, for instance on the extent of father-absence, into all cultures.[26] I also make the early feminist mistake of implying that women do not work in the paid labor-force.

Chapter 3, "Oedipal asymmetries and heterosexual knots," develops the implications of women's mothering for the construction and experience of heterosexual relationships. It also points briefly to a missing and often-sought closeness with other women in women's lives.[27]

The first three chapters take my work up to *The Reproduction of Mothering*. Although I cannot, in a brief introduction, exhaustively describe contemporary academic psychoanalytic feminism, it might be useful to the reader if I situate these essays within the early psychoanalytic feminist project. During this period, until about 1978, there were a few founding contributions and little of the richness and range of the more recent period. "Being and doing" was published in 1971, at a time when feminist treatment of psychoanalysis was entirely critical.[28] "Family structure and feminine personality," written in 1972, was published in 1974, the year during which I completed the dissertation work that subsequently became *The Reproduction of Mothering*, and the year that witnessed publication of the first major argument for psychoanalytic feminism, Juliet Mitchell's *Psychoanalysis and Feminism*. Two anthologies of psychoanalytic writings on women were published in response to the women's movement during the same period. In 1973, Jean Baker Miller's *Psychoanalysis and Women* collected a number of classical and contemporary writings on women in the Neo-Freudian tradition, and in 1974 Jean Strouse's *Women and Analysis* paired classical psychoanalytic essays with modern responses. In 1975, Gayle Rubin published *the* classic psychoanalytic feminist essay, perhaps the classic essay of modern feminism. "The traffic in women: notes toward a 'political economy' of sex" elegantly and succinctly criticized the Marxist–feminist project and tied together the theories of Freud and Lévi-Strauss. "Oedipal asymmetries and heterosexual knots" was published in 1976, the same year as three works foundational to modern psychoanalytic feminism and to the feminist theory of mothering: Dorothy Dinnerstein's *The Mermaid and the Minotaur*, which shares a similar analysis to mine of heterosexual relationships, Jean Baker Miller's *Toward a New Psychology of Women*, and Adrienne Rich's *Of Woman Born*. *The Reproduction of Mothering* appeared in 1978. These works of the period about 1970–8 largely provide the bases for contemporary psychoanalytic feminism.

In chapter 4, "The fantasy of the perfect mother," Susan Contratto and I take the issue of mothering in another direction, toward the kinds of fantasies people (and in particular feminists) develop as a result of being mothered and living in a culture that exalts and debases mothers at the same time. This essay was influenced by Contratto's contemporaneous writing and thinking concerning ideology about mothers.[29]

Part II, "Gender, self, and social theory," moves from an interest in gender to an interest in sometimes and sometimes not gender-related qualities of self. This section is thematically related to its predecessor: it draws upon object-relations theory and feminist analysis, and it assumes the importance of mothering. However, the impact of this mothering, or preoccupation with mother-related issues, is now seen to inhere in masculinist theory as much as in social relations. Chapter 5, "Gender, relation, and difference in psychoanalytic perspective," provides a transition, as it connects an analysis of the general meaning of separateness and self to processes of gender differentiation and to attitudes toward women. Chapter 6, "Beyond drive theory: object relations and the limits of radical individualism," is an exegesis of the psychoanalytic sociologies of Marcuse and Brown demonstrating that drive-theory-based social theories are inevitably individualistic and denying of differentiated human connection. It argues that such purportedly universalistic individualism has gendered foundations, modelling the self as male child and the other as mother. Chapter 7, "Toward a relational individualism" recapitulates both previous essays, as it distills an argument that object-relations theory and clinical practice enable a move beyond the individualism of drive theory and of orthodox psychoanalytic technique.

Part III, "Psychoanalysis, psychoanalysts, and feminism" takes up the psychoanalytic feminist dialogue about gender more as an imagined and actual problem in professional and political communication. Chapter 8, "Feminism, femininity, and Freud" and chapter 9, "Psychoanalytic feminism and the psychoanalytic psychology of women," address feminists and psychoanalysts about the asymmetric approach each takes to questions of gender and psychoanalysis. These essays continue what I have called the woman-related, and even matricentric, theme of the previous two sections. They implicitly and even explicitly pose the problem of connection and difference among people writing about women, contrasting the point of view of psychoanalysts writing about gender, who might well be men but who are likely to be women, with feminist writers. "Psychoanalytic feminism" especially concerns relations among women writers – among feminists as well as between psychoanalysts and feminists – with different points of view about the psychology and sociology of gender.

"Psychoanalytic feminism," as well as the chapters in Part II, begin to locate me in the psychoanalytic feminist debates of the post-1978 period, especially in relation to Lacanian feminism. Chapter 5 was originally written for a conference in which the French feminist anti-Lacanian view of difference was the main arena of debate. Chapter 6 addresses critical theory, and chapter 9 situates my work in relation to Neo-Freudian feminism and to Lacanian theory.

This book begins with reflections on my gender consciousness and how it developed. It concludes also with considerations about gender consciousness, this time playing off mine, and that of my generation, against that of women of another generation. As a further attempt to understand psychoanalysis and women, I began a study in the early 1980s of surviving second-generation women analysts, women who trained in the 1920s, 1930s, and early 1940s, when a relatively large number of women were entering the field. Chapter 10, "Seventies questions for thirties women: gender and generation in a study of early women psychoanalysts," comes from that research. It is a contribution to the growing literature in feminist methodology, reflecting on gender consciousness among "1970s feminists" (women who became feminists during the early second wave) and among women psychoanalysts trained around the 1930s. The essay addresses the cultural and psychological context in which different women ask questions about psychoanalysis and feminism and the kinds of answers they are likely to accept, given their background, training, and cultural and social life situation.

Part III points to another enduring, somewhat defensive, preoccupation in my writing, with who I am and who I am not, intellectually. Such a preoccupation may characterize many interdisciplinary scholars, especially if they adhere to non-traditional and controversial approaches like feminism or psychoanalysis, and it may also characterize women. I am a self-defined "interpretive," or even "humanistic," psychoanalytic sociologist and psychoanalytic feminist. I have been criticized by sociologists for being ungrounded empirically and individualistic theoretically, for not understanding societal determinism, and for underestimating the force of social reality. At the same time, I have been criticized by Lacanian psychoanalytic feminists for the opposite, for being empiricist and socially determinist and for seeing the unconscious as a sociological phenomenon rather than an analytically irreducible and unique register of being and level of analysis.

As a psychoanalytic theorist, I part company with most American psychoanalysts in my reliance on object-relations theory and in that I have always seen psychoanalysis as an interpretive and not a medical or scientific enterprise. However, I differ from many academic humanists in seeing psychoanalysis as a social science that is a theoretically grounded but nonetheless empirically infused study of lives.[30] Recently, as I have been training as a psychoanalyst, I have become more concerned than formerly with claims psychoanalysts, both in their traditional identities and as feminists, make about gender. As I indicate in chapter 9, often what psychoanalysts have to say is narrowly delimited – the little details of how men and women empirically *are*. This is not rich enough or broadsweeping enough, or enough imbued with an understanding of gender as a relation, for the average academic feminist. Even writing by self-defined feminist psychoanalysts sometimes seems too closely focussed on the details of masculinity and femininity, assuming only in a general way that there is something problematic about the larger situation of gender but having no specific analytic categories to invoke to explain or characterize this situation. Reciprocally, the sweeping generalizations of psychoanalytic feminists sometimes seem well beyond utility for the clinical practitioner. I have felt in the middle, and as a result there is often a sense, in the concluding chapters, of someone feeling buffeted around the disciplines, reacting rather than creating.

I have not, in this brief introduction, been able exhaustively to describe contemporary psychoanalytic feminism or to place my ideas within it, and the volume as a whole has the task of documenting and arguing for the psychoanalytic feminist project. In the ten or more years since the major statement I put forth in *Reproduction*, the psychoanalytic–feminist project has proliferated and become more intricate. Psychoanalytic feminism has also become much more institutionalized and has developed a number of proponents (and antagonists) in a variety of academic fields and from a variety of psychoanalytic perspectives. We can now count ourselves, even as we disagree, as part of a collaborative and growing project. The essays that follow provide my own contribution to that rich and complex endeavor.

PART I

The Significance of Women's
Mothering for Gender Personality and
Gender Relations

1

Being and Doing: A Cross-Cultural Examination of the Socialization of Males and Females

There are two crucial issues that people concerned about the liberation of women and men from rigid and limiting sex roles must consider.[1] One is whether there is any basis to the claim that there are biologically derived (and therefore inescapable) psychological or personality characteristics which universally differentiate men and women. The other is to understand why it is that in almost every society women are physically, politically, and/or economically dominated by men and are thought to be (and think themselves to be) inferior to men. This essay refutes the claim for universal and necessary differentiation, and provides an explanation based on a comparison of cultures and socialization practices to account for such differences where and when they occur. It then examines the development of identity in males and females and shows how this development, and in particular the socialization and development of males, leads to and perpetuates the devaluation and oppression of women.

Cross-Cultural Research

Cultural Personality

Cross-cultural research suggests that there are no absolute personality differences between men and women, that many of the characteristics we normally classify as masculine or feminine tend to differentiate *both* the males and females in one culture from those in another, and in still other cultures to be the reverse of our expectations.[2]

Margaret Mead's studies describe societies in which both men and women are gentle and unaggressive (the Arapesh); in which women dislike childbearing and children and both sexes are angry and aggressive (the Mundugumor); in which women are unadorned, brisk and efficient, whether in childrearing, fishing, or marketing, while men are decorated and vain, interested in art, theater, and petty gossip (the Tchambuli); in which adult sex roles follow conventional expectations, but both boys and girls are initially raised alike to be alternately gentle and nurturant or assertive, following which boys undergo severe initiation ceremonies and claim to forget any feminine-type experiences or reactions (the Iatmul).[3] Mead's suggestion, typifying the approach of culture and personality theorists, is that cultures emphasize and reinforce behavior according to many sorts of criteria. Although one culture may have different expectations for male and female behavior, the criteria of differentiation may bear no relation to the criteria of differentiation in other cultures. Male and female personality in one culture may be poles along one continuum of behavior, which is itself differentiated from the continua of behavior of other cultures.

Cross-cultural researchers have also compiled data indicating that children's behavior and socialization tend to differ between cultures along dimensions normally thought to differentiate male from female behavior and socialization. According to Herbert Barry, Irvin Child, and Margaret Bacon, societies with economies relying on "high" or "intermediate high" accumulation of resources ("high" being societies in which the subsistence economy is either pastoral or agricultural with animal husbandry also important; "intermediate high" being agricultural societies without animal husbandry) train *all* children to be more "compliant," that is, to be responsible and obedient (typically feminine).[4] In contrast, societies with economies relying on "low" or "intermediate low" accumulation ("low" being societies with hunting and fishing; "intermediate low" being agricultural societies without animal husbandry but with hunting and fishing) train their children to be more "assertive," that is, to be independent, self-reliant, and oriented toward achievement (typically masculine).

Beatrice B. Whiting and John W. M. Whiting have compared behavior they call "dependent–dominant" (typically masculine) and "nurturant–responsible" (typically feminine) among children of six cultures.[5] They find that in three societies, children's behavior across age and gender is much more nurturant–responsible than in three others, and that, conversely, in the other three societies, children's behavior falls more on the dependent–dominant end of the behavioral spectrum. Similarly, children across age and sex in three of the six societies (a different three) cluster along the "authoritarian–aggressive" ("masculine") end of a different behavioral spectrum, while children in the other three cluster along the "sociable–intimate" ("feminine") end of the same spectrum. Thus, "masculine" behavior seems to characterize children in certain societies, and "feminine" behavior children in others.

Sex Differences within Cultures

This is not to claim that within most cultures, male and female differences do not generally conform to our traditional expectations. George Murdock's and Roy D'Andrade's data on the division of labor by sex indicate that most work is divided regularly between men and women, along conventional lines.[6] Men's work, for instance, is "strenuous, cooperative, and . . . may require long periods of travel";[7] women's work is mainly associated with food gathering and preparation, crafts, clothing manufacture, child care, and so forth. The extent of these differences between the sexes may be large or small. Although in American society we can recognize clear differences between boys' and girls' socialization and between adult sex roles, these differences are relatively small in comparison to many other societies.

Barry, Bacon, and Child show that within cultures where sex differences in pressure toward certain kinds of behavior occur, the socialization of boys tends to be overwhelmingly more achievement oriented and self-reliance oriented, while the socialization of girls tends to be overwhelmingly more nurturance oriented.[8] Although girls are also socialized to be more responsible and more obedient than boys, there is more variation between boys and girls in the socialization of responsibility, and a majority of societies were rated as without sex differences in the socialization of obedience. This seems consistent with their findings on societies differentiated according to type of subsistence economy, in which, for instance, boys in societies emphasizing assertive behavior are more assertive than girls in this same type of society and girls are more compliant than boys. The same is true in societies emphasizing compliant behavior.[9]

Whiting and Whiting also compared behavioral variation by sex and age.[10] They found that young girls across cultures tended to exhibit more intimate–dependent behavior than young boys but that this difference disappeared with age. By contrast, nurturant behavior did not differentiate young children but differentiated older girls sharply from boys, and increasingly so as they got older. Boys of all ages are more aggressive than girls, and while young children of both sexes are equally dominant-dependent, older boys seek dominance and attention more than older girls. These changes make sense: young boys and girls of both sexes exhibit forms of dependent behavior – seeking attention or help. This behavior changes for girls, as their seeking of help and attention soon gives way to offering help and support to younger children. By contrast, boys, who are allowed as very young children to be demanding to adults (especially women) and older children socializers, often lose this privilege as they get older, without receiving in its place a well-defined role in the economy or division of labor. The still-growing boy is then reduced to more illegitimate demands – seeking attention and dominance for their own sake (and these demands are often ignored by the people performing their work around him) – people unlikely to be aware of his role-less status and unsympathetic to his bothering them.[11] In sum, the Whitings find few differences in what we might consider to be masculine and feminine behavior between boys and girls of three to six years old. They find that boys from seven to eleven years old are significantly more dominant and attention-seeking than girls, and girls significantly more nurturant than boys.

Explanations of Cultural and Sexual Differences: Nature or Culture?

These behavioral tendencies should not be taken to reflect biological (hence, necessary) bases for sex roles and the sexual division of labor. With the exception of aggression (and we have seen that authoritarian-aggressive behavior differentiates children of both genders in some societies from children of both genders in others), there are no behaviors that consistently differentiate the sexes across age. In particular, sex differences found in young children's behavior – which might argue for innateness – tend to disappear with age, whereas other more characteristically masculine and feminine behaviors tend to increase as children get older, but well before we could attribute such differentiation to the hormonal changes of puberty. These changes seem to develop as older children learn the actual work expected of them (or are unable to learn this work, and thus are temporarily not integrated meaningfully into the culture). Their personality and behavior facilitate this work or fill time for those without it. In terms of our traditional stereotypes, girls in some societies are more "masculine," and engage in more masculine pursuits, than boys in other societies, and vice versa. In some societies, as Mead has shown, women and men are more similar in terms of personality; in others their personalities diverge widely. In some societies, we find wide gender differences in socialization; in others girls and boys are treated quite similarly.[12]

Barry, Child, and Bacon rely for explanation of cultural differences on differences in subsistence economy. In societies that depend on constant care of animals, or on regular tending of crops, it is necessary to teach children to be obedient and responsible, since disobedience or irresponsibility can endanger or eliminate a food supply for a long period to come. Similarly, experimentation and individual achievement cannot be risked because of the great potential cost. In societies that rely totally or partially on hunting and fishing, disobedience or lack of responsibility is not so crucial: it means missing one day's catch, perhaps, but not ruining a food supply for months to come. In this kind of economy it is worthwhile to be daring and to try new ways of doing things, since success may bring great reward and failure only temporary loss – and perhaps no greater loss than otherwise.

It is clear, however, that those qualities required by the economy in a high-accumulation society are similar, and for the same reasons, to those normally required by woman's work, especially the requirements of child care, but also those of feeding and clothing a family.[13] Because of these more or less constant requirements, girls' socialization in societies of low accumulation cannot be too variable. Although girls are pressured to act assertively as are boys, it is noticeable that in those societies exhibiting pressures toward "masculine" behavior, ranked differences in the strength of socialization of the different kinds of behavior for girls is quite small, whereas the difference for boys between pressure toward assertion and pressure toward compliance is relatively large. The reverse is also true: in those societies which require "feminine" (compliant) behavior, girls' socialization tends to diverge more widely among different kinds of behavior than boys', although the difference is not so extreme.[14]

These differences are accounted for by the fact that men's and boys' work in the two kinds of society can be more radically different than women's and girls' work. Men may *either* hunt, or fish, or farm, or herd. For instance, in societies with animal husbandry, it is often boys who tend livestock, and who thus from an early age must learn to be responsible in the same way that potential child-rearers must learn responsibility.[15] But in societies with hunting and fishing, although women may fish, they still have to take care of children and cook food. Although reliance on gathering and general uncertainty about food supply, along with irregularity of meals and instability of living place, may contribute to differences in female behavior, regularities remain.

Barry, Child, and Bacon do not make clear who does what among the activities they discuss. From general ethnographic knowledge, however, we know that men are the only hunters of large animals in any society; men also generally tend large domestic animals and pastoral herds. Both women and men may fish and participate in various agricultural activities. Accordingly, they find that in societies with hunting, herding, and animal husbandry with large animals and without fishing, the largest sex differences in socialization are found.[16] What seems characteristic of this type of society is not so much that there is specific men's work, but that this work tends to take the men away from the women and children. I would hypothesize that not only is sex-role training most different in these societies, but that they are the ones most characterized by boys' lacking continuous and regular development toward a clearly defined role.

This suggests a possible problem in studies of the relation between socialization and adult economy or culture. While girls are probably consistently and regularly trained to perform a women's role, much of (what is viewed as) the training that boys receive in nurturant behavior particularly, but also in other "feminine" behavior, may not be indicative of or preparatory to an adult role at all. It may reflect the fact that one prevalent societal organization groups women, girls, and boys in opposition to adult men. Since boys are not taught actual woman's work, a natural lot that falls to them is sibling care. This difference may also be true of the Whitings' findings: while nurturant behavior in girls is preparatory to adult role, in boys it may either be this (as, for example, in herding societies) or a time-filler as child-tender where training for an adult male role is unavailable. Dependent, demanding, domineering behavior in both sexes may also simply be an indication that these children have little "real" place in the surrounding adult world.

The preceding consideration of the effect of economy on cultural personality and sex-role distinctions often invokes a "logical" division of labor, or a familial organization and socialization pattern which a particular economy would entail. It is useful to look at these variables by themselves. Whiting and Whiting find that consistent features characterize societies with variant children's behaviors. Cultural complexity – occupational specialization, a monetary economy, and centralized, stratified political and religious systems – differentiates those societies in which children's behavior is characterized by dependent-dominance from those in which it is characterized by nurturant-responsibility. Household organization differentiates authoritarian–aggressive and sociable–intimate children: those in relatively nuclear family cultures exhibit more sociable–intimate behavior; those in more extended family cultures tending toward patrilocality, patrilineality, and polygyny exhibit more authoritarian–aggressive behavior. Barry, Bacon, and Child find that similar societal characteristics relate to sex differences. Large sex differences in socialization are correlated with large family groups with cooperative interaction – either extended families or polygynous families in which co-wives help each other.

Both household structure and complexity of society would seem to entail similar tendencies in child training. In households with few adults, it is likely that more contributions are required from children, both regularly and as temporary substitutes for the mother, than in extended households in which adult substitutes are much more available. In such households as well, it is likely that a man and a woman must be prepared to take each other's role when the other is sick or away; therefore, there cannot be a very large difference in the socialization of sex roles.

Similarly, in less complex societies, children from a very young age can be and are trained toward their already known adult roles. They are functioning members of the economy, and whatever work they do is a necessary and expected contribution. Furthermore, children in this situation can usually understand the reasons for what they are learning and see tangible results of their work: they take part in producing the meal which they eat. In these societies it is also more likely that women participate in the producing economy, making it necessary for children to take care of younger children and to do things at home while their mother is out working. In more complex societies, by contrast, children cannot be as certain of their future role in the division of labor, nor can "work" for them seem as immediately contributory to family welfare as in simpler societies. Crucially, however, these characteristics would probably apply even more to boys than to girls. For girls, there is always some basic household and child-care work whose relevance is immediately perceptible that they can understand and expect to do.

The Genesis and Meaning of Masculine and Feminine Behaviors

Similar sex-role socialization and less sex differentiation in adult work are primarily a reflection of the extent to which boys are socialized to perform more (traditionally) feminine behavior and work. For example, according to Barry, Child, and Bacon, boys in societies stressing compliance are much more compliant according to their ratings than are girls assertive in societies stressing assertion. This is partially a result of the fact that variations in economy still leave women with one element of their economic role certain, thus one aspect of their training assured.

There seem to be differences in how compliant and assertive behavior are learned. All children have the basic experience of being raised primarily by women. In societies that stress masculine behavior, women, however resentful, must perform tasks that require reliability, responsibility, and nurturance. And if both children learn to be more independent, assertive, and achievement-oriented, girls still learn this from women, whereas it is likely that boys learn much of this behavior from men. There is a lack of symmetry in the child-rearing situations of the two kinds of society: both boys and girls learn compliant or nurturant-responsible behavior from women, but while boys may learn assertive behavior from men, girls still learn it from women.

There also seem to be different situational and cultural reasons for pressure toward assertion and actual dominant or authoritarian–aggressive behavior than for pressure toward compliance and actual nurturant–responsible behavior. In the latter case, nurturant, responsible behavior seems to relate to actual learning of role (offering help, offering support, and so forth) and is thus directly supported by pressure toward compliant behavior, that is, toward responsibility and obedience. Boys and girls who exhibit these behavioral characteristics are actually doing things – taking care of siblings, being responsible for livestock, perhaps helping in agricultural work.

Dominant–dependent behavior, by contrast, is likely to be a time-filler for someone who does not have a definite role. There is no necessary relation between this behavior and adult role, although domineering authoritarianism may be an adult personality characteristic. Similarly, it would seem that in societies with pressure toward assertive behavior, the usefulness of this behavior is greater in activities which only older people can do well – hunting, making war, competing in business, and the like. Pressure toward assertion cannot seem immediately relevant to a child nor so tied to successful fulfillment of work role for children. Pressure toward assertion, and dominant–dependent behavior seems to exist in societies where there is no obvious and simple relation between children's role and adult role, societies in which "characters are formed" rather than "roles learned." This seems to be *the* major characteristic of what it means to be trained to be "masculine," to perform a (typically) "male" role.

In most societies, to the extent that an economy or household structure requires that children learn real work as children, they learn what are normally thought of as female patterns of behavior. To the extent that there is no obvious continuity between childhood and adulthood, children learn what are normally male behaviors. Societies in which sex differences in socialization are small might be simple societies in which all children learn early to be responsible, obedient, and nurturant in the performance of real work, or they may be complex societies, such as ours, in which the socialization of both sexes is not perceptibly and immediately contributory to the society's economy and social organization. The extent to which sex-role socialization differs in ways we would expect, whether differentiation is great or small, reflects the difference in the extent to which boys wait, while girls do not, to be integrated into the adult world of work.

What accounts for "feminine" personality and behavior, then, is that a certain part of woman's work in all societies requires particular kinds of behavior, even when the attitude to this behavior is only disdain (women who hate childbearing must bear children and nurse them regularly in non-technological societies where there are no contraceptives or bottles). Men's work, by contrast, varies across cultures both in actual type and in the kinds of personality characteristics it requires. Biological sex differences exist; however, it is clear that all those characteristics that constitute "feminine" experiences and behavior, or feminine "nature," may also characterize men where other sorts of work or role expectations require them. Beyond the minimal requirements of childbearing and nursing, for which even girls can be socialized more or less appropriately, girls' socialization can produce women whose adult personality can range among all those characteristics which we consider male and female. We do not need to confuse statistical predominance with norm, and to explain norms in terms of biological nature. A consideration of specific facts of child training and cultural and sexual division of labor provides a better explanation.

Identity and Sex Role

Female and Male Identity: Being and Doing

There are many ways of characterizing the differences in the processes and goals of female and male socialization. Without trying to evaluate the exactness of these sorts of characterizations, I will describe them briefly. Distinctions can be drawn both between the degree of immediacy of (gender) roles for the child in primitive as opposed to Western societies and between boys and girls in each.

Anthropologists contrast the continuity and clarity of socialization in most primitive societies with modern society. In simpler societies the economic system is relatively understandable to a child. Work training constitutes gradual initiation into different kinds of work that will be expected of the child as an adult. Mothers' work is usually performed near children, and fathers' work, even if it is away, is liable to be a concretely describable, if not observable, task – hunting game or planting and harvesting in near or distant fields – rather than abstract thinking or assembly-line work, to understand which involves understanding the whole process of production in a factory or the structure of the professions. In addition, in societies that are less complex, more parents (especially fathers) do the same kind of work. For an American child, even if his or her father does something concrete and complete, like running a small grocery store or farming, a comparison with other fathers indicates immediately that this particular work cannot be easily equated with *the* male role.

Biological differences too are less apparent. In modern society children's sexuality is played down ("the child must be sexless as far as his family is concerned"[17]), and adult sex and childbearing are hidden. Clothes do their best to hide bodies and bodily differences. Primitive societies often approach bodies and sex differently: children, and often adults, wear much less clothing; families may all sleep in the same room; childbirth takes place in the home. Children's sexual behavior may be either ignored or encouraged rather than actively suppressed.

While these distinctions mean that the learning of adult sex roles is easier for children in less complex societies, it is also probably true that within each of these types of society, similar distinctions ensure that a girl's development into a woman is more continuous and understandable than a boy's development into a man. In some sense feminine identity is more easily and surely attainable than masculine identity. Mead claims that from the time of birth, girls can begin to take on feminine identity through identification with their mothers, while for little boys, masculine identification comes through a process of differentiation. His natural identification, with the person to whom he is closest and upon whom most dependent, is according to cultural values unnatural and works against his attainment of a stable masculine identity. The boy's "earliest experience of self is one in which he is forced, in the relationship to his mother, to realize himself as different, as a creature unlike the mother, as a creature unlike the human beings who make babies in a direct, intelligible way by using their own bodies to make them."[18] This seems to be the paradigmatic situation which describes many of the more general sex-role problems considered below.

I have described how in many non-Western societies, a girl's development and learning of her adult female role is more regular and continuous than a boy's development. Although the case is not so clear in our society (especially because there are more cross-pressures on the girl), it would seem that here also, pressure on girls, and the development of feminine identity, is not as difficult for the girl. Talcott Parsons claims that it is "possible from an early age to initiate girls directly into many important aspects of the adult feminine role."[19] At least part of their mothers' work is around the home, and the meaning of this activity is tangible and easily understandable to the child. Children can also participate in this work or imitate it. For a girl, this is direct training in her adult role; for a boy it is often that part of his socialization which most complicates his development.

In contrast, an urban child's father works away from his home, where his son cannot participate in or observe his work. In addition, masculine functions are "of a relatively abstract and intangible character such that their meaning must remain almost wholly inaccessible to a child."[20] Thus, boys are deprived of the possibility of modeling themselves meaningfully after tangible adult male roles or of being initiated gradually into adult work. Parsons wonders about boys in rural areas whose fathers' work is closer to home and more available to children, and he suggests that these boys tend to be "good" in a sense not typical of urban boys (more like boys in societies where children of both sexes can be gradually integrated into the economy).

This suggests that in both simple and complex societies, girls seem to have an easier time learning their adult role. Their socialization is less conflicted, less irregular, and more continuous, than the socialization of boys. However, socialization for both sexes is more continuous, and thus identity more stable, in simple than in complex societies.

Many different sources reiterate a distinction that both characterizes and explains this difference in the relative ease of girls' and boys' attainment of sex-role identity. These sources claim that girls and women "are," while boys and men "do"; that feminine identity is "ascribed" and masculine identity "achieved." Karen Horney points out that even biological differences reflect this distinction: "the man is actually obliged to go on proving his manhood to the woman. There is no analogous necessity for her: even if she is frigid, she can engage in sexual intercourse and conceive and bear a child. She performs her part by merely *being*, without any *doing*. . . The man on the other hand has to *do* something in order to fulfill himself."[21] Mead claims that the little boy's period of "simple sureness" about his sexuality is short – a brief period during childhood when he knows he has a penis and the potential to be manly, like other "men," but before he finds out that he will not be big or strong enough for a number of years to *act* like a man.[22] This period is the little girl's only period of doubt about her sexual constitution. On either end is sureness about her identity, first through identification with her mother and then because she herself has borne a child.

Culturally as well as psychologically, according to Mead, "maleness . . . is not absolutely defined, it has to be kept and re-earned every day."[23] Parsons suggests that women have an attainable goal – to marry and have children – and that how well they do this may bear on how people judge them but not on their fundamental female status.[24] He contrasts this with male status, which is constantly dependent in a basic way on a man's success at work, at getting promotions, and as a provider.

The need to differentiate himself continues throughout the boy's childhood. Mead points out that the boy "is trained by women to be a male, which involves no identification of the self with the mother–teacher [and when it does, such identification is thought harmful to his attainment of identity]. He is to be a boy by doing the things Mother says but doing them in a manly way."[25] His upbringing, and the attainment of any kind of success, is characterized by its conditional nature: success is always temporary – a failure wipes it out – and love and approval are dependent upon success.

Simone de Beauvoir sees positive rather than negative effects on boys from this differentiation. She describes girls' upbringing and contrasts it with boys', rather than attempting to explain how these contrasts have arisen. For her, boys' "doing" becomes men's transcendence: men are artists, creators, risk their lives, have projects. Women, on the other hand, are carefully trained to "be." A girl's natural inclination would also be to "do," but she learns to make herself into an object, to restrict herself to the sphere of immanence. Female destiny is foreordained and repetitive; men can choose their destiny:

The young boy, be he ambitious, thoughtless, or timid, looks toward an open future; he will be a seaman or an engineer, he will stay on the farm or go away to the city, he will see the world, he will get rich; he feels free, confronting a future in which the unexpected awaits him. The young girl will be wife, grandmother; she will keep house just as her mother did, she will give her children the same care she herself received when young – she is twelve years old and already her story is written in the heavens. She will discover it day after day without ever making it.[26]

The Cultural Universal: Socialization by Females

The common fact in all socialization situations I have mentioned is that women are the primary socializers. Men may also help in child care, but their "work" is elsewhere; for women it is the reverse. I have indicated certain effects that this seems to have on children's development in terms of primary identity, and on the differences between the development of identity in boys and girls. One result for children of both sexes is that, since "it is the mother's and not the father's voice that gives the principal early approval and disapproval, the nagging voice of conscience is feminine in both sexes."[27] Thus, as children of either sex attempt to gain independence – to make decisions on their own that are different from their upbringing – they must do this by consciously or unconsciously rejecting their mother (and people like her) and the things she is associated with. This fact, and the cultural institutions and emphases that it seems to entail, has different consequences for boys and for girls.

Female Socialization and Masculine Dread of Women

One consequence of the fact that women are primary socializers for boys (who later become men) is what Horney calls the "dread of women." This has both psychological and cultural aspects. Psychologically, Horney believes that fear of the mother (women) in men is even greater and more repressed than fear of the father (men). The mother initially has complete power over the child's satisfaction of needs and first forbids instinctual activities, by encouraging the child's first sadistic impulses to be directed against her and her body. This creates enormous anxiety in the child. Fear of the father is not so threatening. It develops later in life, and as a result of specific processes which the boy is more "aware" that he is experiencing. It is not in reaction to the father's total and incomprehensible control over the child's livelihood: "dread of the father is more actual and tangible, less uncanny in quality."[28] In addition, it does not entail a boy's admitting fear of a different sort of being, and "masculine self-regard suffers less in this way."[29] Because all men have mothers, these results are to a greater or lesser degree universal: "the anxiety connected with his self-respect leaves more or less distinct traces in every man and gives to his general attitude to women a particular stamp which either does not exist in women's attitude to men, or if it does, is acquired secondarily. In other words, it is no integral part of their feminine nature."[30]

Individual creations, as well as folk legends and beliefs, are often attempts to cope with this dread: poems and ballads talk about fears of engulfment by whirlpools and allurement by sirens who entice the unwary and kill whom they catch. Women and symbols of women in these creations and fantasies represent for grown men what the all-powerful mother is for the child. For a man, if this power can be named and externalized, it can possibly be conquered. Thus, other ways of coping with dread are to glorify and adore women – "There is no need for me to dread a being so wonderful, so beautiful, nay, so saintly" – or to debase and disparage them – "It would be too ridiculous to dread a creature who, if you take her all round, is such a poor thing."[31]

Culturally, this means that it is important for men to gain power and to insure that the attributes of power and prestige are masculine, or, more precisely, that whatever cultural role accrues to the male is then accorded power and prestige: "If such activities [like cooking and weaving] are appropriate occupations of men, then the whole society, men and women alike, votes them as important. When the same occupations are performed by women, they are regarded as less important."[32] It also becomes necessary to reserve many of these activities for men, to believe that women are unable to do many of the "important" things that contribute to society – to exercise political power, to be artistic or creative, to play an equal role in the economy – and at the same time to devalue whatever it is that women do – whether they are housewives, teachers, or social workers. In fact, "cultures frequently phrase achievement as something that women do not or cannot do, rather than directly as something which men do well."[33]

Melford Spiro's work on the kibbutz provides one empirical illustration of such processes, as he shows how men gain prestige even in this community that is officially trying to eliminate sexual inequality.[34] On the kibbutz where Spiro lived, women's work was not as prestigious as men's work, and this was particularly evident in the socialization institutions most affecting children. Until children are twelve or thirteen, all their nurses and teachers were women. When they reached thirteen and began high school, were more clearly doing serious *work* and not just being brought up, their teachers and supervisors were all men. Female "nurses" in the high school performed mainly menial functions – cleaned buildings and bathrooms, cleaned and repaired clothing. They took care of children only when they were sick. Serving "as an important transitional buffer from an all-female to an all-male [sic] adult environment,"[35] nurses went from being the most available and important adults in the child's world (parents were visited several hours a day and were loving and warm, but were not really the child's socializers or caretakers) to becoming maids. For reasons that Spiro does not specify, they ceded their status to men and became somehow incapable of continuing to play an important socializing role in the children's lives.

Around this time, girls (for reasons not apparent to, or at least not mentioned by, Spiro) ceased to be moral leaders of the students and became less intellectual and artistic than boys, when before they had been more so. Boys became more interested in their work and in politics. Among the adult kibbutz members, women did not serve on important committees, rarely spoke up at meetings (and when they did, were not listened to with the same seriousness as men) and did not participate in the economic administration or intellectual life of the kibbutz. Although they worked harder and longer than most men in order to "prove" themselves and their worth, the men continued to find it necessary not to recognize the value of this work or to accord women equal status.[36]

Dread and Bisexual Identification

Institutionally and culturally, men have often managed to overcome the dread of women through a devaluation of whatever women do and are. But the threat of femininity is internal as well as external: as a result of being socialized by women, men retain within themselves feminine qualities, a partial identification with women, and often a desire to be a woman like one's mother. Several theorists have argued that all people within a culture contain within themselves both what are considered (and tend to be) masculine and what are considered feminine characteristics in that culture. However, such bisexual identification is asymmetrical. In most cultures, the earliest identity for all children is feminine, because women are around them and provide (and do not provide) them with the necessities of life. Moreover, such identification is more threatening to the boy, because more basic, than the elements of masculine identification that a little girl later acquires. Several kinds of evidence attest to the existence (and repression) of feminine elements in boys and men.

One indication of the continuing threat of an internalized femininity to males in our culture is the strength of both external and internal pressure on little boys to conform to masculine ideals and to reject identification with or participation in anything that seems feminine. Initially, this pressure is generated by socializers of both sexes, but it is soon rigidly internalized by young boys, who hold both themselves and their peers to account over it.

The narrowness and severity of this training is far greater than comparable training for femininity in girls. Girls can be tomboys, wear jeans and other masculine clothing, fight, climb trees, play sports, and ride bikes. Their mothers may become somewhat anxious about them, but this behavior will not be cause for great alarm, nor will it be forbidden or cruelly ridiculed. Similarly, they may be considered unfeminine if they continue to be active or to succeed academically or professionally. However, many women do so nonetheless, and without feeling a fundamental challenge to their identity.

The training and subsequent behavior of boys is not so flexible. It would be unheard of for boys to wear dresses, and if they want to cook or play with dolls, do not like sports, or are afraid to fight, this is cause for panic by parents, educators, and psychologists. And in fact, boys conform closely to the masculine goals and behavior required of them. They learn early not to exhibit feminine personality traits – to hide emotions and pretend even to themselves that they do not have them, to be independent participants in activities rather than personally involved with friends. Later, as men, they are careful never to choose women's careers unless they are prepared to bear enormous stigma.

The extent and strength of boys' training not to have or to admit what they consider to be feminine traits is indicated by Daniel Brown's studies on sex-role preference in children.[37] From kindergarten age, boys are much less likely to claim preference for anything feminine than are girls to prefer masculine roles or objects: of girls three to five, about half tend to prefer "feminine" and half to prefer "masculine" toys, roles, and activities; at this age, three-quarters of boys express "masculine" preferences. The differences increase as children get older: from six to nine years old, boys become even more strongly masculine in their preferences, and girls' preferences become *less* feminine. More girls from six to nine make "masculine" choices than "feminine" choices.

The extent of boys' masculine "preferences," particularly in contrast to the willingness of girls to claim cross-sexual preferences, is striking. Part of the reason may be that it is apparent to both boys and girls, and becomes more apparent as they grow older, that in our society male roles and activities are more prestigious and privileged than female roles and activities. However, another interpretation suggests that the extreme unwillingness of boys to make cross-sex choices indicates that they have been taught very early, and have accepted more or less completely, that it is right for them to prefer masculine things. Therefore, they are extremely reluctant to make feminine choices. More important, it would seem that these boys, in contrast to the girls, believe that making such choices helps to insure their masculinity, and, alternatively, that different choices would not just be different choices among a number of possible alternatives, but rather threatening in the deepest sense.

This latter explanation, in terms of fear and attempts to insure masculinity, seems to account better for the regularity with which even very young boys – boys who spend most of their time in a world of female privilege with their mother or female teachers, and who play with children of both sexes – refuse to choose those things that are associated with females and that thus might give them feminine attributes. Studies of parental orientation in young boys also support such an interpretation. At ages when boys are already making strongly "masculine" choices of objects and playmates, they still do not identify with their fathers or male figures as strongly as girls, who are *not* making "feminine" choices, identify with their mothers.[38]

Fear of the feminine may not be so well absorbed and repressed. According to some interpreters, certain cultural or subcultural phenomena attest to direct jealousy of women and attempt to appropriate female roles. In Plains Indian cultures, for example, which stressed extreme bravery and daring for men, transvestism was an institutionalized solution for those men who did not feel able to take on the extremely masculine life required of them. A more important example are cultures in which *all* men perform certain rituals identifying with women. Roger Burton and John Whiting hypothesize that in cultures with both early mother–child sleeping arrangements and matrilocal residence – that is, a world controlled by the child's mother and other female relatives – a boy child will have both primary and secondary feminine "optative identity." In this situation, "the society should provide him some means to act out, symbolically at least, the female role."[39] Their data suggest that an institution that serves this purpose in a large number of societies of this type is the *couvade*, a practice in which men experience certain pregnancy processes along with their wives.

Initiation rites have also been interpreted variously as attempts on the one hand to appropriate or incorporate the feminine role, or, on the other, to exorcise it. On the basis of both anthropological and psychological evidence, Bruno Bettelheim claims that male initiation rites, which often involve subincision and in general include some kind of cutting or wounding of the genitals, are means for symbolically acquiring a vagina, "to assert that men, too, can bear children."[40] At the same time, circumcision and other tests of endurance, strength, and knowledge are ways of proving masculine sexual maturity, of asserting and defining maleness.

Burton and Whiting's cross-cultural evidence provides an explanation of this jealousy in terms of the maternal role in socialization. In certain societies, which Burton and Whiting call "father-absent," children sleep exclusively with their mother during their first two years, and there is a long post-partum sex taboo. All children in such societies develop a "primary feminine optative identity." These societies contrast with ones in which the father and mother continue to sleep together and in which both parents to some extent give and withhold resources. In such societies children's primary optative identity is "adult."[41] Among father-absent societies, there is a contrast between matrilocal and patrilocal societies. In the latter, a boy's secondary identity – which develops when he becomes a "yard child" and observes that in the society at large, it is males who have higher status and power – is masculine. Boys thus develop a "cross-sex identity." Burton and Whiting demonstrate that male initiation ceremonies tend to occur in societies whose sleeping arrangements and residence patterns produce cross-sex identity in boys; the function of these ceremonies is "to brainwash the primary feminine identity and to establish firmly the secondary male identity."[42] In many societies with male initiation rites, sex-identity terms, rather than being the equivalent of "male" and "female" in our society, are instead differentiated so that one term refers to women, girls, and uninitiated boys, while the other refers only to men who have already been initiated.

Evidence from more advanced societies suggests also that father-absence, or "low father-salience" in childhood may lead to reactively masculine behavior which entails the same rejection, although not in a ritual context, of the female world and feminine behavior.[43] Gang and delinquent behavior among American youth often includes strong denial of anything feminine, with corresponding emphasis on masculinity – on risk and daring, sexual prowess, rejection of home life, and physical violence – as well as severe tests, which might be seen as forms of initiation rite, as requirements of gang membership. Similar behavior also seems characteristic of Caribbean men raised in father-absent households.

Beatrice Whiting shows that criminal and other violent behavior occurs more frequently in those two out of the six cultures in which husband and wife may neither sleep nor eat together and seldom work or play together.[44] Sex-identity conflict seems to develop differently in the two societies, however. One is an Indian Rajput caste community, in which children of both sexes score high in dependent–dominant behavior. Boys are around women, perhaps desire their role, and have no role of their own until they grow up. Children in the other community, Nyansongo, Kenya, score highest in nurturant–responsible behavior. Here, boys from a quite young age are herders. Since they are being taught "feminine" behaviors of responsibility and nurturance, and eat and sleep only with women, it is likely that their identity is even more strongly "feminine" than that of the Rajput boys.

Like violent behavior, male narcissism, pride, and phobia toward mature women – other indications of compulsive assertion of masculinity – seem to be prevalent in societies in which boys spend their earlier years exclusively or predominantly with women, and in which the "degree of physical or emotional distance between mother and father as compared with that between mother and child" is great.[45]

All this evidence – of cultural institutions that exorcise or attempt to gain control of feminine powers for men; of institutions that provide for the assertion of compulsively masculine behavior; of the threats of bisexuality or femininity to boys and men – suggests that it is not sufficient to attribute the devaluation of female work roles and personality to external and conscious dread of women, to known fear of woman's power. Rather, it must be attributed to fear of that womanly power which has remained *within* men – the bisexual components of any man's personality. This is so threatening because, in some sense, there is no sure definition of masculinity, no way for the little boy to know if he has really made it, except insofar as he manages to differentiate himself from what he somehow vaguely defines as femininity. "For maleness in America [and, I would suggest, elsewhere] is not absolutely defined, it has to be kept and re-earned every day, and one essential element in the definition is beating women in every game that both sexes play, in every activity in which both sexes engage."[46]

Although reasons for the difficulty in defining male identity are complex, I have tried to indicate one approach which may provide some answers. I have examined how children attain sureness of themselves and an identity which is theirs, and what it means for one sex that there are no people "like me" who are there, and as important as people "not like me," from earliest infancy, as nurturers, as models, as providers and deniers of resources. What it means, according to Mead, is that "the recurrent problem of civilization is to define the male role satisfactorily enough,"[47] both for societies and for individuals who must live up to these undefined roles.

Feminine Development: Identity Versus Performance

When we turn to the development of feminine identity in girls, we discover that this development and sex-role preference are affected by the problems of male socialization I have described. The discussion so far implies that girls should have an easier time than boys developing a stable sexual identity: they are brought up primarily by women; their socialization is fairly gradual and continuous in most societies; the female role is more accessible and understandable to the child. As feminine identity conflict has not preoccupied cross-cultural researchers to the same extent as masculine conflict, in assessing this conflict in what follows I will be concerned primarily with the different forms (and secondary psychological importance) which female envy of males seems to take in Western society.

In contrast to non-Western societies, Western female socialization is not clear or unambiguous, just as the adult feminine role is not seen as an essential or important part of the society. Women get trained partially for traditionally feminine roles like child-rearing and housekeeping and for a personality stressing passivity, compliance, and "goodness." At the same time, they are taught in school goals of achievement and success, and it is made clear to them that their other, feminine role and its values are less desirable and less highly valued in the progress of humanity and the world.

Such a situation is comparable to the problem of cross-sex identity for boys. Girls are initially brought up in a feminine world, with mothers seemingly powerful and prestigious, a world in which it is desirable to acquire a feminine identity. They later go into a world where masculine virtues are important (even if, as in school, these virtues are taught by women) and where males dominate society and its important resources. In a culturally circumscribed, but nonetheless suggestive, way, de Beauvoir describes this situation:

If the little girl at first accepts her feminine vocation, it is not because she intends to abdicate; it is, on the contrary, in order to rule; she wants to be a matron because the matrons' group seems privileged; but, when her company, her studies, her games, her reading, take her out of the maternal circle, she sees that it is not the women but the men who control the world. It is this revelation – much more than the discovery of the penis – that irresistibly alters her conception of herself.[48]

A self-perpetuating cycle of female deprecation apparently develops. Mothers who are anxious and conflicted, even as they produce devaluation of femininity in boys, produce "feminine" qualities in girls. According to Lawrence Kohlberg, those very maternal behaviors conducive to greater conflict and less easy attainment of a secure sense of masculinity in boys – for example, general non-permissiveness, pressures toward inhibition and non-aggression, use of physical punishment and ridicule, high sex anxiety, and severity of toilet training – also encourage in girls the development of "feminine" qualities and femininity.[49] Such maternal behavior, according to Slater and Slater, develops especially in those societies or subcultures where the marriage relationship is distant and where family patterns entail masculine insecurity and compulsively masculine behavior.[50] According to the analysis developed here, however, these tendencies are present to some extent in many – and certainly in the typical modern Western – child-rearing situations, where the mother has major responsibility for children. When a mother's whole life and sense of self depends on rearing "good" or "successful" children, this must produce anxiety over performance and over-identification with children.

Such a situation, then, while producing femininity in girls, must necessarily also produce girls' resentment and conflict over acceptance of this femininity, and thus anxious and resentful behavior toward children in the next generation. However, such conflict does not seem to present the same challenge to fundamental identity as a shift from a female to a male world presents for boys, because in the little girl's case, her primary identity is feminine. These conflicts are not a reflection of a girl's uncertainty about whether she has attained a sufficiently feminine identity. Childhood environment and pressures on both sexes toward "feminine" compliance probably ensure that she has. A girl's conflicts, rather, are about whether or not she wants this identity, an identity reliant on her ability to inhibit herself and to respond to the demands of others, leading eventually to an adult fate where her role and her dependence upon it doom her to bring up sons and daughters resentful of her and the femininity she represents.

It seems clear to the whole society, and especially to the little girl, that this identity and its future leave much to be desired. Brown's findings indicate that not only do small girls "prefer" a masculine role with much more frequency than small boys "prefer" a feminine role, but that this preference for a masculine role increases with age from kindergarten to fourth grade: after the age of five, more girls prefer a masculine role than prefer a feminine role.

Kohlberg, like Brown, presents data from several preference studies of activities, toys, and peer choices. These data do not show the extreme differences that Brown found between boys and girls nor extreme masculine preferences in girls, but they do show that boys' preferences of masculine activities and peers begin and remain high or begin relatively high and increase with age. In contrast, girls' same-sex preferences are never so high as boys and tend to be more erratic. They show no consistent or increasing pattern of preference for feminine activities and peers. Kohlberg also mentions studies which indicate that not only are girls' sex-typed preferences of activities and playmates lower than boys', but also that "girls make fewer judgments than boys that their own sex is better . . . and girls' preferential evaluations of their own sex decrease with age."[51] Girls also tend to make more "feminine" judgments or preferences when they are asked directly "Which do you like?" than they do when asked "Which do girls like?"[52] The former question, it seems, requires the more culturally appropriate response, whereas the latter is a way for girls to express their own real preferences and judgments of value, without indicating to the interviewer that they do not know or believe in what they really ought to like or do.

All of these preferences reflect the clear cultural evaluation of masculine pursuits and characteristics as superior, an evaluation that is probably made more evident to the girl as she grows up and learns more about the world around her. Horney calls this the development of the girl's "flight from womanhood," and she attributes this flight to both unconscious psychological motives and conscious assessment of the world around her. The girl's unconscious motives stem from an attempt to deny an Oedipal attachment to her father by recoiling from femininity and therefore from feminine desires. This is in contrast to the boy, whose fear of his attachment to his mother leads to an increased compensatory masculinity. These unconscious motives "are reinforced and supported by the actual disadvantage under which women labor in social life. . . In actual fact a girl is exposed from birth onwards to the suggestion – inevitable, whether conveyed brutally or delicately – of her inferiority, an experience which must constantly stimulate her masculinity complex."[53] Horney, writing from within the psychoanalytic tradition, defends her emphasis on cultural components of the "flight." Although these cultural reasons may be partially a form of rationalization for less acceptable unconscious motives, she suggests, "we must not forget that this disadvantage is actually a piece of reality" and that there is an "actual social subordination of women."[54] The flight from womanhood is not a flight from uncertainty about feminine identity but from knowledge about it.

Partially because of the social subordination of women and cultural devaluation of feminine qualities, and interacting with masculine need to assert male superiority, girls are allowed and feel themselves free to express masculine preferences and to have much greater freedom than boys – to play boys' games, to dress like boys, and so forth. They are encouraged to achieve in school, and it is considered only natural that they would want to do so. In neither case do the girl or her socializers doubt that her feminine identity is firm – that she will eventually resign herself to her feminine adult role, and that at that time this role will come naturally to her.

As she gets older, however, her peers and the adults around her cease to tolerate overt envy of males and attempts to engage in male activities or to achieve like men: "any self-assertion will diminish her femininity and her attractiveness."[55] She is supposed to begin to be passive and docile, to become interested in her appearance, to cultivate her abilities to charm men, to mold herself to their wants. This is not a one-sided requirement, however. At the same time she is supposed to continue to do well in school but must expect to be stigmatized or reproved if she does. In American society she continues in school to be instilled with "American" (i.e., masculine) goals – success, achievement, competition. She fails as a good citizen, as a successful human being, if she does not succeed, and as a woman if she does. Mead sums up the girl's position:

We end up with the contradictory picture of a society that appears to throw its doors wide open to women, but translates her every step toward success as having been damaging – to her own chances of marriage, and to the men whom she passes on the road.[56]

It seems that society succeeds in imposing its demands. Brown finds that fifth-grade girls make a dramatic switch and suddenly develop strong "preferences" for feminine activities and objects. Girls on the kibbutz, formerly creative, interested in their work, moral and social leaders, and organizers in their children's group, in high school become uninterested in intellectual activities, unconcerned about politics, uncreative, and unartistic. In general, as they grow up, girls are likely to become less successful in school and drop out of the role of equal participant in activities that they once held.

Conclusion

Sex-role ideology and socialization for these roles seem to ensure that neither boys nor girls can attain both stable identity and meaningful roles. The tragedy of woman's socialization is not that she is left unclear, as is the man, about her basic sexual identity. This identity is ascribed to her, and she does not need to prove to herself or to society that she has earned it or continues to have it. Her problem is that this identity is clearly devalued in the society in which she lives. This does not mean that women too should be required to compete for identity, to be assertive and to need to achieve – to *do* like men. Nor does it suggest that it is not crucial for everyone, men and women alike, to have a stable sexual identity. But until masculine identity does not depend on men's proving themselves, their *doing* will be a reaction to insecurity rather than a creative exercise of their humanity, and woman's *being*, far from being an easy and positive acceptance of self, will be a resignation to inferiority. And as long as women must live through their children, and men do not genuinely contribute to socialization and provide easily accessible role models, women will continue to bring up sons whose sexual identity depends on devaluing femininity inside and outside themselves, and daughters who must accept this devalued position and resign themselves to producing more men who will perpetuate the system that devalues them.

2

Family Structure and Feminine Personality

I propose here a model to account for the reproduction within each generation of certain general and nearly universal differences that characterize masculine and feminine personality and roles.[1] My perspective is largely psychoanalytic. Cross-cultural and social-psychological evidence suggests that an argument drawn solely from the universality of biological sex differences is unconvincing.[2] At the same time, explanations based on patterns of deliberate socialization (the most prevalent kind of anthropological, sociological, and social-psychological explanation) are in themselves insufficient to account for the extent to which psychological and value commitments to sex differences are so emotionally laden and tenaciously maintained, for the way gender identity and expectations about sex roles and gender consistency are so deeply central to a person's consistent sense of self.

This chapter suggests that a crucial differentiating experience in male and female development arises out of the fact that women, universally, are largely responsible for early child care and for (at least) later female socialization. This points to the central importance of the mother–daughter relationship for women, and to a focus on the conscious and unconscious effects of early involvement with a female for children of both sexes. The fact that males and females experience this social environment differently as they grow up accounts for the development of basic sex differences in personality. In particular, certain features of the mother–daughter relationship are internalized universally as basic elements of feminine ego structure (although not necessarily what we normally mean by "femininity").

Specifically, I shall propose that, in any given society, feminine personality comes to define itself in relation and connection to other people more than masculine personality does. (In psychoanalytic terms, women are less individuated than men; they have more flexible ego boundaries.[3]) Moreover, issues of dependency are handled and experienced differently by men and women. For boys and men, both individuation and dependency issues become tied up with the sense of masculinity, or masculine identity. For girls and women, by contrast, issues of femininity, or feminine identity, are not problematic in the same way. The structural situation of child-rearing, reinforced by female and male role training, produces these differences, which are replicated and reproduced in the sexual sociology of adult life.

The essay is also a beginning attempt to rectify certain gaps in the social-scientific literature, and a contribution to the reformulation of psychological anthropology. Most traditional accounts of family and socialization tend to emphasize only role training, and not unconscious features of personality. Those few that rely on Freudian theory have abstracted a behaviorist methodology from this theory, concentrating on isolated "significant" behaviors like weaning and toilet-training. The chapter advocates instead a focus on the ongoing interpersonal relationships in which these various behaviors are given meaning.[4]

More empirically, most social-scientific accounts of socialization, child development, and the mother–child relationship refer implicitly or explicitly only to the development and socialization of boys, and to the mother–son relationship. There is a striking lack of systematic description about the mother–daughter relationship, and a basic theoretical discontinuity between, on the one hand, theories about female development, which tend to stress the development of "feminine" qualities in relation to and comparison with men, and, on the other hand, theories about women's ultimate mothering role. This final lack is particularly crucial, because women's motherhood and mothering role seem to be the most important features in accounting for the universal secondary status of women.[5] The present essay describes the development of psychological qualities in women that are central to the perpetuation of this role.

In a formulation of this preliminary nature, there is not a great body of consistent evidence to draw upon. Available evidence is presented that illuminates aspects of the theory – for the most part psychoanalytic and social-psychological accounts based almost entirely on highly industrialized Western society. Because aspects of family structure are discussed that are universal, however, I think it is worth considering the theory as a general model. In any case, this is in some sense a programmatic appeal to people doing research. It points to certain issues that might be especially important in investigations of child development and family relationships, and suggests that researchers look explicitly at female vs male development, and that they consider seriously mother–daughter relationships even if these are not of obvious "structural importance" in a traditional anthropological view of that society.

The Development of Gender Personality

According to psychoanalytic theory, personality is a result of a boy's or girl's social-relational experiences from earliest infancy.[6] Personality development is not the result of conscious parental intention. The nature and quality of the social relationships that the child experiences are appropriated, internalized, and organized by her or him and come to constitute her or his personality. What is internalized from an ongoing relationship continues independent of that original relationship and is generalized and set up as a permanent feature of the personality. The conscious self is usually not aware of many of the features of personality, or of its total structural organization. At the same time, these are important determinants of any person's behavior, both that which is culturally expected and that which is idiosyncratic or unique to the individual. The conscious aspects of personality, like a person's general self-concept and, importantly, her or his gender identity, require and depend upon the consistency and stability of its unconscious organization. In what follows I shall describe how contrasting male and female experiences lead to differences in the way that the developing masculine or feminine psyche resolves certain relational issues.

Separation and Individuation (Pre-Oedipal Development)

All children begin life in a state of what Fairbairn calls "infantile dependence" upon an adult or adults, in most cases their mother. This state consists first in the persistence of primary identification with the mother: the child does not differentiate herself or himself from her or his mother but experiences a sense of oneness with her. (It is important to distinguish this from later forms of identification, from "secondary identification," which presuppose at least some degree of experienced separateness by the person who identifies.) Second, it includes an oral-incorporative mode of relationship to the world, leading, because of the infant's total helplessness, to a strong attachment to and dependence upon whoever nurses and carries her or him.

Both aspects of this state are continuous with the child's prenatal experience of being emotionally and physically part of the mother's body and of the exchange of body material through the placenta. That this relationship continues with the natural mother in most societies stems from the fact that women lactate. For convenience, and not because of biological necessity, this has usually meant that mothers, and females in general, tend to take all care of babies. It is probable that the mother's continuing to have major responsibility for the feeding and care of the child (so that the child interacts almost entirely with her) extends and intensifies her or his period of primary identification with her more than if, for instance, someone else were to take major or total care of the child. A child's earliest experience, then, is usually of identity with and attachment to a single mother, and always with women.

For both boys and girls, the first few years are preoccupied with issues of separation and individuation. This includes breaking or attenuating the primary identification with the mother and beginning to develop an individuated sense of self, and mitigating the totally dependent oral attitude and attachment to the mother. I would suggest that, contrary to the traditional psychoanalytic model, the pre-Oedipal experience is likely to differ for boys and girls. Specifically, the experience of mothering for a woman involves a double identification.[7] A woman identifies with her own mother and, through identification with her child, she (re)experiences herself as a cared-for child. The particular nature of this double identification for the individual mother is closely bound up with her relationship to her own mother. As psychoanalyst Helene Deutsch expresses it, "In relation to her own child, woman repeats her own mother–child history."[8] Given that she was a female child, and that identification with her mother and mothering are so bound up with her being a woman, we might expect that a woman's identification with a girl child might be stronger; that a mother, who is, after all, a person who is a woman and not simply the performer of a formally defined role, would tend to treat infants of different sexes in different ways.

There is some suggestive sociological evidence that this is the case. Mothers in the mother–daughter group (see n. 1), say that they identified more with their girl children than with boy children. The perception and treatment of girl vs boy children in high-caste, extremely patriarchal, patrilocal communities in India are in the same vein. Families express preference for boy children and celebrate when sons are born. At the same time, according to anthropological researchers, Rajput mothers in North India are "as likely as not" to like girl babies better than boy babies once they are born, and they and Havik Brahmins in South India treat their daughters with greater affection and leniency than their sons.[9] People in both groups say that this is out of sympathy for the future plight of their daughters, who will have to leave their natal family for a strange and usually oppressive postmarital household. From the time of their daughters' birth, then, mothers in these communities identify anticipatorily, by re-experiencing their own past, with the experiences of separation that their daughters will go through. They develop a particular attachment to their daughters because of this and by imposing their own reaction to the issue of separation on this new external situation.

It seems, then, that a mother is more likely to identify with a daughter than with a son, to experience her daughter (or parts of her daughter's life) as herself. Psychoanalyst Robert Fliess's description of his neurotic patients who were the children of ambulatory psychotic mothers presents the problem in its psychopathological extreme.[10] The example is interesting, because, although Fliess claims to be writing about people defined only by the fact that their problems were tied to a particular kind of relationship to their mothers, an overwhelmingly large proportion of the cases he presents are women. It seems, then, that this sort of disturbed mother inflicts her pathology predominantly on daughters. The mothers Fliess describes did not allow their daughters to perceive themselves as separate people, but simply acted as if their daughters were narcissistic extensions or doubles of themselves, extensions to whom were attributed the mothers' bodily feelings and who became physical vehicles for their mothers' achievement of autoerotic gratification. The daughters were bound into a mutually dependent "hypersymbiotic" relationship. These mothers, then, perpetuate a mutual relationship with their daughters of both primary identification and infantile dependence.

A son's case is different. Cultural evidence suggests that insofar as a mother treats her son differently, it is usually by emphasizing his masculinity in opposition to herself and by pushing him to assume, or acquiescing in his assumption of, a sexually toned male-role relation to her. John Whiting and Whiting et al. suggest that mothers in societies with mother–child sleeping arrangements and postpartum sex taboos may be seductive toward infant sons.[11] Slater describes the socialization of precarious masculinity in Greek males of the classical period through their mothers' alternation of sexual praise and seductive behavior with hostile deflation and ridicule.[12] This kind of behavior contributes to the son's differentiation from his mother and to the formation of ego boundaries (I will later discuss certain problems that result from this).

Neither form of attitude or treatment is what we would call "good mothering." However, evidence of differentiation of a pathological nature in the mother's behavior toward girls and boys does highlight tendencies in "normal" behavior. It seems likely that from their children's earliest childhood, mothers and women tend to identify more with daughters and to help them to differentiate less, and that processes of separation and individuation are made more difficult for girls. On the other hand, a mother tends to identify less with her son, and to push him toward differentiation and the taking on of a male role unsuitable to his age, and undesirable at any age in his relationship to her.

For boys and girls, the quality of the pre-Oedipal relationship to the mother differs. This, as well as differences in development during the Oedipal period, accounts for the persisting importance of pre-Oedipal issues in female development and personality that many psychoanalytic writers describe.[13] Even before the establishment of gender identity, gender personality differentiation begins.

Gender Identity (Oedipal Crisis and Resolution)

There is only a slight suggestion in the psychological and sociological literature that pre-Oedipal development differs for boys and girls. The pattern becomes explicit at the next developmental level. All theoretical and empirical accounts agree that after about age three (the beginning of the "Oedipal" period, which focuses on the attainment of a stable gender identity) male and female development becomes radically different. It is at this stage that the father, and men in general, begin to become important in the child's primary object world. It is, of course, particularly difficult to generalize about the attainment of gender identity and sex-role assumption, since there is such wide variety in the sexual sociology of different societies. However, to the extent that in all societies women's life tends to be more private and domestic, and men's more public and social, we can make general statements about this kind of development.

In what follows, I shall be talking about the development of gender personality and gender identity in the tradition of psychoanalytic theory. Cognitive psychologists have established that by the age of three, boys and girls have an irreversible conception of what their gender is.[14] I do not dispute these findings. It remains true that children (and adults) may know definitely that they are boys (men) or girls (women), and at the same time experience conflicts or uncertainty about "masculinity" or "femininity," about what these identities require in behavioral or emotional terms, etc. I am discussing the development of "gender identity" in this latter sense.

A boy's masculine gender identification must come to replace his early primary identification with his mother. This masculine identification is usually based on identification with a boy's father or other salient adult males. However, a boy's father is relatively more remote than his mother. He rarely plays a major caretaking role even at this period in his son's life. In most societies, his work and social life take place farther from the home than do those of his wife. He is, then, often relatively inaccessible to his son, and performs his male role activities away from where the son spends most of his life. As a result, a boy's male gender identification often becomes a "positional" identification, with aspects of his father's clearly or not-so-clearly defined male role, rather than a more generalized "personal" identification – a diffuse identification with his father's personality, values, and behavioral traits – that could grow out of a real relationship to his father.[15]

Psychoanalyst and social theorist Mitscherlich, in his discussion of Western advanced capitalist society, provides a useful insight into the problem of male development.[16] The father, because his work takes him outside of the home most of the time, and because his active presence in the family has progressively decreased, has become an "invisible father." For the boy, the tie between affective relations and masculine gender identification and role learning (between libidinal and ego development) is relatively attenuated. He identifies with a fantasied masculine role, because the reality constraint that contact with his father would provide is missing. In all societies characterized by some sex segregation (even those in which a son will eventually lead the same sort of life as his father), much of a boy's masculine identification must be of this sort, that is, with aspects of his father's role, or what he fantasies to be a male role, rather than with his father as a person involved in a relationship to him.

There is another important aspect to this situation, which helps to explain the psychological dynamics of the universal social and cultural devaluation and subordination of women. A boy, in his attempt to gain an elusive masculine identification, often comes to define this masculinity largely in negative terms, as that which is not feminine or involved with women. There is an internal and external aspect to this. Internally, the boy tries to reject his mother and deny his attachment to her and the strong dependence upon her that he still feels. He also tries to deny the deep personal identification with her that has developed during his early years. He does this by repressing whatever he takes to be feminine inside himself, and, importantly, by denigrating and devaluing whatever he considers to be feminine in the outside world. As a societal member, he also appropriates to himself and defines as superior particular social activities and cultural (moral, religious, and creative) spheres – possibly, in fact, "society" and "culture" themselves.[17]

Freud's description of the boy's Oedipal crisis speaks to the issues of rejection of the feminine and identification with the father. As his early attachment to his mother takes on phallic-sexual overtones, and his father enters the picture as an obvious rival (who, in the son's fantasy, has apparent power to kill or castrate his son), the boy must radically deny and repress his attachment to his mother and replace it with an identification with his loved and admired, but also potentially punitive, therefore feared, father. He internalizes a superego.[18]

To summarize, four components of the attainment of masculine gender identity are important. First, masculinity becomes and remains a problematic issue for a boy. Second, it involves denial of attachment or relationship, particularly of what the boy takes to be dependence or need for another, and differentiation of himself from another. Third, it involves the repression and devaluation of femininity on both psychological and cultural levels. Finally, identification with his father does not usually develop in the context of a satisfactory affective relationship, but consists in the attempt to internalize and learn components of a not immediately apprehensible role.

The development of a girl's gender identity contrasts with that of a boy. Most important, femininity and female role activities are immediately apprehensible in the world of her daily life. Her final role identification is with her mother and women, that is, with the person or people with whom she also has her earliest relationship of infantile dependence. The development of her gender identity does not involve a rejection of this early identification, however. Rather, her later identification with her mother is embedded in and influenced by their on-going relationship of both primary identification and pre-Oedipal attachment. Because her mother is around, and she has had a genuine relationship to her as a person, a girl's gender and gender role identification are mediated by and depend upon real affective relations. Identification with her mother is not positional – the narrow learning of particular role behaviors – but rather a personal identification with her mother's general traits of character and values. Feminine identification is based not on fantasied or externally defined characteristics and negative identification, but on the gradual learning of a way of being familiar in everyday life, and exemplified by the person (or kind of people – women) with whom she has been most involved. It is continuous with her early childhood identifications and attachments.

The major discontinuity in the development of a girl's sense of gender identity, and one that has led Freud and other early psychoanalysts to see female development as exceedingly difficult and tortuous, is that at some point she must transfer her primary sexual object choice from her mother and females to her father and males, if she is to attain her expected heterosexual adulthood. Briefly, Freud considers that all children feel that mothers give some cause for complaint and unhappiness: they give too little milk; they have a second child; they arouse and then forbid their child's sexual gratification in the process of caring for her or him. A girl receives a final blow, however: her discovery that she lacks a penis. She blames this lack on her mother, rejects her mother, and turns to her father in reaction.

Problems in this account have been discussed extensively in the general literature that has grown out of the women's movement, and within the psychoanalytic tradition itself. These concern Freud's misogyny and his obvious assumptions that males possess physiological superiority and that a woman's personality is inevitably determined by her lack of a penis.[19]

The psychoanalytic account is not completely unsatisfactory, however. A more detailed consideration of several accounts of the female Oedipus complex reveals important features of female development, especially about the mother–daughter relationship, and at the same time contradicts or mitigates the absoluteness of the more general Freudian outline.[20]

Psychoanalysts emphasize how, in contrast to males, the female Oedipal crisis is not resolved in the same absolute way. A girl cannot and does not completely reject her mother in favor of men, but continues her relationship of dependence upon and attachment to her. In addition, the strength and quality of her relationship to her father is completely dependent upon the strength and quality of her relationship to her mother. Deutsch suggests that a girl wavers in a "bisexual triangle" throughout her childhood and into puberty, normally making a very tentative resolution in favor of her father, but in such a way that issues of separation from and attachment to her mother remain important throughout a woman's life:

It is erroneous to say that the little girl gives up her first mother relation in favor of the father. She only gradually draws him into the alliance, develops from the mother–child exclusiveness toward the triangular parent–child relationship and continues the latter, just as she does the former, although in a weaker and less elemental form, all her life. Only the principal part changes: now the mother, now the father plays it. The ineradicability of affective constellations manifests itself in later repetitions.[21]

We might suggest from this that a girl's internalized and external object relations become and remain more complex, and at the same time more defining of her, than those of a boy. Psychoanalytic preoccupation with constitutionally based libidinal development, and with a normative male model of development, has obscured this fact. Most women are genitally heterosexual. At the same time, their lives always involve other sorts of equally deep and primary relationships, especially with their children, and, importantly, with other women. In these spheres also, even more than in the area of heterosexual relations, a girl imposes the sort of object relations she has internalized in her pre-Oedipal and later relationship to her mother.

Men are also for the most part genitally heterosexual. This grows directly out of their early primary attachment to their mother. We know, however, that in many societies their heterosexual relationships are not embedded in close personal relationship but simply in relations of dominance and power. Furthermore, they do not have the extended personal relations women have. They are not so connected to children, and their relationships with other men tend to be based not on particularistic connection or affective ties, but rather on abstract, universalistic role expectations.

Building on the psychoanalytic assumption that unique individual experiences contribute to the formation of individual personality, culture and personality theory has held that early experiences common to members of a particular society contribute to the formation of "typical" personalities organized around and preoccupied with certain issues: "Prevailing patterns of child-rearing must result in similar internalized situations in the unconscious of the majority of individuals in a culture, and these will be externalized back into the culture again to perpetuate it from generation to generation."[22] In a similar vein, I have tried to show that to the extent males and females, respectively, experience similar interpersonal environments as they grow up, masculine and feminine personality will develop differently.

I have relied on a theory which suggests that features of adult personality and behavior are determined, but which is not biologically determinist. Culturally expected personality and behavior are not simply "taught," however. Rather, certain features of social structure, supported by cultural beliefs, values, and perceptions, are internalized through the family and the child's early social object relationships. This largely unconscious organization is the context in which role training and purposive socialization take place.

Sex-Role Learning and its Social Context

Sex-role training and social interaction in childhood build upon and reinforce the largely unconscious development I have described. In most societies (ours is a complicated exception) a girl is usually with her mother and other female relatives in an interpersonal situation that facilitates continuous and early role learning and emphasizes the mother–daughter identification and particularistic, diffuse, affective relationships between women. A boy, to a greater or lesser extent, is also with women for a large part of his childhood, which prevents continuous or easy masculine role identification. His development is characterized by discontinuity.

Historian of childhood Philippe Ariès, in his discussion of the changing concept of childhood in modern capitalist society, makes a distinction that seems to have more general applicability.[23] Boys, he suggests, became "children" while girls remained "little women." "The idea of childhood profited the boys first of all, while the girls persisted much longer in the traditional way of life which confused them with the adults: we shall have cause to notice more than once this delay on the part of the women in adopting the visible forms of the essentially masculine civilization of modern times." This took place first in the middle classes, as a situation developed in which boys needed special schooling in order to prepare for their future work and could not begin to do this kind of work in childhood. Girls (and working-class boys) could still learn work more directly from their parents, and could begin to participate in the adult economy at an earlier age. Rapid economic change and development have exacerbated the lack of male generational role continuity. Few fathers now have either the opportunity or the ability to pass on a profession or skill to their sons.

Sex-role development of girls in modern society is more complex. On the one hand, they go to school to prepare for life in a technologically and socially complex society. On the other, there is a sense in which this schooling is a pseudo-training. It is not meant to interfere with the much more important training to be "feminine" and a wife and mother, which is embedded in the girl's unconscious development and which her mother teaches her in a family context where she is clearly the salient parent.

This dichotomy is not unique to modern industrial society. Even if special, segregated schooling is not necessary for adult male work (and many male initiation rites remain a form of segregated role training), boys still participate in more activities that characterize them as a category apart from adult life. Their activities grow out of the boy's need to fill time until he can begin to take on an adult male role. Boys may withdraw into isolation and self-involved play or join together in a group that remains more or less unconnected with either the adult world of work and activity or the familial world.

Anthropologist Robert Jay describes this sort of situation in rural Modjokuto, Java.[24] Girls, after the age of five or so, begin gradually to help their mothers in their work and spend time with their mothers. Boys at this early age begin to form bands of age mates who roam and play about the city, relating neither to adult men nor to their mothers and sisters. Boys, then, enter a temporary group based on universalistic membership criteria, while girls continue to participate in particularistic role relations in a group characterized by continuity and relative permanence.

The content of boys' and girls' role training tends in the same direction as the context of this training and its results. Barry, Bacon, and Child, in their well-known study, demonstrate that the socialization of boys tends to be oriented toward achievement and self-reliance and that of girls toward nurturance and responsibility.[25] Girls are thus pressured to be involved with and connected to others, boys to deny this involvement and connection.

Adult Gender Personality and Sex Role

A variety of psychologist's conceptualizations of female and male personality all focus on distinctions around the same issue, and provide alternative confirmation of the developmental model I have proposed. Bakan claims that male personality is preoccupied with the "agentic," and female personality with the "communal." His expanded definition of the two concepts is illuminating:

I have adopted the terms "agency" and "communion" to characterize two fundamental modalities in the existence of living forms, agency for the existence of an organism as an individual and communion for the participation of the individual in some larger organism of which the individual is a part. Agency manifests itself in self-protection, self-assertion, and self-expansion; communion manifests itself in the sense of being at one with other organisms. Agency manifests itself in the formation of separations; communion in the lack of separations. Agency manifests itself in isolation, alienation, and aloneness; communion in contact, openness, and union. Agency manifests itself in the urge to master; communion in noncontractual cooperation. Agency manifests itself in the repression of thought, feeling, and impulse; communion in the lack and removal of repression.[26]

Gutmann contrasts the socialization of male personalities in "allocentric" milieux (milieux in which the individual is part of a larger social organization and system of social bonds) with that of female personalities in "autocentric" milieux (in which the individual herself or himself is a focus of events and ties). He suggests that this leads to a number of systematic differences in ego functioning. Female ego qualities, growing out of participation in autocentric milieux, include more flexible ego boundaries (i.e. less insistent self–other distinctions), present orientation rather than future orientation, and relatively greater subjectivity and less detached objectivity.[27]

Carlson confirms both characterizations. Her tests of Gutmann's claims lead her to conclude that "males represent experiences of self, others, space, and time in individualistic, objective, and distant ways, while females represent experiences in relatively interpersonal, subjective, immediate ways."[28] With reference to Bakan, she claims that men's descriptions of affective experience tend to be in agentic terms and women's in terms of communion, and that an examination of abstracts of a large number of social-psychological articles on sex differences yields an overwhelming confirmation of the agency/communion hypothesis.

Cohen contrasts the development of "analytic" and "relational" cognitive style, the former characterized by a stimulus-centered, parts-specific orientation to reality, the latter centered on the self and responding to the global characteristics of a stimulus in reference to its total context.[29] Although focussing primarily on class differences in cognitive style, she also points out that girls are more likely to mix the two types of functioning (and also to exhibit internal conflict about this). Especially, they are likely to exhibit at the same time both high field dependence and highly developed analytic skills in other areas. She suggests that boys and girls participate in different sorts of interactional subgroups in their families: boys experience their family more as a formally organized primary group; girls experience theirs as a group characterized by shared and less clearly delineated functions. She concludes: "Since embedded responses covered the gamut from abstract categories, through language behaviors, to expressions of embeddedness in their social environments, it is possible that embeddedness may be a distinctive characteristic of female sex-role learning in this society regardless of social class, native ability, ethnic differences, and the cognitive impact of the school."[30]

Preliminary consideration suggests a correspondence between the production of feminine personalities organized around "communal" and "autocentric" issues and characterized by flexible ego boundaries, less detached objectivity, and relational cognitive style, on the one hand, and important aspects of feminine as opposed to masculine social roles, on the other.

Most generally, I would suggest that a quality of embeddedness in social interaction and personal relationships characterizes women's life relative to men's. From childhood, daughters are likely to participate in an intergenerational world with their mother, and often with their aunts and grandmother, whereas boys are on their own or participate in a single-generation world of age mates. In adult life, women's interaction with other women in most societies is kin-based and cuts across generational lines. Their roles tend to be particularistic, and to involve diffuse relationships and responsibilities rather than specific ones. Women in most societies are *defined* relationally (as someone's wife, mother, daughter, daughter-in-law; even a nun becomes the Bride of Christ). Men's association (although it too may be kin-based and intergenerational) is much more likely than women's to cut across kinship units, to be restricted to a single generation, and to be recruited according to universalistic criteria and involve relationships and responsibilities defined by their specificity.

Ego Boundaries and the Mother–Daughter Relationship

The care and socialization of girls by women ensure the production of feminine personalities founded on relation and connection, with flexible rather than rigid ego boundaries, and with a comparatively secure sense of gender identity. This is one explanation for how women's relative embeddedness is reproduced from generation to generation, and why it exists within almost every society. More specific investigation of different social contexts suggests, however, that there are variations in the kind of relationship that can exist between women's role performance and feminine personality.

Various kinds of evidence suggest that separation from the mother, the breaking of dependence, and the establishment and maintenance of a consistently individuated sense of self remain difficult psychological issues for Western middle-class women (i.e. the women who become subjects of psychoanalytic and clinical reports and social-psychological studies). Deutsch in particular provides extensive clinical documentation of these difficulties and of the way they affect women's relationships to men and children and, because of their nature, are reproduced in the next generation of women. Mothers and daughters in the mother–daughter group described their experiences of boundary confusion or equation of self and other, for example, guilt and self-blame for the other's unhappiness; shame and embarrassment at the other's actions; daughters' "discovery" that they are "really" living out their mothers' lives in their choice of career; mothers' not completely conscious reactions to their daughters' bodies as their own (over-identification and therefore often unnecessary concern with supposed weight or skin problems, which the mother is really worried about in herself).

A kind of guilt that Western women express seems to grow out of and to reflect lack of adequate self/other distinctions and a sense of inescapable embeddedness in relationships to others. In an early women's liberation pamphlet Meredith Tax describes this well:

Since our awareness of others is considered our duty, the price we pay when things go wrong is guilt and self-hatred. And things always go wrong. We respond with apologies; we continue to apologize long after the event is forgotten – and *even if it had no causal relation to anything we did to begin with*. If the rain spoils someone's picnic, we apologize. We apologize for taking up space in a room, for living.[31]

As if the woman does not differentiate herself clearly from the rest of the world, she feels a sense of guilt and responsibility for situations that did not come about through her actions and without relation to her actual ability to determine the course of events. This happens, in the most familiar instance, in a sense of diffuse responsibility for everything connected to the welfare of her family and the happiness and success of her children. This loss of self in overwhelming responsibility for and connection to others is described particularly acutely by women writers (in the work, for instance, of Simone de Beauvoir, Kate Chopin, Doris Lessing, Tillie Olsen, Christina Stead, Virginia Woolf).

Slater points to several studies supporting the contention that Western daughters have particular problems about differentiation from their mother. These studies show that though most forms of personal parental identification correlate with psychological adjustment (i.e. freedom from neurosis or psychosis, *not* social acceptability), personal identification of a daughter with her mother does not. The reason is that the mother–daughter relation is the one form of personal identification that, because it results so easily from the normal situation of child development, is liable to be excessive in the direction of allowing no room for separation or difference between mother and daughter.[32]

The situation reinforces itself in circular fashion. A mother, on the one hand, grows up without establishing adequate ego boundaries or a firm sense of self. She tends to experience boundary confusion with her daughter, and does not provide experiences of differentiating ego development for her daughter or encourage the breaking of her daughter's dependence. The daughter, for her part, makes a rather unsatisfactory and artificial attempt to establish boundaries: she projects what she defines as bad within her onto her mother and tries to take what is good into herself. (This, I think, is the best way to understand the girl's Oedipal "rejection" of her mother.) Such an arbitrary mechanism cannot break the underlying psychological unity, however. Projection is never more than a temporary solution to ambivalence or boundary confusion.

The implication is that, contrary to Gutmann's suggestion, "so-called ego pathology" may not be "adaptive" for women.[33] Women's biosexual experiences (menstruation, coitus, pregnancy, childbirth, lactation) all involve some challenge to the boundaries of her body ego ("me"/"not-me" in relation to her blood or milk, to a man who penetrates her, to a child once part of her body). These are important and fundamental human experiences that are probably intrinsically meaningful and at the same time complicated for women everywhere. However, a Western woman's tenuous sense of individuation and of the firmness of her ego boundaries increase the likelihood that experiences challenging these boundaries will be difficult for her and conflictual.

Nor is it clear that this personality structure is "functional" for society as a whole. The evidence presented in this chapter suggests that satisfactory mothering, which does not reproduce particular psychological problems in boys and girls, comes from a person with a firm sense of self and of her own value, whose care is a freely chosen activity rather than a reflection of a conscious and unconscious sense of inescapable connection to and responsibility for her children.

Social Structure and the Mother–Daughter Relationship

Clinical and self-analytic descriptions of women and of the psychological component of mother–daughter relationships are not available from societies and subcultures outside of the Western middle class. However, accounts that are primarily sociological about women in other societies enable us to infer certain aspects of their psychological situation. In what follows, I am not claiming to make any kind of general statement about what constitutes a "healthy society," but only to examine and isolate specific features of social life that seem to contribute to the psychological strength of some members of a society. Consideration of three groups with matrifocal tendencies in their family structure highlights several dimensions of importance in the developmental situation of the girl.[34]

Young and Willmott describe the daily visiting and mutual aid of working-class mothers and daughters in East London. In a situation where household structure is usually nuclear, like the Western middle class, grown daughters look to their mothers for advice, for aid in childbirth and child care, for friendship and companionship, and for financial help. Their mother's house is the ultimate center of the family world. Husbands are in many ways peripheral to family relationships, possibly because of their failure to provide sufficiently for their families as men are expected to do. This becomes apparent if they demand their wife's disloyalty toward or separation from her mother: "The great triangle of childhood is mother–father–child; in Bethnal Green the great triangle of adult life is Mum–wife–husband."[35]

Hildred Geertz and Jay describe Javanese nuclear families in which women are often the more powerful spouse and have primary influence upon how kin relations are expressed and to whom (although these families are formally centered upon a highly valued conjugal relationship based on equality of spouses).[36] Financial and decision-making control in the family often rest largely in the hands of its women. Women are potentially independent of men in a way that men are not independent of women. Geertz points to a woman's ability to participate in most occupations and to own farmland and supervise its cultivation, which contrasts with a man's inability, even if he is financially independent, to do his own household work and cooking.

Women's kin role in Java is important. Their parental role and rights are greater than those of men; children always belong to the woman in case of divorce. When extra members join a nuclear family to constitute an extended family household, they are much more likely to be the wife's relatives than those of the husband. Formal and distant relations between men in a family, and between a man and his children (especially his son), contrast with the informal and close relations between women, and between a woman and her children. Jay and Geertz both emphasize the continuing closeness of the mother–daughter relationship as a daughter is growing up and throughout her married life. Jay suggests that there is a certain amount of ambivalence in the mother–daughter relationship, particularly as a girl grows toward adulthood and before she is married, but points out that at the same time the mother remains a girl's "primary figure of confidence and support."[37]

Siegel describes Atjehnese families in Indonesia in which women stay on the homestead of their parents after marriage and are in total control of the household. Women tolerate men in the household only as long as they provide money, and even then treat them as someone between a child and a guest. Women's stated preference would be to eliminate even this necessary dependence on men: "Women, for instance, envision paradise as the place where they are reunited with their children and their mothers; husbands and fathers are absent, and yet there is an abundance all the same. Quarrels over money reflect the women's idea that men are basically adjuncts who exist only to give their families whatever they can earn"[38]. A woman in this society does not get into conflicts in which she has to choose between her mother and her husband, as happens in the Western working class described by Young and Willmott, where the reigning ideology supports the nuclear family.[39]

In these three settings, the mother–daughter tie and other female kin relations remain important from a woman's childhood through her old age. Daughters stay closer to home in both childhood and adulthood and remain involved in particularistic role relations. Sons and men are more likely to feel uncomfortable at home, and to spend work and play time away from the house. Male activities and spheres emphasize universalistic, distancing qualities: men in Java are the bearers and transmitters of high culture and formal relationships; men in East London spend much of their time in alienated work settings; Atjehnese boys spend their time in school, and their fathers trade in distant places.

Mother–daughter ties in these three societies, described as extremely close, seem to be composed of companionship and mutual cooperation, and to be positively valued by both mother and daughter. The ethnographies do not imply that women are weighed down by the burden of their relationships or by overwhelming guilt and responsibility. On the contrary, they seem to have developed a strong sense of self and self-worth, which continues to grow as they get older and take on their maternal role. The implication is that "ego strength" is not completely dependent on the firmness of the ego's boundaries.

Guntrip's distinction between "immature" and "mature" dependence clarifies the difference between mother–daughter relationships and women's psyche in the Western middle class and in the matrifocal societies described. Women in the Western middle class are caught up to some extent in issues of infantile dependence, while the women in matrifocal societies remain in definite connection with others, but in relationships characterized by mature dependence. As Guntrip describes it: "*Mature dependence* is characterized by full differentiation of ego and object (emergence from primary identification) and therewith a capacity for valuing the object for its own sake and for giving as well as receiving; a condition which should be described not as independence but as mature dependence."[40] This kind of mature dependence is also to be distinguished from the kind of forced independence and denial of need for relationship that I have suggested characterizes masculine personality, and that reflects continuing conflict about infantile dependence. "Maturity is not equated with independence though it includes a certain capacity for independence. . . The independence of the mature person is simply that he does not collapse when he has to stand alone. It is not an independence of needs for other persons with whom to have relationship: *that would not be desired by the mature.*"[41]

Depending on its social setting, women's sense of relation and connection and their embeddedness in social life provide them with a kind of security that men lack. The quality of a mother's relationship to her children and maternal self-esteem, on the one hand, and the nature of a daughter's developing identification with her mother, on the other, make crucial differences in female development.

Women's kin role, and in particular the mother role, is central and positively valued in Atjeh, Java, and East London. Women gain status and prestige as they get older; their major role is not fulfilled in early motherhood. At the same time, women may be important contributors to the family's economic support, as in Java and East London, and in all three societies they have control over real economic resources. All these factors give women a sense of self-esteem independent of their relationship to their children. Finally, strong relationships exist between women in these societies, expressed in mutual cooperation and frequent contact. A mother, then, when her children are young, is likely to spend much of her time in the company of other women, not simply isolated with her children.

These social facts have important positive effects on female psychological development. (It must be emphasized that all the ethnographies indicate that these same social facts make male development difficult and contribute to psychological insecurity and lack of ease in interpersonal relationships in men.) A mother is not invested in keeping her daughter from individuating and becoming less dependent. She has other ongoing contacts and relationships that help fulfill her psychological and social needs. In addition, the people surrounding a mother while a child is growing up become mediators between mother and daughter, by providing a daughter with alternative models for personal identification and objects of attachment, which contribute to her differentiation from her mother. Finally, a daughter's identification with her mother in this kind of setting is with a strong woman with clear control over important spheres of life, whose sense of self-esteem can reflect this. Acceptance of her gender identity involves positive valuation of herself, and not an admission of inferiority. In psychoanalytic terms, we might say it involves identification with a pre-Oedipal, active, caring mother. Bibring points to clinical findings supporting this interpretation: "We find in the analysis of the women who grew up in this 'matriarchal' setting the rejection of the feminine role less frequently than among female patients coming from the patriarchal family culture."[42]

There is another important aspect of the situation in these societies. The continuing structural and practical importance of the mother–daughter tie not only ensures that a daughter develops a positive personal and role identification with her mother, but also requires that the close psychological tie between mother and daughter become firmly grounded in real role expectations. These provide a certain constraint and limitation upon the relationship, as well as an avenue for its expression through common spheres of interest based in the external social world.

All these societal features contrast with the situation of the Western middle-class woman. Kinship relations in the middle class are less important. Kin are not likely to live near each other, and, insofar as husbands are able to provide adequate financial support for their families, there is no need for a network of mutual aid among related wives. As the middle-class woman gets older and becomes a grandmother, she cannot look forward to increased status and prestige in her new role.

The Western middle-class housewife does not have an important economic role in her family. The work she does and the responsibilities that go with it (household management, cooking, entertaining, etc.) do not seem to be really necessary to the economic support of her family (they are crucial contributions to the maintenance and reproduction of her family's class position, but this is not generally recognized as important either by the woman herself or by the society's ideology). If she works outside the home, neither she nor the rest of society is apt to consider this work to be important to her self-definition in the way that her housewife role is.

Child care, on the other hand, is considered to be her crucially important responsibility. Our post-Freudian society in fact assigns to parents (and especially to the mother) nearly total responsibility for how children turn out.[43] A middle-class mother's daily life is not centrally involved in relations with other women. She is isolated with her children for most of her workday. It is not surprising, then, that she is likely to invest a lot of anxious energy and guilt in her concern for her children and to look to them for her own self-affirmation, or that her self-esteem, dependent on the lives of others than herself, is shaky. Her life situation leads her to an over-involvement in her children's lives.

A mother in this situation keeps her daughter from differentiation and from lessening her infantile dependence. (She also perpetuates her son's dependence, but in this case society and his father are more likely to interfere in order to assure that, behaviorally, at least, he doesn't *act* dependent.) And there are not other people around to mediate in the mother–daughter relationship. Insofar as the father is actively involved in a relationship with his daughter and his daughter develops some identification with him, this helps her individuation, but the formation of ego autonomy through identification with and idealization of her father may be at the expense of her positive sense of feminine self. Unlike the situation in matrifocal families, the continuing closeness of the mother–daughter relationship is expressed only on a psychological, interpersonal level. External role expectations do not ground or limit it.

It is difficult, then, for daughters in a Western middle-class family to develop self-esteem. Most psychoanalytic and social theorists claim that the mother inevitably represents to her daughter (and son) regression, passivity, dependence, and lack of orientation to reality, whereas the father represents progression, activity, independence, and reality orientation.[44] Given the value implications of this dichotomy, there are advantages for the son in giving up his mother and identifying with his father. For the daughter, feminine gender identification means identification with a devalued, passive mother, and personal maternal identification is with a mother whose own self-esteem is low. Conscious rejection of her Oedipal maternal identification, however, remains an unconscious rejection and devaluation of herself, because of her continuing pre-Oedipal identification and boundary confusion with her mother.

Cultural devaluation is not the central issue, however. Even in patrilineal, patrilocal societies in which women's status is very low, women do not necessarily translate this cultural devaluation into low self-esteem, nor do girls have to develop difficult boundary problems with their mother. In the Moslem Moroccan family, for example, a large amount of sex segregation and sex antagonism gives women a separate (domestic) sphere in which they have a real productive role and control, and also a life situation in which any young mother is in the company of other women.[45] Women do not need to invest all their psychic energy in their children, and their self-esteem is not dependent on their relationship to their children. In this and other patrilineal, patrilocal societies, what resentment women do have at their oppressive situation is more often expressed toward their sons, whereas daughters are seen as allies against oppression. Conversely, a daughter develops relationships of attachment to and identification with other adult women. Loosening her tie to her mother therefore does not entail the rejection of all women. The close tie that remains between mother and daughter is based not simply on mutual over-involvement but often on mutual understanding of their oppression.

Conclusion

Women's universal mothering role has effects both on the development of masculine and feminine personality and on the relative status of the sexes. This chapter has described the development of relational personality in women and of personalities preoccupied with the denial of relation in men. In its comparison of different societies, it has suggested that men, while guaranteeing to themselves socio-cultural superiority over women, always remain psychologically defensive and insecure. Women, by contrast, although always of secondary social and cultural status, may in favorable circumstances gain psychological security and a firm sense of worth and importance in spite of this.

Social and psychological oppression, then, is perpetuated in the structure of personality. My account here enables us to suggest what social arrangements contribute (and could contribute) to social equality between men and women and their relative freedom from certain sorts of psychological conflict. Daughters and sons must be able to develop a personal identification with more than one adult, and preferably one embedded in a role relationship that gives it a social context of expression and provides some limitation upon it. Most important, boys need to grow up around men who take a major role in child care, and girls around women who, in addition to their child-care responsibilities, have a valued role and recognized spheres of legitimate control. These arrangements could help to ensure that children of both sexes develop a sufficiently individuated and strong sense of self, as well as a positively valued and secure gender identity, that does not bog down either in ego-boundary confusion, low self-esteem, and overwhelming relatedness to others, or in compulsive denial of any connection to others or dependence upon them.

3

Oedipal Asymmetries and Heterosexual Knots

We are faced in our daily lives, in the novels we read, and the movies we see, with a puzzling observation.[1] People, for the most part, marry, and marry heterosexually. At the same time, male–female relationships seem to become strained in regularized ways that we recognize and come to expect. These facts are often taken to be socially accidental or due to the psychological peculiarities of particular women and men. In this article, I suggest that we can make better sense of these same facts if we understand them as part of the routine process of family reproduction. Beginning from Freud's early analysis of family structure and psychosexual development, and the methodology this points us to, I show how the psychological propensities, needs, and wants which lead people to form new family or family-like relationships undermine those very relationships they serve to form.

Drawing on facts often still familiar to us, Freud in "'Civilized' sexual morality and modern nervousness," tells the following story. Sexual repression is a cornerstone of socialization in the bourgeois family. For women, this is an absolute; for men, it is occasionally offset by the double standard permitting, or even requiring, premarital sexual experience. What is most likely to happen is that when a girl is finally "allowed" to fall in love, she isn't really ready, is uncertain of her feelings, and as a result of extensive training in suppression, is sexually unresponsive. Because sex gives her no pleasure, she is unlikely to care much about the potential outcome of sex: children. By the time she matures, separates herself psychologically from her parents, and starts to love and desire her husband, their relationship is beyond repair, and her husband is no longer interested in her or it. She is then liable to turn her interest to her child or children. But it is an inappropriately sexualized interest, which, circularly, awakens precociously in them a sexuality which must be suppressed. As

Freud puts it, "the preparation for marriage frustrates the aims of marriage itself."[2]

This general picture often is exacerbated by two further outcomes of training for marriage and relationship. One, suggests Freud (again pointing to a fact, at least until recently, still with us), is that the verbal message of premarital abstention comes down most heavily on heterosexual coitus. This, he suggests, pushes both young men and women to seek substitute sexual gratification – masturbation, homosexual activity, and what he calls "perversions." In men, he tells us later, it may also lead to a splitting of the erotic heterosexual object into the good non-sexual woman and the sexual woman who can't be respected.[3] Again, faced with their eventual push into heterosexual marriage, neither partner is particularly prepared for coital satisfaction. Secondly, a woman may resent her husband intensely because of her disappointing sexual and marital experience[4] but deny this and try to act the loving wife because her socialization tells her that a wife loves and idealizes her husband. This suppression and turning inward of anger again leads to neurosis, undercutting her marriage, and revenging herself on her husband perhaps even more than straightforward expression of rage might have done. As Freud puts it, "Under the cultural conditions of today, marriage has long ceased to be a panacea for the nervous trouble of women; and if we doctors still advise marriage in such cases, we are nevertheless aware that, on the contrary, a girl must be very healthy if she is to be able to tolerate it . . ."[4]

Freud thus gives a sociological account of the intertwining of the bourgeois Victorian marriage and psyche, the way bourgeois marriage reproduces its dominant sexual modes (sexual repression and heterosexual coitus) while at the same time undermining these. This account gives us some insight into those concrete internal contradictions which must have aided and continue to aid the extra-familial social and economic forces which then as now work to alter the family based on ideals of romantic love and heterosexual intimacy. At the same time, it points to a useful methodology, one capable of yielding a profound analysis of the structural fabric of family relationships, self, and psyche.

It is almost a truism to state that consideration of the woman–man relationship – as a sexual relationship, a core family relationship, a strongly enforced ideological goal and expectation – brings us near the heart of the sociology of gender. In an extremely interesting contribution to the development of feminist theory, Gayle Rubin pushes further Lévi-Strauss's argument that all kinship systems rest at least partly on marriage and the sexual division of labor, by pointing out that the vast world variety of marriage rules, regulating whom one can and cannot marry, all presuppose heterosexual unions, and require that individuals come to be disposed to mate heterosexually. Once stated, this claim becomes obvious, yet it is precisely such a crucially important claim which Lévi-Strauss, and all other family theorists, have assumed and passed over. Heterosexuality is one fundamental organizational principle of the family, and of what Rubin calls the "sex/gender system" of any society.[5]

A second fundamental organizational principle of the family and the social organization of gender, a principle also assumed and not analyzed by theorists of kinship and the family, is the sexual and familial division of labor in which women mother. That is, almost universally, women take primary responsibility for infant care, spend more time with infants and children than men, have primary affectional ties with infants (are the infant's primary attachment figure), and are substitute parents if a biological mother isn't parenting. The amount of time fathers or other men spend with infants and children (and with boys vs with girls) certainly varies widely from society to society, but fathers are never routinely the child's primary parenting person.

Thus, two major organizational rules can describe for us possibly all hitherto extant family systems.[6] We can understand the relations between these as a two-stage process. People enter into marriage, which then legitimates the production of children (this doesn't necessarily mean that the marriage partners produce these children, though this is usually the case), whom women then care for, and for whom men become important second, which, in turn, creates them gendered, heterosexual, and ready to marry.[7]

However, it is the case that the development of this heterosexual object choice, and the nature and meaning of adult heterosexual experience, differ for men and women, and this is *because* women mother. The traditional psychoanalytic account of masculinity and femininity begins from this perception. In our society, marriage has assumed a larger and larger emotional weight supposedly off-setting the strains of increasingly alienated and bureaucratized work in the paid economy.[8] It no longer has the economic and political basis Lévi-Strauss described. As production, education, religion, and care for the sick and aged leave the home, the family in general has collapsed in upon its psychological and personal functions. The contradictions between women's and men's heterosexuality which women's mothering produces now stand out with particular clarity and gain special significance. It is these contradictions that I would now like to discuss – contradictions growing out of the nuclear family of advanced industrial capitalist society, and out of asymmetries in feminine and masculine Oedipal experience which result from women's performing those mothering functions which are expected of them.[9]

According to psychoanalytic theory, heterosexual erotic orientation is a primary outcome of the Oedipus complex for both sexes.[10] Boys and girls differ in this, however. Boys retain one primary love object throughout their boyhood. For this reason, the development of masculine heterosexual object choice is relatively continuous. In theory, the boy resolves his Oedipus complex by repressing his attachment to his mother. He is therefore ready in adulthood to find a primary relationship with someone like his mother. When he does, the relationship is given meaning from its psychological reactivation of what was from its inception and for a long time an intense and exclusive relationship – first an identity, then a "dual-unity," finally a two-person relationship.

Things are not so simple for the girl. Because her first love object is a woman, a girl, in order to attain her proper heterosexual orientation, must transfer her primary object choice to her father and men.[11] Thus, as Johnson argues, drawing upon social-psychological studies for confirmation, the father's behavior and family role, and the girl's relationship to him, are crucial to the development of heterosexual orientation in her.[12] But fathers, in contrast to mothers, are comparatively unavailable physically and emotionally (Mitscherlich talks of the "invisible father" of the mid-century industrial capitalist society.)[13] A father's main familial function is being a breadwinner, and his own training for masculinity may have led him to deny emotionality.

This creates an asymmetry in the feminine and masculine Oedipus complex, and, as the psychoanalytic account stresses, difficulties in the development of female sexuality (given, that is, heterosexuality as a developmental goal). Freud formulates this asymmetry: "It is only in the male child that we find the fateful combination of love for the one parent and simultaneous hatred for the other as a rival."[14] The girl, by contrast, does in all likelihood turn to her father as an object of primary interest from the exclusivity of the relationship to her mother, but the girl's libidinal turning to her father does not substitute for her attachment to her mother. Instead, the girl retains and builds upon her pre-Oedipal tie to her mother (an intense tie characterized by primary identification – a sense of oneness; primary love – not differentiating between her own and her mother's interests: and extensive dependence) together with Oedipal attachments to both her mother and her father. These latter are characterized by eroticized demands for exclusivity, feelings of competition and jealousy. She retains the (internalized) early relationship, including its implications for the nature of her unconscious but fundamental definition of self in relationship, and internalizes these other relationships in addition, and not as replacement.

Thus, for girls there is no absolute change of object nor exclusive attachment to the father. If there is an absolute component to the change of object, it is at most a concentration on her father of genital, or erotic, cathexis. Affective interest, however, remains dual: the clinical corollary to Freud's claim is that love for the father and rivalry with the mother (which would be the mirror image of the masculine Oedipus complex) is always tempered by love for the mother. This happens regardless of the girl's intention, and is the result of the intensity (and ambivalence) of the relation which develops with her mother in a situation of relatively exclusive maternal parenting.

Both Helene Deutsch and Ruth Mack Brunswick, in an article formulated in close collaboration with Freud, and considered to be his final word on the subject of women, speak to this outcome, stressing (we might say, bewailing) the lack of what they would consider to be the final success in the girl's turn to the father and, therefore, the consequent problems of heterosexual attachment. According to Brunswick, the girl, embittered and hostile toward her mother, does "seek to transfer her libido to the father," but "this transference is beset by difficulties arising from the tenacity of the active and passive pre-Oedipal mother-attachment."[15]

Deutsch adds that the girl does normally make a *tentative* choice in favor of her father, turning to him "with greater intensity, although still not exclusively."[16] Brunswick confirms this outcome, pointing to the number of adult women who come for analytic treatment incapable of contact with men, and suggesting that this may be no more than an exaggeration of the normal Oedipal resolution:

Between the exclusive attachment to the mother on the one hand and the complete transfer of the libido to the father on the other hand, the innumerable gradations of normal and abnormal development are to be found. It might also be said that partial success is the rule rather than the exception, so great is the proportion of women whose libido has remained fixed to the mother.[17]

What this account suggests is that the Oedipal situation, and the genesis of heterosexual orientation, is for the girl at least as much a mother–daughter concern as it is that of a daughter and father. The turn to the father is embedded in a girl's external relationship to her mother and in her relation to her mother as an internal object.[18]

What stands out here is the external and internal relational complexity of the feminine Oedipus complex as opposed to the masculine. The girl's internal Oedipus situation (her Oedipal "family," as Laing would call it in "The family and 'the family,'") is multi-layered.[19] Her relationship of dependence and attachment to her mother continues: her Oedipal attachments to her mother, then her father, are simply added on. The implication here is that the relationship to the father is often secondary, and at most emotionally equal, to that of the mother – that the relationships which compose the Oedipus situation are competing for primacy. As Deutsch puts it, the girl oscillates in a bisexual relational triangle, in which her relation to her father is emotionally in reaction to, interwoven, and competing for primacy with, her relation to her mother.

The implications of this are twofold. First, the nature of the heterosexual relationship differs for boy and girl. Most women emerge from their Oedipus complex oriented to their father and men as primary erotic objects, but it is clear that men tend to remain more emotionally secondary, or at most emotionally equal, in contrast to the primacy and exclusivity of the Oedipal boy's emotional tie to his mother and women. Secondly, because the father is a second important love object, who becomes important structurally in the context of a relational triangle, the feminine inner object world is more complex than the masculine.

The girls' relation to her father is not only not of the same exclusivity as that of the boy toward his mother, but because mother and father are not the same kind of parent, its nature and intensity differ as well. Children first experience the social and cognitive world as continuous with themselves; they do not differentiate objects. Their mother, as first caretaking figure, is not a separate person and has no separate interests, and one of their first developmental tasks is the establishment of a self with boundaries, requiring the experience of self and mother as separate. In addition, this lack of separateness is in the context of the infant's total dependence upon the mother for physical and psychological survival. As A. Balint suggests, it is the forced recognition of the mother's separateness and separate interests which constitutes the entrance of the reality principle into the infant's life.[20] The experience of self in the original mother-relation remains both seductive and frightening: unity was bliss, yet means the loss of self and absolute dependence. The father, by contrast, has always been differentiated and known as a separate person with separate interests, and the child has never been totally dependent upon him. He has not posed the original narcissistic threat (the threat to basic ego integrity and boundaries) nor provided the original narcissistic unity (the original experience of oneness) to the girl. Oedipal love for the mother, then, contains a threat to selfhood which love for the father never does. Love for the father, in fact, is not simply the natural emergence of heterosexuality. Rather, it is an attempt on the girl's part to break her primary unity and dependence.

The other side of this attempt also affects the nature of the girl's relation to her father and to men. Janine Chasseguet-Smirgel and Bela Grunberger speak to this issue, and in particular to the peculiar duality of men's secondary yet at the same time primary importance to women.[21] The father and men, while emotionally secondary and not exclusively loved, are also idealized. There are a number of reasons for this. First, the girl's father is a last-ditch escape from maternal omnipotence so it is important that the girl does not drive him away. Secondly, his distance and ideological position of authority in the family, and often her mother's interpretation of his role to her children, make the development of a relationship based on his real strengths and weaknesses difficult. Finally, the girl herself does not receive the same kind of love from her mother as a boy does (i.e., a mother, rather than confirming her daughter's oppositeness and specialness, experiences her as one with herself; her relationship to her daughter is more "narcissistic," that to her son more "anaclitic"). Thus, a daughter turns to her father looking for this kind of confirmation and a sense of separateness from her mother, and cares especially about being loved. She (and the woman she becomes) is willing to deny her father's limitations (and those of her lovers or husband) as long as she feels loved, and she is more able to do this because his distance means that she does not really know him. The relationship, then, because of the father's distance and importance to her, is to a large extent on a level of fantasy and idealization. It lacks the grounded reality which a boy's relation to his mother has.[22]

These differences in the kind of love, and the experience of self in relation to father and mother, are reinforced by temporal differences in entry into the Oedipal situation, which also grow out of the asymmetry in the mother's and father's position in the family. The discovery of the length and intensity of the pre-Oedipal mother–daughter relationship was a major step forward in psychoanalytic theory, and constituted the base for a fundamental reformulation of the psychology of women.[23] Because of the father's relative distance and unavailability, coupled with the intensity of the mother–child relationship, girls tend to enter the Oedipal situation later than boys.

At the same time, the availability of the mother and invisibility of the father may mean early entry of the boy into the Oedipal situation. Slater and J. Whiting et al. have suggested that in the absence of men, mothers, cross-culturally, may early sexualize their relation to sons.[24] Bibring argues that this is indeed the case in many mid-twentieth-century nuclear family households, where there is a strong, active mother who runs the household and exhibits other traits of superiority to her husband (e.g., in cultural or social spheres) and a father who, for a variety of reasons (he is generally ineffectual; he is efficient and competent as a professional but considers the family to be his wife's sphere; he is so busy in his work that he is rarely at home) is uninvolved in and unavailable for family life. In these situations, she suggests, there is too much of mother: "the little boy finds himself . . . faced by a mother who appears to be as much in need of a husband as the son is of a father."[25] The mother, then, sexualizes her relationship to her son early, so that "Oedipal" issues of sexual attraction and connection, and jealousy, become fused with "pre-Oedipal" issues of primary love and oneness. By contrast, since the girl's relationship to her father develops later, her sense of self is more firmly established. If Oedipal and pre-Oedipal issues are fused for her, it is also in relation to her mother, and not to her father.

Finally, a girl does not "resolve" her Oedipus complex to the same extent as the boy. Freud suggests that a boy's Oedipus complex is normally "abandoned, repressed, and . . . entirely destroyed," that in contrast, girls "remain in it for an indeterminate length of time; they demolish it late and, even so, incompletely."[26] A girl represses neither her pre-Oedipal and Oedipal attachment to her mother nor her Oedipal attachment to her father. This means that she grows up with more ongoing preoccupation with internalized object relationships and with external relationships as well.[27] Clinical accounts suggest that Freud's characterization of the masculine resolution may be rather idealized, but that none the less, a boy's repression of his Oedipal maternal attachment (and pre-Oedipal dependence) does tend to be more absolute than the girl's.

The traditional explanation for this difference proposed by Freud is that because the girl is already "castrated," she has no motive for breaking up her infantile sexual world and organization, and can retain a less repressed desire for her father. My reading of the account, stressing the determining primacy of social relational experience and not genital difference, locates this difference in the nature of the Oedipal attachments themselves. The greater intensity and quality of threat in the boy's relationship to his mother requires its repression in the son, whereas the less intense, less reciprocated, non-exclusive relation of a girl to her father enables this relationship, and the whole triangular affective constellation, to remain an ongoing part of her psychic world.

Masculine personality, then, comes to be founded more on the repression of affect and the denial of relational needs and a sense of connection than feminine personality (preparing the boy, parenthetically, for participation in the alienated, affect-free public world of work, where relationships are contractual and universalistically constructed).

By contrast, the girl's situation, in which the father and men, if erotically primary, are most likely affectively secondary, continues into adulthood. Deutsch expresses well the complexity of the developmental layering in women's psyche, and non-exclusive position of men, and the effect of these on the adult woman's participation in relationships:

Let us recall that we left the pubescent girl in a triangular situation and expressed the hope that later she would dissolve the sexually mixed triangle . . . in favor of heterosexuality. This formulation was made for the sake of simplification. Actually, whether a constitutional bisexual factor contributes to the creation of such a triangle or not, this triangle can never be given up completely. The deepest and most ineradicable emotional relations with both parents share in its formation. It succeeds another relation, even older and more enduring – the relationship between mother and child, which every man or woman preserves from his birth to his death. It is erroneous to say that the little girl gives up her first mother relation in favor of the father. She only gradually draws him into the alliance, develops from the mother–child exclusiveness toward the triangular parent–child relation and continues the latter, just as she does the former, although in a weaker and less elemental form, all her life. Only the principal part changes; now the mother, now the father plays it. The ineradicability of affective constellations manifests itself in later repetitions.[28]

The implication of this statement is confirmed by cross-cultural examination of family structure and relations between the sexes, which suggests that conjugal closeness is probably the exception and not the rule.[29]

We can summarize, then, several differences in female and male Oedipal experience, all of which make women important on a basic emotional level to men (and to women) in a way that men are not important to women. Girls enter adulthood with a complex layering of affective ties and a rich, ongoing inner object world. Boys, to begin with, have a simpler Oedipal situation and more direct affective relationships, and this situation is repressed in a way that the girl's is not. Secondly, the mother remains a primary internal object to the girl: the heterosexual relationship is on the model of a non-exclusive, second relationship for her, whereas for the boy it recreates an exclusive, primary relationship.

The complexities of this situation are illuminated by sociological and clinical findings. Conventional wisdom has it, and much of our everyday observation confirms, that women are the romantic ones in our society, the ones for whom love, marriage, and relationships matter. However, several studies point to ways that men love and fall in love romantically, women sensibly and rationally. Most of these studies, rightly, I think, argue that in the current situation, where women are economically dependent on men, women must, in fact, make rational calculations for the provision of themselves and their children.[30] This position suggests that women's apparent romanticism is an emotional and ideological mask for their very real economic dependence. On the societal level, given especially economic inequality, men are exceedingly important to women. The recent tendency for women to initiate divorce and separation more than men – as income becomes more available to them, as recession hits masculine jobs indiscriminately with feminine, as the feminist movement begins to remove the stigma of "divorcee" – further confirms this.

These capacities have their mirror in some of the psychological and developmental differences I have discussed. Just as women, in adulthood, are objectively dependent on men economically, so also in childhood they are objectively dependent on men (their fathers) as escape from maternal domination. Their developed ability on this level to romanticize rational decisions – to not see, or to ignore, the failings of father (and other men) because he is not around to be known well, and because of their dependence – stands women in good stead in this adult situation.

There is another side to this situation, however. On a more profound level, women have acquired developmentally a real capacity for rationality and distance, through the rationality, distance, and emotional secondariness of their earliest relationship to a man in conjunction with their close and emotional relation to a woman. More direct evidence for the psychological primacy and profundity of this latter stance comes from findings about the experience of loss itself. George Goethals reports the clinical finding that loss of at least the first adult relationship for males "throws them into a turmoil and a depression of the most extreme kind", a melancholic reaction to object-loss of the type Freud first describes clinically in which they withdraw and are unable to look elsewhere for new relationships.[31] He implies, by contrast, that first adult loss may not result in as severe a depression for a woman, and claims that his women patients did not withdraw to the same extent and were, in fact, more able to look elsewhere for new relationships. Zick Rubin who studied couples breaking up, reports a similar finding: the men he studied tended to be more depressed and lonely after a break-up than the women.[32] Equally striking, he found that women, more than men, were likely to initiate the break-up of a relationship in which they were more involved than their partner. Jessie Bernard, discussing people at a later age, reports that the frequency of psychological distress, death, and suicide is much higher among recently widowed men than women, and indicates that the same difference can be found in a comparison of divorced men and women.[33]

The implication in all these cases is that women have other resources and a certain distance from the relationship. (In the marriage case, Bernard would argue that women gain from getting out of it.) Internally, my account would argue, the women have a richer, ongoing inner world to fall back on, and the man in their life does not represent the intensity and exclusivity which the woman represents to the man; externally, they also retain and develop more relationships. It is likely then, that, developmentally, men cannot become emotionally important to women on the same fundamental level as women are to men.

This process is furthered by men themselves, who, it turns out, collude in maintaining this distance as a result of their own Oedipal resolution, which has led to the repression of their affective relational needs. According to psychoanalysts Chasseguet-Smirgel and Grunberger, men, in their attempt to deny their own needs for love, come often to be intolerant of those who can express the need for love. Women, by contrast, have not repressed these needs, and still want love and confirmation, and, as I have suggested, may be willing to put up with limitations in their masculine lover or husband in exchange for some evidence of caring and love.[34]

Men, however, must both defend themselves against the threat and, at the same time, because needs for love do not disappear through repression, do tend to find themselves in heterosexual relationships. This is reinforced by their training for masculinity and the sociological situation of their relationships in the public world, both of which make deep primary relationships with other men hard to come by and don't allow children to become important in a way that they are to women. These relationships to women, deriving their meaning and dynamics partly from the man's relation to his mother, must be difficult. In particular, the kind of maternal treatment of sons described by Bibring, Slater, and Whiting, et al. creates relational problems in sons. As Chasseguet-Smirgel and Bibring suggest, and as Slater describes so well, when a boy's mother has treated him as an extension of herself, and, at the same time, as a sexual object, he tends to continue to use his masculinity and possession of a penis as a narcissistic defense. In adulthood, he will tend to look on relationships with women for narcissistic–phallic reassurance rather than for mutual affirmation and love. Chasseguet-Smirgel also suggests that what Brunswick calls the boy's "normal contempt" for women – a standard outcome of the Oedipus complex – is a pathological and defensive reaction to the same sense of inescapable maternal omnipotence, rather than a direct outcome of genital differences.

This situation reinforces in daily life what the woman first experienced developmentally and intrapsychically in relation to men. While she is likely to become and remain erotically heterosexual, she is encouraged by this situation to look elsewhere to fulfill relational needs. One way that women fulfill these needs is through the creation and maintenance of important personal relations with other women. Cross-culturally, social sex segregation is the rule: women tend to have closer personal ties with each other than men have, and to spend more time in the company of women than they do with men. In our society, there is some sociological evidence that women's friendships are affectively richer – a finding certainly confirmed by most writing from the men's liberation movement.[35] In other societies, and in most subcultures of our own, women remain in adulthood involved with female relatives – their mothers, sisters, sisters-in-law (or even co-wives).[36] These relationships are one way of resolving and recreating the mother–daughter bond and are an expression of women's general relational capacities and definition of self in relationship. A second way is by having a child, turning her marriage into a family, and recreating for herself the primary intense unit which a heterosexual relationship tends to recreate for men (both because a relation to a woman is to someone like his mother, his first love object, and because women, for all the developmental reasons I have suggested, tend to be available to relational needs in a way that men are not).

Because women care for children, then, heterosexual symbiosis has a different "meaning" for men and women (just as does mother–infant symbiosis for mother and infant). Freud originally ("a man's love and a woman's are a phase apart psychologically"), and psychoanalytic thinkers after him, all point to a way in which women and men, though "meant for each other," and usually looking for intimacy with each other, are, because of the social organization of parenting, not meant for each other, and do not fulfill each other's needs.[37]

As a result of being parented by a woman, both sexes are looking for a return to this emotional and physical union. A man achieves this directly through the heterosexual bond which replicates for him emotionally the early mother–infant exclusivity which he seeks to recreate. He is supported in this endeavor by women, who, through their own development, have remained open to relational needs, have retained an ongoing inner affective life, and have learned to deny the limitations of masculine lovers for both psychological and practical reasons.

Men, generally, though, both look for and fear exclusivity. Throughout their development, they have tended to repress their affective relational needs and sense of connection, and to develop and be more comfortable with ties based more on categorical and abstract role expectations, particularly in relation to other males. Even when they participate in an intimate heterosexual relationship, it is likely to be with the ambivalence created by an intense relationship which one both wants and fears, demanding from women, then, what they are at the same time afraid of receiving. The relationship to the mother thus builds itself directly into contradictions in masculine heterosexual commitment.

As a result of being parented by a woman and growing up heterosexual, women have different and a more complex set of relational needs, in which exclusive relationship to a man is not enough. This is because women experience themselves as part of a relational triangle in which their father and men are emotionally secondary, or at most equal, in importance to their mother and women. Women, therefore, need primary relationships to women as well as to men. In addition, the relation to the man itself has difficulties. Idealization, growing out of a girl's relation to her father, involves denial of real feelings and to a certain extent an unreal relationship to men.

The contradictions in women's heterosexual relationships, though, do not inhere only in the outcome of early childhood relationships. As I have suggested, men themselves, because of their own development and socialization, grow up rejecting their own and others' needs for love, and, therefore, find it difficult and threatening to meet women's emotional needs. Thus, given the masculine personality which women's mothering produces, the emotional secondariness of men to women, and the social organization of gender and gender roles, a woman's relationship to a man is unlikely to provide satisfaction for the particular relational needs which women's mothering and the concomitant social organization of gender have produced in women.

The two structural principles of the family, then, are in contradiction with each other. The family reproduces itself in form: for the most part people marry, and marry heterosexually; for the most part, people form couples heterosexually. At the same time, it undercuts itself in content: as a result of men and women growing up in families where women mother, these heterosexual relations, married or not, are liable to be strained in the regularized ways I have described.

In an earlier period, father absence was less absolute, production centered in the home, and economic interdependence of the sexes meant that family life and marriage was not and did not have to be a uniquely or fundamentally emotional project. The heterosexual asymmetry which I have been discussing was only one aspect of the total marital enterprise, and, therefore, did not overwhelm it. Women in this earlier period could seek relationships to other women in their daily work and community. With the development of industrial capitalism, however – and the increasingly physically isolated, mobile, and neolocal nuclear family it has produced – other primary relationships are not easy to come by on a routine, daily, ongoing basis. At the same time, the public world of work, consumption, and leisure leaves people increasingly starved for affect, support, and a sense of unique self. The heterosexual relationship itself gains in emotional importance at the very moment when the heterosexual strains which mothering produces are themselves sharpened. In response to these emerging contradictions, divorce rates soar, people flock to multitudes of new therapies, politicians decry and sociologists document the end of the family. And there develops a new feminism.

4

The Fantasy of the Perfect Mother
with Susan Contratto

In the late 1960s and early 1970s, feminists raised initial questions and developed a consensus of sorts about mothering.[1] We pointed to the pervasive pro-natalism of our culture; argued for safe, available abortions and birth control; criticized the health-care system; and advocated maternity and paternity benefits and leaves as well as accessible and subsidized parent- and community-controlled day-care, innovative work-time arrangements, shared parenting, and other non-traditional child-rearing and household arrangements. These consensual positions among feminists all centered on the argument that women's lives should not be totally constrained by child-care or childbearing. Women should be free to choose not to bear children; should have easy access to safe contraception and abortion; should be able to continue their other work if mothers; and should have available to them good day-care. In contrast, recent feminist writing on motherhood focuses more on the experience of mothering: if a woman wants to be a mother, what is or should be her experience? Given that parenting is necessary in any society, who should parent and how should the parenting be done? Feminist writing now recognizes that many women, including many feminists, want to have children and experience mothering as a rich and complex endeavor.

The new feminist writing has turned to mothering even while insisting on women's right to choose not to mother or to do other things in addition to mothering. Feminists often wish to speak to non-feminist or anti-feminist mothers about mothering without succumbing to heterosexism or pro-maternalism. The assumption that women have the right to mother, as well as not to mother, and the recognition that mothering, though it may be conflictual and oppressive, is also emotionally central and gratifying in some women's lives, has created a level of tension and ambivalence in recent writing that was missing in the earlier discussion.

This essay examines certain recurrent psychological themes in recent feminist writing on motherhood.[2] These themes include a sense that mothers are totally responsible for the outcomes of their mothering, even if their behavior is in turn shaped by male-dominant society. Belief in the all-powerful mother spawns a recurrent tendency to blame the mother on the one hand, and a fantasy of maternal perfectibility on the other. The writings also elaborate maternal sexuality or asexuality, aggression and omnipotence in the mother–child relationship, and the isolation of the mother–child dyad. This isolation provides the supercharged environment in which aggression and, to a lesser degree, sexuality become problematic, and the context in which a fantasy of the perfect mother can also be played out.

We point to, and are concerned with, two features of these understandings of motherhood. They have an unprocessed quality; it is as if notions that the personal is political have been interpreted to mean that almost primal fantasies constitute feminist politics or theory. Further, we think there is a striking continuity between these feminist treatments of motherhood and themes found in the culture at large, even among anti-feminists. Feminists differ about the meaning of motherhood and women's mothering, but each of these themes finds its complement in non-feminist or anti-feminist writing. Both these features of the writings we discuss are problematic for feminist theory and politics.

The All-Powerful Mother: Blame and Idealization

Feminist writing on motherhood assumes an all-powerful mother who, because she is totally responsible for how her children turn out, is blamed for everything from her daughter's limitations to the crisis of human existence. Nancy Friday's *My Mother/My Self* exemplifies this genre at its most extreme.[3] The book's central argument is that mothers are noxious to daughters, and that a daughter's subsequent unhappinesses and failings stem from this initial relationship. Friday follows the daughter through the life cycle and shows at each stage how mothers forcefully, intentionally, and often viciously constrain and control daughters, keep them from individuating, and, especially, deny daughters their sexuality and keep them from men.[4] Mothers make daughters in their image. As the mother, in becoming a mother, has denied her own sexuality, so she must deny sexuality to her daughter. Friday even seems to blame mothers for the act of toilet-training their daughters.[5]

Even when Friday points to other causes of a daughter's problems, it is still the mother's fault. Sexual information learned in school or from friends doesn't alter a mother's impact; women are ultimately responsible even for obstetrical atrocities performed by men in the interests of male power. Friday relates Seymour Fisher's finding that good female relationships with men depend on the belief that a daughter's father will not desert her, but then she asks, "But who put on the sexual brakes to begin with?"[6] Friday makes occasional disclaimers; for example, blaming mother is not taking responsibility for oneself.[7] But these disclaimers are buried in 460 pages of the opposite message. They are certainly not the message we remember from the book.

It is not clear whether Friday considers herself a feminist (though she certainly claims to be a woman's advocate and many see her as a feminist). In any event, she reflects in extreme form a widespread feminist position, one that also argues that mothers are the agents of their daughters' oppression and also pays lip-service (or more) to the fact that mothers themselves are oppressed and are therefore not responsible. Judith Arcana's *Our Mothers' Daughters*, for instance, written out of explicit feminist commitment and concern, gives us an account almost exactly like Friday's.[8] The only difference from Friday is that Arcana claims that maternal behavior is a product of mothers' entrapment within patriarchy rather than a product of their evil intentions.

While Friday and Arcana condemn mothers for what they do to their daughters, Dorothy Dinnerstein in *The Mermaid and the Minotaur* discusses the disastrous impact of maternal caretaking on sons, daughters, and society as a whole.[9] Dinnerstein claims that, as a result of "mother-dominated infancy," adult men and women are "semi-human, monstrous" – grown-up children acting out a species-suicidal pathology.[10] In Dinnerstein's account the mother is an object of children's fury and desperation, and children will put up with and create anything to escape her evil influence: "The deepest root of our acquiescence to the maiming and mutual imprisonment of men and women lies in the monolithic fact of human childhood: under the arrangements that now prevail, a woman is the parental person who is every infant's first love, first witness, and first boss, the person who presides over the infant's first encounters with the natural surroundings and who exists for the infant as the first representative of the flesh."[11]

Dinnerstein's account, like Friday's and Arcana's, confuses infantile fantasy with the actuality of maternal behavior. Thus, even as Dinnerstein describes the infantile fantasies that emerge from female-dominated child-care, she also asserts that mothers are in fact all-powerful, fearsome creatures. She emphasizes the *"absolute power"* of the *"mother's life-and-death control over helpless infancy: an intimately carnal control"* whose *"wrath is all-potent"* and whose *"intentionality is so formidable – so terrifying and . . . so alluring."*[12] This potency engages with the infant's totally helpless need and dependence; it humiliates, controls, and dominates as it seduces, succors, and saves. As a result, according to Dinnerstein, the mother (or whoever would care for the child) is inevitably the child's adversary.

Dinnerstein says that women's exclusive mothering affects the child's relationship to mother and father, attitudes toward the body, and adult erotic capacities. It shapes the later ambivalence toward nature and nature's resources, creates an unhealthy split between love and work, produces adults who parent differently according to sex, fosters particular kinds of destructive power and ensures patriarchal control of that power, and forms the nature of our history-making impulse.[13] In short, women's all-powerful mothering shapes the child's entire psychological, social, and political experience and is responsible for a species life that "is cancerous, out of control."[14]

The other side of blaming the mother is idealization of her and her possibilities: If only the mother wouldn't do what she is doing, she would be perfect. Friday's perfect mother is self-sacrificing and giving (though ultimately in the interest of her own deferred emotional rewards): "The truly loving mother is one whose interest and happiness is in seeing her daughter as a person, not just a possession. It is a process of being so generous and loving that she will forego some of her own pleasure and security to add to her daughter's development. If she does this in a genuine way, she really does end up with that Love Insurance Policy." "It is a noble role that mother must play here."[15] Friday, the new woman's advocate, sounds like the most traditional traditionalist.

Most feminist writing does not expect mothers to change on their own. As feminists locate blame, they also focus on the conditions – those of patriarchy – in which bad mothering takes place, in which mothers are victims and powerless in the perpetuation of evil. But this implies that if only we could remove these patriarchal constraints, mothering could be perfect. Arcana, in pointing to women who have broken out of the traditional mold, wants to turn these women into perfect mothers: "Such women may mother us all."[16]

These writings suggest not only that mothers can be perfect but also that the child's needs (e.g., those of the daughters in the books by Friday and Arcana) are necessarily legitimate and must be met. Such an implication persists in the most subtle and sophisticated feminist accounts. Jane Flax, for instance, offers an analysis of the psychodynamics of the mother–daughter relationship in which she writes of the difficulties of being a mother in a male-dominant society and of the psychological conflicts that setting generates.[17] She offers perceptive insights into the contradictory needs that emerge from being mothered by a woman. But her article still implies that mothers can be perfect and that the child's felt desires are absolute needs: "As a result of all these conflicts, it is more difficult for the mother to be as emotionally available as her infant daughter needs her to be."[18] The "needs" to which she refers are those of women patients talking about their mothers, and Flax accepts their accounts. She does not suggest that a child's "needs" might be unrealistic or unreasonable.

We find the idealization of maternal possibility not only in those accounts that blame the mother but also in another strain of feminist writing on motherhood, one that begins from identification with the mother rather than with the daughter. Adrienne Rich and Alice Rossi also premise their investigations of motherhood on the assumption that a maternal ideal or perfection could emerge with the overthrow of patriarchy.[19] Both discuss mothering as it has been affected by patriarchy and describe how patriarchy has controlled – as Rich observes, even killed – mothers and children. Mothers are not powerful, but powerless under patriarchy.

Rich provides a moving account of maternal love and concern and a vision of the potential power of women's maternal bodies, which could enable women to be intellectually, spiritually, and sexually transformative, and which could forge nurturant, sexual, and spiritual linkages among women:

The repossession by women of our bodies will bring far more essential change to human society than the seizing of the means of production by workers. . . We need to imagine a world in which every woman is the presiding genius of her own body. In such a world, women will truly create new life, bringing forth not only children (if and as we choose), but the visions and the thinking necessary to sustain, console and alter human existence – a new relationship to the universe. Sexuality, politics intelligence, position, motherhood, work, community, intimacy will develop new meanings; thinking itself will be transformed. This is where we have to begin.[20]

Rossi, like Rich, turn to women's maternalism, but she focusses less on the global social and cultural implications of the freeing of motherhood from patriarchal technological constraints and more on the possibilities of the mothering experience. Rossi argues that women have a "biological edge" in parental capacities and implies that children will do best with their natural mothers if these mothers can reclaim their bodies and become in touch with their innate mothering potential, and if their experience can be removed from male-dominant social organization. Rossi stresses the natural and untutored quality of some of women's intuitive responses to infants and the potential interconnection of sexual and maternal gratification. All these qualities could be enhanced if their expression were not distorted or destroyed by doctor-centered obstetric management, by industrial threats to fetuses and pregnant women, by too-close spacing of children, by women mothering according to a male life script (i.e., self-involved instead of nurturant). The return to a more natural mothering relationship would also sustain and further connections among women, the "women's culture" that the feminist movement has emphasized. Like Rich, Rossi implies that mothering could be wonderful if women could recognize and take pleasure in their procreative and maternal capacities and if these were not taken over by institutional constraints and alienated understandings of mothering.

Sexuality

Contradictory fantasies and expectations about maternity/mothering and sexuality also emerge in the new feminist literature. In *The Dialectic of Sex*, an influential early feminist work, Shulamith Firestone argued that biological sex is the basic social category and contradiction.[21] The reproductive difference between the sexes – that women bear children – leads to a sexual division of labor that is the root of all women's oppression by men, as well as oppressions of class and race. Since the fact of their biological childbearing capacities causes women's oppression, women must be freed from this biology. According to Firestone, the solution would be a technology that eliminates biological reproduction, untied to anyone's procreative body. This would end both biological and social motherhood.

In place of a male-dominant society based on women's biology and the biological family, Firestone envisions a society with total sexual liberation and a positively valued polymorphous perversity. By implication, freeing women from their reproductive biology leads to, and is a prerequisite of, sexual liberation. According to Firestone, pregnant bodies are ugly, and motherhood and sexuality are incompatible. In the new society, people would have individual freedom to move in and out of relationships, children could live where and with whom they want, and there would be no parental relationships as we know them. "Down with childhood" is the other side of "down with mothers." Firestone argues that the only alternative to the inequities of the family is no family at all, no long-term commitments of anyone to anyone; everyone must be an individual without ties. Thus, for Firestone, individualism goes along with a liberated sexuality, and both are inherently opposed to motherhood. For Nancy Friday, also, women's goal in life is to attain sexual individuality, which is the opposite of being a mother. Womanhood is non-maternal (hetero)sexuality. Relationships between mother and daughter – and between women generally – are entirely negative. From early childhood, little girls try to do one another in. Sexual relationships with men offer the only positive direction and the best thing a mother can do for her daughter is to promote her heterosexuality.

One strand of feminism, then, is represented by Shulamith Firestone, who would wipe out women's procreative capacities altogether, and by Nancy Friday, who poses a choice for women between exercising their procreative capacities and expressing their sexuality. Both imply a radical split between sexuality and maternity and opt for sexuality, either in its polymorphous perverse or its genital heterosexual form.

We find an opposing strand in Rossi and Rich, who identify motherhood with sexuality and would locate one foundation of women's liberation and fulfillment in the repossession (in the broadest sense) of their maternal bodies. Rich and Rossi imply that patriarchal institutions have distorted a natural maternal essence and potential for the mother–child bond. Rossi points to the inherent sexual pleasures of the mothering experience, and Rich suggests a connection between the physical pleasures of the mother–infant (especially mother–daughter) relationship and sexual bonds between women.

Aggression and Death

If having a child makes a mother all-powerful or totally powerless, if women's maternal potential requires the desexing of women or enables fully embodied power, then the child who evokes this arrangement must also be all-powerful. The child's existence or potential existence can dominate the mother's. This leads to a fourth theme that emerges in recent feminist writing on motherhood, a theme that grows out of the writer's identification as a mother or potential mother: an almost primal aggression in the mother–child relationship, an aggression that goes from mother to child, from child to mother, from mother-as-child to her own mother. Cemented by maternal and infantile rage, motherhood becomes linked to destruction and death. Rich, for instance, introduces and concludes her account of mothering within patriarchy with the story of a depressed suburban housewife and mother who decapitated her two youngest children.

Feminist Studies, one of the major scholarly feminist journals, published a special issue, "Toward a feminist theory of motherhood," on this theme.[22] With four exceptions, the issue is about motherhood, horror, and death. We read articles, poems, and autobiographical accounts about maternal death, children's deaths, the blood of childbirth, spontaneous abortions, stillbirths, the inability to conceive, childbirth as an experience of death, nineteenth-century obstetric torture techniques, unmothered monsters, child murder, and incest. Some of these articles, poems, and accounts are beautifully written, finely constructed, powerful, and persuasive. They illuminate women's fantasies and fears and guide us insightfully to themes and preoccupations we had not previously considered. Yet, the whole obliterates the parts: We are left, not with memories of these individual creations, but with impressions of an inextricable linkage of motherhood, blood, gore, destruction, and death.

Rachel Blau DuPlessis, the issue editor, points out that the contributions to the issue, in stressing the intertwining of birth, life, and death, react to cultural images of the mother as idealized nurturer. DuPlessis points out that there is, as yet, no synthesis, but she also does not seem to want to create one.[23] On the contrary, polarities are writ large; an almost satanic imagery of blood, guts, and destruction and subjective expostulation substitutes for cultural idealization. There is little attempt to investigate reality in its complex subjective and objective breadth.

Kate Millett's *The Basement: meditations on a human sacrifice*, further extends the linkage of motherhood, violence, and death.[24] The book is a true account of a woman, her seven children, and their torture-murder of a sixteen-year-old girl who was left in the woman's charge by her parents. Millett portrays the torturer–protagonist as society's victim: The squalor and poverty that surround her and her abandonment by men are not of her making. Therefore, her craziness is inevitable and understandable. Motherood contributes to the violence she feels: She is supposed to be the "responsible" adult with her children, in a situation where she has little power, and she visits her rage and frustration on one of them. The victim-mother creates a victim-child.

Jane Lazarre's feminist and autobiographical *The Mother Knot*, certainly less absolute and bleak than *The Basement*, also tells a story of maternal anger and victimization, and of the link between mother as victim and child as victim.[25] Lazarre sets out to tell the story of maternal ambivalence – the only "eternal and natural" feature of motherhood. Motherhood turns the woman's love relationship into the formal role pattern of Husband and Wife and brings her to the brink of madness. The protagonist's ambivalence is her profoundest reality. She desperately loves and resents her child, feels tenderness and rage at her husband. Hate and love, fury and overwhelming joy, remain unfused and unresolved, experienced only in their pure and alternating forms.[26]

In these accounts, a fantasied omnipotence, played out in the realm of aggression and anger, oscillates between mother and child. On the one hand, we have an all-powerful mother and a powerless child. On the other hand, we have the child who identifies with the all-powerful mother and whose very being casts its mother into the role of total victim or angel. Thus, in the *Feminist Studies* special issue, in Millett's story, and in Rich's account of the woman who murders her children, we find the notion that having a child is enough to kill a woman or make a woman into a murderer. Being a mother is a matter of life and death; having a child destroys the mother or the child. If anti-feminists have tended more than feminists to blame the mother, feminists tend to blame the child, or the having of children.

Why? There is, of course, historical and psychological truth here. Women's lives change radically when they have children, and caring for children in our society is difficult. The institution of motherhood, as Rich shows, is indeed oppressive to mothers and to those who are not mothers. Moreover, millions of women have died in childbirth throughout history, often as a direct result of obstetrical interference. In the past, infant mortality was often as likely as infant survival. Even today, the United States ranks high in infant mortality rates when compared with other industrialized nations. Moreover, surviving a child, or experiencing one's infant's death, in an age when we expect orderly generational progression, is a tragedy that can leave a permanent scar.

And yet death and destruction are by no means the whole experience or institution of motherhood. Rich and Millett suggest that the continuity of violence from men to women and women to children accounts for the link of motherhood and death, and we feel this is partly correct. The *Feminist Studies* issue seems to suggest an even deeper, more inevitable link. The writer is the mother whose individuality and separateness are threatened by the child and whose fantasy therefore kills it; and she is the child who is both the destroyer of the mother and the object of destruction. In this rendition, mother and child seem caught in a fantasied exclusive and exclusionary dyad where aggression, frustration, and rage hold sway. These writers merge fantasies of maternal omnipotence into the totalizing quality of the experience of the mother–child relationship.

Maternal Isolation

Another assumption apparent in recent feminist literature is that mother and child are an isolated dyad. Mother and child are seen as both physically and psychologically apart from the world, existing within a magic (or cursed) circle. Sometimes, as in Millett's work, the isolation has a physical boundary to it. The woman's home is her castle, in which she is isolated and all-powerful in motherhood. The children's fathers have left her. Her neighbors, hearing the screams from her basement, choose to leave her alone; they say it is her right and responsibility to discipline her children, and besides, they do not want to get involved. Other adults – social workers, the school personnel, the minister – are also loath to tread on a mother's space.

More often, the isolation is psychological. Rich talks of the isolation that comes from responsibility, that of the single adult woman who, though physically surrounded by others, bears the total task of mothering. The successes, failures, and day-to-day burdens of child-care are particularly hers. Lazarre chillingly describes the isolation of responsibility she faces (and creates). And she shows how that isolation helps lead to her desolation, rage, and destructiveness. Dinnerstein sees the isolation from the point of view of the child's development and describes how it magnifies the relation to the mother and creates in the child a desperate need to escape.

At the same time, some feminist writing wishes to maintain a form of isolated mother–child relationship but to make it unique and special in a positive way. The protagonist of *The Mother Knot* sets herself off from others and wishes to retreat into the perfect unit of infant and mother. Rich and Rossi wish conditions to change so that mothers receive the community support that would enable the specialness of the mothering relation to emerge.

In these accounts, this isolation, in which mother and child live in a unique and potent relationship, explains and even justifies the effects of mothering. It explains why mothers (even in their oppression by patriarchy) are so all-powerful in relation to their children, and why the mother–child relation is likely to be so bound up with powerful feelings. Mother and child are on a psychological desert island. Having only each other, each is continually impinging and intruding on the other, and there is no possibility of escape. As a result, the other becomes the object of aggressive fantasies and behaviors, and mothering becomes linked to extremist expectations about sexuality.

Cultural and Psychological Roots of Feminist Interpretations of Mothering

We have discussed four interrelated psychological themes that emerge from recent feminist work on mothering: (1) blaming and idealizing the mother, assuming that mothers are or can be all-powerful and perfect and that mothering either destroys the world or generates world perfection; (2) extreme expectations of maternal sexuality, asserting the incompatibility of motherhood and sexuality or romanticizing maternal sexuality; (3) a link between motherhood and aggression or death; and (4) an emphasis on the isolation of mother and child. All these themes share common characteristics: their continuity with dominant cultural understandings of mothering and their rootedness in unprocessed, infantile fantasies about mothers.

Our cultural understandings of mothering have a long history, but reached a peak in the nineteenth century. That century witnessed the growth of a sexual division of spheres that materially grounded mother–child isolation and bequeathed us a picture of the ideal mother who would guarantee both morally perfect children and a morally desirable world.[27] At a time when everyone's life was being affected by the frenzied growth of developing industrial capitalism, somehow mothers were seen as having total control and unlimited power in the creation of their children.

Post-Freudian psychology assumes the mother–child isolated unit that nineteenth-century industrial development produced and elaborates the notion that the early mother–infant relationship is central to later psychological development and to the psychological, emotional, and relational life of the child. As a result of this assumption, virtually all developmental research of the last thirty-five years has been directed to this early period. This has further reinforced and seemed to substantiate the popular view that the relationship of mother and infant has extraordinary significance. The assumption has also often led to a psychological determinism and reductionism that argues that what happens in the earliest mother–infant relationship determines the whole of history, society, and culture.[28]

Both nineteenth-century cultural ideology about motherhood and post-Freudian psychological theory blame mothers for any failings in their children and idealize possible maternal perfection. Blaming the mother, a major outcome of these theories and a major theme in feminist writings, has a long social history. David Levy's *Maternal Overprotection*, the Momism of Wylie and Erikson, literature on the schizophrenogenic mother, Rheingold's analysis of maternal aggression as the primary pathogenic influence on the child, Slater's discussion of the Oedipally titillating, overwhelming mother, and Lasch's account of the mother "impos[ing] her madness on everyone else," all suggest the terrible outcome of the omnipotent mother.[29] With the exception of Slater, they ignore any conditions that determine or foster maternal behavior in the first place and accept a completely deterministic view of child development.[30]

More recently, as women have entered the paid labor force and some have chosen not to become mothers, mothers have been blamed more for what is called "maternal deprivation" than for "maternal overprotection." Selma Fraiberg's *Every Child's Birthright: in defense of mothering* is a good example.[31] Describing herself as the child's advocate, Fraiberg has no sympathy for women who choose to work. Her message is clear: A good mother does not use regular substitute child care before the age of three.

Thus, feminists' tendency to blame the mother (the perspective of feminist-as-child) fits into cultural patterning. Feminists simply add on to this picture the notion that conditions other than the mother's incompetence or intentional malevolence create this maternal behavior. But feminists do not question the accuracy of this characterization of maternal behavior, nor its effects.

As we suggested, idealization and blaming the mother are two sides of the same belief in the all-powerful mother. In the nineteenth century, the bourgeois mother received moral training and guidance to enhance her motherly performance, guidance that, if followed, would lead children and the world to moral perfection. In contemporary child-rearing manuals, the good mother knows naturally how to mother if she will only follow her instincts,[32] or can be perfect if she will only stay home full-time,[33] or can provide proper stimulation and gentle teaching to her child.[34] Feminists take issue with the notion that a mother can be perfect in the here and now, given male dominance, lack of equality in marriage, and inadequate resources and support, but the fantasy of the perfect mother remains: If current limitations on mothers were eliminated, mothers would know naturally how to be good.

Blame and idealization of mothers have become our cultural ideology. This ideology, however, gains meaning from and is partially produced by infantile fantasies that are themselves the outcome of being mothered exclusively by one woman. If mothers have exclusive responsibility for infants who are totally dependent, then to the infant they are the source of all good and evil.[35] Times of closeness, oneness, and joy are the quintessence of perfect understanding; times of distress, frustration, discomfort, and too great separation are entirely the mother's fault. For the infant, the mother is not someone with her own life, wants, needs, history, other social relationships, work. She is known only in her capacity as mother. Growing up means learning that she, like other people in one's life, has and wants a life of her own, and that loving her means recognizing her subjectivity and appreciating her separateness. But people have trouble doing this and continue, condoned and supported by the ideology about mothers they subsequently learn, to experience mothers solely as people who did or did not live up to their child's expectations. This creates the quality of rage we find in "blame-the-mother" literature and the unrealistic expectation that perfection would result if only a mother would devote her life completely to her child and all impediments to doing so were removed. Psyche and culture merge here and reflexively create one another.

Originally, idealization of mothers is an infantile fantasy: No human being can be perfect. Thus, although the idealization of maternal life found in both Rich's and Rossi's writing is more from the perspective of mothers, their accounts are also informed by some identification with the stance of the child, who *needs* certain things in order to develop. One focus of Rossi's argument is the biological tie of infant to mother. Rich also claims that the child has powerful, strong feelings for the mother, "authentic" need – "a need vaster than any single human being could satisfy, except by loving continuously, unconditionally, from dawn to dark, and often in the middle of the night."[36] This need is evoked by the sense of uniqueness of the mother, by her singularity. This leads us to ask: What will happen to these "authentic" needs, and who will fulfill them? Does Rich think these intense feelings will disappear in a non-male-dominant world? Or are they inherent in mothering and, therefore, unavoidable? To what degree are they a product of the institution of motherhood under patriarchy and the experience of mothering it generates? And once there are "needs" and feelings like this, won't we start evaluating and idealizing mothers who do and do not meet them, and do and do not feel them?[37]

Fantasy and cultural ideology also meet in themes about maternal sexuality. An assumed incompatibility between sexuality and motherhood is largely a product of our nineteenth-century heritage, and some women psychoanalysts have helped perpetuate this cultural and psychological belief. In *The Psychology of Women*, Helene Deutsch claims clinical and literary support for the view that there is a natural and desirable psychological split between motherliness and erotic feelings.[38] Therese Benedek suggests that "mature" (i.e., motherly) women are simply less sexual than "immature" women.[39]

Ambivalence about maternal bodies, especially around sexuality, is present in the experience of many women, both as mothers and as daughters/children or would-be mothers. The trend, ideologically and for individual women, has been to opt for asexual motherhood. Rossi and Rich argue strongly against the view that motherhood and sexuality are incompatible; other feminists, like Firestone and Friday, accept the traditional view of incompatibility yet, unlike the analysts, argue in favor of sexuality.[40]

The understandings of motherhood we have been describing are larger than life and seen only in extremes. For Dinnerstein, women's mothering generates conditions that threaten to destroy human existence. For DuPlessis, a feminist theory of motherhood must begin with the inextricable link of motherhood and death; motherhood, she says, relates to heaven and hell, and to speech and silence; the overcoming of the institution of motherhood will be the end of dualism. For Friday, we must choose to be sexual or maternal. For Firestone, we must either accept inequality or give up our reproductive biology.

Rage is an inevitable outcome of this extremism. Psychological theory and cultural ideology have focused on the harm that mothers can do to their children, and some feminists continue to focus on this harm. We magnify the impact of one individual, the mother, and when the child in us suffers the inevitable frustrations of living, we blame our mothers. *My*

Mother/My Self has been extraordinarily popular. It speaks to the daughter in all women and tells them that their problems are not political, social, personal, or, heaven forbid, caused by men; their problems are caused solely by their mothers. We are all prone to mother-hating, for we live in a society that says that mothers can and should do all for their children. Moreover, we were all mothered, and our psyches retain the imprint of these origins.

Other feminists move beyond this position. They describe aggression done to women first by men and then by children, which leads to mothers' rageful fantasies and behaviors. Children's aggression in this model is expectation as much as actuality. Starting from the belief that "perfect" mothering is both centrally important and possible, if only a mother is totally devoted and attentive, as these feminists become mothers, or imagine being mothers, they fear the experience as all-consuming and come unconsciously and consciously to resent, fear, and feel devoured by their children. The outcome is the powerful aggressive feelings and behaviors and preoccupation with death we described above. The outcome also is to experience a total and overwhelming isolation of self with child.

Thus we can see a progressive logic to feminist themes about motherhood, a logic that moves a woman from an identification as daughter or child to an identification as mother. Drawing from and reflecting a cultural ideology and infantile sense of infantile need and maternal responsibility for the outcomes of child rearing, feminists begin by identifying with the child and blaming the mother, or by expecting her to be more than perfect. Cultural ideology and fantasy can also lead to idealization of maternal life from the point of view of the mother, as in the writing of Rossi and Rich. More often, the belief in total infantile need and maternal responsibility, and identification with the angry child, lead to a maternal identification that is in its turn full of rage and fear, and a sense that the conditions of patriarchy totally oppress mothers and isolate them with their child.

Feminism and Mothering: Moving Beyond a Politics of Primary Process

Where does this analysis lead us? In our identities as women, theoretically and programmatically, feminists need to move beyond the extremist assumptions and fantasies we have described. Insofar as we treat mothers as larger than life, omnipotent, all-powerful, or all-powerless, and motherhood as intimately connected to death, we deny mothers the complexity of their lives, their selfhood, their agency in creating from institutional context and experienced feelings. We deny them their place in a two-way relationship with their children, manifold relationships with the rest of the world, and we deny ourselves as mothers. But insofar as mothers are women, this involves a denial of all women as active subjects and a denial and split in our self-identities as children/daughters and people as well. This reflexively self-denying split of self from mother who is a fantasy partially accounts for the ambivalence and anger found in much of this writing.

As political beings, we must also question our involvement in child-centered assumptions about mothers. As individuals we can lament the past, wish we had gotten more than we had, wish we had been "better" mothered, and so forth. Although this stance may provide some temporary catharsis, it does not in itself help us to understand what we might do, personally or politically, in the present. We may think "our mothers" got us into this situation, but this knowledge alone can never tell us how to get out of it. Catharsis and rage may be a first step to political activity or working to change one's situation, but by themselves they lead nowhere. Rather, they trap us in our private psychical reality, and they dissipate energy.

In particular, feminists need to be especially self-conscious about the way they draw upon fantasy to inform theory and politics. Much of the feminist writing we have considered puts forth fantasy, or primary process thinking as the whole of reality or as a self-evident basis for theory and politics.[41] Fantasies are obviously fundamental experiences, and we must take them into account in creating a feminism that speaks to women's lives, but they cannot in themselves constitute theory or justify political choices. We need to analyze and reflect upon them, to allow secondary process thinking to mediate and interpret primary process reality. Moreover, it is not enough simply to claim that a particular fantasy, feeling, or behavior is a product of patriarchy, or women's oppression, and that therefore it cannot be further evaluated.

A striking instance of the problem created by accepting fantasy as the self-evident basis of theory or politics – of believing that it is enough to know that a woman's feeling or behavior is a product of her oppression – is a peculiar preoccupation with and moral paralysis around acts of maternal violence in some of the accounts discussed. In the case of violence against women, feminists have been outraged. We have focussed on the fact of this violence and have worked to protect women from the wife-beater, rapist, and assaulter. We have been properly angered by research and policies whose goal is to understand the individual motivations and causes of this violence rather than to eliminate it and protect its victims. By contrast, when we read Rich on maternal violence, Millett on maternal torture–murder, and the rampant aggression conveyed in the *Feminist Studies* issue, we find that maternal violence is described but not opposed.

These writings focus on the cause and motivation of maternal violence – "patriarchy" – to the exclusion of the fact of the violence.

The preoccupation with fantasies and their sources in oppression has embroiled us in violence, has allowed us to understand but not to condemn it, as we do in the case of violence against women. This preoccupation does not allow for the necessary political and moral argument that people, even within oppressive systems, can choose among a variety of actions; that although unreflected-upon feeling may determine action, it need not.

These accounts thus reflect the assumption that any act motivated by an internal emotional state, if that state reacts to women's oppression, is by definition political. Further, they lead to the conclusion that all acts motivated in this way are equally correct as political actions. But it is inadequate to imply that women's fantasies are automatically an extension of the personal that is political. Consider, for example, an abused wife who has murderous fantasies toward an abusive husband and kills him. We might call her act political, and we would in many circumstances defend her in the courts. But most of us would have preferred that she had left him and started a new life with the aid of friends, kin, a support group or a shelter for battered wives. We would consider this a better individual and political strategy. That the personal is political, that we can understand motherhood as experience and institution, implies that fantasies and feelings inform but do not directly determine our thoughtful, analyzed political decisions and judgments. The feminist accounts of mothering we discussed do not take that step. They do not move beyond seeing personal experience (feeling) and political institution (patriarchy) as absolute.

Feminist writing on motherhood has moved us forward in many areas. Adrienne Rich has transformed our ability to locate the many facets of motherhood as institution and has written powerfully of the complexity of maternal feeling and experience. Other feminists have called attention to the constraints, if not horrors, of mothering in a male-dominant society that devalues mothering, a society in which many mothers have no economic, communal, familial, or medical resources. Dorothy Dinnerstein persuaded many feminists of the serious consequences of exclusively female mothering. The *Feminist Studies* special issue, Nancy Friday, and Jane Lazarre have all revealed how overwhelmed women may feel as mothers or as children (daughters) of mothers. Rich, Rossi, and Lazarre have begun to articulate for us, sometimes in idealized ways (or ways that threaten to maintain the equation of woman and mother), what a non-patriarchal motherhood or nurturance might be.

But all this writing has been limited in a particular way: feminist theories of motherhood have not been able to move further because, as we have suggested, they are trapped in the dominant cultural assumptions and fantasies about mothering, *which in turn* rest on fantasied and unexamined notions of child development. Feminists have analyzed assumptions and biases in various disciplines, and feminism early on led us to notice cultural assumptions about gender (e.g., about sexual orientation) in society. But feminists have been trying to build a theory of mothering without examining or noticing that a theory of mothering requires a theory of childhood and child development as well.

Instead of developing this theory, feminists have built their theories of mothering on the dominant cultural and psychological assumptions about childhood. Drawing on psychoanalysis, these assumptions include an idealization of early infancy, in which development is seen exclusively as a painful process. The baby is most peaceful *in utero*, and birth is the first trauma and fraught with inevitable anxiety. There is now a trend toward trying to take the edge off this experience by non-violent birth. After initial bonding to a primary caretaker – a process both fragile and portentous – the infant begins the slow and often reluctant process of individuation, separation, and growth. Infantile rage, frustration, anxiety, loss, and fear spur emotional and cognitive development. Total dependency gives way to ambivalent independence, insatiable needs are grudgingly put aside when faced with reality, and impulses are tamed and controlled.

In this account children inevitably grow up with a residue of rage against those who frustrate their needs, even though they can grow up only if their needs are frustrated. In this model of development, mother and child are adversaries. The good mother helps the child grow up for his or her own good, and we expect and therefore allow children to be furious with their mothers for doing so. Rich's discussion of children's needs suggests such a model, as does Jane Flax's lack of differentiation between needs and wants. Dinnerstein's argument is based on the inevitable adversary relationship of parent and child. Her recommendation for shared parenting stems from her wish that the inevitable rage toward caretakers be shared between women and men.

A second set of assumptions in some feminist work draws from a simple role-learning theory of development. In the writings of Friday, Firestone, and Arcana we find the notion that children (daughters) are victims and recipients of pressures from their mothers in particular and from the culture in general. Mothers and the culture expect the repression of sexuality, feminine passivity and dependence, and docile role acceptance; and daughters passively conform to these expectations.

These models of child development seriously constrain feminist accounts of mothering. We would suggest that feminists draw upon and work to develop theories of child development that are interactive and that accord the infant and child agency and intentionality, rather than characterize it as a passive reactor to drives or environmental pressures.

We need to build theories that recognize collaboration and compromise as well as conflict. We should look to theories that stress relational capacities and experiences instead of insatiable, insistent drives; to theories in which needs do not equal wants; in which separation is not equivalent to deprivation, and in which autonomy is different from abandonment; in which the child is thought to have some interest in growth and development. We need to separate what we take to be the infant's or child's subjective feelings from a more inclusive appraisal of the state of the infant or child. And we need theories that examine how the tie to primary caretakers develops and changes for both caretakers and child, and that examine the rewards of non-infantile modes of relating and cognizing. We must begin to look at times other than infancy in the developmental life-span and relationships over time to people other than the mother to get a more accurate picture of what growing up is about.[42]

In the feminist writing we have discussed, there is an extraordinary current of energy and searching. To the extent that these accounts speak to shared feelings, they communicate with other women. The fantasy of the perfect mother, however, has led to the cultural oppression of women in the interest of a child whose needs are also fantasied. Although feminists did not invent this vision of motherhood and childhood, they have borrowed it. Feminist views of mothering, as mother and as daughter, have united infantile fantasies and a culturally child-centered perspective with a myth of maternal omnipotence, creating a totalistic, extreme, yet fragmented view of mothering and the mother–child relation in which both mother and child are paradoxically victim yet omnipotent. To begin to transform the relations of parenting and the relations of gender, to begin to transform women's lives, we must move beyond the myths and misconceptions embodied in the fantasy of the perfect mother.

PART II

Gender, Self, and Social Theory

5

Gender, Relation, and Difference in Psychoanalytic Perspective

I would go so far as to say that even before slavery or class domination existed, men built an approach to women that would serve one day to introduce differences among us all.

Claude Lévi-Strauss

In both the nineteenth- and twentieth-century women's movements, many feminists have argued that the degendering of society, so that gender and sex no longer determined social existence, would eliminate male dominance.[1] This view assumes that gender differentiating characteristics are acquired. An alternate sexual politics and analysis of sexual inequality has tended toward an essentialist position, posing male–female difference as innate. Not the degendering of society, but its appropriation by women, with women's virtues, is seen as the solution to male dominance. These virtues are uniquely feminine, and usually thought to emerge from women's biology, which is then seen as intrinsically connected to or entailing a particular psyche, a particular social role (such as mothering), a particular body image (more diffuse, holistic, non-phallocentric), or a particular sexuality (not centered on a particular organ; at times, lesbianism). In this view, women are intrinsically better than men and their virtues are not available to men. Proponents of the degendering model have sometimes also held that "female" virtues or qualities – nurturance, for instance – should be spread throughout society and replace aggression and competitiveness; but these virtues are nevertheless seen as acquired, a product of women's development or social location, and acquirable by men, given appropriate development, experience and social reorganization. (Others who argue for degendering have at times held that women need to acquire certain "male" characteristics and modes of action – autonomy, independence, assertiveness – again, assuming that such characteristics are acquired.)

This essay evaluates the essentialist view of difference and examines the contribution that psychoanalytic theory can make to understanding the question of sex or gender difference. It asks whether gender is best understood by focussing on differences between men and women and on the uniqueness of each and whether gender difference should be a central organizing concept for feminism. The concept of difference to which I refer here is abstract and irreducible.[2] It assumes the existence of an essence of gender, so that differences between men and women are seen to establish and define each gender as a unique and absolute category.

I will not discuss differences among women. I think we have something else in mind when we speak of differences in this connection. Differences among women – of class, race, sexual preference, nationality, and ethnicity, between mothers and non-mothers – are all significant for feminist theory and practice, but these remain concrete differences, analyzable in terms of specific categories and modes of understanding. We can see how they are socially situated and how they grow from particular social relations and organization; how they may contain physiological elements (race and sexual preference, for example) yet only gain a specific meaning in particular historical contexts and social formations.

I suggest that gender difference is not absolute, abstract, or irreducible; it does not involve an essence of gender. Gender differences, and the experience of difference, like differences among women, are socially and psychologically created and situated. In addition, I want to suggest a relational notion of difference. Difference and gender difference do not exist as things in themselves; they are created relationally, that is, in relationship. We cannot understand difference apart from this relational construction.

The issues I consider here are relevant both to feminist theory and to particular strands of feminist politics. In contrast to the beginning of the contemporary women's movement, there is now a widespread view that gender differences are essential, that women are fundamentally different from men, and that these differences must be recognized, theorized, and maintained. This finds some political counterpart in notions that women's special nature guarantees the emergence of a good society after the feminist revolution and legitimates female dominance, if not an exclusively female society. My conclusions lead me to reject those currents of contemporary feminism that would found a politics on essentialist conceptions of the feminine.

There is also a preoccupation among some women with psychological separateness and autonomy, with individuality as a necessary women's goal. This preoccupation grows out of many women's feelings of not having distinct autonomy as separate selves, in comparison, say, to men. This finds some political counterpart in equal rights arguments, ultimately based on notions of women exclusively as individuals rather than as part of a collectivity or social group. I suggest that we need to situate such a goal in an understanding of psychological development and to indicate the relationship between our culture's individualism and gender differentiation.

Psychoanalysis clarifies for us many of the issues involved in questions of difference by providing a developmental history of the emergence of separateness, differentiation, and the perception of difference in early childhood. Thus it provides a particularly useful arena in which to see the relational and situated construction of difference, and of gender difference. Moreover, psychoanalysis gives an account of these issues from a general psychological perspective, as well as with specific relation to the question of gender. In this context, I will discuss two aspects of the general subject of separateness, differentiation, and perceptions of difference and their emergence. First, I will consider how separation–individuation occurs relationally in the first "me" – "not-me" division, in the development of the "I," or self. I will suggest that we have to understand this separation–individuation in relation to other aspects of development, that it has particular implications for women, and that differentiation is not synonymous with difference or separateness. Second, I will talk about the ways that difference and gender difference are created distinctly, in different relational contexts, for girls and boys, and, hence, for women and men. The argument here advances a reading of psychoanalysis that stresses the relational ego. It contrasts with certain prevalent (Lacan-influenced) feminist readings of psychoanalysis, in particular with the views advanced by French theorists of difference like Luce Irigaray and with the Freudian orthodoxy of Juliet Mitchell.

I do not deal in this essay with the male and female body. We clearly live an embodied life; we live with those genital and reproductive organs and capacities, those hormones and chromosomes, that locate us physiologically as male or female. But, as psychoanalysis has shown us, there is nothing self-evident about this biology. How anyone experiences, fantasizes about, or internally represents her or his embodiment grows from experience, learning, and self-definition in the family and in the culture. Such self-definitions may be shaped by completely non-biological considerations, which may also shape perceptions of anatomical "sex differences" and the psychological development of these differences into forms of sexual object choice, mode, or aim; into femininity or masculinity; into activity or passivity; into one's choice of the organ of erotic pleasure; and so forth. We cannot know what people would make of their bodies in a non-gender or non-sexually organized world, what kind of sexual structuration or gender identities would develop. We do know that the cultural, social, and psychological significance of biological sex differences, gender difference, and different sexualities is not obvious. There might be a multiplicity of sexual organizations, identities, and practices, and perhaps even of genders themselves. Bodies would be bodies (we do not want to deny people their bodily experience). But particular bodily attributes would not necessarily be so determining of who we are, what we do, how we are perceived, and who are our sexual partners.

Differentiation

Psychoanalysis talks of the process of "differentiation" or "separation–individuation."[3] A child of either gender is born originally with what is called a "narcissistic relation to reality": cognitively and libidinally it experiences itself as merged and continuous with the world in general, and with its mother or caretaker in particular. Differentiation, or separation–individuation, means coming to perceive a demarcation between the self and the object world, coming to perceive the subject/self as distinct, or separate from, the object/other. An essential early task of infantile development, it involves the development of ego boundaries (a sense of personal psychological division from the rest of the world) and of a body ego (a sense of the permanence of one's physical separateness and the predictable boundedness of one's own body, of a distinction between inside and outside).

This differentiation requires physiological maturation (for instance, the ability to perceive object constancy), but such maturation is not enough. Differentiation happens *in relation to* the mother, or to the child's primary caretaker. It develops through experiences of the mother's departure and return, and through frustration, which emphasizes the child's separateness and the fact that it doesn't control all its own experiences and gratifications. Some of these experiences and gratifications come from within, some from without. If it were not for these frustrations, these disruptions of the experience of primary oneness, total holding, and gratification, the child would not need to begin to perceive the other, the "outer world," as separate, rather than as an extension of itself. Developing separateness thus involves, in particular, perceiving the mother or primary caretaker as separate and "not-me," where once these were an undifferentiated symbiotic unity.

Separateness, then, is not simply given from birth, nor does it emerge from the individual alone. Rather, separateness is defined relationally; differentiation occurs in relationship: "*I*" am "*not-you*". Moreover, "*you*," or the other, is also distinguished. The child learns to see the particularity of the mother or primary caretaker in contrast to the rest of the world.

Thus, as the self is differentiated from the object world, the object world is itself differentiated into its component parts.

Now, from a psychoanalytic perspective, learning to distinguish me and not-me is necessary for a person to grow into a functioning human being. It is also inevitable, since experiences of departure, of discontinuity in handling, feeding, where one sleeps, how one is picked up and by whom, of less than total relational and physical gratification, are unavoidable. But for our understanding of "difference" in this connection, the concept of differentiation and the processes that characterize it need elaboration.

First, in most psychoanalytic formulations, and in prevalent under-standings of development, the mother, or the outside world, is depicted simply as the other, not-me, one who does or does not fulfill an expectation. This perception arises originally from the infant's cognitive inability to differentiate self and world; the infant does not distinguish between its desires for love and satisfaction and those of its primary love-object and object of identification. The self here is the infant or growing child, and psychoanalytic accounts take the viewpoint of this child.

However, adequate separation, or differentiation, involves not merely perceiving the separateness, or otherness, of the other. It involves perceiving the person's subjectivity and selfhood as well. Differentiation, separation, and disruption of the narcissistic relation to reality are developed through learning that the mother is a separate being with separate interests and activities that do not always coincide with just what the infant wants at the time. They involve the ability to experience and perceive the object/other (the mother) in aspects apart from its sole relation to the ability to gratify the infant's/subject's needs and wants; they involve seeing the object as separate from the self and from the self's needs.[4] The infant must change here from a "relationship to a subjectively conceived object to a relationship to an object objectively perceived."[5]

In infantile development this change requires cognitive sophistication, the growing ability to integrate various images and experiences of the mother that comes with the development of ego capacities. But these capacities are not enough. The ability to perceive the other as a self, finally, requires an emotional shift and a form of emotional growth. The adult self not only experiences the other as distinct and separate. It also does not experience the other solely in terms of its own needs for gratification and its own desires.

This interpretation implies that true differentiation, true separateness, cannot be simply a perception and experience of self–other, of presence–absence. It must precisely involve two selves, two presences, two subjects. Recognizing the other as a subject is possible only to the extent that one is not dominated by felt need and one's own exclusive subjectivity. Such recognition permits appreciation and perception of many aspects of the other person, of her or his existence apart from the child's/the self's. Thus, how we understand differentiation – only from the viewpoint of the infant as a self, or from the viewpoint of two interacting selves – has consequences for what we think of as a mature self. If the mature self grows only out of the infant as a self, the other need never be accorded her or his own selfhood.

The view that adequate separation–individuation, or differentiation, involves not simply perceiving the otherness of the other, but her or his selfhood/subjectivity as well, has important consequences, not only for an understanding of the development of selfhood, but also for perceptions of women. Hence, it seems to me absolutely essential to a feminist appropriation of psychoanalytic conceptions of differentiation. Since women, as mothers, are the primary caretakers of infants, if the child (or the psychoanalytic account) only takes the viewpoint of the infant as a (developing) self, then the mother will be perceived (or depicted) only as an object. But, from a feminist perspective, perceiving the particularity of the mother must involve according the mother her own selfhood. This is a necessary part of the developmental process, though it is also often resisted and experienced only conflictually and partially. Throughout life, perceptions of the mother fluctuate between perceiving her particularity and selfhood and perceiving her as a narcissistic extension, a not-separate other whose sole reason for existence is to gratify one's own wants and needs.

Few accounts recognize the import of this particular stance toward the mother. Alice Balint's marvelous protofeminist account is the best I know of the infantile origins of adult perceptions of mother as object:

Most men (and women) – even when otherwise quite normal and capable of an "adult," altruistic form of love which acknowledges the interests of the partner – retain towards their own mothers this naive egoistic attitude throughout their lives. For all of us it remains self-evident that the interests of mother and child are identical, and it is the generally acknowledged measure of the goodness or badness of the mother how far she really feels this identity of interests.[6]

Now, these perceptions, as a product of infantile development, are somewhat inevitable as long as women have nearly exclusive maternal responsibilities, and they are one major reason why I advocate equal parenting as a necessary basis of sexual equality. But I think that, even within the ongoing context of women's mothering, as women we can and must liberate ourselves from such perceptions in our personal emotional lives as much as possible, and certainly in our theorizing and politics.[7]

A second elaboration of psychoanalytic accounts of differentiation concerns the affective or emotional distinction between differentiation or separation–individuation, and *difference*. Difference and differentiation are, of course, related to and feed into one another; it is in some sense true that cognitive or linguistic distinction, or division, must imply difference. However, it is possible to be separate, to be differentiated, without caring about or emphasizing difference, without turning the cognitive fact into an emotional, moral, or political one. In fact, assimilating difference to differentiation is defensive and reactive, a reaction to not feeling separate enough. Such assimilation involves arbitrary boundary creation and an assertion of hyper-separateness to reinforce a lack of security in a person's sense of self as a separate person. But one can be separate from and similar to someone at the same time. For example, one can recognize another's subjectivity and humanity as one recognizes one's own, seeing the commonality of both as active subjects. Or a woman can recognize her similarity, commonality, even continuity, with her mother, because she has developed enough of an unproblematic sense of separate self. At the same time, the other side of being able to experience separateness and commonality, of recognizing the other's subjectivity, is the ability to recognize differences with a small "d," differences that are produced and situated historically – for instance, the kinds of meaningful differences among women that I mentioned earlier.

The distinction between differentiation/separateness and difference relates to a third consideration, even more significant to our assessment of difference and gender difference. Following Mahler, much psychoanalytic theory has centered its account of early infant development on separation–individuation, on the creation of the separate self, on the "me" – "not-me" distinction. Yet there are other ways of looking at the development of self, other important and fundamental aspects to the self: "me" – "not-me" is not all there is to "me." Separation, the "me" – "not-me" division, looms larger, both in our psychological life and theoretically, to the extent that these other aspects of the self are not developed either in individual lives or in theoretical accounts.

Object-relations theory shows that in the development of self the primary task is not the development of ego boundaries and a body ego.[8] Along with the earliest development of its sense of separateness, the infant constructs an internal set of unconscious, affectively loaded representations of others in relation to its self, and an internal sense of self in relationship emerges. Images of felt good and bad aspects of the mother or primary caretaker, caretaking experiences, and the mothering relationship become part of the self, of a relational ego structure, through unconscious mental processes that appropriate and incorporate these images. With maturation, these early images and fragments of perceived experience become put together into a self. As externality and internality are established, therefore, what comes to be internal includes what originally were aspects of the other and the relation to the other. (Similarly, what is experienced as external may include what was originally part of the developing self's experience.) Externality and internality, then, do not follow easily observable physiological boundaries but are constituted by psychological and emotional processes as well.

These unconscious early internalizations that affect and constitute the internal quality of selfhood may remain more or less fragmented, or they may develop a quality of wholeness. A sense of continuity of experience and the opportunity to integrate a complex of (at least somewhat) complementary and consistent images enables the "I" to emerge as a continuous being with an identity. This more internal sense of self, or of "I," is not dependent on separateness or difference from an other. A "true self," or "central self," emerges through the experience of continuity that the mother or caretaker helps to provide, by protecting the infant from having continually to react to and ward off environmental intrusions and from being continually in need.

The integration of a "true self" that feels alive and whole involves a particular set of internalized feelings about others in relation to the self. These include developing a sense that one is able to affect others and one's environment (a sense that one has not been inhibited by over-anticipation of all one's needs), a sense that one has been accorded one's own feelings and a spontaneity about these feelings (a sense that one's feelings or needs have not been projected onto one), and a sense that there is a fit between one's feelings and needs and those of the mother or caretaker. These feelings all give the self a sense of agency and authenticity.

This sense of agency, then, is fostered by caretakers who do not project experiences or feelings onto the child and who do not let the environment impinge indiscriminately. It is evoked by empathic caretakers who understand and validate the infant as a self in its own right, and the infant's experience as real. Thus, the sense of agency, which is one basis of the inner sense of continuity and wholeness, grows out of the nature of the parent–infant relationship.

Another important aspect of internalized feelings about others in relation to the self concerns a certain wholeness that develops through an internal sense of relationship with another.[9] The "thereness" of the primary parenting person grows into an internal sense of the presence of another who is caring and affirming. The self comes into being here first through feeling confidently alone in the presence of its mother, and then through this presence's becoming internalized. Part of its self becomes a good internal mother. This suggests that the central core of self is, internally, a relational ego, a sense of self-in-good-relationship. The presence or absence of others, their sameness or difference, does not then become an issue touching the infant's very existence. A "capacity to be alone," a relational rather than a reactive autonomy, develops because of a sense of the ongoing presence of another.

These several senses of agency, of a true self that does not develop reactively, of a relational self or ego core, and of an internal continuity of being, are fundamental to an unproblematic sense of self, and provide the basis of both autonomy and spontaneity. The strength, or wholeness, of the self, in this view, does not depend only or even centrally on its degree of separateness, although the extent of confident distinctness certainly affects and is part of the sense of self. The more secure the central self, or ego core, the less one has to define one's self through separateness from others. Separateness becomes, then, a more rigid, defensive, rather fragile, secondary criterion of the strength of the self and of the "success" of individuation.

This view suggests that no one has a separateness consisting only of "me" – "not-me" distinctions. Part of myself is always that which I have taken in; we are all to some degree incorporations and extensions of others. Separateness from the mother, defining oneself as apart from her (and from other women), is not the only or final goal for women's ego strength and autonomy, even if many women must also attain some sense of reliable separateness. In the process of differentiation, leading to a genuine autonomy, people maintain contact with those with whom they had their earliest relationships: indeed this contact is part of who we are. "I am" is not definition through negation, is not "who I am not." Developing a sense of confident separateness must be a part of all children's development. But once this confident separateness is established, one's relational self can become more central to one's life. Differentiation is not distinctness and separateness, but a particular way of being connected to others. This connection to others, based on early incorporations, in turn enables us to feel that empathy and confidence that are basic to the recognition of the other as a self.

What does all this have to do with male–female difference and male dominance? Before turning to the question of gender difference, I want to reiterate what we as feminists learn from the general inquiry into "differentiation." First, we learn that we can only think of differentiation and the emergence of the self relationally. Differentiation occurs, and separation emerges, in relationship; they are not givens. Second, we learn that to single out separation as the core of a notion of self and of the process of differentiation may well be inadequate; it is certainly not the only way to discuss the emergence of self or what constitutes a strong self. Differentiation includes the internalization of aspects of the primary caretaker and of the caretaking relationship.

Finally, we learn that essential, important attitudes toward mothers and expectations of mothers – attitudes and expectations that enter into experiences of women more generally – emerge in the earliest differentiation of self. These attitudes and expectations arise during the emergence of separateness. Given that differentiation and separation are developmentally problematic, and given that women are primary caretakers, the mother, who is a woman, becomes and remains for children of both genders the other, or object. She is not accorded autonomy or selfness on her side. Such attitudes arise also from the gender-specific character of the early, emotionally charged self and object images that affect the development of self and the sense of autonomy and spontaneity. They are internalizations of feelings about the self in relation to the mother, who is then often experienced as either overwhelming or over-denying. These attitudes are often unconscious and always have a basis in unconscious, emotionally charged feelings and conflicts. A precipitate of the early relationship to the mother and of an unconscious sense of self, they may be more fundamental and determining of psychic life than more conscious and explicit attitudes to "sex differences" or "gender differences" themselves.

This inquiry suggests a psychoanalytic grounding for goals of emotional psychic life other than autonomy and separateness. It suggests, instead, an individuality that emphasizes our connectedness with, rather than our separation from, one another. Feelings of inadequate separateness, the fear of merger, are indeed issues for women, because of the ongoing sense of oneness and primary identification with our mothers (and children). A transformed organization of parenting would help women to resolve these issues. However, autonomy, spontaneity, and a sense of agency need not be based on self–other distinctions, on the individual as individual. They can be based on the fundamental interconnectedness, not synonymous with merger, that grows out of our earliest unconscious developmental experience, and that enables the creation of a non-reactive separateness.[10]

Gender Differences in the Creation of Difference

I turn now to the question of gender differences. We are not born with perceptions of gender differences; these emerge developmentally. In the traditional psychoanalytic view, however, when sexual difference is first seen it has self-evident value. A girl perceives her lack of a penis, knows instantly that she wants one, and subsequently defines herself and her mother as lacking, inadequate, castrated; a boy instantly knows having a penis is better, and fears the loss of his own.[11] This traditional account violates a fundamental rule of psychoanalytic interpretation. When the analyst finds trauma, shock, strong fears, or conflict, it is a signal to look for the roots of such feelings.[12] Because of his inability to focus on the pre-Oedipal years and the relationship of mother to child, Freud could not follow his own rule here.

Clinical and theoretical writings since Freud suggest another interpretation of the emergence of perceptions of gender difference. This view reverses the perception of which gender experiences greater trauma, and retains only the claim that gender identity and the sense of masculinity and femininity develop differently for men and women.[13] These accounts suggest that core gender identity and masculinity are conflictual for men, and are bound up with the masculine sense of self in a way that core gender identity and femininity are not for women. "Core gender identity" here refers to a cognitive sense of gendered self, the sense that one is male or female. It is established in the first two years concomitantly with the development of the sense of self. Later evaluations of the desirability of one's gender and of the activities and modes of behavior associated with it, or of one's own sense of adequacy at fulfilling gender role expectations, are built upon this fundamental gender identity. They do not create or change it.

Most people develop an unambiguous core gender identity, a sense that they are female or male. But because women mother, the sense of maleness in men differs from the sense of femaleness in women. Maleness is more conflictual and more problematic. Underlying, or built into, core male gender identity is an early, non-verbal, unconscious, almost somatic sense of primary oneness with the mother, an underlying sense of femaleness that continually, usually unnoticeably, but sometimes insistently, challenges and undermines the sense of maleness. Thus, because of a primary oneness and identification with his mother, a primary femaleness, a boy's and a man's core gender identity itself – the seemingly unproblematic cognitive sense of being male – is an issue. A boy must learn his gender identity as being not-female, or not-mother. Subsequently, again because of the primacy of the mother in early life and because of the absence of concrete, real, available male figures of identification and love who are as salient for him as female figures, learning what it is to be masculine comes to mean learning to be not-feminine, or not-womanly.

Because of early developed, conflictual core gender identity problems, and later problems of adequate masculinity, it becomes important to men to have a clear sense of gender difference, of what is masculine and what is feminine, and to maintain rigid boundaries between these. Researchers find, for example, that fathers sex-type children more than mothers. They treat sons and daughters more differently and enforce gender role expectations more vigorously than mothers do.[14] Boys and men come to deny the feminine identification within themselves and those feelings they experience as feminine: feelings of dependence, relational needs, emotions generally. They come to emphasize differences, not commonalities or continuities, between themselves and women, especially in situations that evoke anxiety, because these commonalities and continuities threaten to challenge gender difference or to remind boys and men consciously of their potentially feminine attributes.

These conflicts concerning core gender identity interact with and build upon particular ways that boys experience the processes of differentiation and the formation of the self.[15] Both sexes establish separateness in relation to their mother, and internalizations in the development of self take in aspects of the mother as well. But because the mother is a woman, these experiences differ by gender. Though children of both sexes are originally part of herself, a mother unconsciously and often consciously experiences her son as more of an "other" than her daughter. Reciprocally, a son's male core gender identity develops away from his mother. The male's self, as a result, becomes based on a more fixed "me" – "not-me" distinction. Separateness and difference as a component of differentiation become more salient. By contrast, the female's self is less separate and involves a less fixed "me" – "not-me" distinction, creating the difficulties with a sense of separateness and autonomy that I mentioned above.

At the same time, core gender identity for a girl is not problematic in the sense that it is for boys. It is built upon, and does not contradict, her primary sense of oneness and identification with her mother and is assumed easily along with her developing sense of self. Girls grow up with a sense of continuity and similarity to their mother, a relational connection to the world. For them, difference is not originally problematic or fundamental to their psychological being or identity. They do not define themselves as "not-men," or "not-male," but as "I, who am female." Girls and women may have problems with their sense of continuity and similarity, if it is too strong and they have no sense of a separate self. However, these problems are not the inevitable products of having a sense of continuity and similarity, since, as I argue here, selfhood does not depend only on the strength and impermeability of ego boundaries. Nor are these problems bound up with questions of gender; rather, they are bound up with questions of self.

In the development of gender identification for girls it is not the existence of core gender identity, the unquestioned knowledge that one is female, that is problematic. Rather, it is the later-developed conflicts concerning this identity, and the identifications, learning, and cognitive choices that it implies. The difficulties that girls have in establishing a "feminine" identity do not stem from the inaccessibility and negative definition of this identity, or its assumption by denial (as in the case of boys). They arise from identification with a negatively valued gender category, and an ambivalently experienced maternal figure, whose mothering and femininity, often conflictual for the mother herself, are accessible, but devalued. Conflicts here arise from questions of relative power, and social and cultural value. I would argue that these conflicts come later in development, and are less pervasively determining of psychological life for women than are masculine conflicts around core gender identity and gender difference.

Men's and women's understanding of difference, and gender difference, must thus be understood in the relational context in which these are created. They stem from the respective relation of boys and girls to their mother, who is their primary caretaker, love-object, and object of identification, and who is a woman in a sexually and gender-organized world. This relational context contrasts profoundly for girls and boys in a way that makes difference, and gender difference, central for males – one of the earliest, most basic male developmental issues – and not central for females. It gives men a psychological investment in difference that women do not have.

According to psychoanalytic accounts since Freud, it is very clear that males are "not females" in earliest development. Core gender identity and the sense of masculinity are defined more negatively, in terms of that which is not female or not-mother, than positively. By contrast, females do not develop as "not-males." Female core gender identity and the sense of femininity are defined positively, as that which is female, or like mother. Difference from males is not so salient. An alternative way to put this is to suggest that, developmentally, the maternal identification represents and is experienced as generically human for children of both genders.[16]

But, because men have power and cultural hegemony in our society, a notable thing happens. Men use and have used this hegemony to appropriate and transform these experiences. Both in everyday life and in theoretical and intellectual formulations, men have come to define maleness as that which is basically human, and to define women as not-men. This transformation is first learned in, and helps to constitute, the Oedipal transition – the cultural, affective, and sexual learnings of the meaning and valuation of sex differences.[17] Because Freud was not attentive to pre-Oedipal development (and because of his sexism), he took this meaning and valuation as a self-evident given, rather than a developmental and cultural product.

We must remember that this transformed interpretation of difference, an interpretation learned in the Oedipal transition, is produced by means of male cultural hegemony and power. Men have the means to institutionalize their unconscious defenses against repressed yet strongly experienced developmental conflicts. This interpretation of difference is imposed on earlier developmental processes; it is not the deepest, unconscious root of either the female or the male sense of gendered self. In fact, the primary sense of gendered self that emerges in earliest development constantly challenges and threatens men, and gives a certain potential psychological security, even liberation, to women. The transformed interpretation of difference is not inevitable, given other parenting arrangements and other arrangements of power between the sexes. It is especially insofar as women's lives and self-definition become oriented to men that difference becomes more salient for us, as does differential evaluation of the sexes. Insofar as women's lives and self-definition become more oriented toward themselves, differences from men become less salient.

Evaluating Difference

What are the implications of this inquiry into psychoanalytic understandings of differentiation and gender difference for our understanding of difference, and for our evaluation of the view that difference is central to feminist theory? My investigation suggests that our own sense of differentiation, of separateness from others, as well as our psychological and cultural experience and interpretation of gender or sexual difference, are created through psychological, social, and cultural processes, and through relational experiences. We can only understand gender difference, and human distinctness and separation, relationally and situationally.[18] They are part of a system of asymmetrical social relationships embedded in inequalities of power, in which we grow up as selves, and as women and men. Our experience and perception of gender are processual; they are produced developmentally and in our daily social and cultural lives.

Difference is psychologically salient for men in a way that it is not for women, because of gender differences in early formative developmental processes and the particular unconscious conflicts and defenses these produce. This salience, in turn, has been transmuted into a conscious cultural preoccupation with gender difference. It has also become intertwined with and has helped to produce more general cultural notions, particularly, that individualism, separateness, and distance from others are desirable and requisite to autonomy and human fulfillment.[19] Throughout these processes, it is women, as mothers, who become the objects apart from which separateness, difference, and autonomy are defined.

It is crucial for us as feminists to recognize that the ideologies of difference which define us as women and as men, as well as inequality itself, are produced, socially, psychologically, and culturally, by people living in and creating their social, psychological, and cultural worlds.

Women participate in the creation of these worlds and ideologies, even if our ultimate power and access to cultural hegemony are less than those of men. To speak of difference as a final, irreducible concept and to focus on gender differences as central is to reify them and to deny the reality of those processes which create the meaning and significance of gender. To see men and women as qualitatively different kinds of people, rather than seeing gender as processual, reflexive, and constructed, is to reify and deny relations of gender, to see gender differences as permanent rather than as created and situated.

We certainly need to understand how difference comes to be important, how it is produced as salient, and how it reproduces sexual inequality. But we should not appropriate differentiation and separation, or difference, for ourselves and take it as a given. Feminist theories and feminist inquiry based on the notion of essential difference, or focused on demonstrating difference, are doing feminism a disservice. They ultimately rely on the defensively constructed masculine models of gender that are presented to us as our cultural heritage, rather than creating feminist understandings of gender and difference that grow from our own politics, theorizing, and experience.

6

Beyond Drive Theory: Object Relations and the Limits of Radical Individualism

Psychoanalysis continues, as it has since Freud's earliest writings, to inspire social theory, social critique, and visions of liberation, as well as vociferous debates concerning psychological theory and clinical practice.[1] One continuing basis of these discussions concerns the question of the "true Freud." Psychoanalysts, even as they have developed ego psychology, object-relations theory, new theories of narcissism, Kleinian theory, cultural and interpersonal theory, always find an obligatory opening quote or passage to prove that they are extending and not modifying Freud, or they risk disenfranchisement or ouster by the mainstream establishment. As Robert Wallerstein remarks in his contribution to a symposium on "The Identity of the Psychoanalyst," psychoanalysts have not yet come to terms with the death of Freud. They have never fully mourned Freud, incorporated their ambivalence toward him, or consolidated their identifications with him. Thus they have been unable definitively to move beyond him.[2]

In the world of critical psychoanalytic social and cultural theory, there has also been a reluctance to move beyond Freud. Here also, revisionists are excoriated and seen as major purveyors and defenders of the worst evils of the contemporary psyche and contemporary society. The major locus of debate in this latter case, as often in the former, concerns the status of the drives. Starting with Wilhelm Reich, and continuing to the present, strands of social critique, liberatory and utopian theory, and popular therapeutic practices have turned to a psychoanalytically derived conception of drive liberation, or sexual liberation, as their basis. In this chapter, I examine an important contribution to this debate. The critical psychoanalytic social theories of Norman O. Brown and Herbert Marcuse, put forth especially in *Life against Death* and *Eros and Civilization*, provide the fullest and most substantial expression of a position that characteristically rejects any attempt to question the full psychoanalytic truth of the late drive theory, and argues that post-Freudian psychoanalytic theory – especially Neo-Freudianism, but also ego psychology and its derivatives – eliminates the radical core of psychoanalytic insight into the drives, repression, and the unconscious.[3] I indicate crucial problems in an interpretation of Freud that stresses the drive metapsychology and the drive-repression dynamic and suggest that a drive theory interpretation of psychoanalysis ultimately results in Brown and Marcuse offering profoundly limited social theories and visions of liberation, radical individualist visions that sees all sociality as constraint, and that (unlike Freud) do not see sociality as necessary or desirable.[4] Liberation here becomes either freedom from society – the individual apart from social relations – or, alternatively, dissolving all social relations into the self. We are left with little understanding of how new human relations could be constructed or of how people could participate in social bonds or political activity. As well, their theories and visions involve a particularly problematic view of women, gender relations, and generation. I conclude by suggesting that object-relations theory provides a more adequate basis for a critical psychoanalytic social theory and social vision.

My point here is not globally to criticize Brown and Marcuse as social thinkers, but to draw upon their extensively and carefully worked-out accounts to demonstrate the consequences of using certain psychoanalytic approaches to underpin social thought.[5] As I will suggest, their reliance on the drive theory and its derivatives leads not only to the problems I describe but also to contradictions in their accounts. In the case of Marcuse, the psychoanalytic theory he embraces undermines the social vision and analysis he puts forth in other works and even in parts of *Eros and Civilization* itself. In Brown, contradictions emerge within his interpretation of psychoanalysis, both within *Life against Death* and between *Life against Death* and *Love's Body*.

Nor do I wish to suggest that Brown's and Marcuse's accounts are exactly the same. I will point out divergences below. In spite of Marcuse's and Brown's debate about *Love's Body*, however, I think that in terms of the fundamental features at issue Brown and Marcuse are sufficiently similar to warrant discussing them together.[6] *Life against Death* and *Eros and Civilization* share many basic psychoanalytic assumptions and present a nearly identical vision of liberation; *Eros and Civilization* exhibits many of those very features that Marcuse later criticizes in *Love's Body*.

The Analysis and Vision of Brown and Marcuse

Civilization and Its Discontents, of course, provides us with Freud's fullest exposition of a drive-theory-based psychoanalytic social theory.[7] Freud argues that unconscious drives fundamentally determine psychic life; repression, which transforms or suppresses these drives, is the fundamental psychodynamic experience and the *sine qua non* of social life. Social connections are compromise formations (like symptoms) that derive from repression. Freud's book thus contains an implicit assumption that people are originally anti-social: we need to explain both the fact that people form social bonds and the processes through which they do so when it is not really their nature. Freud constructs an opposition between the oceanic feeling – human connectedness – and human nature – our individual primal aggressive and libidinal drives.

Thus, *Civilization and Its Discontents*, Freud's most important work of social theory, provides a sobering argument based on the drive theory for the necessity of human unhappiness. The drives and civilization are unalterably opposed, and the former must be repressed in the interests of the latter. Individuals pay the price of this repression in neurosis and guilt.

Drives as Truth

Following Freud, Marcuse and Brown claim that the drive theory constitutes the core of psychoanalysis and that the repression of drives is the core of civilization, even as they offer different interpretations of how drives are repressed and how they have been repressed in the past. This repression requires condemnation: contemporary civilization, or culture, threatens to dominate if not annihilate the individual. In such a context, the major contribution of psychoanalysis is not its account of the necessity of repression but its account of the fundamental opposition between the individual and culture. The individual's core – her or his drives – cannot be completely dominated; the instincts can be a center of resistance and opposition.

The drive theory provides the basis for a radical critique of society and a vision of human liberation and true human life. In stressing the independence of drives from culture, it is revolutionary and liberating. Thus, *Eros and Civilization* and *Life against Death* wish to use the drive theory to reverse Freud's vision: if the drive theory is the revolutionary core of psychoanalysis and culture is a major threat to the individual, then freedom from domination and constraint must be based on instinctual liberation.[8] Marcuse and Brown argue that an understanding of the drives allowing happiness and lack of repression is possible and necessary. If repression and guilt are the price of civilization and serve civilization against the individual, then liberation must consist in the expansion of instinctual gratification and freedom from repression. Drive repression is the same thing as oppression, as the drives offer the only potential for liberation and true human existence.

Drive theory is not only the true core of psychoanalysis; it also provides a measure for evaluating individual life and society. The extent to which a culture is fulfilling is the extent to which it enables or encourages drive fulfillment. Marcuse and Brown both acknowledge a debt to Reich for first insisting on the link between domination and sexual repression and for arguing for sexual liberation as a foundation of social liberation. Yet both theorists go substantially beyond Reich's notion of heterosexual genital fulfillment in their vision of drive liberation.[9]

Brown and Marcuse begin by arguing that drive theory is the only legitimate reading of psychoanalysis.[10] They assume not only that drive theory is the revolutionary truth of psychoanalysis, but also that drives are needs, and that these needs are authentic and legitimate, and deserve to be fully satisfied. Thus, Brown claims that the only alternative to the current regime of repression, in which the ego is allied to the reality principle against the id, is to ally ego and id against reality. This is the only solution, Brown claims, "if we hold fast to the Freudian insight into the immortal strength of our repressed desires,"[11] recognizing that the instincts are our only link to our true, bodily, animal nature. Brown tells us:

[Freud's] realism and his humanitarianism could come together only on the platform of instinctual liberation. All Freud's work demonstrates that the allegiance of the human psyche to the pleasure principle is indestructible and that the path of instinctual renunciation is the path of sickness and self-destruction.[12]

Similarly, for Marcuse, drive gratification – Marcuse uses this concept interchangeably with the concept of need satisfaction – measures happiness, which is equivalent to freedom. Authenticity inheres in the unconscious, whose demands are the measure of freedom and happiness. Happiness equals freedom equals drive gratification equals needs satisfaction:

But as Freud exposes their scope and their depth, he upholds the tabooed aspirations of humanity: the claim for a state where freedom and necessity coincide. Whatever liberty exists in the realm of the developed consciousness, and in the world it has created, is only derivative, compromised freedom, gained at the expense of the full satisfaction of needs. And insofar as the full satisfaction of the needs is happiness, freedom in civilization is essentially antagonistic to happiness: it involves the repressive modification (*sublimation*) of happiness. Conversely, the unconscious, the deepest and oldest layer of the mental personality, *is* the drive for integral gratification, which is absence of want and repression. As such it is the immediate identity of necessity and freedom.[13]

Brown's and Marcuse's vehement claim to adhere to the true Freudian position leads to a passionate polemic against Neo-Freudian revisionism. As Brown puts it, speaking of "the catastrophe"[14] of Neo-Freudianism, "it takes only the capacity to endure unpleasant truth to prefer the bleak pessimism of *Civilization and Its Discontents* to the lullabies of sweetness and light which the Neo-Freudians serve up as psychoanalysis."[15] Marcuse devotes an appendix to criticizing the Neo-Freudian revisionists, particularly Fromm, who assimilate theory to therapy, and derogate sexuality and the unconscious in favor of the clinical and of discussions of "human relationships," instead of understanding that the non-clinically verifiable metapsychological and speculative core of psychoanalysis – the death instinct, the account of the primal horde – are its explosive core.[16] Compared to instinctual dynamics, rooted in our biological materiality, the "'total personality' in its 'relatedness to the world'"[17] is an idealist illusion that advocates adjustment to a sick society.

Even as they excoriate the revisionists for moving away from the true Freud, Brown and Marcuse themselves challenge a fundamental Freudian tenet concerning the necessity of repression. As Marcuse puts it:

The notion that a non-repressive civilization is impossible is a cornerstone of Freudian theory. However, his theory contains elements that break through this rationalization; they shatter the predominant tradition of Western thought and even suggest its reversal.[18]

Marcuse acknowledges that his vision of drive liberation requires a transformation of the current reality principle. Unmitigated drive liberation under current conditions would lead to chaos and disaster:

These prospects seem to confirm the expectation that instinctual liberation can lead only to a society of sex maniacs – that is, to no society. However, the process just outlined involves not simply a release but a *transformation* of libido: from sexuality constrained under genital supremacy to erotization of the entire personality. It is a spread rather than an explosion of libido – a spread over private and societal relations which bridges the gap maintained between them by a repressive reality principle. This transformation of the libido would be the result of a societal transformation that released the free play of individual needs and faculties.[19]

Marcuse, unlike Brown, implies that some repression is necessary: "*Surplus-repression*: the restrictions necessitated by social domination . . . is distinguished from (basic) *repression*: the 'modification' of the instincts necessary for the perpetuation of the human race in civilization."[20] He argues that the abolition of scarcity made possible by the technological advances of capitalism lays the foundation for the end of repression. Eros would not need to be repressed at all in the current historical period were it not for domination, and the necessary transformation (sublimation) of the death drives could serve useful technological progress.

Yet Marcuse never fully evaluates the toll basic repression might take in a society without domination or scarcity. As I read *Eros and Civilization*, this is because he believes that the repression necessary for human and social continuity has already been encoded in the phylogenetic modification of the instincts resulting from conflict in the primal horde; all further repression has been either in the interests of domination or because of genuine scarcity. Thus as the historical basis for repression diminishes, all necessary repression is already phylogenetically encoded. No further repression of either libidinal or death drives will be necessary: "The sex instincts, after the elimination of all surplus-repression, can develop a 'libidinal rationality.'"[21]

Brown breaks through Freud's therapeutic and social pessimism somewhat differently, arguing that the instinctual ambivalence and mental conflict that Freud saw as basic to human nature, as well as the destructive threat of the death instinct, are not inherent in all life but a uniquely human product of the flight from death. A return to nature and recognition of death could overcome the human sickness, instinctual dualism and conflict that require repression: "Psychoanalytical consciousness can only be the vision of the possibility of human living not based on repression."[22]

In one sense, these analyses are fundamentally different. Marcuse holds that civilization under the repressive order of the performance principle creates repression and neurosis in the individual. The end of domination will then lead to the end of repression and to gratification. Brown argues that the repression, instinctual ambivalence, and neurosis that arise from anxiety and the individual flight from death create an oppressive and distorted culture and history. Thus, it is the elimination of human self-repression, the rise of gratification, and the recognition of death that will lead to social historical change. Between the two, then, Marcuse is more the critical Marxist, for whom Freudian theory helps illuminate and solve social questions. Brown is more the critical Freudian, whose sociology is accounted for by psychoanalytic processes.[23] The causal order is reversed in the two cases.[24]

In spite of this major difference in causal interpretation, however, Marcuse and Brown both believe that ontogenetic repression is not (or no longer) necessary, and they give us a multifaceted vision of freedom from repression – of authentic, fulfilling human life. Both would dissolve adult genitality into an eroticization of the whole body and a return to the polymorphous perverse pleasure ego of childhood. This dissolution is necessary both because adult genitality does not allow genuine gratification and because it is tied to inauthentic causes, psychological in Brown's case, social in Marcuse's.

Brown argues that adult genitality (like the other psychosexual stages) results from morbid, death-denying, transformations of infantile sexuality: adult sexuality is "a tyranny"[25] of one component of infantile sexuality that suppresses and dominates the others, a product of death not life, subordinating pleasure to reality. Libidinal development is not a natural maturational unfolding but a series of ego and sexual compromises. He advocates that we "abolish the unnatural concentrations of libido in certain particular bodily organs"[26] in favor of a "Dionysian ego . . . freed from genital organization."[27] *Love's Body* extends the critique of genitality found in *Life against Death* to suggest that politics is itself a genital product, in which the political leader represents the penis and politics expresses phallic power. The citizen has assumed a false external identity through internalization of the father or ancestor, and the concept of representation takes its meaning from a split between the active phallic father and the passive child observing parental coitus.

Marcuse similarly views the supersession of genital sexuality as necessary to human liberation. Genital sexuality is by definition repressive because this sexuality is dominated by the performance principle: is purposive, structured by the interests of reproduction and the upholding of a set of repressive institutions, especially the monogamous patriarchal family, that organize and restrict interpersonal relations. Doing away with genitality first re-eroticizes the body:

The regression involved in this spread of the libido would first manifest itself in a reactivation of all erotogenic zones and, consequently, in a resurgence of pregenital polymorphous sexuality and in a decline of genital supremacy. The body in its entirety would become an object of cathexis, a thing to be enjoyed – an instrument of pleasure.[28]

Marcuse argues for a return to the perversions, which would have a different content in a non-repressive society: "The inhuman, compulsive, coercive, and destructive forms of these perversions seem to be linked with the general perversion of the human existence in a repressive culture, but the perversions have an instinctual substance distinct from these forms."[29] The repression of the perversions is sometimes in the interests of actual human development. More often, it is in the interests of "the purity, regularity, cleanliness, and reproduction required by the performance principle."[30] The perversions may be progressive rather than regressive: "And the reactivation of prehistoric and childhood wishes and attitudes is not necessarily regression; it may well be the opposite – proximity to a happiness that has always been the repressed promise of a better future."[31] Marcuse here takes Orpheus and Narcissus, who reject the constraints of "normal Eros . . . the repressive order of procreative sexuality,"[32] as models for libidinal freedom and pleasure and for the rejection of the performance principle and normal sublimation.

Sexuality, Play, and Art

Marcuse and Brown link the freeing of sexuality from genital supremacy to a transformation of culture and activity in much wider arenas, in a new "self-sublimation"[33] of sexuality. Non-repression would not only re-eroticize previously repressed and tabooed infantile sexual mores and zones; it transforms the content of these stages and spills over into other arenas of life, including work, until all aspects of life are "sustained by free libidinal relations."[34] The final goal of life is "delight in the active life of the human body,"[35] "eroticization of the entire organism,"[36] people freed to return to their real – libidinal – interests and thus attaining happiness and freedom. The "resurrection of the body" allows a "way out of the human neurosis into that simple health that animals enjoy, but not man."[37]

A playful, non-purposive creativity and aesthetic relation to life, in which people recover the paradise of the polymorphous perverse pleasure principle of childhood in embodied play and delight, would replace the normal, repressive sublimation that is culture. Marcuse considers this as "non-repressive sublimation," in which:

> The instinct is not "deflected" from its aim; it is gratified in activities and relations that are not sexual in the sense of "organized" genital sexuality and yet are libidinal and erotic. Where repressive sublimation prevails and determines the culture, non-repressive sublimation must manifest itself in contradiction to the entire sphere of social usefulness; viewed from this sphere, it is the negation of all accepted productivity and purpose.[38]

For Marcuse, the orphic and narcissistic Eros, against the purposive promethean repression of the performance principle, sustain song, play, beauty, and contemplation – the "aesthetic dimension."[39]

For both Brown and Marcuse, art is the true path to a fused libidinal and cognitive liberation. For Marcuse, the aesthetic demonstrates the "connection between pleasure, sensuousness, beauty, truth, art, and freedom,"[40] reconciling "sensuousness and intellect, pleasure and reason."[41] The sensuous appreciation of beauty fuses cognition and appetite, undoing the repressions of reason, purpose, and the reality principle, and giving unrepressive form and purpose to instinctual desire. This freedom and lack of constraint make "sensuousness rational and reason sensuous."[42]

Brown, like Marcuse, claims that art both adheres to the pleasure principle and exhibits organization. He celebrates art as a model of "conscious play . . . Art as pleasure, art as play, art as the recovery of childhood, art as making conscious the unconscious, art as a model of instinctual liberation."[43] Thus art is unlike dreams or neurosis, which give expression to the unconscious but only in distorted form – to wishes which are already products of repression. Art, because it challenges repression, subverts civilization. Art demands communication between artist and audience, and because that communication is attained through the audience's identification with those unconscious repressions that the artist expresses, art "form[s] a subversive group, the opposite of that authoritarian group"[44] Freud describes in *Group Psychology*. Artists make contact with that "ultimate essence of humanity"[45] which is repressed and needs liberating; art asserts itself for both artist and audience against the "hostility"[46] of the reality principle.

Human Fulfillment

Linked to the abolition of adult genitality and the eroticization of the body in aesthetic play, Marcuse and Brown exalt a relation to the world that extends primary narcissism. Marcuse thus appeals to Narcissus not only as a model for preoccupation with beauty and (self)contemplation, but as the original model for Freud's labelling of the "primary narcissism" of the baby who does not differentiate self and other. According to Marcuse, "The Orphic–Narcissistic images are those of the Great Refusal: refusal to accept separation from the libidinous object (or subject). The refusal aims at liberation – at the reunion of what has become separated."[47] Freud's primary narcissism provides an alternative to and advance upon traditional Eros; "with it there came in sight, the archetype of another existential relation to *reality*. Primary narcissism is more than autoeroticism; it engulfs the 'environment.'"[48] Marcuse re-evaluates the oceanic feeling that Freud criticizes in the opening of *Civilization and Its Discontents* to suggest that narcissism is a "constitutive element in the construction of reality, coexisting with the mature reality ego."[49] The "limitless narcissism" and "oneness with the universe" that the oceanic feeling seeks to re-establish "denot[e] a fundamental relatedness to reality which may generate a comprehensive existential order."[50] "Narcissism may contain the germ of a different reality principle: the libidinal cathexis of the ego (one's own body) may become the source and reservoir for a new libidinal cathexis of the objective world,"[51] especially through the overflow of narcissistic libido to objects in a non-repressive sublimation.

Brown also argues that a superior and desirable relation to the world, that of primary narcissism, preceded subject–object dualism, instinctual ambivalence, and the split into identification and object choice. In infancy there is only one kind of relation, fusion – "A relation of being-one-with-the-world."[52] Throughout life, "Eros is fundamentally a desire for union (being one) with objects in the world."[53] This contrasts with "true object-love," Freud's anaclitic love that grows out of and relies on self-preservative needs and dependence and desires possession. Originally, Brown argues, the child's desire is not possession but union and incorporation of the breast, desires indistinguishable from identification. A narcissistic mode reproduces this original fusion, aimed both at union with objects outside the self and at self-loving. The fusion can occur because the infant's original pleasure is bodily and sexual: narcissistic love, as infantile love, grows out of the desire for pleasurable activity in one's own body, and the search for gratification leads to other bodies: "loving as the relation of the ego to its sources of pleasure."[54] The infant has an "unreal sense of reality. Reality is his mother, that is to say, love and pleasure; infantile sexuality affirms the union of the self with a whole world of love and pleasure."[55] The "pure pleasure ego" of the infant "absorbs into identity with itself the sources of its pleasure, its world, its mother."[56]

Brown, like Marcuse, turns to the oceanic feeling that Freud rejected: "human ego-feeling once embraced the world, and Eros drives the ego to recover that feeling... In primal narcissism the self is at one with a world of love and pleasure; hence the ultimate aim of the human ego is to reinstate what Freud calls 'limitless narcissism'."[57] Human perfection consists in an expansion of the self until it enjoys the world as it enjoys itself":[58] "the proper question . . . for our time . . . is to develop a love based on . . . self-acceptance, self-activity, self enjoyment,"[59] narcissistic Eros "overflow[ing] outward into the world [in] erotic exuberance."[60]

In *Love's Body*, Brown extends his vision to reject all separations and boundaries. Mind, individual, self, and soul, as forms of separation, are falls from grace. The reality principle is "a false boundary drawn between inside and outside; subject and object; real and imaginary; physical and mental."[61] "Separation (on the outside) is repression (on the inside) . . . separateness, then, is the fall – the fall into division, the original lie."[62] Brown argues for "the Dionysian, or drunken, principle of union, or communion,"[63] proposing a mystical unity of humankind, and within the mind–body unity, a reintegration of "self and world, self and environment."[64] Male and female are also false divisions: "if we are all members of one body, then in that one body there is neither male nor female . . . it is an androgynous or hermaphroditic body, containing both sexes."[65]

At the same time as they exalt, throughout these works, the dissolution of boundaries and narcissistic oneness, Marcuse and Brown also both insist on the importance of individuality and separateness. This is true especially of the core argument of *Life against Death*, in which Brown claims that only animals, because they accept death, are able to live the individual lives appropriate to their species. Humans directly deny death and separateness, and thus individuality, and all the morbid transformations of sexuality serve further to deny these. Society itself, – Brown here follows psychoanalyst and cultural theorist Geza Roheim's conception of society as a defensive huddled horde – also results from people, in their weakness, coming together to deny separateness from parents. The recognition of death would enable individual life. As we have seen, *Love's Body*, as other parts of *Life against Death*, reverse this concern, and it is this reversal that Marcuse challenges in "Love mystified: a critique of Norman O. Brown," when he says, agreeing with the individualist Brown, that "all pleasure and all happiness and all humanity originate and live in and with these divisions and these boundaries."[66]

These two positions seem contradictory, and I think are so; yet there is also a link between them: primary narcissism, as they describe it, is *the* source of infantile gratification. Brown claims that "the sexual instinct seeks, over and beyond bodily pleasure, some appropriate form of union with objects in the world," a narcissistic union.[67] Thus, for the satisfied infant, relatedness and drive gratification are conflated. One major concern for both writers is the loss of individual gratification resulting from self-repression and a repressive society. This is clear in Brown's images of Dionysian exuberance and in Marcuse's claims for a new ontology based on a "logic of gratification" in which "being is essentially the striving for pleasure."[68] Thus, both Brown and Marcuse propose primary narcissism as the model for a mode of relating which maintains non-repressive bodily gratification and pleasurable union with the world.

Marcuse and Brown thus appropriate and transform Freud's analysis of the relation among drives, repression, and civilization to argue that freedom and happiness inhere in the abolition of repression, a new form of love, and the transformation of civilization. Theirs is a powerful and at times attractive vision. They are both, following Nietzsche, profoundly critical of the rationalism and ascetic denial of pleasure that they find in modern society and in prevalent philosophical and political traditions, of the deadening denial of self that Marcuse locates as a result of modern capitalism and Brown in the society and history that repression produces. Both would criticize strands of Marxism that devalue the individual and deny the importance of pleasure. At the same time, both criticize the hyper-individualism that characterizes capitalist man and modern masculinity.

Yet a close examination of this initially powerful critique shows it to be extremely problematic. Their social theory and vision of liberation founder on the way they choose to appropriate psychoanalysis. Though they wish to turn toward ideals of union and communion as a reaction to their critique of hyper-individualism, their reliance on drive theory to do so ends up with a radical individualist view itself. When they do discuss union, their use of primary narcissism as a model, in the drive-theory context, maintains a focus on individual gratification and denies gratification and selfhood to the other. Brown and Marcuse often put forth contradictory claims and rely on contradictory theories. These contradictions, however, help point toward a more consistent and persuasive psychoanalytic social theory and vision of social possibility.

Problems and Contradictions in the Brown–Marcuse Vision

Radical Individualism

Throughout *Life against Death* and *Eros and Civilization* we are told again and again that human relations – all social bonds – are exclusively constraining and oppressive. Brown claims that childhood dependence and the desire to be loved, growing out of life in the family, are morbid and to be overcome. Family relations, because they are intense, create anxiety about separateness, and are exclusively negative. Recognizing one's mortality and thus one's individuality would eliminate anxiety by overcoming the sense of dependency on and love for others. Similarly, Brown criticizes the impulse to have children as a rejection of individuality and a morbid attempt to deny death. Group formation in general, in which people submit themselves to an authoritarian leader or huddle together in groups as a substitute for the parents they had to give up, is exclusively negative and morbid. In this view, there are no primary, positive reasons for relationship. Desires for omnipotent indulgence in pleasure and complete body absorption – though also growing out of early experience – should form the basis of human existence. For Marcuse, also, all social relations hitherto have been based on domination, from those in the primal horde family to those under the performance principle of class society.

Marcuse's critique and vision are shaped by Frankfurt School Marxism (the performance principle rests on "alienated labor," though Marcuse implies that play opposes the performance principle as well), and accordingly we expect and get from him more of a social theory. In one visionary chapter, "The transformation of sexuality into Eros," he claims that "the sex instincts can, by virtue of their own dynamic and under changed existential and societal conditions, generate lasting erotic relations among mature individuals,"[69] and that "sexuality can, under specific conditions, create highly civilized human relations."[70] Moreover, "libido can take the road of self-sublimation only as a *social* phenomenon: as an unrepressed force, it can promote the formation of culture only under conditions which relate associated individuals to each other in the cultivation of the environment for their developing needs and faculties."[71] He envisions a "civilization evolving from and sustained by free libidinal relations,"[72] so that the extension of Eros (which, according to Freud, leads toward "ever greater unities") under conditions of non-repressive sublimation would lead to a "system of expanding and enduring libidinal relations which are in themselves work relations."[73]

But *Eros and Civilization* in many ways seems to counter Marcuse's

Marxism, as his critique of collectivism and conformity moves him to a hyper-individualism and lack of ability to envision a concrete total social formation or an effective politics. His account of the effects of alienated labor, for instance, emphasizes more the stifling of individual drive gratification than the quality of human relations that alienated labor creates, and the unalienated labor (and play) he envisions are in the first instance self-expression and the sociality they entail a lucky outcome if instincts (which are, as we have seen, needs) seek *individual* gratification under non-repressive conditions:

Reactivation of polymorphous and narcissistic sexuality ceases to be a threat to culture and can itself lead to culture-building if the organism exists not as an instrument of alienated labor but as a subject of self-realization – in other words, if socially useful work is at the same time the transparent satisfaction of an individual need. . . Under such conditions, the impulse to "obtain pleasure from the zones of the body" may extend to seek its objective in lasting and expanding libidinal relations because this expansion increases and intensifies the instinct's grati-fication. . . The culture-building power of Eros *is* non-repressive sublimation; sexuality is neither deflected from nor blocked in its objective; rather, in attaining its objective, it transcends it to others, searching for fuller gratification.[74]

Moreover, Marcuse's claims for a vision that includes relationships, certainly not to be criticized in themselves, are not motivated or sustainable by the psychological and developmental arguments that form the core of *Eros and Civilization*. They appear tacked on, in one chapter only, while the central psychodynamic of individual gratification and the Great Refusal and other social claims in the book remain individual. For instance, while we would certainly want to consider the "aesthetic dimension" a part of a full human life, Marcuse's account of it is in terms of the *individual's* impulses and capacities: the fusion of cognition and appetite, reason and sensuousness. Marcuse mentions Narcissus' "relation-ships," but these are with nature, not other people: "The contemplation of Narcissus repels all other activity in the erotic surrender to beauty, inseparably uniting his own existence with nature."[75]

Thus, Marcuse seems unable to free his vision from a focus on individual gratification and the self-evident truth and meaningfulness of instincts, if only these could be freed under different "existential and social conditions." That "lasting erotic relations among mature individuals" will follow from centering on individual drive gratification is a wish that does not follow, and, as I will argue, is unlikely to follow, from the drive logic. Moreover Marcuse, because he is implicitly arguing against ascetic and what he sees as overly collectivist social theories, never deals directly with the problems of a social vision in which individual gratification, rather than forms of community and relatedness, remains the primary goal.[76]

Brown gives a different view of desirable social relations. In *Life Against Death*, art, rather than unalienated labor, epitomizes self-expression and sociality, and his only mention of unoppressive relations concerns the subversive group formed by artists and their audience. He suggests that art, unlike more neurotic transformations of instinct, must be intelligible and serve a communicative function (though there is contradiction even here, since Brown also argues that all sublimations are bad because they deny and desexualize the body).

In *Love's Body* Brown formulates a radically communal vision, perhaps as radical as the individualism in *Life against Death* and *Eros and Civilization*. The themes introduced in *Life against Death* – limitless narcissism, the expansion of self, and the Dionysian ego – appear in *Love's Body* as claims that all separations within the individual and between individuals are repressions and false. We are all one body, and these separations must be overcome in "unity,"[77] the overcoming of "boundary,"[78] and "fusion": "In freedom is fusion . . . Fusion: the distinction between inner self and outside world, between subject and object, overcome. To the enlightened man, the universe becomes his body. . . Fusion, mystical participation."[79]

This vision might indicate that Brown has changed his mind, or that he is at least ambivalent about the radical individualism of *Life against Death*. Yet Brown still maintains his critique of "normal sociability." This radical communal vision, like the radical individualist vision, makes it hard to get a sense of what a fabric of social relations might or ought to look like. Instead, we have sociality, or communality, as total merger of all people and all qualities. For Brown, we are all isolated individuals, or there is no differentiation at all among or within us.

Thus though they attack the morbidity of existing social relations, Marcuse and Brown have very limited views of what social relations might be – of how individuals might become part of a social formation. We are left with hopes – that art might enable subversive and even liberatory communication, or that instinctual gratification in a non-repressive society will lead to sustained work and erotic relations. Yet we have little sense of what social relations might actually look like without repression, beyond the *absence* of the performance principle and the flight from death on the one hand or the total merging of "limitless narcissism" on the other.[80] We have instead a notion of how the individual would live his life, treating the world as a narcissistic extension of himself.

The Marcuse–Brown solution, then, frees individuals from concrete relationships so that each can individually experience the world in body pleasure, play, unrepressed drive gratification, and artistic creativity. Orpheus does seek love for boys, but Narcissus seeks self-love. Both, in

Marcuse's account, aim to revive pre-genital pleasures in which the world is an extension of myself.[81]

Marcuse and Brown wish to transform the Freudian assessment: polymorphous perversity constitutes the height of sexual freedom and pleasure, a narcissistic relation to reality the height of ego development. Exclusive focus on pre-genital pleasure, as Marcuse and Brown describe it, means exclusive focus on one's own body as the source and standard for pleasure, freedom, and genuine progress. The other becomes purely an instrument of gratification. Marcuse's and Brown's desire to valorize pleasure here becomes profoundly anti-social and individualist, and their argument against genital sexuality becomes more than an argument against repressively derived pleasure limited to particular body parts or for particular goals. Its logic, perhaps against their intentions, constitutes an argument against relational sexuality, where the partner is important, itself. Similarly, their argument against sublimation implies that culture, currently a product of repression, should be built solely out of *individual* drive gratification.

Thus, Marcuse and Brown offer views of liberation that are virtually individualistic and anti-social. What may have begun as a critique of oppressive social forms here becomes a critique of sociality. Not only, as in Freud's view, are people originally anti-social, narcissistic bundles of drives – this anti-sociality is desirable and all development away from it is bemoaned. Brown uses the instinct theory to prove the "morbidity of human sociability," to tell us that "sociability is a sickness."[82] Marcuse criticizes the Neo-Freudian revisionists for "succumb[ing] to the mystification of societal relations."[83] The instinctual gratification of the individual becomes the basis of human freedom and happiness. Marcuse hopes that this will also be the basis for lasting ties; Brown interweaves this extreme arelationalism with an equally extreme vision of oneness and union, where there is no differentiated person to become part of society or culture.

The Role of Drive Theory

Brown and Marcuse, two major theorists of human liberation, alternately hold asocial visions or see sociality as mystical union or a secondary by-product of drive gratification. With little exception, their books develop not so much an alternate vision of community and society as a defense of super-individualism. They do so partially because of the social context in which Brown and Marcuse were writing. Like many other social critics, they respond to what they see as the successful domination of the individual and dulling of autonomy that result from late-capitalist mass society in the West and the crushing weight of Stalinist collectivism in the

East. (Marcuse, of course, retains a vivid memory of the authoritarian conformity of fascism.) On the one hand, then, Marcuse and Brown reassert a creative individuality in the face of perceived totalitarian and totalist tendencies; contemporary distortions of individuality are contrasted with accounts of undistorted or unrepressed individuality. On the other hand, institutions and community are by definition oppressive ("sociability is a sickness"), and "limitless narcissism" is as close as they can come to reclaiming or constructing alternate forms of community or collectivity. Marcuse offers vague notions of free libidinal relations, and Brown alternates extreme individualism with total merging.

However, it is not only Brown's and Marcuse's social critique that leads to their individualist emphasis. Their (often inconsistent and contradictory) appropriation of psychoanalytic theory, relying upon the late drive theory and pleasure principle as their basic metapsychology contributes decisively to this outcome. Marcuse and Brown turn to drive theory because, given their view that existing social life is completely distorted and that the individual does not really exist, they take the clinical to be based on an illusion of psychological autonomy. Thus the immutable drives serve both as a measure of repression or alienation, and as the only possibility for anchoring resistance to domination and grounding a vision of an alternative. But an exclusive focus on drives and the drive-repression dynamic is inadequate both as an interpretation of psychoanalysis and as a basis for social theory. It eliminates both a concept of the person as agent and of the person as related. Moreover, the claim for drive theory as liberating psychoanalytic truth leads to a focus on restricted aspects of human experience, on people as children and as male, that masks the very contradictions that their drive-theory-based social theory creates.

Linked to the elevation of the late drive theory is the downplay and even disdain for Freud's clinical contribution. Marcuse claims disinterest in the "technical discipline which psychoanalysis has become" and wishes to move "exclusively in the field of theory."[84] Brown contrasts "the psychoanalytical movement as a method of therapy controlled by professional adepts and available only to a select and wealthy few" with "psychoanalysis [as] a wider general theory of human nature, culture, and history, to be appropriated by the consciousness of mankind as a whole."[85]

Marcuse, and to a lesser extent Brown, here conflate the clinical as a source of evidence for theory with the therapeutic as a goal of psychoanalysis. Much of the psychoanalytic theory they accept – the discovery of repression and of unconscious fantasy, for instance and, as Brown willingly recognizes, the late anxiety theory – rests on clinical material elicited by Freud and other early psychoanalysts. This same psychoanalytic work was directed towards a "psychoanalytic cure," but even in Freud these two uses of the clinical were conceptually distinct.

Moreover, disdaining the clinical, because it emerges in the interpersonal setting of analyst and analysand and the transference relationship, means disdaining the interactional and relational. Marcuse and Brown want no part of "societal relations"; they want the individual alone, in fact, the individual's drives. Needs here are entirely (as in the drive theory they must be) individualistic and individually determined and experienced. "Freedom" and "gratification," likewise, are opposed to the constraint that relationship implies. Insisting on a non-clinically based psychoanalytic orthodoxy concerning the dual-instinct theory and the determinism of the drives drastically limits the importance of relationships and the individual as an agent and participant in these relationships.

Marcuse's argument does not eliminate interaction or relationships *per se*. But in this work he is interested not so much in how people interact or relate, or in what such interaction might look like in a liberated society, but, like Freud in *Beyond the Pleasure Principle*, in how *instincts* interact.[86] In the late drive theory, as Marcuse uses it, Eros and death are the significant forces. The instincts express themselves, interact, and are repressed. Society (even the mature erotic relations Marcuse mentions) expresses instinctual principles and drive outcomes. At most, people (the ego, the "I") are simply the passive vehicle through which the instincts are expressed or repressed; they are not agents themselves. As Marcuse describes it, the new reality principle comes first, and that new reality principle (however it comes about), will lead to or enable a different, liberated, drive expression. Even in his vision of liberation, then, people, rather than creating their lives, simply express their new drive organization. Humans enter into Marcuse's vision only in the form of the two men, Orpheus and Narcissus, with their Great Refusal of separation, performance, and genital sexuality. Thus Marcuse reproduces the very image of people as alienated and lacking in agency that he uses the drive theory to criticize.

While Marcuse's reliance on the drive theory contradicts the social and relational goals he puts forth near the end of *Eros and Civilization* and in his other works, the contradiction between drives and relationship inheres more centrally throughout Brown's psychoanalytic–social account itself. Brown claims a theoretical *need* for a dual-instinct theory, and cites approvingly Freud's effort to find an organic basis for the human ambivalence between Eros and aggression and to give intentions to the drives: that "organisms die for internal reasons," that "death is an intrinsic part of life" means, as Freud put it, that "the *goal* of all life is death."[87] Freud's argument, says Brown, is logical, not empirical or clinical. But Brown in fact rests his own arguments concerning the death instinct on empirical and clinical claims.[88] He points to the origins of anxiety in the fear of separation from the mother and points to Freud's claim that the ego fears an "overthrow or extinction" when it experiences anxiety. This creates a link, he claims, between separation and the death instinct: anxiety is fear of separation which is felt "as death." Death is thus experienced psychologically every day.

But to say that the infant's (or anyone's) desire to avoid separation is a refusal to face death is a metaphoric claim that, taken literally, brings irrelevant instinctual considerations into a clearly object-related and ego experience. In *Life against Death*, even as he gives theoretical primacy to drives, Brown discusses love, hate, ambivalence, desires for union – *affects* of people, not drives. Thus, like Roheim, upon whose account of group formation Brown relies, Brown can often be read as starting from a theory of relationship, with instincts tacked on. For instance, though Brown asserts that omnipotent body eroticism and indulgence in pleasure are primary in childhood, he also claims that development results from the conflict between this pleasurable omnipotence on the one hand and childhood dependence and the need for love on the other. The parent–child relation is both "a new mode of . . . interdependent union which is the essence of life [and] a new mode of individual independence which is the essence of death."[89] This "intenser mode of love"[90] makes the child fearful of separation and anxious about loss.

All this is completely in the sphere of interpersonal and intrapsychic relationships. But Brown has started from the instincts, and this is where he wants to end. Thus, in a long syllogism he has reasoned that since Eros seeks unification and immortality, death must seek separation and mortality. Moreover, the theory of anxiety describes the flight from death, since Freud has argued that anxiety stems from fear and ambivalence toward separateness. Brown claims: "It is because the child loves the mother so much that it feels separation from the mother *as* death,"[91] that the ego's point of departure is the denial of separation, which is the denial of death. But he also argues that, because individuality implies mortality and stems from separation, separation and death are equivalent. Thus Brown explains what he takes to be the basic spur of development in relational terms – fear of separating from the mother – and recognizes that the new anxiety theory is *par excellence* a relational theory, but insists that his explanation refers to instincts and their denial. He also implies that all these relational experiences, because they are equivalent to the denial of death, are to be overcome in the interests of the return to pure instinctual life.

In *Love's Body*, Brown moves beyond Freud to draw on Klein and Roheim – both drive theorists, but with strong object-relational admixtures. This further reinforces his tendency to develop a more complex and less purely drive-based psychoanalytic position than Marcuse. In one instance, his use of Klein draws him to to a view of connection and the overcoming of boundaries that does not collapse into the complete fusion and lack of recognition of any individuality that primary narcissism entails. In a richly evocative passage, he claims:

> The existence of the "let's pretend" boundary does not prevent the continuance of the real traffic across it. Projection and introjection, the process whereby the self as distinct from the other is constituted, is not past history, an event in childhood, but a present process of continuous creation. The dualism of self and external world is built up by a constant process of reciprocal exchange between the two. The self as a stable substance enduring through time, an identity, is maintained by constantly absorbing good parts (or people) from the outside world and expelling bad parts from the inner world. "There is a continual unconscious wandering of other personalities into ourselves."
>
> Every person, then, is many persons; a multitude made into one person . . . we are members of one another.[92]

Repression and the Problem of Agency

While he insists on psychoanalytic orthodoxy regarding the centrality of sexuality and the dual-instinct theory, Marcuse ignores the psychodynamic specificity of repression. This has the effect of further denying agency to the human actor. He tells us early in his book that "'repression' and 'repressive' are used in the non-technical sense to designate both conscious and unconscious, internal and external processes of restraint, constraint, and suppression."[93] This metaphoric usage has the consequence of eliminating perhaps the most important distinction in psychoanalysis: that between conscious and unconscious, interpersonal and intrapsychic. (By contrast, Brown works with the notion that repression is intrapsychic and not simply socially imposed. The morbid ego is not, as in Marcuse, a direct product of external reality but an intrapsychic product of the transformations aimed at avoiding the recognition of death.)

This strategy does not simply mean that Marcuse applies standards to others that he does not hold for himself. Rather, his choice seems both to arise from and deepen a crucial problem in his political vision and vision of human possibility. Marcuse's social theory and account of individual development paint a picture of total domination, of repression both external and internal, conscious and unconscious. At the same time, the way out is through the instincts, which give us both principles opposed to civilization and a vision of liberation.

In fact, it would be hard to find a more extreme conception of instinctual malleability than that presented in *Eros and Civilization*. On the one hand, no aspect of the psyche or the instinctual structure escapes total penetration; history inheres in the deepest instinctual structure of the individual. The performance principle has created vast institutional and organizational structures that perpetuate control of the individual, the most totalistic control and organization so far in history. On the other, Marcuse's argument in favor of a new reality principle rests on the capacity of the supposedly fixed drives to develop a "libidinal rationality" that allows in essence a non-repressive repression. His critique of Fromm and the Neo-Freudians becomes somewhat disingenuous, to the extent that he castigates them for a view that downplays the role of fixed drives and portrays their aims in too pleasant a manner.[94] In Marcuse's perspective, the drives are both claimed to be immutable and characterized as mutable, as reified second nature. The war between Eros and Thanatos disappears without really being resolved.

Because Marcuse has such an absolute notion of repression, and because he fuses social domination and constraint with intrapsychic repression, he misses the essence of repression: internal psychic *conflict*. For Freud, repression never becomes absolute but yields dynamic tension.[95] For Freud, the discovery of repression led to the discovery of the multiplicity of ego activities and compromise formations that testify to diverse human possibilities for symbolization, transformation, substitution, and splitting. In place of this view, Marcuse offers a unidimensional measure and account of psychic life that asks only how far culture represses the drives. What goes on unconsciously and mentally, even with the drives themselves, is unexamined. We see only the products of this unconscious mental life: genital sexual orientation and submission to work.[96]

By starting from the drive theory as Marcuse interprets it, ego functions can only be conformist and externally determined. There can be no agentic ego or self – even if the agency and creativity available to that ego are not all they could be, given psychic conflict and defenses. Society has directly appropriated and controls all ego functions and possibilities, which all morbidly conform to the reality principle, and it has almost entirely come to dominate the id as well. Depth psychology disappears as the individual conforms totally to external institutions and an external reality principle.

Marcuse does insist on the need to construct a new reality principle and this suggests that change is possible. But his argument is purely contingent: the gradual overcoming of scarcity makes transcending the performance principle possible. Yet given total repression, and an analysis that makes drives, and not people, into actors, it is hard to envision any human activity or politics that could create this new reality principle: that someone could engage in a Great Refusal does not follow from Marcuse's developmental account. Marcuse also claims that fantasy remains split off from the rest of the mental apparatus and committed to the pleasure principle. But if the rest of the psyche is totally dominated and "organized [by] society," so that "neither [the person's] desires nor his alteration of reality are henceforth his own,"[97] there is no rational or ego faculty left to translate fantasy into reality, to create the "conscious rationality of mature civilization."[98]

Marcuse's theory of total domination is sustained not only by his elimination of the psychodynamic notion of repression, but also by his inconsistent and partial developmental account. He draws first on the primal horde story to account for the origins of repression. Here, domination and repression originate in the family, in which the female as sexual object is appropriated by the primal father and made scarce. Similarly, as Marcuse implies (in his wish to deny separation from the libidinous object), the female as mother is unnecessarily scarce. The origins of repression, then, lie in phylogenetic sexual scarcity and the ontogenetic scarcity of drive gratification.

Marcuse, having drawn on a myth that links repression in the family to sexual scarcity and sexual and aggressive domination, then claims that domination and the performance principle can be measured in terms of the manipulation of economic scarcity and the domination of labor. But the never indicates the mechanism by which economic domination might lead to repression, nor how patriarchal domination in the family or the primal horde becomes renunciation for labor. He reduces Freud's notion of repression to repression for work: "Originally the organism in its totality and in all its activities and relationships is a potential field for sexuality, dominated by the pleasure principle. And precisely for this reason it must be *desexualized* in order to carry out unpleasurable work."[99]

Having given a psychodynamic account only of the origins of repression in false sexual scarcity, Marcuse then claims, without evidence or alternate psychodynamic account, that the elimination of false economic scarcity imposed in the interests of domination will eliminate that repression. He thus presents an account of sexual scarcity and its effects, asserts that what is at issue now is economic scarcity, and finally claims that the elimination of economic scarcity will transform that which, by his own account, it never created in the first place.

Marcuse, then, has simply asserted a correspondence between society and personality organization; he has not given us an account of how it happens. He seems to follow Frankfurt Institute colleagues like Horkheimer here, pointing to the decline of father–son conflict and consequently of the superego: "the ego seems to be prematurely socialized by a whole system of extra-familial agents and agencies . . . gangs, radio, and television."[100] Somehow, in the absence of the father, these agencies directly form the psyche and repress the drives. But we have no idea how. The implication – one consistent with Marcuse's view of total domination – is that a behaviorist passivity allows direct cultural determinism of all parts of the psyche – the very Neo-Freudian view that Marcuse criticizes.

Brown, like Marcuse, also begins from the insistent power of the instincts, whose constant striving for release and acceptance drives people to ever more contorted sexual and ego organizations and ever more problematic historical projects. As with Marcuse, people passively express instincts. The repression of the instincts, and refusal to recognize death, preclude the natural animal "activity without motion or change . . . not in time,"[101] the unreflective living of an individual life proper to one's species. The unsatisfied instincts continually seek a return to nature.

Brown offers an extreme account of the domination of the drives, and a unidimensional measure of psychic life: as with Marcuse, how much are the drives repressed? Yet he also sees people as actors and gives us a much more active sense of the individual constructing [his] self, even if this construction is morbid and reactive. His interest in the intrapsychic means that his account centers on conflict, contradiction, restless striving, and discontent, rather than total domination. His argument for change, whatever the problems with its substance, is at least a possible outcome of the activity of the people he has described, whose morbid egos are at least active egos, and could presumably engage in projects other than the negative ones that now preoccupy them.

Intersubjectivity and the Perspective of the Child

Brown's and Marcuse's idealization of a narcissistic mode of relating and of drive gratification based on the pleasure principle precludes those very intersubjective relationships that should form the core of any social and political vision.[102] "Refusal to accept separation from the libidinous object (or subject)," "the union of the self with a whole world of love and pleasure" denies that object or external world its own separateness and choice, requiring that others be objects, not subjects, and denying subjectivity to the other, who can only be a narcissistic extension of the self and an object instrumental for one's own gratification.

Marcuse and Brown do not consider that two different people will each have their own narcissism, their own body pleasure, and their own drive gratification, that many people will have many narcissisms, many body pleasures, and many drive gratifications. Precisely for this reason development must include growing away from primary narcissism, from treating and experiencing the world as an extension of the self. We are never told what invisible hand would guarantee that even two people's narcissisms would mesh, let alone those of an entire society. Narcissus limited his relationships to himself and "nature"; the narcissistic person organizes relationships in order that another can serve as an extension of the self and gratify the self's pleasures. In the classic account of infantile primary narcissism, the other does not exist at all, but fuses with the infant and begins to exist only as a gratifier of wants.[103]

Marcuse and Brown do not intend to end up in this impasse. As I noted, Brown does suggest the possibility of combining differentiation and connectedness, thereby enabling a view of psychological intersubjectivity. But this one claim is an exception to a predominant vision of total communion and merging in which all separations or differentiations are false repressions. Marcuse speaks of "mature relations," and "free libidinal relations," but when he puts forth an alternative to promethean acquiescence in the performance principle, the only relations he specifies are those of the narcissistic Great Refusal. Those relations do not allow recognition of the other – do not allow, that is, the other's freedom.

Another subject by definition limits one's own narcissism and body pleasure. Thus, the exaltation of the narcissistic mode of relating, like the insistence on the authenticity of drives, implies that relationships in which the other is a subject must be repressive. The only model of primary social needs here is that a person not be constrained or interfered with, by, for instance, a libidinous subject (not object) who wants some separation from Narcissus.

Marcuse and Brown are right that the reality principle imposes limits on body pleasure and infantile omnipotence. But the reality principle does not simply signify an abstract, repressive civilization based on the performance principle and domination, or on a morbid and neurotic history and culture. Rather, the reality principle is in the first instance the subjectivity of others – the recognition that others have their own intentions, goals, and experiences of pleasure and pain. For the child, learning the meaning of the self–other distinction and of one's relatedness to a differentiated other is the same thing as the reality principle, and is intrinsic to the construction of self.[104] When Marcuse discusses "the limitations imposed upon freedom and happiness by the reality principle,"[105] which he sees as "surplus repression," he is conflating what might indeed be unnecessary domination with the constraints intrinsic to living with others who are not solely extensions of the self. The narcissistic mode of relating to the world and unconstrained body pleasure retain the psychological stance of the infant and make intersubjectivity impossible. It is no accident that drive liberationists like Marcuse and Brown have little vision of a liberated society but only a vision of liberated individuals.

Through maintaining the psychological stance of the child, Marcuse and Brown are able to ignore the contradiction implicit in a conception of a society generated by mutual narcissisms and mutual treating of the other as an object of body pleasure or drive gratification.[106] The problem of the other's wants only presents itself to the adult; it does not at first appear to the child, but is in fact the essence of childhood learning. If the infant is originally cognitively narcissistic – unable to distinguish the rest of the world from the self – then it cannot understand that the other might have different wants and needs or an alternate subjectivity. Marcuse and Brown, as we have seen, insist on the authenticity of drives and of childhood wishes. In doing so, they take the point of view of the child (or the fantasied point of view of the child), see its unmitigated striving for drive gratification as a model for all life, and idealize its cognitive narcissism. But while the infant is not separate and cannot be said to use the other instrumentally, once separateness is established, such assumptions can only instrumentalize and deny the other.[107] Marcuse and Brown have borrowed a vision of erotic fusion suggested by the "limitless narcissism" of Freud's oceanic feeling in an attempt to get away from repressive, distorted separations (Brown) and unequal relations of domination (Marcuse). Yet by not recognizing the developmental setting of primary narcissism, they do not recognize that a fusion that takes its interpersonal meaning from primary narcissism constitutes an asymmetrical, even tyrannical, subsumption of the one by the other.

By idealizing childhood and the authenticity of drives, Marcuse and Brown give us an account of the kind of development they do not want, but little account of what development should or could consist in. Marcuse extols the "reactivation of prehistoric and childhood wishes"[108] and the Great Refusal of separation and libidinal change and organization. Fantasy, he suggests, refuses "to forget what *can be*,"[109] remembers that past time before the "reality principle" imposed limits on freedom and happiness. Brown also talks of the "tyranny" of adult sexuality and glorifies childhood play and immaturity in contrast to "capitulation to the reality principle which we call education or maturity."[110] Between Freud's two methods of salvation – instinctual renunciation that recognizes reality for what it is and involves growing up, and instinctual liberation, whose goal is to change reality to recover lost pleasure – Brown chooses the latter and argues that it is the only choice consistent with psychoanalysis: "All Freud's work demonstrates that the allegiance of the human psyche to the pleasure-principle is indestructible and that the path of instinctual renunciation is the path of sickness and self-destruction."[111]

Conflating the entirety of human life with childhood, Brown claims that artists are "spokesmen for the essence [of humanity] and for the future . . . for what is repressed in the present . . . a way of life faithful to the natural instincts and therefore faithful to childhood."[112] The artist is Brown's version of the Great Refusal: "The artist is the man who refuses initiation through education into the existing order, remains faithful to his own childhood being."[113] As does Marcuse, Brown idealizes the refusal to grow up; real pleasure is infantile and individual. Childhood is the state of nature, and all experience beyond childhood a fall from grace. Humankind is committed to the unconscious project of overcoming instinctual ambivalence

and restoring the unity of opposites that exists in childhood and animals –
committed only to return, not to growth.

Brown and Marcuse have taken Freud's drive theory and account of
primary narcissism not only as an account of who we originally are, or how
we are; they have also taken it as an account of how we ought to be.
Because Freud has told us that drives always tend toward their own release
and gratification, we cannot evaluate these drives or any person's claim for
drive gratification. Drives are given and good; their gratification is the
essence of freedom. But, as Marcuse implies in his developmental account
and account of total repression, and as Brown also suggests in his account
of the development of the psychosexual organizations, which result from
the ego's compromises with its anxiety and fear of death, instinctual wants
are shaped and modified from the day an individual is born.[114]

Psychoanalysis by and large agrees that a good part of our unconscious
life seeks (remembered) earlier states and forms of gratification. But,
following Freud in *Civilization and Its Discontents*, it also argues that we
wouldn't have life if we could keep childhood. Development, change, and
growth are constitutive of human life. What we need therefore, and what
Brown and Marcuse do not provide us, is an alternative developmental
theory to the "morbid" development they describe. Their works do not
recognize that infancy or childhood *necessarily* differ from adulthood.
Brown, in complaining that the human family creates childhood dependence,
even seems to imply that infants could survive on their own without any
kind of primary care.

It is one thing to advocate incorporating the pleasures of the child into
those of the adult; it is another to advocate never growing up or moving
beyond childhood. Neither Brown nor Marcuse considers the possibility
of adult pleasures or experiences beyond those of childhood. Both talk of
union as the goal of Eros and idealize the seeking of non-genital body
pleasure, but they have little notion that there might be adult forms of
union which are not simply fusion and subsumption of the other to the
self. Brown talks of "loving as the relation of the ego to its sources of
pleasure,"[115] thereby following Freud's dictum that love arises from
gratification. The love-object here is an object instrumental to gratification.
But he does not acknowledge that development means coming to see these
sources as differentiated subjects in their own right and not just extensions
of the self or objects that give pleasure.

Marcuse and Brown focus on procreative genital sexuality as a goal-
oriented limit upon sexual options and narrowing of body pleasure. They
dispute the traditional psychoanalytic critique of the perversions on this
score, and wish to open up possibilities for body pleasure. They realize
that the perversions as they now develop can be narrowly purposive and
monolithic – Marcuse links this "with the general perversion of the human

existence in a repressive culture"[116] – but claim that they are arguing for a non-repressive, non-exclusive polymorphous perversity.

Yet Brown and Marcuse fail to note another element of the psychoanalytic critique. It is true that Freud posits genital sexuality as the final goal of erotic development largely because of teleological assumptions about reproduction as the major sexual aim.[117] But psychoanalysts (often incorrectly) criticize the "perversions" not only for their non-heterosexual, non-genital centrism but also for their fixation on a body pleasure for its own sake that entails instrumental and objectifying treatment of the other (such a critique is of course also true of much heterosexual genital sexuality and of more extreme forms of coercive heterosex). Both exclusivity in libidinized body organs, and an exclusive focus on body pleasure distinguish certain forms of genital sex and some "perversions" from what psychoanalysts call "genital love," "mature object-love," or "true object-love." The differentiating criterion concerns the extent to which the sex is object-oriented, involving "genital identification": does the sex depend on assimilation of the other to the self, or the self to the other – primary identification – or do "interests, wishes, feelings, sensitivity, shortcomings of the partner attain about the same importance as our own."[118] Such sexual practices are mistakenly called "*genital* love" and "*genital* identification," and they certainly need not be heterosexual; they involve a particular mode of loving the sexual object and not the gender of that object. But they differ sharply from sex and love based on refusal to allow the separateness of the object and on loving as a relation to "sources of pleasure." Such a view opens the possibility of sexual pleasure and love beyond the child's; giving love and pleasure to others, taking their needs and wants into account. Marcuse and Brown argue for the pleasure symbolized by Eros in its non-exclusive focus, but have no conception of the role or wishes of the sexual object; hence, the idealization of Narcissus.

As we should expect in a child-centered perspective, a second major arena of adult experience and pleasure, in addition to that of mature object-love, is absent from the drive liberation/limitless narcissism perspective. That is the experience of parenting, or nurturance. The neglect and even condemnation of parenting emerges from and sustains Marcuse and Brown's arelational vision, since parenting must be relational, and must involve a psychic organization beyond fusion and unmediated narcissistic drive gratification. Parenting requires conscious, mature, goal-oriented thinking that combines rationality, and orientation to reality, with attentive caring for the wants and perceived needs of another.[119] Marcuse ignores the issue. When he mentions "mature relations," these concern work, and not procreation and nurturance. Brown goes further, to cite approvingly Nietzsche's condemnation of the desire for children as no more than a denial of self and self-involvement[120] and Frye's claim that "The 'sin' in the sex act is not that of love but that of parentage."[121]

The Perspective of the Male and the Disappearance of Women as Subjects

The exaltation of drives, narcissism, childhood pleasures, and the refusal to grow up allows Brown and Marcuse not to recognize the contradictions that inhere in the problem of mutual narcissisms, and treating the other instrumentally for one's own gratification. They therefore do not see that their social solutions are in fact individualistic and asocial. This perspective, as I have indicated, is exemplified in their denial of adult experiences of relational sexuality, and their neglect of nurturance and parenting. This denial in turn reflects particularly clearly another major characteristic in their account. In addition to maintaining the stance of the child, *Eros and Civilization*, *Life against Death*, and *Love's Body*, while exhibiting a definite anti-masculinist stance, manifest a near-complete invisibility or denial of women as subjects and of considerations about gender. Both the specific focus on men (Orpheus, Narcissus, Dionysus) as liberators, and their general analyses, reveal this tendency.[122]

The argument against adult genitality and procreative sexuality – the rejection of "normal Eros" – amounts implicitly to an argument against relations with women, a rejection of women. Marcuse and Brown both idealize Narcissus, who chooses himself rather than a woman. Marcuse in addition idealizes Orpheus, who loves only boys and whose unfortunate end occurred when "he was torn to pieces by the crazed Thracian women."[123] (Marcuse almost takes a woman seriously. He points to Pandora, "the female principle, sexuality and pleasure"[124] as the major challenge to the Promethean world of the performance principle. But he immediately drops this view and asserts that Orpheus and Narcissus, who are "akin"[125] to Dionysus, Brown's hero, stand as the symbols of an alternate reality principle to Prometheus. A woman, it seems, could not stand for anything.)

Like the argument against "normal" sexuality, the denial of inter-subjectivity involved in the narcissistic vision implicitly argues that women constrain, and denies women as subjects. It is of course the mother who is experienced as a narcissistic extension of the child and who imposes drive organization and modification. The mother's subjectivity is the reality principle for the child, and the mother requires that the infant separate from her and give up its primary narcissistic relation to reality. The narcissistic refusal to accept separation from the libidinous object is not refusal to separate from just any object or subject. A woman directly enforces the primary restraints that seem to be the essence of unfreedom from the perspective of drive liberation and limitless narcissism.

Only by assuming that the mother is an object, and emphatically not a subject, can we envision narcissistic union and the complete satisfaction of pre-genital demands and desires as progressive social principles. Marcuse and Brown do not notice that there can be no intersubjective world in their vision inasmuch as they ignore that mothers, in particular, and women, in general, are subjects. We can refuse to grow up, remain in the pre-ambivalent childhood state, only if others are objects or extensions of us; the mother – symbolizing women in general – is this object.

The drive-liberation formulation requires constraining some people in the interests of others.[126] The adult projects I discussed earlier must get done: procreation and procreative sexuality are required for human, let alone social, continuity, as is parenting. Brown does not really think infants could survive without care nor does Marcuse think humanity could survive without procreative sex. Brown and Marcuse somehow assume that parenting will get done – but do not theorize this. Yet mothers (or any primary parents), as the original "libidinous objects," must modify and transform their primary drives for goal-oriented reasons – that of caring for a child. They must, even while experiencing a sense of oneness and primary identification with a child, also be constantly exercising mature, reality oriented ego functions. It is only the child himself who can treat his caretaker as nothing but one with the self or a source of gratification. The unstated division of the world between female mothers/objects and male children/subjects conveniently obscures this problem.

The development and experience of self in the world that Brown and Marcuse describe cannot be generically human. At every step it denies women their own development and self-experience, and demands they be objects for gratification, serving the self's narcissistic interests and wants. The way out of Nirvana and death, the way to overcome that separateness that equals death, is to subsume the other to oneself. Whereas Freud in *Civilization and Its Discontents* wants to deny the importance of oceanic feelings, thereby denying the tie to the mother, Brown and Marcuse want to return to these feelings and this tie.

There is a hidden developmental argument here, one that helps us to understand a contradiction in both Brown's and Marcuse's formulations. I have pointed out that Brown wants to recognize separateness, individuality, and death while also wanting an exuberant Dionysian erotic union, which denies the separateness of the other. The resolution reverses the original infantile situation: rather than losing oneself in the other, one makes the other an extension of the self, thereby gaining individuality and freedom from relations entailing obligation or dependence while maintaining union. One substitutes active narcissistic subsumption of the other, in which she exists only to fulfill one's own needs, for passive dependence upon her. Similarly in Marcuse, one overcomes the threat of Nirvana – the return to the mother and death – by a reversal, in which the mother is subsumed into one's own omnipotence. One re-establishes union, with the direction of dependence and connection reversed. A new power relation institutes power over the mother and denies the mother herself. A separate individuality and narcissistic union can coexist, because the mother is not an individual subject but either an extension of self, an object from whom one is separate, or an object for need-gratification.[127]

While women are sometimes present in Brown's and Marcuse's accounts, they appear as objects, not subjects. Marcuse locates the origins of instinctual renunciation and domination in the original social act (that of the brothers in the primal horde) resulting from struggle between males, but does not notice that the instinctual liberation the brothers were fighting for was the equal right to dominate women, against the father's claim that only he had that right. These women struggled over by the primary group of brothers, Pandora, who appears in one paragraph, and the women who tear Orpheus to pieces, are the only women explicitly present in *Eros and Civilization*. The Nirvana principle and the desire for death and quiescence are also implicitly the desire for merging with the mother; thus, women are also implicitly present as equivalent to death.

Marcuse rightly criticizes Reich for his view that genital liberation is real drive liberation. But he ignores Reich's critique of male–female power relationships in the traditional family. Focussing both ontogenetically and phylogenetically only on Oedipal struggle and resolution, he also ignores the family dynamics involved in the pre-genital period that he extols. Recognizing these relationships and dynamics would require recognizing that the narcissistic vision entails the constraining of some people in the interests of others.

Although the thrust of his argument begins from and concerns a male ego, Brown is much more explicitly concerned with the role of women and the problem of male dominance. In *Love's Body*, he offers androgyny as a goal. This difference is partly because Brown recognizes the significance of the pre-Oedipal period – of the relation to the breast and the mother and the problem of separation – in the construction of the psyche and in later object choice. Unlike Marcuse, Brown in *Life against Death* discusses Freud's psychology of women and the pre-Oedipal mother–daughter relationship (though largely to set up a discussion of male development). In the boy's case too, Brown suggests, "the role of the father must be quite secondary,"[128] certainly in pre-Oedipal development but even in the development of the Oedipus and castration complexes, which "can be generated in principle without any reference to the father-figure."[129] What is important here, Brown suggests, is "not the image of the castrating father, but the image of the castrated mother":[130] "the Oedipal relation to the father [is] a superstructure on top of a substructure of Oedipal relations to the mother."[131]

Brown not only recognizes male dominance: he takes Freud to task for not recognizing it, and takes both male dominance and aggressiveness as in need of explanation: "the Primal Father was once a boy, and, if there is anything to psychoanalysis, owes his disposition to his boyhood. . . In the myth of the Primal Father Freud abandons psychological explanation and invokes the category of brute natural force to cover the gap."[132] He claims, "the proper starting point for a Freudian anthropology is the pre-Oedipal mother. What is given by nature, in the family, is the dependence of the child on the mother. Male domination must be grasped as a secondary formation, the product of the child's revolt against the primary mother."[133]

In *Love's Body*, Brown focusses even more on the importance of the mother, but as he does so, she becomes more emphatically an object rather than the starting-point for a Freudian anthropology. The goal of individuation and separation from the mother and all she represents, stressed in *Life against Death*, here gives way to a goal of total union with her. Brown claims, drawing on the female-centric Kleinian writings and the writings of Roheim, that the world and environment, from which the self should not separate, is the mother – "the world is our mother. The outside world is 'the mother's body in an extended sense'. . . To explore is to penetrate; the world is the insides of the mother."[134] "The dreamer" creates himself by

split[ting] himself into both self and world, self and environment, mother and child. . . Out of the body of the dreamer is made both a phallus and a womb; and the basic dream is of phallic movement in a female environment (space) . . . from mother, to mother, in mother.[135]

The mother here is no longer a person at all, but the whole world. At the same time, because the dreamer (still with the psyche of the narcissistic infant) "make[s] a world *out of himself*,"[136] the world and mother are only a fantasied emanation of the self. Maintaining the stance of the child, Brown takes a Kleinian view of unconscious childhood fantasy and idealizes it as the whole of reality, borrowing the infantile view of the mother in the process. And in keeping with his implicit view of men as subjects, he characterizes all life-activity as phallic.

There is little question that Brown and Marcuse reject many of the gender-defined qualities of traditional masculinity. Orpheus and Narcissus oppose the achievement-oriented promethean performance principle with song, contemplation, merging, and beauty, with images of soft receptivity that oppose aggressive mastery of the world. Brown turns from the super-masculine Apollonian image to the bisexual, almost androgynous,

Dionysus, and calls for androgyny ("if we are all members of one body, then in that one body there is neither male or female").

But these images use women, or feminine qualities, as symbols of alternative principles of civilization, so that the image of the perfect person, the image of liberation, is the man – Orpheus, Narcissus, Dionysus – who incorporates feminine qualities.[137] Marcuse, moreover, sees nothing problematic in the primal horde theory. Even in Brown's claim for androgyny, which does not subsume the feminine into the male but speaks to a reconciliation and merger between them, there is no mention of the lives of women themselves or of the actual relations between men and women. Brown does take male dominance and male aggressiveness as in need of attention, but in his account they are not so much problems for women as problems for men and for the full expression of male humanity. Thus, in spite of their strong critique of traditional masculinity, and in spite of Brown's "Freudian anthropology" and recognition of the important role of the pre-Oedipal mother, the logic of the Marcuse–Brown view of liberation is, finally, liberation from women, from the woman who represents, for her own sake as a human subject as well as in the interests of "socializing" her child, the restrictions upon that narcissistic oneness and that pre-genital gratification which they take to be equivalent to liberation. Liberation is also escape from sexual association with the female, who, as she is symbolized by genitality, is rejected by Orpheus, and who, as she is symbolized by society and social constraint, is rejected by Narcissus. She represents that relational sexuality and recognition of the sexual partner as a person rather than object of gratification that Marcuse and Brown pass over. For the consistency of the theory, women must be constrainers of freedom and objects: a woman does not have the option to remain a child or to be constrained but must be the mother/woman who does not require separation but serves as a narcissistic mirror and extension or even as the life environment. At most, she represents idealized feminine qualities which can be incorporated into the ideal total person – who is a male. In not seeing women as people, the drive liberation/primary narcissism view yields an individualistic version of liberation in which childhood is truth, without noticing the internal inconsistencies of such a position.

Toward an Alternative Psychoanalytic Social Theory

Brown and Marcuse made a major contribution in recognizing the need to ground social theory, social criticism, and social vision in more than purely sociological factors. They recognized that social theory must take account of the intertwining of social and psychological life, that society and culture, as Freud suggested, inhere in the deepest intrapsychic experience of the individual. But in their zeal to discredit the Neo-Freudians and remain true to Freud, they end up with an incomplete and asocial social vision and inconsistent and inaccurate accounts of mental life.

Brown and Marcuse give us glimpses of an alternate social vision – in Marcuse's social sublimation and mature erotic work relations among individuals, in Brown's account of the communicative creative world of artists and of a world in which "we are members one of another" – but their accounts keep collapsing back upon a radical individualist position that conceives of instinctual gratification as the basis for human freedom and happiness. This position embraces either freedom from human relations (rather than a liberated form of relations), or relations in which the world and others are only extensions of the self and instrumental to the self's pleasures. In both variants, repression is oppression, and relations with differentiated others only constrain. Brown and Marcuse are caught in a dilemma, in which a search for meaningful subjectivity and intersubjectivity is undercut by drive theory as a basis for such a search. Despite their radical individualism, the psychoanalytic approach chosen by Brown and Marcuse precludes individual agency, and there is little place for organized activity or relations with any goal other than immediate individual drive gratification or merging. In a life of narcissistically centered pre-genital play, since there is no constraint or recognition of the other as a subject, the ego need not develop at all. Moreover, neither drive gratification nor fusion respect or allow the individuality of the other. Finally, such a child-centered perspective, in which the mother is an object, accords little room to a gendered world – either for analyzing the inequities of current gender arrangements, or for according subjectivity to women. In spite of Marcuse's condemnation of the ego-lessness of modern man, and Brown's condemnation of the morbid ego, their account of moving "Beyond the Reality Principle" (*Eros and Civilization*) to "the Resurrection of the Body" (*Life against Death*) has no real place for the ego at all; their vision is of free individuals who are all id, or all primary pleasure ego. In their accounts here, and against Marcuse's desires elsewhere for "boundaries to be enjoyed by you and by me"[138] and Brown's for an ego "strong enough to die; and strong enough to set aside guilt,"[139] there is no notion of a mature "I" engaged in work or reciprocal human relations; there are only the drives with their inherent truth, or the quest for primary oneness. We must assume that for Marcuse the Orphic–Narcissistic solution will also bind destructiveness, but there is no ego nor society to organize such binding. The instincts both are and are not historicized; Eros and death are and are not at war. For Brown, the collapse of all duality – of instinctual dualism in *Life against Death* and all other separations in *Love's Body* – returns us to a natural ego-less state of life as oneness.[140]

Freud's Dual Theory

Brown's and Marcuse's vision and critique clearly require an alternative interpretation of psychoanalysis – an interpretation that could generate a social theory that moves us beyond the poles of radical individualism and radical individualist fusion. We can find the kernel of such an alternative in Freud, even in *Civilization and Its Discontents*. The work that Brown, Marcuse, and Freud claim as the source of a drive-repression theory of society also relies on a clinically based, object-relational account.[141] There, Freud gives us a rich account of the complex social connections formed through repression – connections that form work, love, sex, friendship, politics (though Freud still assumes that these social bonds are derivative, and that they are paid for in human unhappiness). Moreover, Freud offers object-relational as well as drive motivations for development. Aggression, in *Civilization and Its Discontents*, is in the first instance an inexorable drive, and a basic threat to society. At the same time, as Freud describes its transformation in superego formation, aggression emerges in relation to the parents and to the fear of loss of love. Freud also claims, in an argument for the drive origins of aggression, that the severity of the superego is not directly proportional to parental strictness, but his account does not rule out such severity being proportional instead to the strength of the child's love. These accounts arise not from the drive metapsychology but from Freud's clinical experience and observations of human life.

Civilization and Its Discontents and *Group Psychology and the Analysis of the Ego*, Freud's major late statements on society, exemplify a dualism found throughout his work; an oscillation between the clinical and the metapsychological, in which he often presents the clinical in rich, immediate detail, and then postulates the drives and the metapsychology to "explain" the clinical findings.[142] The metapsychology does not emerge from the clinical, however, but from Freud's psychobiological assumptions. Although there has been debate about the scientific status of clinical findings as evidence, these findings (along with some observational research) are *the* evidential source of psychoanalytic claims about unconscious mental processes. It is unlikely that further psychoanalytic work – situated, interpersonal, clinical work – can provide evidence for postulated quasi-biological drives, which are a different order of phenomena. Yet Brown and Marcuse disdain the clinical and wish to draw exclusively on the drive-repression metapsychology, without examining its evidential basis or logical status.

A focus on the clinical provides a view of psychological complexity and agency and of object relationships that an exclusive focus on drives and their repression lacks. The theory of unconscious mental functioning that Freud first developed through clinical and self-analytic experience describes and requires an acting (quite creative) subject who represses, resists, condenses, symbolizes, displaces, substitutes, transforms drives and drive representations, and engages in manifold ego defenses. This subject *makes something* both of drives and social experiences. An understanding of these processes emerges in Brown's complex account of morbid ego and libidinal development, but is completely missing throughout Marcuse as well as in Brown's liberatory vision.

Freud's later structural theory, like the theory of unconscious mental processes, focuses on psychological complexity and agency. In the late anxiety theory, Freud argues that anxiety is not simply a direct physical reaction to drive repression. Rather, the ego, as Brown also makes clear, *experiences* anxiety, leading it to institute repression of drives. The person no longer passively reacts to drive repression; she or he is an agent experiencing something.[143]

The account of superego formation through the Oedipus complex emphasizes concrete relational influences.[144] The Oedipus complex arises not only from fear of the father but from *love* for him and the mother as well, and Freud implies that the boy wants a relationship to the father for its own sake, and not simply to protect himself from his father's wrath. It is hard to see this love for the parents as originally and purely a drive phenomenon (this may be even truer of love for the father than of love for the mother, since Freud can argue that the latter arises out of the need for food). The formation of the superego and ego ideal occur in relation to the father.[145]

But Freud's structural theory is more than an account of id, ego, and superego. The theory of narcissism argues strongly for the relational nature and complex construction of the ego as well.[146] The ego in this theory yields object cathexis, modifies and constructs itself to incorporate relationships, and represents and experiences itself in external and internal relation to others. Psychic experience and structure here become an internal constellation of self in relation to others; the ego constructs itself through its object attachments. Even in *Group Psychology*, the "narcissistic libido" that attaches to the leader and to other community members has an object-based component (though it is couched in the language of drives and libido).

This suggests that we draw upon the theory of narcissism not simply to extol primary narcissism, where the world is an extension of myself. Rather, the theory sustains the view that we are all incorporations and extensions of – take in and provide aspects of – one another. The theory of narcissism is a basis not for a new individualism (even if expressed in seemingly relational visions of fusion and merging), but for a vision of (inner and outer) community and mutual relationship in which, to quote psychoanalyst Joan Rivière, "we are members one of another."[147]

Just as Freud's theory of the unconscious is a theory of the richness and complexity of mental processes, and not simply of repression, the structural theory portrays mental experience as more than drive expression or the experience of a superego (or "society") grinding down the drives. Rather, basic mental experience includes an ego (even an unformed ego) with agency, the capacity to experience anxiety and ways to make something of relationships. Just as these processes speak to the complexity of psychological development and experience, indicating an actor who engages in mental experience and processes, and in relationships, the structural theory indicates that the outcome of development is not simply a monolithic repression instituted by a single-function superego which is the internalization of the father. The outcome of development consists in a self constituted by multiple internalizations and transformations of experienced relationships. Thus the total domination pictured by Marcuse is impossible because *any* mental process requires an agent, however alienated or depersonalized that person's experience of self may be.

Object-Relations Theory as a Basis for Psychoanalytic Social Theory

Freud's theory, then, is a dual theory – a theory starting from drives and a theory starting from object relations. This dualism permits and has permitted a rich and complex account of psychic functioning and agency that portrays a person in intrapsychic and interpersonal relationship. Brown also gives us a dual account, mediated by the dual theories of Klein and Roheim. But in *Life against Death* he consistently underplays this component of his work, and in *Love's Body* he collapses object relations into merging and total oneness.[148] Object-relations theory has tried to disentangle this duality and to reverse the causality implicit in drive theory.[149] A clinically based, object-relations perspective seems to give us a better account of and standard of evaluation for some of the same issues that preoccupy critical psychoanalytic social theories based on a drive perspective.[150]

Object-relations theory, rooting itself in the clinical, requires by definition attention to the historically situated engagement with others as subjects, an attention to the processes of transference and counter-transference that constitute the clinical situation and do so by bringing each person's relational history to it. This theory argues, through clinical example, that people are fundamentally social, even that there is a fundamental social "need." For Alice and Michael Balint, "primary love", not primary narcissism, is the original infantile state; for Fairbairn, libido is object-seeking rather than pleasure-seeking. People manipulate and transform drives in the process of relating to others, rather than desiring in the first instance to reduce the tension of drives. Clinically, this theory argues, where we find narcissism, anti-sociality, insistent separateness, preoccupation with drive gratification for its own sake (all Marcuse's and Brown's goals), we explain these as defenses, in relation to the individual's life history, rather than in terms of universal human nature.

Object-relations theory develops its account of primary sociality by describing the relational construction of the self, both developmentally and in daily life. Because it is clinically rooted, it need not appeal to a vaguely defined, extra-individual, unsubstantiateable Eros as a force for unity. Extending Freud's structural theory and theory of narcissism and Melanie Klein's account of internal objects, it characterizes the relational ego as consisting in unconscious, affectively loaded representations of experienced relationships and senses of self-relationship. The personal environment and quality of care experienced by the developing individual – not innate, pre-formed drives experienced in a universal developmental sequence – provide the context and material from which the individual forms and shapes her or his psyche. Thus, images of early experiences with primary caretakers and early relationships become part of the self, even as these representations can be more or less integrated. If a person is to develop at all, the self must come to include what were originally aspects of the other and the relation to the other (despite Brown's claim that any such internalizations and representations are false and morbid). The object-relations view enables, even requires, an image of psychological *development* as a necessary concomitant of living in the world.

We become a person, then, in internal relation with the social world. This social world, even at its worst, is not purely constraining, as Brown and Marcuse would have it (the mother's presence *mitigates* anxiety more than it creates it), nor could it ever completely eliminate the individual. People inevitably incorporate one another; our sociality is built into our psychic structure and there is no easy separation of individual and society or possibility of the individual apart from society. Extolling the primary narcissistic relation to the world denies this *mutual* constitution of selves and relational input to differentiation, as does an insistent individualism which defensively asserts a separation between self and other or posits the other only as a projection of the self and instrument of the self's needs.

Object-relations theory asks us to rethink not only our conceptualization of psychic structure, but also our conceptualization of the drives. Just as there is no pristine, asocial self, but only an ego potential that develops in relationship, so there are no pristine drives that are or are not repressed. In Jacobson's view, the infant is born with undifferentiated drive potentials which are transformed and used in the process of development, in the interests of internal and external relationships, to become aggressive and libidinal drives.[151] Drive potentials are structured in early experience, becoming part of an internal self–object constellation. The infant may be a bundle of unintegrated drive energies, but it can't move beyond infancy without drive organization and structuralization. Drive organization is inevitable, and intrinsically linked to self–object organization. And organization is not the same thing as repression.

Clinically and theoretically, object relations writers examine the ways that sexuality, eroticism, anger, and aggression are experienced and structure intrapsychic and interpersonal experience from earliest infancy. However, like other post-Freudian traditions within psychoanalysis (for instance, ego psychology), they do not privilege those drive experiences above other fundamental mental experiences, such as the construction of the self, the nature of the inner-object world, and the choice of ego defenses. Nor do they see the drives as fixed, operating in an unvarying sequence, insisting on release apart from individual intrapsychic context, as the early Freudian account would have it.[152]

Such a view does not preclude evaluating the role of sexuality and aggression in the individual psyche, or in the psychic organization of typical members of a society. But this evaluation, or an assessment of sexual repression, must be in terms of the total psychic structure and characterization of dominant mental processes, in which drives play only one (integral) part. When drives come to develop independently of these other features of mental life, when individual drive gratification comes to dominate psychological goals, this is a neurotic developmental product.

By putting forth a different model of psychological development and psychic life, object-relations theory leads us to focus on alternate criteria of social critique and on an alternate vision of a liberatory social life.[153] To begin from an object-relations-based account one could not easily derive the conception of total domination, or totally distorted history, that Marcuse and Brown find attractive. Object-relations theory suggests that we look at a range of criteria in our evaluation of psychological life, and it suggests that most of our evaluation will be in relative rather than absolute terms.

Both Marcuse and Brown, in spite of themselves, are led away from the pure drive theory with which they begin. Marcuse begins from the unchanging truth and insistence of the drives, which, though repressed, incorporate our only hold-out against total domination. Yet he also pictures the drives as totally transformed by the repressive reality principle, and puts forth a vision of liberation in which the drives are equally malleable and transformed, though still to be judged in terms of their gratification. Brown, recognizing the problems in an account based on the truth of the embodied, material drives that are part of our animal nature, turns to a mystical vision of "Love's Body" as the bodily unity of humankind. Object-relations theory (along with post-Freudian psychoanalytic theory generally) has confronted the limitations of the hydraulic energy model implicit in the original drive theory. At the same time, it leaves us with criteria for evaluating the role of the drives, in terms not of their global repression, but of how insistent and isolated drive expressions and drive demands are – how split off from and unintegrated with the rest of psychic life. This does not eliminate the claim for pleasure as a social and individual goal or right, but it suggests that this claim must be seen in the psychic totality and evaluated in terms of the extent to which there are asymmetries in the claims for and abilities to gain pleasure among people in different structural locations.

As well as limiting drives and drive development to one aspect of psychological life, the object-relations perspective removes repression from the central (or only) role among the defenses and ego processes. Moreover, repression affects not only immutable drives, but repudiated aspects of object-relational experience and unacceptable or fearsome aspects of self, both of these affectively laden and laden with sexual and aggressive (drive-derivative) meanings. To the extent that a large amount of a person's unconscious psychic life is preoccupied with maintaining these repressions, such repression would certainly be taken as problematic. However, because repression concerns differentiated aspects of emotionally charged psychic identity and structure, it must be understood in terms of the complexity of psychic structure and emotional life as a whole, and cannot be measured in any unidimensional way.

Unlike the drive theory, this view of psychological life permits a complex approach to the members of a particular society. Evaluations can be made in terms not of one monolithic repression or liberation, but of the pervasiveness of repression, along with the greater or lesser integration of unconscious early internalizations and representations, the quality of relatedness, the more or less meshing or fragmentation of these, the degree of sense of continuity and authenticity of self, the extent of felt agency as opposed to felt reactivity. None of these is an absolute measure, for in the process of development some repression, some splitting, some discontinuity, some feeling acted upon, are inevitable. Moreover, as psychological life is a totality, none of its elements can be fully evaluated without reference to the others.

Because it pictures a complex whole, object-relations theory always recognizes some part of the self, however small, that remains actively striving and not totally dominated – minimally, that part of the ego available to the analyst in the clinical situation; potentially, a part of the ego available for transformative activity. Freud's experience of resistance in patients led to his discovery of repression. Both discoveries turned the field of psychoanalytic inquiry to the question of the varieties of ego activity and eventually to the complex construction of the self-in-relationship. Marcuse and Brown wish to appropriate the discovery of repression while rejecting all the implications for ego activity and self-construction that follow from that discovery, Marcuse by denying ego activity altogether, Brown by seeing it as morbid and reactive. The view of the construction of self proposed by clinically based, post-Freudian theories of object relations, in which differentiation consists in particular forms of relatedness, enables us to envision two selves, each developing in relation to the other yet unique, in which a "mature dependence"[154] enables access to feelings of identity and oneness while also maintaining individuality. We thus have a theory more able to incorporate inter-subjectivity, and a theory which directs attention to the interrelations of individuality and collectivity or community. Such a theory refuses the alternatives of individualism run wild or extreme fusion that becomes solipsism – alternatives offered by combining drive theory with an unspecified wishful communal vision.

Object-relations theory also points to a social theory that includes women. Its focus on pre-Oedipal development means a focus on the mother–child relationship, though a thorough reinterpretation is needed to make this mother into a subject.[155] The drive-repression dynamic, by contrast, is an Oedipal theory – a theory of generation and potentially of relationship to be sure – but a theory of the father. It does not require women other than as Oedipal object of cathexis. Accordingly, as we have seen, Marcuse, who does not move beyond the drive-repression dynamic, never incorporates women into his account, whereas Brown, who discusses the pre-Oedipal period in *Life against Death* and a Kleinian interpretation of childhood fantasy in *Love's Body*, is much more consciously attuned to the role of the mother in development and in culture, even as this mother remains mainly an object of (male) childhood fantasy.

Finally, object-relations theory suggests alternate possibilities for a psychoanalytic interpretation of culture and creativity. In Freud, Brown, and Marcuse, we have mainly individualistic interpretations of creativity or visions of creative possibility, either drive repression and sublimation, or erotic exuberance. But Marcuse calls for "social sublimation" and Brown for an artistic community, and Winnicott suggests, in *Playing and Reality*, such a fully relational conception. He describes the "transitional object," both physically present in the objective world (an object "objectively perceived") and, in its meaning, created by the child ("a subjectively conceived of" object),[156] and the "transitional space" – that area between mother and child which, as the child develops, is neither "me" nor "not-me," where there is neither merging nor insistent separation. The transitional object thus inhabits a transitional space where boundaries are and aren't, where the world is both subjective and objective, where mother and child accept this lack of definition.

The transitional space grows to become first the arena of play, and then the "location of cultural experience," to which each participant brings a history, knowledge, and identity, which can be creatively used in the further mutual development of histories, knowledge and identities. Culture and creativity emerge through the imaginative ability to both enter into the world of the other, or the observed, in the transitional space and also to assess and evaluate one's experience in the full confidence of the "I," or self. Winnicott's view thus also shows how childhood experience and the childhood subjective world come to be integrated into the adult's creative life and culture as a whole without seeing creativity as simply a return to childhood wishes, fantasies, and fears.[157]

In Freud, it is very difficult to derive primary relationships out of drive theory and the pleasure principle. Yet Freud, even as he denied it, assumed a primary relatedness which drive-liberation theorists like Brown and Marcuse pass over. Post-Freudian theories that privilege clinical and object-relational perspectives, by starting from a view of the individual as relationally constituted, can solve the contradictions in critical social theories that rest on the drive-repression dynamic.

Beginning from the clinical and object-relational in creating a psycho-analytic social theory means that the *form* of intersubjectivity and the political and social process creating a particular intersubjectivity need accounting, both on an individual and on a societal basis. Yet inter-subjectivity itself is not problematic; rather, it is rooted in a sense of multiple internal relatedness, of the complexity of psychodynamic possibilities and mental processes, of an actor who is a historical and social actor and who is also a (more or less integrated, more or less agentic, more or less unproblematically both individuated and related) psychological actor. On this basis one could begin to look at individual commitment to, interpretation of, resistance to, reshaping of a variety of social experience and institutions; one could evaluate both the quality of individuality and the quality of community, beyond the alternatives of a super-individualism or a radical collectivism. At the same time, such an approach does not see the individual simply as a reflection of society. Rather, the self has its own psychodynamic experience and multiple relations to others – both individuals and institutions. With a notion of primary sociality and intersubjectivity, with a theory that includes, in addition to sociality in a general sense, gender, generation, and sexuality in a specific historical sense, with an account that sees life as a developmental and relational process, one could even begin to imagine not only liberated individuals, but individuals mutually engaged in a society built on liberated forms of social life.

7

Toward a Relational Individualism: The Mediation of Self Through Psychoanalysis

Psychoanalysis begins with a radical challenge to traditional notions of the individual self.[1] As Freud, with characteristic modesty, puts it:

In the course of centuries the *naive* self-love of men has had to submit to two major blows at the hands of science. The first was when they learnt that our earth was not the centre of the universe but only a tiny fragment of a cosmic system of scarcely imaginable vastness. This is associated in our minds with the name of Copernicus, though something similar had already been asserted by Alexandrian science. The second blow fell when biological research destroyed man's supposedly privileged place in creation and proved his descent from the animal kingdom and his ineradicable animal nature. This revaluation has been accomplished in our own days by Darwin, Wallace and their predecessors, though not without the most violent contemporary opposition. But human megalomania will have suffered its third and most wounding blow from the psychological research of the present time which seeks to prove to the ego that it is not even master in its own house, but must content itself with scanty information of what is going on unconsciously in its mind.[2]

According to Freud, then, we are not who or what we think we are: we do not know our own centers; in fact, we probably do not have a center at all. Psychoanalysis radically undermines notions about autonomy, individual choice, will, responsibility, and rationality, showing that we do not control our own lives in the most fundamental sense. It makes it impossible to think about the self in any simple way, to talk blithely about the individual.

At the same time, however, psychoanalysis gives us an extraordinarily rich, deep, and complex understanding of whatever it is that is not the simple self we once thought we were, and it explains how whatever this is develops. "What is going on unconsciously in its mind" are forces and structures beyond conscious control or even knowledge: sexual and aggressive drives within the id; primary process thinking with no respect for time, logic, reality, or consistency; powerful ideas and wishes that anxiety and repression have removed from consciousness and that defenses like resistance, isolation, and denial work to ensure will not reappear there; conflict, as these wishes and ideas seek recognition and meet with resistances and defenses; superego pressures that once were felt to come from recognized external forces but now operate relatively independently, fed by aggressive drives turned inward. This fragmentation of structure, function, and process that the psychoanalytic metapsychology describes affects the everyday subjective experience of self, lending what Freud recognized as a certain unease to expressed certainties about autonomous individuality and sparking a fierce opposition to his theories.

Even though Freud radically undermined notions of the unitary and autonomous individual, we can also see psychoanalysis, in its endless, reflexive involvement with self-investigation, as a particularly intense scrutiny of the individual, the apogee of the development of individualism in Western culture.[3] From the earliest days of psychoanalysis until the present, cultural thinkers, artists, and writers have celebrated the fragmented self that psychoanalysis portrays, denigrating character in literature, romanticizing the lack of agency, meaning, morality, and authorship.

Freud, however, wanted to resolve the paradox he created, to use the scrutiny of individual and self not to celebrate fragmentation but to restore wholeness. He could not accept that the self is the outcome of messy unconscious processes and a warring structure, that it disallows individual morality, autonomy, and responsibility; he wanted to reconstitute the individual and the self he had dissected. That metapsychological dissection shows who we are, but the clinical project of psychoanalysis is to develop individual autonomy and control in the self. As Freud put it, "Where id was, there shall ego be. It is a work of culture – not unlike the draining of the Zuider Zee."[4] And where an overwhelming, punitive superego was, there shall a conscious ego be. These goals, I think, have to be made very clear. Freud, and later psychoanalysts, did not just give up in despair; that is, although he did despair that the dikes could keep back the Zuider Zee entirely, he certainly wanted to give it a good try. All analysts probably want to restore a certain wholeness and agency to the self.

In this chapter, I discuss two psychoanalytic solutions to the dilemma posed by Freud's challenge to individualism and the self, two different conceptions of wholeness and agency. These solutions are not mutually exclusive: they overlap each other in psychoanalytic thought and in theory and therapy. One solution is, in essence, to reconstitute, or resuscitate, the traditional autonomous self of the pristine individual; the other is to reconstruct a self that is in its very structure fundamentally implicated in relations with others. Because the mediation of self through psychoanalysis happens within the psychoanalytic process, we must examine this mediation in clinical practice as well as in theory.[5]

In the traditional model, based on Freud's drive theory along with his late structural theory, "where id was, there shall ego be," maturation and psychic health consist in rational ego control over the insistent drives, reducing the tyranny of the superego in order to harmonize conscience and wish, ego-ideal and ego-actuality. Internal conflict, then, is between different aspects of the psychical personality; reduction of this conflict will presumably lead to fulfillment in the external world, although traditional psychoanalysis does not specify how that will happen. The developmental model here is the Oedipal struggle between self and father, where the Oedipus complex – the relational complex itself – is "smashed to pieces" and leaves in its wake a superego "so inexorable, so impersonal, so independent of its emotional origins."[6] Autonomy is key: although the superego is originally formed in response to parental prohibitions and the relationship to parents, this relational history ceases to be actively part of one's psychic make-up. The focus on individual autonomy is extended in Heinz Hartmann's work on ego psychology, which contributes to psychoanalytic metapsychology the notion of autonomous, conflict-free ego spheres; it is also reflected in the work of Heinz Kohut, who assesses the psychic functioning of the bipolar self in terms of ambitions and ideals.[7]

An alternative psychoanalytic view of the individual and the self emerges, not from Freud's structural discussions or from the exhortation that "where id was, there shall ego be," but from his essay "On narcissism." Here, Freud notes how libido can be directed alternately toward objects (other people) or toward the self. He calls these forms "object libido" and "ego libido," and he locates psychic wholeness in a delicate balance between them. In Freud's view here, exclusive investment in the self with no connection to the other creates the narcissistic neuroses and psychoses; relatedness is the *sine qua non* of mental health. At the same time, he warns against the opposite danger, complete investment in the object – as in slavish unrequited love, which debases the self and deprives it of energy. As he puts it, "A strong egoism is a protection against falling ill, but in the last resort we must begin to love in order not to fall ill, and we are bound to fall ill if, in consequence of frustration, we are unable to love."[8]

The developmental theory Freud begins to describe in the same essay points toward a maturation of belongingness or connectedness (such as Carol Gilligan outlines)[9] instead of ego autonomy and control. He proposes that in its original libidinal state the infant has two love-objects, "itself and the woman who tends it," and conceptualizes development in terms of what happens to these two libidinal attachments: in the best case, unproblematic self-regard and lack of self-punitiveness on the one hand, and "true object love," loving a person as a complement to and not an extension of the self, on the other.

Just as Hartmann and others picked up from Freud's metapsychology and developmental theory an emphasis on the autonomous ego and rational superego, so other post-Freudian psychoanalysts have expanded upon the theory of narcissism. Object-relations theorists conceptualize the infant in terms of its cognitive narcissism and primary libidinal relatedness – that is, its inability to distinguish itself conceptually from its primary caretaker and other objects in the world, even while it feels itself in, and gets gratification from, a relationship to an other.[10] As cognitive narcissism gives way to a sense of bounded self, internality and externality come to have both a simple cognitive and a complex affective reality.[11] On the physical level, the infant comes to be unproblematically aware of its own boundaries and separateness. On the affective level, as the infant defines a self out of the mother–child matrix, the early flux of projections and introjections ensures that some aspects of that self are likely to have originally been perceived or experienced as aspects of the primary other or others, and aspects of the other may have originally been felt as aspects of the self.[12] On a psychological level, then, even the apparent boundaries of the individual do not separate in any simple way the pristine individual from the rest of the world.

The core of the self, or self-feeling, is also constructed relationally. Michael Balint locates the primary feeling of self in terms of the sense of fit or lack of fit with the primary caretaker; Winnicott characterizes as "the capacity to be alone" a sense of individuality and autonomy that includes the internalization of the benign but uninvolved presence of the mother. The development of psychic structure begins with this basic self-feeling and self-structure, which includes relatedness to and aspects of the other, and it continues through internalizations and splittings-off of internalized self–other representations to create an inner world consisting of different aspects of an "I" in relation to different aspects of the other. Psychological disorders, the problem of the fragmented individual, are seen here not so much in terms of conflict and defenses but rather in terms of problematic self–other relationships, which themselves internally constitute low self-esteem, self-punitiveness, lack of control, and so forth.[13]

Thus, the object-relations perspective gives us a very different notion of the construction of individuality than does the classical analytic account. In the classical account, the inner world is conceived in terms of different aspects of the psychical personality, and the goal is reduction of conflict among these. The classical account accords some recognition to the implicit relatedness of the individual: Freud claims that "the superego continues to play the part of an external world for the ego, although it has become a portion of the internal world," and he also mentions the role of identifications in the formation of the ego-ideal.[14] But these origins are not stressed in accounts of psychic functioning or models of the psychic constitution; instead, autonomy and the resolution of conflict are seen in terms of modes of ego functioning.

By contrast, the object-relations model, although it recognizes the role of defenses in ego functioning (understanding these defenses as operating in terms of an internal sense of self in relationship and of internal objects) and acknowledges the desirability of conflict-free ego spheres, conceptualizes the self as inexorably social and intrinsically connected. Thus, both views challenge the traditional notion of the pristine individual, but one does so without fundamental recourse to the "outside world." In neither view is the self unitary, but in object-relations theory it is also not apart from the other. Joan Rivière – an associate of Melanie Klein, who first made projection, introjection, and the role of internal objects central in psychoanalytic theory – puts the position as follows:

We tend to think of any one individual in isolation; it is a convenient fiction. We may isolate him physically, as in the analytic room; in two minutes we find he has brought his world in with him, and that, even before he set eyes on the analyst, he had developed inside himself an elaborate relation with him. There is no such thing as a single human being, pure and simple, unmixed with other human beings. Each personality is a world in himself, a company of many. That self, that life of one's own, which is in fact so precious though so casually taken for granted, is a composite structure which has been and is being formed and built up since the day of our birth out of countless never-ending influences and exchanges between ourselves and others. . . These other persons are in fact therefore parts of ourselves, not indeed the whole of them but such parts or aspects of them as we had our relation with, and as have thus become parts of us. And we ourselves similarly have and have had effects and influences, intended or not, on all others who have an emotional relation to us, have loved or hated us. We are members one of another.[15]

Rivière, like Freud, points to the threat that this conception of the individual poses:

The "inner world," like other psychoanalytical concepts, meets with a twofold resistance; on the one hand, the incapacity to understand it, and on the other a direct emotional rejection of it . . . an acute reaction which arises, as experience teaches, from an acute anxiety. . . When this proposition meets with an intense emotional rejection there is clearly a direct association in the hearer's mind of this idea with danger, as though anything inside one which is not "oneself" pure and simple is and must be dangerous – or pathological.[16]

Object-relations theory does not need to idealize a hyper-individualism; it assumes a fundamental internal as well as external relatedness to the other. The question is then what kind of relation this can or should be. The relational individual is not reconstructed in terms of his or her drives and defenses but in terms of the greater or lesser fragmentation of his or her inner world and the extent to which the core self feels spontaneous and whole within, rather than driven by, this world. Even the sense of agency and autonomy remain relational in the object-relations model, because agency develops in the context of the early relationship with the mother and bears the meaning of her collaboration in and response to it. Separation and autonomy are not so crucial to development, because the model assumes the permeability of boundaries and focusses instead on the nature of the inner world and the inner core of self, whose implicit relatedness is acknowledged in its very structure. Paraphrasing Freud, we might say that the goal in the object-relational reconstruction of the individual is: where fragmented internal objects were, there shall harmoniously related objects be; and where false, reactive self was, there shall true, agentic self be, with its relationally based capacity both to be alone and to participate in the transitional space between self and other self that creates play, intimacy, and culture.

Object-relations psychoanalysis, in reformulating the psychoanalytic conception of self, also reformulates a self for social theory and analysis. This self is intrinsically social, and, because it is constructed in a relational matrix and includes aspects of the other, it can better recognize the other as a self and, ultimately, attain the intersubjectivity that creates society. This self's full historical grounding contrasts with that of the drive-determined individual. The grounding of the object-relational self derives from an appropriation and interpretation of experienced relationships and accordingly varies by individual, culture, period, gender, and so forth. By contrast, the self of the drive-determined individual is originally constructed not through historically grounded experience but from universal and unchanging drives; this leads to a more abstract and universalist view of the self. (Insofar as this latter self has historical grounding, that grounding also derives from its object-relational history, the "precipitate of abandoned object-cathexes"[17] that it contains.) We might speculate that a fully social and historical conception of self provides an alternative to the autonomous ego and responsible, non-punitive superego as a solution to the problems of morality, responsibility, and so forth posed by the psychoanalytic dissolution of the individual.

Psychoanalytic knowledge of the individual and the self is developed in theoretical and in metapsychological writings, but this knowledge is originally derived from the clinical setting, the analytic situation. Thus, an investigation of this setting can give further insight into the differentiated or relational self and help us decide between classical and object-relations models.

It would seem that the epistemological setting provided by the analytic situation requires that the knowledge of self emerging within it be relational, because this situation is a reflexively constructed collaboration in which analyst and analysand, through their interaction, create a history, or story, of the analysand's life.[18] Engagement with others as subjects (an engagement moderated by objectivity) is central to clinical practice, as opposed to metapsychology. In fact, this practical activity, empathetically involved with and taking account of another's interests, while objectively assessing the other and the self, in some ways illustrates a desirable sociality in general. A clinically derived view of the self also seems to require a historical as well as a social view of the self because of this concretely based engagement. Thus, a clinical perspective on the self same to require engagement with the other, no matter what your theory.

Nevertheless, psychoanalysts have developed two clinical approaches, which reflect – though less starkly than the theory, for reasons I have suggested – the two approaches to the individual I have discussed. The first approach is popularly caricatured in the silent, uninvolved, blank-wall analyst, the object of a transference brought entirely from past experiences and relationships, who says little except, "What comes to mind?" or "umhmm," and occasionally offers brief nuggets of inter-pretation.[19] Analytic technique here consists in analyzing resistances and defenses that prevent the analysand from acknowledging transference feelings. The relentless analysis of all the analysand says in terms of these resistances will eventually lead to an acknowledged transference relationship, which can then be analyzed to bring out and resolve early developmental material. This assumes that what is going on in the analysis has nothing to do with any actual relationship to the analyst or with the reality of the person of the analyst, that this relationship is entirely transference and as such is entirely one way. There is also a "therapeutic" or "working" alliance between analyst and analysand,[20] but this is merely an agreement made with the un-neurotic parts of the analysand's ego to work on change, in tandem as it were, and does not involve any reciprocity or acknowledged connection.[21]

In this view, what the analyst does is to help the analysand reorganize a psychic organization and mental processes conceived as drives, superego, ego defenses, and resistances. In Freud's original view, counter-transference – strong feelings about the analysand or about particular moments in the analysis, feelings perhaps evoked by the analysand – was always an unwelcome intrusion and a sign of the analyst's own inadequate analysis. The later classical model recognizes countertransference but prescribes that it should count for little in the analysis.

This view of the analytic process corresponds with and nicely reinforces a metapsychology that posits a pristine individual who is all ego and id, and whose autonomous ego must take more and more spheres of control from id, unconscious ego defenses, and superego. Nonetheless, in spite of formal intention the clinical situation almost requires some recognition of the interpersonal construction (and reconstruction) of a self. Various residual concepts in the classical account of technique (none formally acknowledged in theory and all requiring justification and scrutiny in the individual case), much like the Ptolemaic epicycles, point to an alternative formulation of the analytic process and the selves involved in it. The relentless interpretation of resistances is sometimes avoided for considerations of "tact" and "timing" – if pointing them out might lead to the creation of even more ego defenses by the analysand. Deviations from technique (in revealing information about yourself, in allowing the analysand to sit up, in responding to questions) are occasionally allowed if these will help the analytic work by making the analysand more secure. Similarly, building a therapeutic alliance may depend partly on the analysand's trust in the analyst's good intent and may therefore require the analyst to indicate such intent.

All of these, of course, are ways to acknowledge that the actual relationship between analyst and analysand matters, that change in the analysand depends at least partly on the nature and meaning of that relationship. An alternative clinical position makes this engagement and its consequences more explicit. Formulated variously by Michael Balint, Heinz Kohut, Frieda Fromm-Reichman, Margaret Little, Leo Stone, Harold Searles, D. W. Winnicott, and others, this position proposes, not that the analyst should participate equally in a real relationship (always answering questions about her or himself, always being supportive and responsive), but that what is central to an analysis and must be constantly kept at the forefront of the analyst's awareness is an affective and cognitive exchange between two people.[22] Choices in technique accordingly have the aim of enhancing this relationship so that the analytic work can progress; analysis focusses primarily on experiences of the self in both internal and external relationship rather than on the analysis of resistances and defenses.

In this model the analyst's attentiveness to and investigation of countertransference is a crucial part of every analysis, not a hold-over to be avoided. Moreover, countertransference involves all feelings evoked in the analyst, and these feelings are not seen as purely neurotic. As Elizabeth Zetzel puts it: "Many analysts to-day believe that the classical conception of analytic objectivity and anonymity cannot be maintained. Instead, thorough analysis of reality aspects of the analyst's personality and point of view is advocated as an essential feature of transference analysis and an indispensable prerequisite for the dynamic changes."[23] These "many analysts" would claim that a focus on the analyst's own reactions will provide the best clue to what is going on with the patient (and with the analyst's self as well). Thus, they would explicitly recognize that the analysand's self is reconstructed in and through both conscious and unconscious interaction with the analyst.

The focus on countertransference points to a final, important part of the first psychoanalytic formulations of the self: psychoanalytic knowledge of the self originally concerned the self of the analyst as well as the self of the patient. Thus, Freud first learned about the unconscious, resistance, and repression from his hysterical patients, but he learned about dreams and the Oedipus complex from self-analysis.[24] And in the countertransference, perhaps not only the self of the analysand is reconstructed or reconstituted; the analyst's self may be changed, or at least better understood, as well.[25] Thus, knowledge of the other and knowledge of the self, construction of the self and construction of the other, are intimately related.

Psychoanalytic theory radically challenges our understanding of ourselves as whole, autonomous individuals, then seeks to reconstruct that wholeness and autonomy. It poses two solutions to this goal in its metapsychology and attempts them in its therapeutic technique and understanding. But the therapeutic setting can, finally, produce knowledge and self-knowledge only of a relational self. And psychoanalysis can only know the self in the analytic situation; anything else is ungrounded speculation. Thus, when we investigate psychoanalytic theory and practice, we see a historical progression from a view favoring a pure, differentiated individuality based on rigid notions of autonomous separateness toward a relational individualism.

PART III

Psychoanalysis, Psychoanalysts, and
Feminism

8

Feminism, Femininity, and Freud

Feminists have evinced significant interest in psychoanalytic theory and have drawn upon psychoanalysis as one basis of theory in many and varied ways.[1] Such interest would have surprised members of the women's movement in the late 1960s and early 1970s. The dominant feminist stance during this period, beginning with Betty Friedan, and continuing with major statements by Firestone, Millett, Weisstein, and others, was an enormous hostility to and condemnation of Freud. Freudian theory and therapy were taken as major factors in women's oppression.[2]

The response to this feminist debate was quite mixed within psychoanalysis itself. On the one hand, the women's movement has spurred extensive rethinking, revision, and critique of Freud, especially in what are considered the Neo-Freudian or cultural schools – Sullivanians, the followers of Horney and Thompson, and so forth.[3] Within orthodox psychoanalysis as well, there has been a resurgence of interest in questions of female sexuality, female development, and the psychology of women more generally.[4] But also, it seems, there has been a strict attempt to keep this new research and interest scientific and sober, to make sure it is not influenced by what are seen as extraneous considerations like politics or cultural values.

In this chapter I address two general questions (or objections) posed by feminists and Freudians which are related to these developments and to each other. Mainly, I address questions asked by feminists, but I also address questions asked by Freudian scholars and clinicians. Both sets of questions concern a claim put forth by feminist psychoanalytic theory: that femininity, feminism, and Freud are in many ways related and gain meaning one from the other.

What are these two general questions? The feminist asks: what does Freud, or psychoanalysis, have to do with feminism? Does psychoanalysis have anything to do with feminism, or anything meaningful to say about women and "femininity"? The Freudian's question is the obverse. The clinician or psychoanalyst asks, what does feminism have to do with Freud? Does feminism have anything to do with Freud, or with our psychoanalytic understanding of female psychology?

The Feminist's Questions

Let us expand the feminist's question. The person who asks what Freud has to do with feminism may have in mind a number of objections. The first and most extreme position holds that women's oppression is political, economic, and social, and that psychology has nothing to do with it.

A second position claims that women are certainly psychologically oppressed, but that we do not need a theory as mystified or complicated – relying on the unconscious and intrapsychic – to explain and understand female socialization and how women turn out the way they do. It has nothing to do with the unconscious but is obvious in daily life. Children grow up in a male-dominated society, channeled from the day they are born into pink and blue blankets, into playing with trucks or dolls, through books with sexist messages and a gender-differentiating school. Girls learn that they are supposed to be good and to please men, boys to be strong, and so forth. "Society" imposes values on people and they have to behave according to societal expectations. "Society" expects that women will not achieve or be active, so they are not. People respond according to the social situation they are in and the rewards they get. This was the argument made early by Betty Friedan, and, in her widely influential piece, by Naomi Weisstein. It is made repeatedly by many others.[5]

Third, the feminist argues, Freud's theory was sexist, anti-woman, misogynist. Freud denied women their own orgasms; he thought that women were without as great a sense of justice as men, that they were vain, jealous, full of shame, and have made no contributions to civilization except for weaving. He thought it was obvious that any three-year-old would think the masculine genitalia better than the feminine.

The Freudian's Questions

We can also expand the Freudian's question. The person who asks what feminism has to do with Freud may also have several objections in mind. First, according to the Freudian, psychoanalysis is a psychological theory and clinical practice; by contrast, feminism is a political movement, or at most a political theory. Psychoanalysis does not have to do with questions of politics, equality, or inequality.

The Freudian makes a second, related claim, the methodological claim that psychoanalysis is a value-free science, simply recording the truth about human development and human psychological life and not taking sides. Feminism, by contrast, is value-laden, and has an axe to grind.[6]

These are the sorts of questions and considerations I will discuss here. I will address the feminist questions first, because I believe that this provides insight into the clinician's, or Freudian's, questions as well. Let me say parenthetically that I consider feminism here as a theory and practice. Feminist theory must understand the social organization and dynamics of women and men in their life situations – of sexual inequality and asymmetry, of sexuality, of gender, parenting, children, of the relations between the sexes. But feminist theory must also contribute to a liberatory practice, to a practice that will free us from sexual inequality and enable us to change things.

Answering the Feminist: The Importance of Freud for Feminism

To take on the feminist's questions: what does Freud have to do with feminism? Does psychoanalysis have anything meaningful to say about women and "femininity"? Recall the first objection: women's oppression is social and not psychological. It is concerned with wage inequality, job segregation, rape, wife-abuse, the unequal sexual division of labor in the home, men's power over women. Let us develop an answer.

To start, this social and political organization of gender does not exist apart from the fact that we are all sexed and gendered in the first place – that we all have a particular sexual organization and orientation, that we are all either men or women – which is a part of our fundamental identity and being in the world. We cannot understand the social and political organization and history of gender without simultaneously taking people's sexualization and engendering into account. So we are not talking here about external roles, as, for instance, sociologists might want us to do, that people are workers, parents, teachers; that we differentiate occupational from family roles, the mother role from the father role, that people are personifications of economic categories. This is not the case with gender. People do not just play out a gender role that combines with other roles, or that they can step out of. We cannot step out of being sexed and gendered; this is who we are. We do not exist apart from being gendered, or have a separate self apart from our engendering. So, when we are interested in questions of gender and sexuality – even when our questions are in the first instance social, political, or economic questions – there is no easy line between psyche and society. The social organization of gender, and people as sexed and gendered, are an inextricable totality or unity: the social organization of gender is built right into our heads and divides the world into females and males; our being sexed and gendered (our sexuality and our gender identity) is built right into social organization. They are only given meaning one from the other.

Feminist theory must be able to encompass these linkages, this totality. For our purposes here, feminist theory must include the fact that we are psychologically gendered and sexed as part of who we are. The social organization of gender is not an organization of empty places or role categories that anyone can fill, as people have argued about places in the economy or polity. In the social organization of gender, only particular people can fill particular places.

But feminism also wishes to change the social organization and psychology of sex and gender. Its basic argument is that gender and sexuality, whatever the biology that helps to inform these, are created culturally and socially; they are not immutable givens. Therefore, feminism demands a theory of how we become sexed and gendered.

Freud has given us such a theory. He has given us a rich account of the organization and reproduction of sex and gender, of how we are produced as gendered and sexed. Psychoanalytic theory is almost by definition a theory of sexuality and the way sexuality develops in women and men. Freud shows us why we do not exist apart from our particular sexualization and gender identification, even though that sexualization and that gender identification are created. Let me mention a few important elements in Freud's argument.

First, Freud divorced, or liberated, sexuality from gender and procreation. As Freud argues, there is nothing inevitable about the development of sexual object choice, mode, or aim; there is no innate femininity or masculinity. We are all potentially bisexual, active or passive, polymorphous perverse and not just genital. How any woman or man understands, fantasizes about, symbolizes, internally represents, and feels about her or his physiology is a developmental product, and these feelings and fantasies may be shaped by considerations completely apart from biology. Woman is made, not born, Freud tells us, and he describes quite openly the special difficulty girls have in attaining an expected passive, heterosexual genital adulthood. Freud argued as well that both homosexuality and heterosexuality, for both sexes, are products of development. Neither is innate.

Freud demonstrated that all sex – procreative and non-procreative, genital and non-genital, heterosexual and homosexual, autoerotic and other-oriented, child and adult – is on a continuum and related in manifold ways. There is nothing special about heterosexual coitus for purposes of reproduction, which is just one kind of sex among many. Any organ, almost any object, can have erotic significance.

Freud, secondly, tells us how, in spite of the fact that sexual and gender development as we know them are not inevitable, the development of gender personality and sexual orientation tends to happen in regularized ways for women and for men. We find this in the classic account of the Oedipus complex, which explains the development of masculine identity, the development of female heterosexuality and love for the father, and differential forms of superego formation. We find it in the important, late account of the special nature of the pre-Oedipal mother–daughter relationship and the effect this relationship has on a woman's later life. And we find that Freud is quite candid about the fact that "normal" female development is very costly to women. In a passage in his lecture "Femininity," he says:

I cannot help mentioning an impression that we are constantly receiving during analytic practice. A man of about thirty strikes us as a youthful, somewhat unformed individual, whom we expect to make powerful use of the possibilities for development opened up to him by analysis. A woman of the same age, however, often frightens us by her psychical rigidity and unchangeability. Her libido has taken up final positions and seems incapable of exchanging them for others. There are no paths open to further development; it is as though the whole process had already run its course and remains thenceforward insusceptible to influence – as though, indeed, the difficult development to femininity had exhausted the possibilities of the person concerned.[7]

In this discussion of how gender personality and sexual orientation develop in regularized ways for women and for men, there are two things of particular note for feminist theory.

First, Freud demonstrates that women's heterosexual attraction to men is very tenuously achieved and even then only partially. In the developmental account, a girl wants a penis from her father, not him for his own sake. Or she wants him as a refuge from mother, and always remains involved with mother, taking the character of her relationship with her mother to her relationships with men. Freud also implies that women only achieve "true" object-love in relation to children, not to men (he never looks to see if women achieve true object-love with women, which would be the logical extension of his theory).[8] Women have no "natural" attraction to men; this attraction must be created.

Second, the theory of the masculine Oedipus complex is a theory of the reproduction of male dominance. Contempt for women, as penis-less creatures, and identification with his father in their common masculine superiority, are normal outcomes of the masculine Oedipus complex. The masculine Oedipus complex results in what Freud's follower, Ruth M. Brunswick, calls "what we have come to consider the normal masculine contempt of women."[9] This is the manner by which a boy comes to give up his mother as a love-object and the reason he is willing to do so. Freud doesn't extend his insight here, but later analysts, like Karen Horney and Grete Bibring, were able to do so, to demonstrate the intertwining of contempt for women, fear of women, and devaluation of women, feminine activities, and ways of being as a developmental product of a boy's first love-object and primary parent being a woman.[10] (Women, also, as a normal outcome of their Oedipus complex, come to devalue their own gender. We become who we are as men and women with a differential valuation of masculinity and femininity.)

Finally, Freud provided perceptive social analyses concerning oppressions of gender and sexuality. Two examples must suffice here. First, in "'Civilized' sexual morality and modern nervousness," Freud analysed how sexual repression in childhood created conflictual and strained marital relationships which in turn affected the children of these marriages in ways that would reproduce the whole situation in the next generation.[11] A bourgeois woman, Freud argues, brings the sexual repression forced upon her into marriage, along with her dependence on her parents. These together lead her husband to turn elsewhere for sexual satisfaction. As she matures, however, her sexual interests awaken, but by then her husband is no longer around. As a substitute, she sexualizes her relationship to her children, awakening their sexuality, which must then be repressed (helping to create their neuroses). She also feels guilty about the resentment she feels towards her husband because of his marital and sexual failures, and she turns this resentment inward into neurosis, which hurts her, her children, and her marriage. Second, *Studies on Hysteria* gives us the glimmering of an argument for a relationship between constraint on women and neurosis. Here, Freud argues against the view prevalent in his time that hysterics are degenerate and weak, and for the view that the women he treated were especially intelligent, creative, and moral. It was confinement, he suggested, for instance in caring for the sick, that did not allow the expression of a woman's gifts and capacities. Her neurosis was a reaction.[12]

Thus, in answer to the first feminist question, I would suggest that Freud demonstrates the intertwining of psychological and social forms of gender oppression, and especially that he provides an account of the genesis of psychological aspects of gender and sexuality in their social context.

To turn to the second feminist objection: why do we need such a complicated theory, one relying on unconscious mental processes, when it is obvious that society treats women and girls differently and pushes them into certain roles? Two issues are relevant here. First, we need to explain and understand the tenacity of people's commitment to our social organization of gender and sex: the intensity of the taboo on homosexuality; why people often cannot change even when they want to; why a "liberated" man still has difficulty parenting equally or being completely happy about his successful, independent, liberated wife; or why a feminist woman might find it hard to be attracted to a non-macho, non-traditionally masculine man just because he's "nice" and egalitarian or to be unambivalent about choosing not to have children. Psychoanalysis helps here, because it shows us that we also live our past in the present. We do not just react to our contemporary situation and conscious wishes, nor can we easily change values, feelings, and behavior simply if we have an encouraging social setting. Moreover, psychoanalysis explains our commitment to this past, which arose at a time of huge feelings of helplessness and dependency, a commitment which is now repressed, unconscious, and inaccessible to our conscious self. It is who we are, and changing that is very difficult. Role-training theories, social-learning theories, situational theories, cannot explain this tenacity as well. They suggest that gender and sexuality are added onto something else, to our "real" selves, and that they can presumably be dropped at will. They also suggest that changing the social setting and nature of reinforcement should automatically change behavior, which we know from experience is not true. (This is not to say that change is impossible. Psychoanalysis also argues for the replacement of unconscious determination by conscious choice: "where id was, there shall ego be." It is only to say that change is more, and often much more, than a matter of will, and that – as we know from contemporary politics – people's feelings about changes in the organization of sex and gender run very deep.) We need a theory which includes unconscious mental factors to understand what we observe about gender psychology and behavior.

Second, role-learning theories and theories of situational reinforcement in fact make people (women in this case) into passive reactors to society. Where can the initiative for change come from in a theory where people only react? Psychoanalysis, by contrast, is a theory founded on people's creativity. People always make something of their situation, even if that something is neurotic. (Neurosis, as we know from Freud's case studies, is highly original and individual.) People appropriate, fantasize, transform, react against, repress, resist, and symbolize their experiences. They create their inner object world and self. The goal of psychoanalysis is to make this individually created unconscious conscious, to move beyond being powered or directed by these active, though not always desirable to the individual, fantasies. Psychoanalysis, then, is a theory of human nature with positive, liberatory implications, a theory of people as active and creative.

Let us turn now to the third feminist objection, that Freud was sexist, and that psychoanalytic theory and practice have been oppressive to women. A few words will have to suffice on this very complex topic.[13] First, we have to acknowledge that this criticism is not entirely wrong; Freud was indeed sexist. He wrote basically from a male norm and ignored women. He repeated cultural ideology in a context where it can be mistaken for scientific findings. He talks, for instance, about women's lesser sense of justice, of their jealousy, shame, vanity, and lack of contribution to civilization as if these were clinical findings, but then claims that these are "character-traits which critics [masculine critics, we may assume] of every epoch have brought up against women."[14] He finds it perfectly natural that girls would find their own genitals inferior, talks of these girls' "genital deficiency" and the "fact [note, not the fantasy] of her being castrated."[15] He recognizes the costs to women of female development, as I mentioned, but he is quite cavalier about it and does not care much. It seems that "Nature" has taken less care of the feminine function than the masculine, but this does not really matter, since the "accomplishment of the aim of biology [i.e., procreation] has been entrusted to man's aggressiveness and left to some extent independent of women's consent."[16] And so forth. Moreover, the evidence seems clear that psychoanalytic theory has been used against women, for instance, when they were labelled frigid because they did not have what turned out to be a non-existent vaginal orgasm, when they were called masculine for wanting careers.

But there is a method to Freud's misogyny, and this method can be used against him.[17] Freud goes wrong, it turns out, when he undercuts his own psychoanalytic methodology and findings. I will give a few examples here. I suggest, however, that this lack of methodological consistency is very widespread.

First, as we have seen, psychoanalysis is founded on Freud's discoveries that there is nothing inevitable about the development of sexual object choice, mode, or aim, and that all sexuality is qualitatively continuous. Freud argues explicitly in the *Three Essays on Sexuality* and the *Introductory Lectures* that nothing inherently distinguishes procreative sex from any other sex. But Freud implicitly has a functionalist, teleological theory that gender differentiation is for the purposes of procreation. And he defines procreative sexuality in a particular way: Procreation is a product of active, genital masculine heterosexuality and passive, genital feminine heterosexuality.[18] The theory becomes coercive, as Freud talks of Oedipal "tasks," and claims that "anatomy is destiny," in a functionalist sense rather than a maturational sense. These tasks, and this destiny, are not at all inevitable biologically, but they "must" happen for nature's requirements to be met.

But, this functionalism is not inherent to psychoanalysis; it comes in as

Freud's value system. Similarly, women's passivity is not biologically inevitable, or even necessary to procreation. It is only necessary to male dominant sex, which Freud also takes for granted.[19]

Secondly, in psychoanalytic theory, traumas need explaining: Psychoanalysis always looks for the history of something conflictual and powerful in previous individual history, except in the case of penis envy. Penis envy is self-evident, and not in need of any explanation: "she sees one and she knows she wants one." If we employ psychoanalytic methodology and look to the history of this powerful conflict, we can learn a lot about the origins of penis envy. We can learn about the pre-Oedipal girl's relation to her mother and early development; about her desire for autonomy and for something that can symbolize that autonomy; about symbols of male supremacy in the culture and in her family.

In addition to the male genitals being self-evidently better than female genitals, penis envy is "necessary" to the creation of female passivity. This is another reason why Freud does not take it as problematic or in need of explanation. In Freud's theory, girls come to want babies as a substitute for the penis (the penis–baby equation). But Freud also admits that girls already may want babies as part of their identification with their mother. This won't do for Freud, however, who has to get the girl's passive heterosexuality and a man into the baby picture. So, he claims, wanting a baby as identification with mother is "not an expression of femininity"! Only when the baby becomes a baby from the father as a substitute for a penis is it a feminine wish. Penis envy here becomes a developmental task, not inevitable or biologically determined but necessary for a girl to achieve her "destiny."

A third example of Freud's undercutting his own methodology is his claim that "woman is made, not born." The little girl is originally a "little man," because she loves her mother with an active sexuality. Both sexes are originally masculine. But there is a peculiar asymmetry in the developmental account here. Either, it would seem, you need to take a biological determinist view, in which case both women and men are born, or a developmental/cultural view, in which case both women and men are made. But if the little girl is a little man, then, seemingly, man is born but woman is made.

I could go on. The point is that unless one thinks that Freud took an extreme "biology of the sexes" position, and he did not (although many psychoanalysts do), his anti-woman statements are not intrinsic to psychoanalytic theory and modes of theorizing or to clinical interpretation, but counter to them. This is why there has been, and has needed to be, such extensive feminist critique and revision of Freud. But because the theory is so useful, this critique and revision have often been rich and provocative.

Answering the Freudian: Why Psychoanalysis and Feminism are Intrinsically Linked

I now turn briefly to address the questions of the Freudian who wonders what feminism has to do with Freud, who thinks and argues that feminism has nothing to do with Freud. We can use our insights from the previous discussion to address these questions. The first question, or objection, argued that psychoanalysis is only a psychological theory. Clinical practice, interested in psychic structure, mental processes, and the development of sexuality, has nothing to do with politics, equality, or inequality.

My argument for why feminists must incorporate an understanding of Freud into their theory and practice should make the response here obvious. First, Freud made gender and sexuality central to his theory. Psychoanalysis is first and foremost a theory of femininity and masculinity, a theory of gender inequality, and a theory of the development of heterosexuality. Freud did not develop just any theory or clinical practice, but this specific one. Moreover, psychoanalysis makes a feminist argument that women (and men) are made and not born, that biology is not enough to explain sexual orientation or gender personality.

Just as we cannot have a theory of the social organization of gender and sexuality apart from a psychological theory, so we cannot have a psychological theory of sex and gender apart from the social and political. Freud's theory is a social and political theory. The analysis of development that Freud puts forth is not the analysis of any development, but of development in a particular social situation which is intrinsic to the theory. That children develop in a family where women mother or perform primary parenting functions explains the development that Freud found; biology does not explain this development. Psychoanalysis shows that women and men and male dominance are reproduced in each generation as a result of a social division of labor in which women mother (recall the account of men's psychology and ideology of male superiority, of the nature of women's heterosexuality and connections to women and children, of women's self-valuation, of the development of attitudes toward women). That people develop in a society with a heterosexual norm and with parents who are heterosexual is also intrinsic to Freud's theory and explains development, whereas biology does not (otherwise, why should a girl turn from the mother whom she loves? Why should the mother experience her son and daughter differently and treat them differently? Why should father–daughter attraction develop?).

Further, Freud's theory assumes, and is founded on, "politics" in a wide sense. The inequality of child and adult, the child's powerlessness, is central to the explanation of character and neurosis development and of the formation of defenses. The inequality of women and men is central to the theory. Freud does not give us a theory which explains what is necessary for species survival or the survival of any society. He constructs his theory around what is necessary for the perpetuation of a male dominant social organization, for the restriction of women's sexuality to be oriented to men's, for the perpetuation of heterosexual dominance.

What about the second psychoanalytic objection, that psychoanalysis is a value-free science with no axe to grind, that psychoanalysis doesn't take sides about anything, whereas feminism is value-laden and by definition takes sides. I would give two kinds of answers to this objection. Most generally, I would say, psychoanalysis is not a behavioral or medical science; it cannot be, and should not be, a value-free positivistic description and explanation of behavior. Rather, it is an interpretive theory of mental processes, and with an interpretive theory, we can only say that an interpretation makes better or worse sense, not that it is true or false, right or wrong. Similarly, psychoanalysis is not founded on the objective description of someone out there about someone studied. It comes out of the transference situation, a mutually created interpersonal situation which in its turn reflexively informs the processes of free association, interpretation, and the further working through of the transference. "Observer" and "observed" together create psychoanalytic theory and clinical practice, through their interaction and the interpretation of that interaction.

On a completely different track, but in answer to the same objection, it must be pointed out that Freud himself made the "mistake" of constantly intertwining ideological positions with clinical interpretation and theory. Freud made an insistence on inequality central. There is nothing, for instance, inherently valuational in saying that women and men have differently formed superegos, or different modes of object-choice, or differently formed body images. But Freud insisted on introducing value and judgment, in arguing that men's mode of superego development and function, that men's mode of object choice, that men's body image, were better and more desirable.

Finally, we must recognize that Freud did not content himself with simply making *ad hominem* claims about women. He actively threw down the political gauntlet at feminists, in ways which make unclear whether it was he himself or feminists who first chose to make psychoanalysis a center of ideological struggle. In "The dissolution of the Oedipus complex," published in 1924, he claims that "the feminist demand for equal rights for the sexes does not take us far."[20] In 1925, in "Some psychical consequences of the anatomical distinction between the sexes," he argues that "we must not allow ourselves to be deflected from [conclusions about women's lesser sense of justice, their vanity, envy, etc.] by the denials of the feminists, who are anxious to force us to regard the two sexes as completely equal in position and worth."[21] When such criticism begins to creep into the psychoanalytic ranks themselves, and women psychoanalysts begin to object to his characterizations of women and claim that it may be biased, he responds with a more subtle anti-woman put-down: women psychoanalysts were not afflicted with the negative characteristics of femininity but were special and unlike other women. As he puts it in his lecture on femininity: "This doesn't apply to *you*. You're the exception; on this point you're more masculine than feminine."[22]

Conclusions

Let me try to bring my original query together, a query about the relation of femininity, feminism, and Freud. We started with the justifiable anger of past feminists. Freud does give us a prime example of an *ad hominem*, distorted ideology about women and women's inferiority, an ideology which feminists must confront, challenge, and transform.

But, more importantly, Freudian theory does not just oppress women. Rather, Freud gives us a theory concerning how people – women and men – become gendered and sexed, how femininity and masculinity develop, how sexual inequality is reproduced. With the exception of anthropological kinship theorists like Malinowski, Fortes, Lévi-Strauss, Schneider, and others, no major classical social theorist has made sex and gender central to his theory. In telling us how we come to organize sexuality, gender, procreation, parenting, according to psychological patterns, Freud tells us how nature becomes culture and how this culture comes to appear as and to be experienced as "second nature" – appears as natural. Psychoanalytic theory helps to demonstrate how sexual inequality and the social organization of gender are reproduced. It demonstrates that this reproduction happens in central ways via transformations in consciousness in the psyche, and not only via social and cultural institutions. It demonstrates that this reproduction is an unintended product of the structure of the sex–gender system itself – of a family division of labor in which women mother, of a sexual system founded on heterosexual norm, of a culture that assumes and transmits sexual inequality. Freud, or psychoanalysis, tells us how people become heterosexual in their family development (how the originally matrisexual girl comes to be heterosexual rather than lesbian); how a family structure in which women mother produces in men (and in women, to some extent) a psychology and ideology of male dominance, masculine superiority, and the devaluation of women and things feminine; how women develop maternal capacities through their relationship to their own mother. Thus, psychoanalysis demonstrates the internal mechanisms of the socio-cultural organization of gender and sexuality and confirms the early feminist argument that the "personal is political." It argues for the rootedness and basic-ness of psychological forms of inequality and oppression.

But psychoanalysis does not stop at this demonstration. Freud suggests that these processes do not happen so smoothly, that this reproduction of gender and sexuality is rife with contradictions and strains. People develop conflicting desires, discontents, neuroses. Psychoanalysis begins from psychic conflict; this is what Freud was first trying to explain. Thus, heterosexuality is not constituted smoothly for all time: Women still want relationships and closeness to women, and male heterosexuality is embedded in Oedipal devaluation, fear and contempt of women as well as a fear of the overwhelmingness of mother and of acknowledging emotional demands and needs. Male dominance on a psychological level is a masculine defense and a major psychic cost to men, built on fears and insecurity; it is not straightforward power. Psychoanalysis demonstrates, against theories of over-socialization and total domination, a lack of total socialization. It demonstrates discontent, resistance, and an undercutting of sexual modes and the institutions of sexual inequality.

Psychoanalysis is also a theory that people actively appropriate and respond to their life environment and experiences, make something of these psychologically, and, therefore, presumably can act to change them.

9

Psychoanalytic Feminism and the Psychoanalytic Psychology of Women

There is, in the current period, a striking lack of theoretical or empirical consensus among people who write and think about psychoanalysis and women.[1] On the one side, among psychoanalysts, debate that exhibits a range of positions and interests about women and femininity has become a topic of burgeoning concern in recent years. On the other side, psychoanalytic feminists – academic feminist literary critics, philosophers, social scientists, and epistemologists – engage in a distinctly different set of discourses, about different questions.[2] Different discussions are going on, with rare mutual recognition, among different sets of people.

Briefly, psychoanalytic feminists begin, somewhat in the manner of the Freud of *Studies on Hysteria, Three Essays on Sexuality*, and " 'Civilized' sexual morality and modern nervousness," from a critical and evaluative theoretical position. We take gender and sexuality as we typically know these to be socially, culturally, and psychologically problematic and wish to understand how this gender and sexuality develop and are reproduced in the individual and thereby in society. Psychoanalysts begin, somewhat in the manner of the Freud who asks "how [a woman] comes into being,"[3] from a query about how gender and sexuality develop and are played out in life, and how, in individual cases, these do not follow the route prescribed or described as normal. Their evaluative stance tends to assume a bifurcation of masculinity and femininity in more or less traditional cultural terms and a heterosexuality with partners in complementary but different roles and sexual stances. A small but growing number of feminist psychoanalysts – practicing psychoanalysts who identify themselves explicitly as feminists – borrows from and elaborates clinically upon the theoretical contributions of some psychoanalytic feminist theory, and a few psychoanalytic feminists make efforts to follow the changing psychology of women in the psychoanalytic literature.

We are compellingly reminded of the professional and intellectual separation of worlds. For the most part, psychoanalysts do not seem to be aware of or to care much about the enormous exciting ferment in psychoanalytic feminist theory that is in the forefront of a number of academic disciplines. They tend to identify themselves as scientists, practitioners of a scientific psychology or branch of psychiatry, for whom empirical reality and direct clinical application have definite primacy, if not exclusive claim to document truth. They are more likely to think that science can be value-free and have tended to see feminism as a political or politicized practice rather than as a theory that is relevant to their own theory or practice.[4] Reciprocally, psychoanalytic feminists often seem to go about their work paying little attention to the claims of those who by profession, as clinicians and researchers, would seem to have a strong right to decide among, or at least be consulted in decisions about, psychoanalytic claims. Psychoanalytic feminist literary critics, philosophers, and epistemologists, who work more exclusively from text, "story" or theoretical argument, and who often adhere to a postmodernist skepticism about truth, in particular often feel that evidential claims need not affect their assessments about persuasive arguments. We are faced with creating an account when one group claims scientific data as proof but debates what the "correct" data is, while others rely on interpretive strategies about data, on theoretical or narrative coherence or plausibility, on accord with experience, on interpretive relevance to other texts, or on congruence with socio-political analysis.

I have found these questions to be particularly vexing and problematic. My discomfort here could be taken to rest on individual biography and identity: I am a social scientist who writes in the field of object-relations psychoanalytic feminism and practices as a clinician. Questions about the varieties of psychoanalytic theories of gender seem particularly problematic for social scientists, who stand epistemologically between the empiricist scientism of psychoanalysts and the interpretive relativism of humanists, as we privilege both empirical "reality" and theory, draw upon a variety of interpretive and explanatory strategies, and tend to grant that there is no such thing as value-free science. I would argue, however, that it is generally necessary for psychoanalytic feminists, who claim to draw upon psychoanalysis, to come to terms with what psychoanalysts say gender is about, even if and as we want to say something different. By complement, since psychoanalysis is a deeply embedded cultural discourse and not just a therapeutic practice or value-free science, psychoanalysts would do well to consider seriously the debates and claims of psychoanalytic feminism.

Psychoanalytic Theories of Women and Gender

All modern developments, both psychoanalytic and feminist, are in dialogue with the traditional Freudian theory of the development of femininity. Three features of this view are relevant here. First, sex difference doesn't matter until the phallic phase, around age four, at which stage "the little girl is a little man" with a masculine sexuality.[5] Second, for both sexes sexual knowledge until puberty is monistic: sexual difference is presence or absence of the penis, and the vagina (for classical psychoanalysts, *the* female sexual organ) is unknown, both consciously and unconsciously. Third, the development of heterosexuality and maternality in the girl are a secondary product of her sense of failed masculinity.

The classical view, followed by some modern theorists, speaks not so much of gender as of sex and sexuality. Freud and his colleagues were concerned with the nature and meaning of erotic experience as this is mediated through body zones and organs, and with sexual object choice. Insofar as we can infer from this account, conceptions of gender identity (how we cognize and what we make of our own gender; our sense of feminine or masculine self) and gender personality (males' and females' character, psychic structure, and psychological processes) are in the first instance tied to apprehension of genital constitution: Does a boy give up his mother (or his father, in case he is tempted into a passive sexual position *vis-à-vis* this father) in exchange for his penis? Does a girl accept her "castration" or protest against it? Does she go through life seeking a penis? The creation of sexual orientation, the desire for parenthood, masculine and feminine identifications with the same-sex parent, all result from what the child does with her or his sense of genital difference.

There was, of course, a major dissident position on female sexuality from almost as early as Freud discussed it, but active debate about the nature of femininity nevertheless disappeared for some time. The topic was kept alive indirectly through clinical case discussion, but rarely in ways that maintained or constructed any fundamental challenge to the theory. In the last fifteen years or so, however, theoretical, clinical, and empirical discussion has emerged into active reformulation and debate. As I read the literature, contemporary psychoanalytic debate centers on three issues, two developmental and one clinical.[6]

First, attention has been focused especially on the question of genital awareness, when and how it develops, and what its impact is on gender identity, gender personality, and the sense of self. Specifically, psychoanalysts now claim, against Freud's view that sex difference doesn't matter until the phallic phase, that genital awareness develops in the second year, in what would have formerly been called the pre-genital period.

There are two positions within this view. Galenson and Roiphe follow Freud, in that they understand early genital awareness as an awareness of sexual difference, and difference in the traditional sense: Presence or absence of the penis is what matters.[7] They claim that the one-year-old girl's response to her discovered castration is the organizing influence, both inhibiting and enhancing, from this time onward, not just on psychosexual development, sexuality, and the girl's turn to her father, but on ego and object-relational development as well.

Other recent psychoanalytic accounts agree with Galenson and Roiphe's claim for early genital schematization, but they provide different views of what this schematization is and its role in the formation of gender identity and gender personality. In one way or another, these formulations all challenge Freud's view that the little girl is a little man with a "phallic" (active, clitoral) sexuality who doesn't know her own feminine organs consciously or unconsciously. They rely on a notion of primary femininity, arguing that in both boys and girls a primary genital awareness, involving a primary cathexis of their own genital organs, precedes the observation or schematization of genital difference. Such awareness proceeds directly out of body experience, though for different writers it can be more or less affected by parental labelling and treatment.

I include several people in this group. Chasseguet-Smirgel argues along with Horney that sexual monism in either sex does not result from lack of knowledge but from repression or a splitting of the ego. For her, the Freudian picture of the woman who lacks vagina, penis, an adequate erotic object, or any intrinsic feminine qualities she could enjoy is *"exactly the opposite of the primal maternal imago* as it is revealed in the clinical material of both sexes."[8] Kestenberg not only argues for knowledge of the vagina but also develops a positive conception of its role, or the role of inner-genital experience and an inner-genital phase preceding the phallic phase (which Kestenberg might prefer to call the outer- or external-genital phase) in the libidinal development of both sexes. Her conception paves the way for what we might call a libidinally based feminine developmental line, drawing us from a conception of femininity solely in terms of passive vaginal heterosexuality in relation to men to one that stresses maternality as well.[9] Kleeman, Lerner, and others point to the role of vague and inaccurate parental labelling of the external female genitalia – vulva and clitoris, often generically called vagina – in hindering schematization of that part of her genitals which a girl can most directly see and touch.[10] Mayer suggests that the mental representations defining a sense of femaleness for a girl begin not with vaginal awareness but with conceptions of the vulva, leading girls to experience their genitals as having an opening and potential inside space. Women's valuation of this genital openness may be observed in derivative symbolic form, as they value emotional openness, access to inner feelings, empathetic capacities, and receptivity. Castration anxiety in this context involves the fear of being closed over both genitally and emotionally. Women's characterizations of men as emotionally closed and unable to be receptive or aware of inner feeling are a symbolic reflection of a more basic genital fear.[11]

A second strand of recent psychoanalytic theories of feminine (and masculine) development focusses not so much on genital awareness as on gender identity, enlarging on the argument developed by Money and Ehrhardt and others that cognitive labelling of gender, or core gender identity – the sense of femaleness and maleness – develops in the first few years of life. As with the issue of genital awareness, we can find two positions on the question of gender identity. The first and dominant position – like Freud's implicit view that gender identity is a matter of sexual orientation and genital constitution – hinges gender identity, even if it is cognitively developed and not necessarily based on invidious comparison of the girl's with the boy's genitals, on genital awareness.[12] Tyson, for instance, claims that the boy's first task in the establishment of his core gender identity is the discovery of his penis and its integration into his body image and that his first step in gender role assumption is upright urination in identification with his father. She discusses body experience and body representation as central to the establishment of the girl's core feminine gender identity as well.

An alternate account of the development of gender identity is found in the work of Kleeman and Stoller, who hinge gender identity on cognitive and interpersonal factors and make genital experience distinctly derivative.[13] Kleeman argues that although genital experience and self-stimulation occur in the young child, such behavior is no more important than object relations, self-development, cognitive development, and other aspects of behavior. Against Freud's early claims, Stoller argues that the sense of femaleness is more easily attained than the sense of maleness, and that male gender identity development runs a continual risk of being undermined by a primary feminine identification that emerges from a close tie to the mother. Thus, against the psychoanalytic mainstream, these theorists accord much more weight to interpersonal psychodynamics in gender development than to genital awareness and genital difference. For them, core gender identity is a composite result of biological forces, sex assignment, and parental labelling at birth and in the early years, parental attitudes about that sex, family psychodynamics, and the infant's interpretation of these experiences. The Stoller–Kleeman position has been influential in establishing gender identity as a feature of cognitive self-concept that is not the same as sexual orientation and in stressing the importance of labelling and object relations in the creation of gender identity and genital experience.[14]

To review, with the exception of the Stoller–Kleeman account, modern psychoanalytic developmental interest in female psychology has centered on female sexuality, defined as what girls make of their own genitals and genital difference. In a sense, this modern attempt to deal with the empirically incorrect (as well as sexist) early Freudian theory of primary masculinity turns further toward an essentialist view of gender identity and gender role. Whereas classical psychoanalytic theory begins from a more generically conceived sexuality and mobile unconscious drives that in turn create genital experience (and character), in contemporary theories of gender, direct genital awareness and experience become primary determinants, and sexuality (as well as object relations and character) becomes more derivative.

The third central area of contemporary psychoanalytic debate is clinical rather than developmental, and it concerns cross-gender transference. Much of the early discussion of psychoanalytic technique and process derived from cases of women hysterics treated by male analysts, and Freud pointed out that women analysts had made fundamental discoveries about the psychology of women as a result of the specific transferences they experienced from women patients.[15] Recently, psychoanalysts have become concerned with the nature of the transference that men patients develop toward women analysts, and some have argued that men do not develop an erotic or a paternal transference to their female analysts.[16] Moreover, they have not seen these "findings" as differences. Rather, they imply that an analysis is not complete without an erotic or paternal transference.

Responses to these claims have taken several forms (forms that incidentally move us toward psychoanalytic feminism). The simplest challenge is empirical, providing clinical evidence of male patients who have developed such transferences.[17] A more sophisticated version of the empirical claim holds that analysts of either gender are more likely to recognize certain transferences than others because they are more culturally and psychologically consonant, and that we must recognize and analyse latent as well as manifest transferences in different gendered pairs.[18] Thus, men may be less likely to recognize a maternal transference whereas they easily recognize an erotic transference from a younger woman, and women may not as easily recognize an erotic transference from a younger man. A different kind of argument, suggested by Person, takes issue with the evaluative schema itself.[19] The issue is not whether we can find some men who develop a manifest or latent erotic transference to their women analysts, but why many men, or most men – men who, according to psychoanalytic views, act out sexually more than women, are more likely to engage in various perversions, and so forth – can't become, or must deny becoming, erotically attracted to women in the analytic situation.

Psychoanalytic Feminism

As with psychoanalytic writings on gender and women, any division of psychoanalytic feminism is partly arbitrary. Three self-identified approaches stand out, and I think we can see large commonalities between the first two in comparison to the third. Here, I distinguish an object-relations and interpersonal psychoanalytic feminism from a Lacanian psychoanalytic feminism.[20]

Following for the most part British object-relations theory, object-relations feminists put self–other relations and the development of a self (whether whole or fragmented, agentic or reactive) as it is constituted through its consciously and unconsciously experienced relations in the center of development. The object-relations school has itself hardly dealt with gender difference or the development of gender, but we argue that their approach can be drawn upon in such a venture.[21] The outlines of the object-relations perspective on feminine development and personality can be summarized from my own writing.[22] I have argued that, as a result of being parented primarily by a woman, men and women develop differently constructed selves and different experiences of their gender and gender identity. Through their early relationship with their mother, women develop a sense of self continuous with others and a richly constructed, bisexual, Oedipal-oscillating-with-pre-Oedipal inner self–object world that continuously engages unconscious and conscious activity: "The basic feminine sense of self is connected to the world."[23] This psychic structure and self–other process in turn help to reproduce mothering: "Because women themselves are mothered by women, they grow up with the relational capacities and needs, and psychological definition of self-in-relationship, which commits them to mothering."[24]

Men develop by contrast a self based more on denial of relation and connection and on a more fixed and firmly split and repressed inner self–object world: "the basic masculine sense of self is separate."[25] The object-relations view argues that as a result of being parented primarily by a woman, masculinity develops a more reactive and defensive quality than femininity in women. Dinnerstein and I point to the mother blame, misogyny, and fear of women and femininity that develops in both sexes, but especially in men, in reaction to the powerfully experienced mother (and internal mother-image), and we suggest that this fuels male dominance in culture and society and creates systematic tensions and conflicts in heterosexual relationships.[26]

Writers in the object-relations tradition like Benjamin, Flax, and Fox Keller have described how this arelational masculinity, based on a need to dominate and deny women, the feminine, and human and natural interconnectedness has become institutionalized in notions of scientific objectivity and the technical rationality of advanced capitalism (in reality defensive institutionalizations of a rigid separateness needed by the masculine psyche and built on a latent structure of anger and the repudiation of women), in individualistic political and social theories that assume the inevitability of hierarchy and the need to create society out of asocial individuals, and in practices of erotic, scientific, and technical domination.[27] Feminist literary critics, represented by Elizabeth Abel, Janet Adelman, Marianne Hirsch, Coppelia Kahn, and others, draw from an object-relations perspective to investigate woman's voice, the mother-image, inner worlds and qualities of relatedness in women writers, and male writers' unconscious attitudes to mothers and feminine power.[28]

Thus the object-relations perspective takes the construction of masculinity and femininity to be interconnected and constitutes a critique of masculinity as well as a reformulation of our understanding of the female self. It stands the traditional Freudian understanding on its head, as it to some extent revalorizes women's construction of self and makes normal masculinity extremely problematic. Feminist object-relations theorists have also argued strongly for theoretical and developmental treatment of the mother as a subject, against psychoanalytic (including object-relational) tendencies to treat her as an object whose role is evaluated in terms of the presumed needs and fantasies of the child alone.[29] This leads to a reformulation of the psychoanalytic self as well, as it emphasizes not only that separateness, not connectedness, needs explaining, but that intersubjectivity and the mutual recognition of the other and the self are fundamental to satisfactory development.

The interpersonal (or cultural, or "Neo-Freudian") group has created an account of female psychology for our purposes similar to the object-relations perspective. Baker Miller, a Sullivanian analyst, enunciated the main features of the cultural psychoanalytic perspective, and the group also draws on the theories of Gilligan.[30] Miller argues that women are repositories of qualities of affiliativeness, relatedness, empathy, and nurturance – qualities that object-relations feminism also describes – that are devalued and distorted in male dominant culture and by men. She wants women to reclaim and revalorize these qualities. Much of the writing of the interpersonal group is based on clinical cases, and in these case descriptions, women's problems are seen to inhere mainly in the denial and devaluation of affiliative qualities both by others and by themselves. Cure consists in women's recognizing and accepting these qualities, in being caring and empathetic toward themselves. A second, less prominent strand in the cultural perspective focusses on problems women have in asserting anger and aggression, both of which have been repressed and denied by our male dominant culture. Clinical work should also focus in this area.[31]

Miller's original work attributed the developmental origins of the feminine qualities she described in a general way to cultural learning, and the group continues to attribute women's qualities to cultural prescription and suppression. In the recent work of the group, however, the implicit and articulated view seems to follow the object-relations perspective as well, emphasizing the influence of the mother–daughter relationship on the development of what they now call the "self-in-relation."[32]

This general feminist perspective is definitely bifurcated. As psycho-analytic theorists, object-relations feminists pay more attention to the complexities of the inner object world, to internalizations, to unconscious defenses and conflicts, and to the unconscious structuring of self. Interpersonal theorists tend not to emphasize unconscious dynamics as much but to pay more attention to cultural and personal evaluation of different qualities and capacities. Object-relations feminists, whose roots are in critical social theory as much as in psychoanalysis, tend to see the psychology of men and women as an intertwined conflictual whole, as part of a totality of social and psychological relations. Cultural school feminists do not discuss the psychology of masculinity except by comparative implication and seem to operate more in the context of an empirical psychology of sex differences and a separate spheres feminism.

Object-relations theorists focus more on the problems that, along with strengths, inhere in women's psychological qualities, and we are more likely to focus on male development as a problem. Although we may also valorize women's qualities, both our social analysis and our greater attention to unconscious conflict lead object-relations theorists to hold a more tempered and critical view of these qualities. I argue, for example, that women's relational self can be both a strength or a pitfall in feminine psychic life, as it enables empathy, nurturance, and intimacy but can also threaten lack of autonomy and dissolution of self into others. Women's mothering itself shares this ambivalent position, as it often generates pleasure and fulfillment and at the same time is fundamentally related to women's secondary position in society and to the fear of women in men. Flax stresses the difficulties women can have in recognizing differences with other women and argues that women's empathetic, different-voiced, relational self rests on the repression of selves bound up with autonomy, aggression, intellectual and interpersonal mastery, and active sexual desire. Benjamin describes women's tendency to seek separateness and recognition through a love for the father that becomes masochistically tinged.[33] By contrast, recent interpersonal writing seems to see women's relationality more exclusively in positive terms.

But these views have several features in common. Although we (especially the object-relations group) focus, like contemporary psycho-analysts, on the early infantile and pre-Oedipal period as crucial to gender development and therefore on the crucial importance of the relation to the mother, we emphatically and by definition do not understand genital apperception and genital difference to be causal and central in gender identity and gender personality. We focus on the experience of self with other and how that comes to be organized and appropriated. When feminine development and sexuality are seen as problematic, such problems are seen to inhere centrally and originally in relational and self issues – conflict in the mother, devaluation by the father, experiences of lack of fit, inadequately resolved Narcissistic development and development of agency and wholeness – or in problems of cultural valuation. These are not built upon a more primary conflicted genital schematization or problematic genital awareness (though they may be played out partly around such issues).

The object-relations–interpersonal perspective separates gender identity and gender personality. Qualities of self or self-in-relation (and denial of relation is equally important here) become more important than unconsciously or consciously experienced gender identity and cognition and assessment of gender difference. It is not because she knows she is female that a girl or woman experiences her self in relationship (though by contrast, a boy's or man's denial of relationality may very well be a product of his sense of appropriate masculinity). Her self in relation is a developmental product, tied to her mother's sense of self, but not only to gender identity or gender-role learning. The object-relations–cultural perspective does not ignore conscious gender identity and the construction of gender or unconscious meanings of these, but it claims that this is not all there is to gender, and it embeds these in object-relations or cultural sense of self. Because of this focus on qualities of self, the object-relations perspective in particular moves radically away from essentialist views of gender toward a view that constructs feminine and masculine personality and male dominance in a contingent, relationally constructed context.

Lacanian feminism, the second branch of psychoanalytic feminism, like the first, reacts to the original psychoanalytic theory, but it also reacts to the object-relations position.[34] Lacanian feminists argue that Freud's account of how we become sexed shows how our very sexualization is asymmetrical and unequal. In the Lacanian view, the unconscious (as opposed to the ego or internalized object relations) is the fundament of psychic life, and this linguistically constructed and structured unconscious *is* our sexuality: Subjectivity emerges out of unconscious sexual drives. This sexualization and subjectivity are by definition constituted in terms of the difference, or opposition, between the sexes, an opposition that is structured linguistically and not biologically. We are also born into this sexual/linguistic setting; it precedes us and makes inevitable our developmental situation.

A person takes their place in the world as a subject only through entry into the "symbolic," into language and culture. This acquisition of subjectivity takes place through the intervention of a third person, or term, into the "imaginary" mother–child dyad, which is conceived to lie conceptually and emotionally outside of language and culture. The father, symbolized by his phallus (which in turn symbolizes the prohibition of desire for the mother and the threat of castration) institutes and constitutes this symbolic intervention. The phallus thus stands for entrance into the symbolic. In this view, then, subjectivity is sexuality, and sexuality is defined exclusively in terms of sexual difference, in terms of the presence or absence of the phallus. Sexuality and subjectivity, rooted in the unconscious, are precarious for both sexes, as they hinge on resolution of the castration complex.

In contrast to recent psychoanalytic views, in the Lacanian view there can be no primary genital awareness that is not tied to the awareness and cognizing of genital difference, which, in turn, is located and mediated in language. Nor can there be pre-Oedipal knowledge of genital difference, since such knowledge is by definition tied to the Oedipal transition and the castration complex. In contrast to object-relations feminism, there can be no subjectivity apart from schematized sexual identity: gender difference is all there is when it comes to our selfhood or subjectivity, and gender difference is experienced and cognized (through our placement in language) in terms of sexuality and genital schematization. Subjectivity and sexuality are interdependent; neither can develop without the other.

One reading of Lacan holds that the resolution of the castration complex differs for men and women and thereby institutes (and documents) sexual difference. Sexual constitution and subjectivity is different for he who possesses the phallus and she who does not. As the phallus comes to stand for itself in the theory of desire, and not even to stand in relation to the mother's desire, the woman becomes not a subject in her own right – even one who can never have the phallus – but simply a symbol or a symptom in the masculine psyche.

Another reading, and some Lacanian feminists argue that the sexually critical and liberatory potential of Lacan lies here, is that although one sex has an anatomical penis, neither sex, finally, can possess the phallus. Sexuality is incomplete and fractured for both sexes. Moreover, as men and women must line themselves up on one or another side of the linguistic/sexual divide, they need not do so on the side isomorphic with their anatomy.

Lacanian feminism makes radical psychoanalytic and feminist claims. It argues that there are no other aspects to gender division, identity, or personality than sexuality and symbolized genital difference and that there is no subjectivity outside of sexuality: any speaking being must locate him or herself in relation to the phallus. Such a theory locates every action firmly in an unequal sexual world and never loses sight of our developmentally inevitable placement in a phallocentric culture. It speaks to women's lack of self and sense of being the Other, to her fundamental alienation from and objectification in culture.[35] On a more sociological plane, Lacanian-inspired theorists argue for the importance of the son's generational Oedipal change of object, as he goes from involvement with the powerful pre-Oedipal mother to a position of power in relation to women, and they point to the girl's accession to a passive heterosexuality, as men gain rights to her sexuality that she neither gains in theirs nor retains in her own.[36]

Lacanians bring up, against object-relations feminists and primary femininity theorists the point that, in focussing on the mother–daughter relationship, or on femininity defined not only in relation to masculinity, we fail to see the totality and all encompassing nature of these systematically unequal social and psychological relations.[37] They criticize views that idealize women's qualities or ignore women's situation in a male-dominant culture and language, arguing that there can be neither wholeness nor positive qualities for either men or women in such a culture. There can be no experiences not generated by male dominance nor can there be a femininity defined in itself. The critique of sexual difference here combines with Lacan's anti-humanistic account of the fragmented, necessarily alienated, subject.[38]

We are presented in the contemporary period, then, with three theories and three epistemological approaches to the question of psychoanalysis and gender. Psychoanalysts are interested in when genital awareness develops and whether boys and girls develop an awareness of their own genitals first or of the boy's only, whether they value their own genitals or only the boy's. They are interested in what gender identity means, and for the most part they tie this to questions of genital awareness. Object-relations and interpersonal feminists are concerned with questions of self as this is separate from but related to gender identity and have developed theories that contrast the female and male self. They argue that qualities that are traditionally considered desirable and normal – firm ego boundaries, an emphasis on autonomy, an independent morality and impersonal superego, objectivity, are male defenses against connections to others and deeply inherent in a male dominant society and culture. Whereas they may recognize that women need more access to autonomy, assertion, and an active sexuality, they also see women's relational qualities as desirable and more fully human than masculine autonomy. Lacanian feminists, by contrast, argue that such revaluation is wrong, that all people, but perhaps especially women, are stunted, perhaps inevitably, by a fractured subjectivity and sexuality imposed by placement in a phallocentric culture and language. Psychoanalysis cannot describe desirable qualities but is rather the best account we have of the iron cage of sexual inequality and male dominance.

What are the relations among these theories? Lacanians and French anti-Lacanians seem to have fundamental assumptions in common with the dominant psychoanalytic mainstream, locating gender difference in genital difference, but this is an accidental commonality. It encompasses the scope neither of psychoanalysis, with its complex developmental account of the emotional meanings of the genitals, nor of Lacanian theory, with its specifically linguistic account of the relationship of sexuality and subjectivity. For most classical analysts (as for object-relations feminists) there is a distinction between sexuality and subjectivity, and it makes a difference whether we have primarily a speaking subject, in which location in language predominates, or a sexual subject, in which sexual difference and the phallus predominate. It is not clear that anything genital or sexual as psychoanalysts think of this (or relational as object-relations theorists think of this) matters to Lacanians.

More important, the Lacanian argument is a logical argument about the structure of language and us as its speakers: As developing beings, we must break out of the dyadic mother–child relationship that does not understand itself to be constituted by an order beyond. There must be a third term to institute this break, and the father, symbolized by his phallus, is this third term. Evidence cannot oppose this logic, since it is a logic, and Lacanians even have a language for dismissing evidence: anything pre-given, natural, or "real" is repudiated by definition on the symbolic level. We can linguistically describe or experience nothing outside of the symbolic, which places us in that very phallic order against which we might want to find evidence.

In this context, claims for primary femininity must be inadequate, as are conceptions of gender that are not constituted as sexual difference. Evidential claims about a genital phase in the second year or about the early mother–child relationship cannot have impact on the account. Cognitive and developmental psychological research about language development or innate linguistic structures cannot impinge on the Lacanian claim that language only reacts to loss and that symbolization occurs only in the absence of an object. Against queries about whether the actual presence or absence of the father makes a difference, Lacanians claim that the father is a symbol, definitionally present in language; his actual presence is irrelevant.

Such views diametrically oppose those of most practicing analysts, certainly in this country and probably in many other countries as well. Psychoanalysts see their work as scientific, as a product of the steady development of clinical and observational evidence. "Discoveries" are made and "evidence" comes to light; theory is "confirmed" by clinical and research "findings." Psychoanalytic debates, certainly in the area of gender psychology, concern the nature and interpretation of evidence; they are rarely cast in the language of theoretical logic.[39] Thus, the psychoanalytic position, though apparently congruent with the Lacanian, fundamentally contrasts with it.

A different contrast holds between object-relations and interpersonal psychoanalytic feminism and psychoanalytic gender theory. Contemporary psychoanalysts certainly take object relations and the self seriously, but they have not applied these concerns to their approaches to gender, which still tend to be based in drive theory and genital experience.[40] Object-relations feminists make the development, structure, and experience of self and self–other relations into a primary phenomenon in our consideration of gender and not a secondary reaction to drive development or genital experience. They do not hinge gender personality on genital apperception or cognition, or even necessarily on gender identity, as do psychoanalysts. Here, the closing-off of debate is substantively theoretical rather than epistemological.

Overlap and commonality between object-relations feminism and psychoanalysis, as in the Lacanian case, are often accidental and not intentional. For instance, Kestenberg developed a theory of libidinal phase development that leads to maternality and the potential for nurturance in both sexes, just as object-relations feminists have developed a relational account of the same outcome. Both object-relations feminists and psychoanalysts have developed a version of a theory of primary femininity, but the former is rooted in mother–daughter identification and shared selfhood, and the latter is rooted in primary genital awareness. The object-relations developmental account concerning the role of fear of women, especially powerful women, in the development of masculinity seems to explain clinical findings about erotic transference in male patients of female analysts at least as well as and perhaps better than classic accounts about primary genital awareness or castration anxiety, but against "research" on genital awareness object-relations feminists can only claim that other things are psychologically more important.

Such a situation can lead to radically different interpretations of the same situation by people who both hold that clinical "evidence" matters.

For instance, consider a woman who has enormous performance anxiety and does much worse than she could in school and in testing situations.[41] A classical analyst might say that she unconsciously experiences success as gaining a penis, that this reminds her of the early narcissistic injury when she learned that she could never have one, and that she therefore develops inhibitions against success. Alternately, this fantasy of gaining (stealing) a penis induces Oedipal guilt or fear of punishment. An interpersonal psychoanalytic feminist might understand this same woman to symbolize success unconsciously as a denial of connection to other students and friends, in which case her refusal to succeed becomes an affirmation of her self in relationship and her desires for affiliation and connection to other women.

There are complex divisions between and within the two feminist positions. First, substantive disagreements exist concerning whether we should conceptualize psychological development in terms of object-relational and self experience or of linguistic placement in culture; whether we should conceptualize gender and male dominance in terms of consciously and unconsciously cognized sexual difference *per se* – in which case the genders can only exist and have meaning in relation one to the other – or in terms of qualities we can attribute to or feel as people of different genders; whether we should see sexuality as a product of relational development and its unconscious sequelae or as a lingustic location. Choices here hinge also on our developmental theories. In reaction to the nearly exclusive traditional psychoanalytic focus on the Oedipus complex and the central role of the father in creating gender and sexuality, object-relations feminists center attention on the role of the mother in both pre-Oedipal and Oedipal periods. Lacanians retain and even extend the traditional position, arguing against the psychological centrality of the pre-Oedipal and even Oedipal mother and making the Oedipal period and the relation to the father exclusively generative of sexuality and subjectivity.

Second, equally fundamental epistemological and evidential differences pose a Lacanian feminist analysis of language and logical argument against the claims of some object-relations and interpersonal feminists for empirical and clinical reality. Here things are more complicated, because academic object-relations feminists arrange themselves on a spectrum in relation to textual versus empirical truth. In an internal division mirroring what begins to emerge as a deep divide within academic feminism, object-relations literary critics often share the Lacanian feminist commitment to textual analysis and a postmodernist skepticism concerning empirical reality, whereas object-relations social critics, while in no way part of the positivist mainstream of their fields, still wish to argue on empirical and clinical as well as theoretical grounds.[42]

Even as we argue among ourselves, all psychoanalytic feminists unite in opposition to what we perceive as overly biological psychoanalytic interpretations and to psychoanalytic claims to a value-free "scientific" study of gender and gender difference, a study that notices only by happenstance and in the occasional case that there is something problematic in the construction and organization of gender. We also to varying extents and in different ways see masculine and feminine personality, development, and identity as interrelated, as part of a larger set of social, cultural, and psychological relations.

The various discourses, then, have different truth criteria and different definitional realities. Logic is relevant to Lacanians: sex difference inheres in a sexuality that is cognized, Oedipal, and defined *vis-à-vis* the phallus. Object-relations and interpersonal feminists criticize traditional psychoanalysts for focusing in an atomized way on genital possession rather than on relations of gender, self–other relations, and the establishment of self. At the same time, some feminists appeal to clinical and research evidence for their own theoretical claims against psychoanalysts, Lacanians, and if necessary other textual-theoretical psychoanalytic feminists. Psychoanalysts, by virtue of the professional separation of spheres not bound into the feminist debates, simply do their work, arguing only among themselves. Because the discourse that I am discussing is, after all, psychoanalytic, and they are psychoanalysts, they needn't care so much what the feminists think (except when they find them on the couch). But in terms of the larger culture and even of the broad range of modern psychotherapies, both of which currently challenge psychoanalytic dominance, psychoanalysts who ignore or pass over feminist debate run the risk, as in their theory and practice in general, of themselves in turn being bypassed and ignored.

Clearly, this chapter is a call for dialogue. On one side, psychoanalysis confronts a psychoanalytic feminism that has by and large considered only the psychoanalytic theory of women developed in the early years of psychoanalysis. Our problem as psychoanalytic feminists is the nature of our claim to appropriate psychoanalytic theory and findings and the grounds by which we choose what to accept and reject, both as theory and as clinical or empirical claim. Relying as we do on what we claim to be psychoanalysis, we cannot dismiss or ignore modern psychoanalytic work. In considering modern psychoanalytic claims, we must evaluate the extent to which female development is embedded in sexual difference and genital evaluation and experience: how does genital apprehension affect gender identity and sexuality? How central is it compared to other areas of experience, to cognitive labelling, cultural categories, object relations, the development of sense of self more generally? Even, we might ask, how important is gender identity, in the broadest sense, to women's sense of self?

Such a challenge has different meanings for different psychoanalytic feminists. Literary or philosophical critics, including most Lacanian feminists as well as some object-relations feminists, take psychoanalysis in whatever variety as a text or story. For them, evidence is less important and persuasiveness is measured in terms of consistency with a larger cultural story and resonance with other texts. By contrast, because we are more concerned, however interpretively, with how things empirically "are," object-relations and interpersonal feminists who are social scientists or practicing clinicians must engage directly with psychoanalytic evidence. In this latter context, the potential contribution of contemporary psychoanalysis to object-relations and interpersonal psychoanalytic feminism is great. Like the schools they draw upon, these theories are insightful about questions of self, other, and (both hetero and homo) emotional orientation, but they have downplayed sexuality. A reconsideration of recent psychoanalytic views of primary femininity and genital awareness – if we can situate these socially and interactively, and not as essentialist, automatic dichotomies – might help to reincorporate such a focus.

On the other side, psychoanalytic feminism makes important demands upon psychoanalysis and points to areas of potential expansion and revision. The gender of the analyst is a useful place to begin. As some psychoanalytic writers make clear, findings about male analysands and female analysts can only be understood in a socially and culturally, as well as psychologically, gendered context. In a setting where they are passive and dependent upon a woman or mother-figure in a position of power or authority, men's sexuality freezes or is denied. Both psychoanalytic and feminist object-relations developmental accounts have shown how male development involves denying and avoiding attachment to and dependence upon strong women, but psychoanalytic feminism in particular has stressed that the very definition of heterosexuality involves dominance and inequality, that the Oedipal transition for the boy involves a reversal of relative power as absolute as the girl's gendered change of object.

Object-relations and interpersonal psychoanalytic feminism also constitutes a basic challenge to and revision of classical psychoanalytic (and Lacanian feminist) developmental theory and theories of gender identity, as this feminism removes the centering of the gendered psyche from the body and drives toward a recentering in the self and self with other. In questioning the extent to which female development is embedded in sexual difference and genital evaluation, this view argues against the centrality of genital apprehension in comparison to other areas of experience like object relations and the development of sense of self. Psychoanalysts of course focus on object relations clinically, but this focus has not been central to theory in the case of gender. Such a refocussing is suggested by some of those who have written on perversion but not at all by those interested in normal sexual and gender development.[43]

Lacanian feminism makes another kind of challenge to both psycho-analytic theories of gender and to object-relations feminism. It provides a persuasive argument that heterosexual desire is rooted in unequal relations and meanings of gender, and it stresses the problematic and conflictual nature of all sexual identity and desire. This is an interpretation taken directly from Freud, but psychoanalysis has tended in the meantime to make problematic deviant and conflictual sexualities while seeming to assume that normal heterosexuality is relatively conflict- and problem-free. Such a normative theory, supplemented by a theory of perversion, cannot account for major features of heterosexuality, for instance, the pervasive intertwining of sexuality and aggression in men and of radical asymmetries in violent sexual behavior. Such an account needs a firmly psychoanalytic understanding of the dynamics of sexuality, but it needs this in a strongly feminist context that does not lose sight of dominance as a normative feature of masculinity.

In a challenge to primary femininity theories of both libidinal and object-relations varieties and to gender and self theories, Lacanian feminism, as a structuralist theory, also demands that we examine assumptions that gender need not be thought of in terms of gender relation. Can masculinity have meaning apart from femininity? How can the genitals of either sex have meaning in themselves, and not in the context of a structure of related meanings of the genitals of both?

I am stressing here relative and not absolute difference between psychoanalytic theory and psychoanalytic feminism. Many psychoanalysts think that women have been severely misunderstood by their theory, and they want to claim value for women's traditional role and genital and reproductive physiology. Occasionally they criticize male blindness and male power in the creation of theory, and some discuss the just role of anger in feminine emotional life. But by and large in the revisions of theory, one does not hear much challenge to the division of gender and parental roles, to normative notions of sexuality, to normal masculinity and femininity. Femininity may be resuscitated and revalorized, but there is little sense that masculinity is problematic. Psychoanalytic theory tends toward normatively generated, essentialist, and absolutist views of gender and sexuality, and it does not incorporate or allow for the incorporation of a critical stance. Psychoanalytic feminism challenges psychoanalysis in all these arenas.[44]

Paradoxically, that psychoanalytic approach that seems closest to at least one branch of psychoanalytic feminism particularly exemplifies these problems. Following Freud, traditional psychoanalysts continue to stress the internal, endogenous components of infantile sexuality. In the case of rape and incest, for instance, psychoanalysts have found it hard to give up the view that unconscious desires on the part of the female victim are involved.[45] By contrast, English and American object-relations theorists and self-psychologists have tended to focus on the actual behavior of the pre-Oedipal mother, and Stoller appropriates this stance as he develops an object-relations theory of male development. Stoller tends to see the actual behavior of the mother as directly causal of psychopathology and not to pay attention to the reciprocal role of the boy nor of his internal unconscious processes in creating gender-identity problems and perversion. Like other analysts, Stoller also never questions the traditional view of masculinity against which he measures the males he studies, and he makes claims about unproblematic femininity as well. In a cultural context of radical questioning of traditional gender norms, one wonders about the meaning of the claim that "clear cut femininity is routinely seen [in girls] by a year or so of age."[46] Psychoanalytic feminists, by contrast, have been especially focussed on demonstrating the fundamentally problematic nature of psychological masculinity, defined negatively and reactively in terms of that which is not feminine and based in heterosexual dominance of women and defensive denial of relationality.

There is a final problem with all the psychoanalytic theories of gender I have discussed. In other arenas in feminist theory, we have begun to look at gender-salience, or prominence, in social and cultural life, and to see that we must understand gender as it relates to other identities and other situated aspects of social and cultural organization.[47] I believe this is true psychologically as well. When, how, and why is gender or sexuality psychologically invoked, and how does it become relevant and in relation to what other aspects of psychological and emotional life? Psychoanalytic theories speak in global terms of "the girl," "the boy," "the man," "the woman." Is gender a continuing identity or feature of personality? Is it always a dominant identity or feature of personality? Are there characteristics that tend to differentiate the genders but which are not necessarily conceptualized psychologically as a part of gender identity?

Neither the psychoanalytic theorists of gender nor the feminist psychoanalytic theorists discuss gender salience, or, in fact, have much way to conceptualize it. Such a situation is tautologically true for Lacanian feminists, since sexuality is subjectivity. Interpersonal and object-relations feminists could build gender salience into their theories, but they haven't. Galenson and Roiphe assert that gender, as genital apprehension and apperception, determines identity and psyche, but those psychoanalytic accounts that stress primary femininity also do not locate this femininity in a more general or varied sense of self. Gender is certainly part of what is often on people's minds, and it is part of what constructs (and constricts) their life consciously and unconsciously, but it is also certainly not all, and it is differentially salient at different times and places. A next step for all psychoanalytic feminists and psychoanalysts who reflect on women and gender will be to build gender salience into our theories and practice.

In this context, clinical psychoanalysis has something important to teach both psychoanalytic feminists and psychoanalytic theorists of sex and gender. Object-relations feminism has been interpreted to mean that the pre-Oedipal mother–daughter relationship is almost all there is to female development and identity; Lacanian feminism seems to claim that the phallus is the phallus is the phallus; primary femininity psychoanalysts imply that the developmental meaning of the female genitals is self-evident. By contrast, the clinical encounter reminds us forcefully that the symbolizations and transference meanings of relationships and body parts are manifold. It argues that any development and identity will build on multiple internal relationships and interpretations of experience, and that no person, symbol, or organ can hold a singular and unvarying place in any other person's psyche or symbolic system.

A melding of object-relations feminism and recent psychoanalysis might take us further in the right direction. Against the essentialism of psychoanalytic gender theory, object-relations feminism enables an understanding of variability and fluidity in gender salience, because it sees development as contingently determined by experience and what one makes of this experience, and because it incorporates an understanding of gender characteristics like the self-in-relationship that are not necessarily available as gender conceptions. At the same time, as a feminist theory it remains continuously cognizant of gender hierarchy and relations of inequality, even as it also sees these as multiplex and situationally variable. Like clinical psychoanalysis, object-relations theory enables many developmental and psychological stories and leads to a recognition of variation, of ways that identities may or may not be invoked or experienced in different contexts and interpersonal or intrapsychic situations. At the same time, a theory of gender must include understanding of sexuality and body experience, and object-relations and interpersonal theorists have tended to downplay this area that psychoanalysis has so intricately and intimately studied. Lacanian feminism also reintroduces sexual difference and sexuality, and it does remind us forcefully of the intertwining of the psychodynamics of gender, sexuality, and male dominance as a constitutive cultural force – another lacuna in the psychoanalytic approach – but Lacan puts us in an absolute sexual and subjective world with no room for salience or fluidity: you can only accept or refuse previously given sexual positions which are always and invariably present.

This chapter outlines epistemological, theoretical, and substantive problems in professional communication, but it does not synthesize or create an adequate psychoanalytic and feminist understanding of women and men. On the former issue, I simply suggest that we need to talk. On the latter, I have suggested initial steps: We need to develop an approach to gender that enables understandings (1) of the selves and object-relational patterns of women and men; (2) of the senses of maleness and femaleness; (3) of sexual identities and interpretations of bodily experiences; (4) of masculinities and femininities; (5) of the fundamental interrelation of unequal social and cultural organizations of gender and their psychodynamics; and (6) of the fact that we are not always and in every instance determined by or calling upon these gendered and sexualized psychological experiences. Gender and sexuality are situated in, as they help to create, life in general.

10

Seventies Questions for Thirties Women: Gender and Generation in a Study of Early Women Psychoanalysts

One of the earliest articulated and still most important goals of feminist sociology has been to allow women's voices to be heard.[1] We have been aware of ways that dominant ideologies have shaped our discourse and understandings so that women have had to see things from male perspectives or have had their own, perhaps less articulated, perspective ignored or silenced. Because of this goal, feminist sociologists have often chosen to employ qualitative and reflexive methods, which, traditionally, allow the subjects of inquiry to speak and make subjects' perceptions and understandings central. They argue that we need to recognize and articulate women's double consciousness, the "disjunction between experience and the forms in which experience is socially expressed," and that we need to pay attention to the researcher's own subjectivity and to the relation between her and her research subjects.[2]

When a researcher wants to respect the voices of other women and is concerned about a history of dissolving differences into a hegemonic unity, she runs into problems when the voices she wants to respect seem not to recognize the central categories in her research. This essay discusses such a methodological problem that arose as I sought answers to questions about gender consciousness in interviews with early women psychoanalysts, when I discovered that, from the point of view of a hyper-gender-sensitive 1970s feminist, these women were relatively gender-blind, or unattuned to gender, regarding both their role in the profession and their profession's theory. I was thus faced with two kinds of questions. First, how can and should we conceptualize the gender-consciousness of women for whom gender itself does not seem like a salient category? Second, does the discovery that the very topic of inquiry is not salient to research subjects raise problems for methodologies like qualitative and reflexive sociology or feminism that privilege the perspective and voice of the subject? Are we left imposing categories on people that are not otherwise important to them, implying false consciousness in a group of women and thereby undercutting one major reason why we were doing feminist sociology in the first place? A tension arose between the feminist injunction to let women's voices be heard and the feminist injunction to analyze the social and cultural relations of gender.

My own attempt to resolve this dilemma went through several stages.[3] I had come to the study with what I self-mockingly called "unresolved positive transference" to my research subjects: they were somewhat idealized grand old women and foremothers.[4] I had images of the half-dozen women – Grete Bibring, Florence Clothier, Helene Deutsch, Eleanor Pavenstedt, Eveoleen Rexford, and Helen Tartakoff – who had sat on the dais at a symposium I attended on early psychoanalysis in New England, of the women in the totalizing culture of Viennese psychoanalysis idealized in much psychoanalytic history, of Horney and Klein making their individual and powerful ways against the psychoanalytic mainstream, of Lampl-de Groot and Deutsch debating and discussing the psychology of women with Freud. I wanted such women to hold views like myself, and was dismayed (for this reason as well as for the reason that I could not conceive how to proceed with my study) if they did not think gender had been important in their professional lives.[5] My second step was to consider that these women were (to accuse them of being) gender-blind, and to look for the cognitive and emotional functions that such gender-blindness served. As a feminist sociologist drawing upon interpretive traditions like psychoanalysis, Marxism, structuralism, and functionalism that claim to reveal underlying meanings or patterns, or to demonstrate the significance of particular forms of consciousness for the maintenance of social structure, identity, or hegemony, I thought in terms of false consciousness, rationalization, denial, defense, and the resolution of cognitive dissonance.

My suspicion of an analysis that invokes false consciousness as an explanatory category led me, finally, to relativize and expand my understanding of my own gender-consciousness and of the varieties of gender-consciousness and female self-understanding available to women of different eras and milieux. Drawing on a basic premise of the sociology of knowledge and on the feminist methodological injunction that we pay particular attention to the relationship of researcher to researched, I came to see that my ideas, as well as those of my interview subjects, were rooted in our different social and cultural conditions, that differences in women's interpretations of a situation may be understood not only in terms of structural categories like class and race but also historically, culturally, and generationally. I came to conclude that my interviewees, rather than being gender-blind, had different forms of gender-consciousness than I and experienced a different salience of gender as a social category and aspect of professional identity. Gender salience became a central concept in my research.[6]

Studying Early Women Psychoanalysts

I began an interview study of early women psychoanalysts – women who trained in the 1920s, 1930s, and early 1940s – in the early 1980s. My central research questions arose from the fact that, unlike most male-dominant professions, psychoanalysis seemed to have been extraordinarily open to women, to have counted a fair proportion of women in its ranks and to have recognized many of these women as significant, eminent, and even great.[7] I wanted to know how such a situation came about, and what the experiences of women were in a field that seemed to have facilitated their participation rather than to have mitigated against it. I wanted to ask these women the kinds of questions that we often want to know about women in the professions, for example, about friendships, colleagueship, mentors, the gendered tone of professional culture, family, and career.

That these women were psychoanalysts posed a particularly interesting problem concerning the role of culture and consciousness in the creation of gender relations, and vice versa. A major part of the professional knowledge and practice of psychoanalysis concerns psychologies of gender, parenthood, and sexuality. Prevalent cultural conceptions, especially feminist conceptions, of psychoanalysis might lead us to speculate that the field would be particularly *in*hospitable to women, one in which women would not want to participate. Psychoanalysis seems often to argue sexist and even misogynist views of women's lives, that women's lives are dominated by penis envy, that women must stay home full-time with their children during these children's early years or risk serious consequences, that women are naturally passive, that career achievement is a substitute for or expression of unresolved penis envy, and so forth. Such theories lead one to ask how a field with a radically dichotomous understanding of male and female personality and capacities can admit both as presumably equal practitioners; how the early women practitioners reconciled a theory that seems to devalue them with their own self-esteem, life situation, and practice; how and whether they related their lives as women, wives, and mothers to psychoanalytic theory; whether the issue of penis envy was salient for them; what they made of the feminist challenge to psychoanalysis. My study, then, called out for an investigation of women practitioners' consciousness in relation to the field's theories.[8]

Gender-Consciousness among Early Women Psychoanalysts

Throughout my interviews, I found that their gender, and that of colleagues, had simply not been salient professionally to the women I was studying. That I would make women problematic at all was even striking. As one European trained in Vienna said:

And with your problem. I don't understand your problem. Why is it so peculiar that women? . . . there are many professional women in the world; why shouldn't they be analysts too?

When I pointed to my emphasis on *proportionately* more, this woman responded with the example of Marie Curie and her daughter. I demurred.

Not so many, you think? But there are many male analysts too.

As an American trained in Vienna more bluntly put it:

You interest me in your question about were there women, what did the women do? I don't know, what did the women eat? Where did the . . . I just took it as a matter of course. . . The thing that struck *me* the most and was hardest for *me* was doing all this in German, seeing as I didn't know German.

Some interviewees could, when asked, notice the relative prominence of women in the field of psychoanalysis and speculate about the reasons for this. One British analyst, asked about the impact of women analysts on the field, pointed out that because so many of the leading analysts were women, the impact had to be big. Their impact, however, was because they were important individuals, not because they were women. I asked:

Did it make a difference that so many of the leading analysts are women? What if it had all been men?

She answered:

I don't know. I find it difficult to *lump* together women, you know. I can think of *special* women; it would have been different without *them*. But women, when you *lump* them into a *whole*, I don't know.

She followed this by an association to Winnicott's (a male analyst's) "immense identification with mothers."

An American analyst, asked whether relations among women analysts were different from those among men – a mainstay claim in most studies of women in the professions – said:

I think we were all analysts. We kept pretty much to talking about things of that sort . . . I don't think of them any different.

The same British analyst, reflecting a typical pattern, went back and forth.

When I asked why there were so many women, she suggested that psychoanalysis was a

passive sort of thing, lots of men are too assertive and active. It is difficult for the *ordinary* sort of male to do a lot of sitting all day in a passive analysis, sit still all day . . . that sort of receptiveness is easier for women, don't you think? But then again one thinks of how bossy some of the women are; they're not very receptive. You know bisexuality is very real to me. I could never get 'round the fact that a lot of the women are very masculine. So how can one generalize?

In contrast to these women, other interviewees disagreed with my basic premise: "I didn't know there were so many; I don't see anything so many about it," said one Viennese-trained American, echoing many of her colleagues. Upon reflection:

I guess it was the period when women were getting involved, but I never thought of it so much. The feminine part, I didn't know anything about feminist movements, feminist activity. I never even thought of such a thing. Because it seemed to me pretty easy as a woman to do what you wanted.

If I noted that their major trainers – their training analyst, their two supervisors, the people who first interviewed them when they applied for training – were all women, they said, as one Viennese put it:

I took it as a matter of course. It didn't matter, and I didn't notice. Look, training was so easy going; people were consumed by our interests in psychoanalysis.

Some, when I asked about women analysts as a category (as people who study women in other professions seem to be able to do), had no associations, emphasized that they simply did not and never had thought of their colleagues that way, or laughingly, almost scornfully, claimed that of course the men and women were different: women are women; men are men. Nor did they think of their own professional histories in terms of being women; they did what they did because they wanted to do it.

There were a few areas where interviewees perceived gender differences in professional experience. A very few had noticed discriminatory treatment or patterns in the ways men and women psychoanalysts conducted themselves, related to the profession and to each other, and so forth. Many stressed discrimination in medical school and medical school admissions and contrasted this with the favorable situation in psychoanalysis. A couple noted areas of inequity in the arena of formal leadership, where there was a tendency not to have female psychoanalytic society officers proportional to their numbers in the field. A few talked of the general societal discrimination against women. One Kleinian spoke of her relief when men came into the Kleinian ranks: "one did feel uneasy [when the women were dominant] whereas previously one didn't feel in the past uneasy if there was a predominance of men." And she attributed some of this unease to the content of Melanie Klein's theories, which center on the importance of the mother.

In keeping with the position that there are natural gender differences – that women are women and men are men – many women analysts could see the influence of gender in the analytic situation itself.[9] They talked of the different transference toward women – that women more easily elicit a mother transference and the expression of pre-Oedipal issues – and of the fact that women analysts are particularly good for patients with certain kinds of problems. At the same time, one suggested, another reason for the low salience of gender to women analysts was precisely this same transference, which does not respect gender boundaries: "in a complete analysis, the analyst is experienced as father, mother, monster, anything." Several interviewees remarked that women analysts were more maternal, more open, warmer, less threatening, or "gifted." One said, "more of us have a feeling for the unconscious, maybe," and another suggested that it was easier to confide in a woman. Others noted that women had made major contributions to our understanding of children. One claimed, without specifying how, that women were just special and different. A few, indicating identification with women, pointed to the fact that they didn't engage in mother-blaming in their developmental theories. In the analytic situation, then, gender was relevant and interviewees expected that they would be treated as women; otherwise gender was not particularly salient in their professional life.

How could the early women psychoanalysts be unattuned to gender, in a field that makes a theory of gender so central? Could one be a psychoanalyst without noticing the theory of femininity?

For the most part, early women psychoanalysts were more interested clinically in individual women than they were in the "theory of femininity" writ large. Some women might be narcissistic, some exhibit penis envy, but these were matters for individual interpretation. When pressed, however, most could reflect on the theory, and a few were quite critical:

We strongly have the feeling that it's nonsense to think that every woman thinks she has a terrible lot and then finally makes the best of it, the way Freud really presents it

said one Viennese woman, who then went on to defend psychoanalysis by pointing to the many recent revaluations and revisions of the theory.

Interviewees were more likely, however, to modulate their criticism or to defend only part of the theory, to argue that penis envy is a developmental stage rather than a major determinant of women's lives, that anyone can see that little girls envy the penis just as boys have castration anxiety, or that boys have womb envy just as girls have penis envy: "envy is a human quality," said one. Some claimed that Helene Deutsch just wanted to please Freud or personally disliked women. One woman, trained in New York when Karen Horney and Clara Thompson (both dissidents against the Freudian theory of femininity) were still members of the New York Society, claimed that she and her friends held the "secret theory" that penis envy was socially derived. Others emphasized alternate aspects of female psychology. Kestenberg, for instance, modified the theory of libidinal development, holding that an "inner-genital" phase precedes the phallic phase in both girls and boys and is the early libidinal origin of parentalism; Kleinians opposed Freud's phallocentrism with, in one interviewee's phrase, Klein's "mammo-centrism," or focussed on women's internal organs, internal organ integrity, and the role of feelings about internal organs in conflicts about reproduction and motherhood.[10]

Early women analysts employed another strategy of accommodation. They split their concept of the personal, familial side of femininity and women's lives into the areas of sexuality and maternality. By making this separation, they could valorize femininity in terms of maternal interests, could even conceptualize psychoanalysis itself as a womanly endeavor and understand their own professional practice to grow out of women's empathy and maternality, and they could pay not too much attention to the sexual theories. In these latter areas, Freudian theory may be misguided, as it emphasizes inevitable passivity and masochism (though Freud did, as several pointed out, affirm women as desiring sexual beings rather than sex objects).

Interviewees' assessment of the Freudian theory of femininity must be seen in the context of a firm belief in gender difference, and such a belief also affected their reaction to the contemporary feminist challenge. Most see themselves to some degree as critical of contemporary feminists, who in their view disparage women's maternality and the child's need for its mother and want to get rid of men. Feminists deny basic physiological sex differences, going without bras as if they don't have breasts. My interviewees often attributed feminist denial of gender difference to a deep-seated fear on our part that women are in fact inferior: we ourselves haven't gotten past the early penis-envy stage, where only presence or absence of maleness matters, to a true genital stage where the sexes are different but equal:[11]

I don't quite agree with the feminist ideas that the theory is discriminating. Again, there is after all a reality of difference, and I think many of these, you know, ultra-feminists are more, feeling themselves really inferior, and have to fight it that way . . . I don't see that one is inferior because one has no penis.

Between the two, then – on the one hand Freud's theory with its perhaps problematic notion of penis envy but its firm assertion of gender difference, and on the other what they see as the feminist denial of any sex difference – interviewees were more comfortable ignoring or modifying the former than accepting what they take to be the fundamentally flawed basic assumptions of the latter.

Problems in differential attunement to gender were particularly acute when I asked what I came to call "seventies" questions for "thirties women." These questions were developed in order to elicit reflections, not upon women's role in the profession nor upon the theory of femininity, but upon the relationship of their own self-understanding as women to their understanding of psychoanalytic theory. Had one affected the other? Had one led them to try and change the other? This set of questions also asked interviewees to address directly the feminist critique of psychoanalytic theory in relation to their own obvious professional success and active public careers. I wanted to know not only what they thought about the theory of femininity, penis envy, and so forth, but whether they thought about this theory in relation to being a woman.

I seem to have been intuitively clued in to the problematic nature of these questions, because even in my original interview schedule, they are quite lengthy and seem to require a lot of explanation. When I asked them, they were always extraordinarily convoluted and almost incomprehensible in their reflexivity. The following example comes from the end of an early interview. I clearly knew that such a question would not work:

One of the things that people always ask me because, you know, I'm a product of this recent women's movement and a feminist, and yet obviously very committed to psychoanalytic theories and studies, how do you reconcile being, you know, a feminist and believing or thinking that this theory – which ranges from anywhere from, you know, it's male-centered or it's sexist or misogynist or phallocentric, I mean people use a lot of different terms – and I'm wondering whether in your history as an analyst or when you were in training – I don't mean the sort of accusations, although I'm interested in that too – but did that come up for you or for other women? Did you think of yourselves, I mean the issue of the theory of femininity in relation to yourselves, was that something you talked about or did it come up?

These "seventies questions" were asked in the early to mid-seventies of any feminist who was passionate about psychoanalytic theory, or even any feminist who underwent an analysis, and such suspicions are still widely articulated among feminists. But they had neither been thought of nor did they seem relevant to most of the women with whom I spoke. They did not see themselves in relation to psychoanalytic theory or vice versa:

You know, it wasn't something that was more, much more central for me than many other questions, perhaps even less important.

I asked an American:

As you were bringing up your children and also being in training, [did] the kinds of theories about femininity you were learning, or motherhood, seem to be compatible?

No, they didn't seem to conflict. Because I took such pleasure in my children . . . I had these two really strong interests, getting an analytic background . . . and also my fascination by my children. But I was never bothered in a theoretical sort of way. I can see it from the point of view of patients. I never bothered myself.

I asked an early theorist of female and pre-Oedipal development:

Do you think that the fact of your being a woman influenced what you chose to work on in psychoanalysis?

No, not because I was a woman, but because I was an analyst, and I learned from my patients. [She did go on to concede that for the *very* early period in life women may have more understanding because of their experiences as mothers. *Maybe.*]

Thus, the psychoanalytic theory of femininity may have been relevant to patients, but not to practitioners' selves.[12] One European interviewee had been very articulate about the low feminine self-esteem which she had felt since early childhood. This low self-esteem provided one personal reason why she went into analysis and analytic training. I asked if the psychoanalytic theory of femininity contributed to her understanding of this low self-esteem or to her sense of how she ought to be feminine. At first she did not understand my question. I repeated:

Do you think, when you started learning about the psychoanalytic theory of femininity, did that increase your sense, or did that affect your sense, of whether you were feminine or not?

No, it didn't go through my brain, no.

I asked an American if she thought about the psychology of women in training at all:

Did you think about it in relation to yourself, or did women think about it in relation to themselves?

Uh uh . . . It doesn't figure at all. [I reformulated my question, again using myself as an example of someone who had had such thoughts.] Those didn't surface, at least as far as I was concerned. The mother part did because I felt I was missing something, as I told you before.

But you didn't think it was harmful to your child not to have. . .?

Well, I didn't think it was the greatest thing in the whole world, but I also didn't . . . I felt I was giving enough prime time to offset it. I don't think he always felt that way. [She went on about how she spent as much time as did "full-time" mothers who went off to social activities.] So I didn't feel guilty on that score. I just felt deprived that *I* didn't have as much time with him as I'd like to have. But otherwise I didn't. I don't think this women's issue came up until really. . .

Thus, although some interviewees criticized the theory of femininity, they almost never arrived at their conclusions by measuring the theory against their own lives.

These findings must be seen in context. The early women psychoanalysts were *not* docile, passive, unthoughtful women. Some opposed parental wishes in becoming professionals; many, depending on country of origin, were part of the earliest wave of women to enter the university. They identified themselves with what was felt to be a small, highly embattled avant-garde radical movement. Many thought of themselves as unconventional and as cultural radicals. They were often involved politically as antifascists, social democrats, or in farther left movements.[13] How, then, are we to understand their beliefs and claims?

Interviewees themselves begin to give us the answer, pointing implicitly and explicitly to their own historical and social situation. When, near the end of her interview, I asked the woman who said "what did the women eat?" if her mother had worked, I had finally come up with a question that situated things historically *for her*.

Did my mother work! Now you make me see the difference between men and women . . . I can't imagine my mother working . . . I can't imagine any woman working, of our acquaintanceship.

The more sociologically minded themselves commented on my questions as historically grounded. When I asked one about the relation between her consciousness as a woman, wife, or mother and the analytic theories she was learning, she did not answer directly but said:

Well, I think you have to keep in mind that these theories became attacked, under attack, at a time when I'd way already passed my participation in the analytic world.

Another said "I don't think those issues were as important then as they are now."

Context and Consciousness

Structural–organizational and cultural aspects of women analysts' lives situate and explain the consciousness I found. The context of their psychoanalytic training is in the first instance relevant to understanding interviewees' accounts. According to one, non-clinical training consisted in reading and rereading *The Interpretation of Dreams*, along with the case histories and the works on technique. These works do not give theoretical prominence to gender or to gender-specific sexuality, and these latter topics were not much discussed or thought about. The theory of femininity was simply not a salient part of their training.[14]

We know that there were written debates about the theory of femininity in the 1920s and early 1930s, when some of my interviewees were in training and beginning to practice, and these debates were sometimes quite passionate. It may well be, as Fliegel claims, that these early debates suffered a sort of repression by the collective consciousness of the field.[15] It is not clear, however, that they were central to most psychoanalysts, and, by contrast, it is quite clear that on many of the issues that concern contemporary feminists, all protagonists would have been on the same side. They believed in sex differences and recognized the developmental importance, if not overarching determinism, of penis envy.[16] More important, most analysts of both sexes felt themselves actively engaged in other struggles that were more salient – in cultural and medical struggle, controversy and debate about Freud's theories of the unconscious and infantile sexuality. In these debates, they were certainly on Freud's side.

Professional and personal experience also seem to have helped keep the early women psychoanalysts from personally reflective notice of Freud's theory of femininity. The extent of real discrimination or invidious differential treatment in the field against early women practitioners cannot be definitively measured. In later years there clearly was some, both in terms of access to certain kinds of positions and in terms of male attitudes to at least some female practitioners: my own discussions with men produced memories of being the only man in the Anna Freud Seminar in Vienna or at the Putnam Center in Boston and of the powerful women whose presence dominated the Boston, Washington, and London Societies. Men referred to the "lovely women" who were active in psychoanalytic affairs, to the Kleinian "phalanx of women who all wore black," and to the "Boston matriarchy."[17] But women clearly received substantial recognition. Male analysts I spoke with also respected women, referred patients to them, thought they were as good or better as practitioners. As the field developed, moreover, male analysts themselves often had women of an earlier generation as training analysts and retained a positive transference to them. Equally important, the early women analysts did not perceive much discrimintion, but felt that they were treated without regard to gendered status.

Cohort features of their life cycle and beliefs about femininity also seem to have shaped the consciousness of early women practitioners. Modally, they married in their early to mid-thirties and had children in their mid- to late thirties; even those who seem the most domestic members of psychoanalytic couples didn't marry until at least their late twenties. Thus, their careers were already established by the time they were confronted by the demands of motherhood. Culturally, women of this cohort were not confronting a post-World War II feminine mystique version of psychoanalytic theory. The Europeans all assumed they would have careers. As one put it, "we were told you *have* to be independent." People asked her after she had immigrated why she was not married. Such a question would have been "unthinkable" in Vienna. Some pointed to the greater sexism which shocked them upon arrival in the United States, and claimed that they did not notice the phallocentrism of the theory until they were in the context of a sexist culture. The Americans, though more aware of the practical conflicts of family and career – as one said, "the Americans were a more domesticated brood" – were nonetheless of the 1890–1910 cohort which married late and had few children (and for whom becoming a psychoanalyst and doctor was often so foreign to their origins that it could not even be compared to the cult of domesticity).

The early women psychoanalysts did have a concept of femininity and the female life cycle, but it was one that implicitly or explicitly included work and career. Even Freud had said that the psychoanalytic theory of femininity only describes "women in so far as their nature is determined by their sexual function," acknowledging that "an individual woman may be a human being in other respects as well."[18] Judith Kestenberg, who began to develop her reformulation of the theory of femininity in the 1950s, extends the theorizing of these other respects, in a way that I think reflects the conceptions of other women analysts of the thirties generation. There were, for these women, "three faces of femininity," motherhood, eroticism, and career or intellectual development.[19] In Kestenberg's account, each of these faces draws on different aspects of drives, unconscious processes, object relations, and developmental phase, but *all* are part of a full female life.

Partly because of class background and partly because of European background, almost none (and the few who did were not themselves mothers) operated under the assumption often attributed to their theories that children need 24-hour maternal care – as one put it, "a very American phenomenon that women should be home full time." Many did not have children, and most were quite accepting of this option for those contemporary women who have chosen it.[20] Those who did have children all talked of the competing claims of their different roles and said that they had cut back on work when their children were small. "I had a husband, two houses, and two children, so I never really fulfilled my destiny," said one American who had a private practice, wrote two books, and was a training and supervising analyst at a major institute. As another put it:

You have a feeling now, well, should I be there or should I be there? I mean I'm having fun with my child, but should I be reading a book? And you read the book and you wonder what they're doing now.

About professional women with children, she said:

They're enriched intellectually by what they do, and they're enriched emotionally by the little person upstairs.

But, she concluded, "one doesn't have to be too ambitious, I think." Mothers did tend to express their own regrets – for *their* sake rather than that of their children – that they could not spend more time with their children, and one claimed that she had to work and would have liked to be a full-time mother.

A few felt that their children had been harmed by not enough maternal care, but others were quite comfortable with afternoons or a couple of hours contact a day. One talked about her great delight in domesticity and her children, said that she "did a good deal of the child-rearing," and claimed that "the high point of the day [was] the time I spent with the children." I asked: Was that a couple of hours in the evening? and she said, "it would be about that." A younger American analyst who had trained in the "feminine mystique" 1950s talked about asking an older, very busy and eminent analyst of Viennese origin when she had had time to crochet a series of little table-cloths used for entertaining. This woman had answered, "when I was with the children." As the younger woman, who had had to contend as she was in training with American fifties cultural theories of mothering, interpreted this, "being with the children" seems to have comfortably consisted for the older woman in visits to the nursery where she sat on a chair and crocheted.[21] Several early women psychoanalysts had long separations from children, one when she was able to emigrate to the United States and left her son for six months with her husband until she was settled, another upon arrival sending her German-speaking children off to the country for the summer, ostensibly so they could get fresh air. Another, ready to give up her analysis in Zurich because her small son was living with his father and grandmother several hours away, was told by her analyst to stick with it and just go visit her son when she couldn't stand to be away any longer.[22]

The early women analysts, then, were not gender-blind or unattuned to gender. Low gender-salience did not characterize all aspects of their lives. Rather, as products of their era, they split their public and domestic interpretations of gender. As European social democrats and socialists, as products of the American women's colleges or of Bloomsbury, as cultural radicals, they believed in women's right to work. As post-World War I Europeans, they often knew that they had to work: the former Austro-Hungarian Empire was devastated; the Weimar monetary system collapsed in the early 1920s; their own once-substantial families might be currently needy, and millions of men of their generation had been killed, so that marriage was by no means a certain future. If they were feminist, it was as participants in socialist or social democratic politics, which argued for women's rights to equality in the public sphere, where there was no reason for difference:

You see the sociological side of it in the patriarchal societies, of course, and that I am against: Why should a woman who works not have the same payment and the same status as the man? But otherwise, it is very good to be a woman. And a mother.

Another claimed that feminists have a point about sexual inequality but that over her lifetime, she had been more preoccupied with social-democratic politics, anti-fascism, economic inequality, and social legislation. Currently, she likes Friedan's second-stage feminism, which wants to resuscitate concern for preservation of the family and family values:

We've done sort of the rough job, and the Pankhurst-like [things], you know, but now we have to get down to what are the *real* issues for women. And I am more inner-directed, and more interested in the internal issues.

She spoke of the "complexity" of the "inner conflicts" and "inner tasks," which include such things as how to reconcile career and family. Another said:

I'm not the right person really because at my time it was absolutely taken for granted that a woman is as good as a man, can do as much, has an absolute free choice.

There were, they recognized, still some inequalities in the higher echelons of power and status to work out, but with social democracy, they had believed, these would be taken care of as well. She concluded, with rueful hindsight, "instead of that, Hitler came."

Even as they believed in sex similarity and equality in the public sphere, they believed passionately, in keeping with their commitments to psychoanalytic theory, in natural differences in the domestic sphere. Women psychoanalysts did not think that they were challenging basic notions of women's nature. Their move away from tradition was in the public (professional, economic, political) realm, and they did not feel the need to transform or uproot the domestic sexual division of spheres. They continued to take major responsibility for child- and home-care and for entertaining (particular early women psychoanalysts were famous party-givers), and they believed that women have special nurturant capacities. For example, the woman for whom it had been "absolutely taken for granted that a woman is as good as a man" worried about why women had been put into inferior positions over the millennia. But she disagreed strongly with contemporary feminist advocacy of shared parenting, claiming that men don't have the right body configuration and aren't cuddly enough to take care of infants. In her career, the only time gender was relevant was when she had children. Another said, in remarkably clear reflection of the notion that what differentiates women is their family and sexual role: "being a woman was fully satisfied by having a very good husband and two children; my psychoanalytic interests emerged out of my literary concerns."

Low gender-salience, then, did not characterize all aspects of women psychoanalysts' lives or identity. Participation in an exciting professional movement as equals and notions of socialist comradeship characterized their experience of work relations, women's natural role as mothers and (equal but different) wives their experience of home roles. They assumed a division of labor in the home, assumed women's natural maternality, assumed innate, and desirable, gender personality differences.[23]

Their views, then, are in sharp contrast to the contemporary feminist challenge to the domestic division of labor and notions of innate gender differences. However, they are in equally sharp contrast to the view that innate differences between women and men or women's natural domestic location entail that women shouldn't be in the public world of work and politics. Their firm sense of gender difference did not feel like a life restriction, requiring 24-hour mothering or women's dependence on men.

This division of conceptions of gender into public and domestic aspects provides a first step in answering questions about how early women analysts dealt with the psychoanalytic theory of femininity in relation to their own professional success: it applies to the domestic side of women's lives. A further, more abstract, metafeature of their gender-consciousness is equally important. The recent women's movement began with the slogan that the personal is political. For the students and scholars in this movement, this also meant that the personal was theoretical and, conversely, that the theoretical had to be validated by the personal. In sharp contrast, as I describe above, it had not occurred to most of my interviewees to think of the theoretical as personal: their personal life and their personal analysis were personal; their reading and evaluation of theory was as professional practitioners. When an interviewee, reflecting historically, claimed that "these theories became under attack" after she had passed her participation in the analytic world, she did not mean to imply that she had never thought about them. She in fact *had* thought about the issue of penis envy and its cultural determination at that earlier time, but she rightly saw *my* question, which related these issues to her own life, as a product of the contemporary debate where the personal is theoretical and vice versa. Such thoughts "go through one's brain" when they are in the cultural air. In the deepest sense, self-reflection here seems culturally shaped and delimited, even for practitioners in a field that invites and insists upon self-reflection.[24]

Seventies questions about psychoanalytic theory, it seems, become salient under two conditions: first, if that theory seems dissonant with your identity, and, second, helping to condition the first, when it is a subject of historically situated cultural discourse. For the early women psychoanalysts, it felt largely consonant with their identity, and it was not a subject of discourse or debate. They did not experience the theory to constrain *them*, and it is even unclear if they imposed it in negative ways on their patients. One told about a miserable woman painter with a two-year-old who was staying home full-time with her child: "I said why don't you paint *and* be a mother? And I never saw her again after I made that suggestion."[25]

We have seen how cultural and historical setting served to make early women psychoanalysts, from the viewpoint of seventies feminism, relatively unattuned to gender in some aspects of their lives. We can understand this low gender-salience not only in terms of the internal structure of interviewees' gender-consciousness, but also in relation to other aspects of social location and self-categorization. Cynthia Epstein has argued that social categorizations that cross gender lines can minimize the salience of gender in women's lives, and Sherry Ortner also suggests we can understand the actions of some women better if we focus on structural characteristics shared between particular men and women that lead them to act in parallel ways. Our analyses need not always polarize women and men.[26] For many of the Europeans, Jewishness was certainly a more salient self-categorization, and this was a characteristic shared with men. Participation in psychoanalytic families and couples, in a psycho-analytic social world, and in the radical social movement that was psychoanalysis itself, being a lay analyst in medical psychoanalytic America, socialist youth movement membership, and participation in other avant-garde movements or social groups like Bloomsbury also created identities, all held in common with some male psychoanalysts, that modulated the salience of gender identity.

Interviewees could see this in relation to both selves and others. "She probably felt handicapped by being Polish and Jewish, but not as a woman," said one about another, who said that it had also been much harder for her to be Jewish. She described the anti-Semitism that drove her from her native country to anti-Semitic Germany, where students demonstrated against her and she was almost ousted from the university for being Jewish. The issue of being non-medical dominated the entire interview of another woman, an American who had trained in Vienna and through independently gained supervision (and such informal training was common in the 1920s) and was probably the first child analyst in New York. This woman was never made a regular member of the New York Psychoanalytic Society and spent her long professional career with special visiting privileges. Another, whose father was a card-playing partner of

Freud's and whose husband also became a prominent analyst, was first cousin to another woman analyst and related to yet another, each themselves married to analysts. For all these women, non-gender-linked structural characteristics were more personally and culturally salient than was their gender.

Portraying Self and Other: Generation

My interviewees had different forms of gender-consciousness and experienced a different salience of gender as a social category and aspect of professional identity than second-wave feminist professionals like myself (including those in their own field).[27] They interpret and interpreted their situation differently than we, imaginatively placed within it, might do, leading us to wonder at their ability to reduce what to us seem such striking instances of cognitive dissonance. Of course, my interviews draw upon retrospective accounts – and accounts of considerably distant experience – so we cannot be certain that interviewees describe how they really felt at the time. And we also know that psychoanalysis as a field has not always been kind to its internal dissidents: interviewees may have had practical motives for their ways of experiencing and interpreting the situation. Cognitive dissonance reduction, faulty memory, and instrumental motives for avoiding punishment for dissent may all have contributed to the accounts I found.

However, I found it methodologically and empirically more illuminating to assume that interviewees' accounts reflect how they in fact feel and felt. This position enabled me to see how cultural and historical processes, as well as social situation, make certain conceptualizations and not others more probable, even as it also problematized and relativized my own expectations and understandings. Gender-emphasis on the one hand, the relative downplay of gender issues on the other, are not only objectively determined by a structural situation. They are also subjective features of identity and culture. I needed to learn that feminist analysis could focus on subjects who minimized the importance of gender and on situations of low gender salience.

To return to myself as an historically situated seventies feminist researcher: in our time the existence of unconscious mental phenomena and childhood sexuality is widely accepted, and the theory of femininity has been a major contested arena both within the field and without. I therefore notice a lack of attention to this theory. I think about comparative historical statistics on women in the professions, as well as about the less measurable question of prominence of women in other fields, when I think that women seem so prominent in psychoanalysis. I note that even in fields like anthropology and child development, percentages were never as high, and practitioners did not find it easy to obtain regularized high-status institutional positions. My few interviewees who "don't see so many about it" trained when membership was growing from about 20 percent to 30–40 percent women, depending on location, and when one-third of trainees might be women. This is certainly a minority and, in the United States in particular, membership figures for women have declined since the 1950s and are now lower than in many other professions.

On the other side, comparative statistics also help us to understand interviewees' seeming false consciousness. We can point to the theory of femininity, to sexist remarks by colleagues, to ways some were passed over for positions, but it is hard to argue that something was radically wrong and they should have noticed. We can probably, with some accuracy, characterize their professional lives as a 90 percent advance over the lives of women of the previous generation, and an 80 percent advantage over most women of theirs. Is it really false consciousness, in such a situation, not to focus on the remaining arenas of discrimination or difference? Are they denying gender stratification in their profession, or justifiably conscious of the extent of gender equality within it?

There is another reason for the generation gap that I have labelled "seventies questions for thirties women." The gender-consciousness and gender-unattunedness of my interviewees was not only different from mine; they were in some ways the reverse of my own. For our part as feminists, even as we want to eliminate gender inequality, hierarchy, and difference, we expect to find such features in most social settings. In our effort to demonstrate the importance of social and cultural relations of gender, to put women, or put gender, in the center, we have begun from the assumption that gender is always a salient feature of social life, and we do not have theoretical approaches that emphasize sex similarities over sex differences. As Jane Atkinson puts it, feminist ethnographers do best with extreme practices that "fairly scream out for" comment, and less well with societies exhibiting low gender-salience.[28] But low gender-salience characterizes the women analysts' interpretation of their lives and their situation as psychoanalysts – characterizes their cultural meaning system, and, it seems at least to some extent, characterized their objective professional situation as well. This contrasts with my own situation, and with the assumptions of contemporary gender theory. At the same time, feminist sociologists hold a psychological theory that downgrades or eliminates notions of innate or desirable sex differences. A psychological theory of innate and desirable sex difference is precisely what women psychoanalysts held.

Feminist researchers, I think, need to be especially careful about our own normative patterns of gender-consciousness and gender-blindness. In my study, the situation was compounded. My interviewees were not the disadvantaged or silenced women of color, class, or sexual orientation that white, heterosexual, middle-class professionals have been admonished not to subsume under a monolithic feminist hegemony, but long-time, leading professionals in an important field. We are moreover in parallel situations, both in fields that center on issues of gender and that attribute underlying meanings and causes to stated beliefs. Just as feminists are liable to impute false consciousness to women who do not see our gendered truth, so psychoanalysts are liable to impute to us denial, fixation, or regression.

My research suggests a tension, but a productive tension, in feminist research. In the most consistently phenomenological qualitative methods, the researcher privileges research subjects' understandings. The feminist methodological imperative to let women's voices be heard and women's consciousness be expressed leads to a similar position. But feminists also ask structural, or organizational, questions, which depend on our concerns with gender inequality, asymmetry, or difference. Such questions do not necessarily arise from subjects' understandings. Thus, even as my structural and organizational conclusions draw upon what my interviewees told me, my questions often did not have much salience for them. We had, in fact, basically different interpretations of the importance of gender in different settings, and perhaps in social life more generally.

Gender as a feature of professional life and knowledge was minimized by the particular way that the women analysts interpreted gender – as relevant in the domestic sphere but not the public; by the fact that non-gender-linked social characteristics were personally and culturally salient to them; and by their interpretation of the psychoanalytic theory of femininity – as not to be evaluated in relation to their own lives and as not as important as the theory of the unconscious. Low gender-salience, or lack of attunement to gender, characterized my interviewees' interpretation of their professional lives – characterized their cultural meaning system. As I have described it, this variable and situated quality of gender came to me in a forceful way, as I was talking to interviewees. The pervasiveness of gender as a category to me simply did not resonate with their own life experiences, and I began to realize how much my perceptual and analytic categories had been shaped by my coming of age in the women's movement and my immersion in the recent literature of gender theory. Only with this recognition, that the salience and meaning of gender were products of one's time and place, could I come to understand gender within the fabric of my interviewees' lives.

Some feminist theorists have argued recently for situating gender, for gender as a relational, and relative, category both in itself and in relation to the social and cultural whole.[29] The methodological requirements that we let women's voices be heard, and that we examine our own relationship to our research subjects, and the theoretical concept of gender-salience, enable us to do this, to go beyond conceptualizing gender in absolute terms. They guide us to look at gender as a situated phenomenon, both in itself, as it can be more or less salient in different arenas or at different times of life, and in relation to other aspects of social and cultural categorization. Social, historical, and cultural context – on the one hand a social situation of low gender-salience and a relative lack of feminist politics, or a politics that assumed natural differences between the sexes, on the other a social, professional, and political situation that stresses high gender-salience – served to create what I considered to be normative patterns of gender-blindness in early women psychoanalysts, and what I came to see as normative patterns of hyper-gender-sensitivity in contemporary feminists like myself. At the same time, these variations in the organization of gender and in gender as a social and structural category are, partially, reciprocally created by these situated interpretations. An examination of interpretations of gender, and of the dialogue between those with different interpretations, informs our understanding of the social, historical, and cultural context that these interpretations help to produce and that help to produce them.

Notes

Introduction

1 See Beatrice B. Whiting (ed.), *Six Cultures: studies in child rearing* (New York, John Wiley and Sons, 1963); Beatrice B. Whiting and John W. M. Whiting, *Children of Six Cultures: a psycho-cultural analysis* (Cambridge, Mass., Harvard University Press, 1975); and John W. M. Whiting and Irvin L. Child, *Child Training and Personality* (New Haven, Yale University Press, 1953).

2 Philip Slater, *The Glory of Hera: Greek mythology and the Greek family* (Boston, Beacon Press, 1968). See also *The Pursuit of Loneliness* (Boston, Beacon Press, 1970) and *Earthwalk* (New York, Doubleday, 1974). Slater is eloquent about the entrapment of women in the home, both in ancient Greece and in the contemporary United States, but he does tend to accept psychiatric and psychoanalytic views of willfully resentful and destructive mothers that feminists must feel, at the least, ambivalent about. The still unresolved complexity for feminists of issues of maternal power and mother-blame are addressed throughout this book.

3 This argument first appeared in "Family structure and feminine personality," chapter 2 of this volume, and it is elaborated most explicitly in chapter 8.

4 See Karen Horney, *Feminine Psychology* (New York, W. W. Norton, 1967). Ernest Jones' arguments on femininity are largely indebted to Horney, although his role as emissary from London to Vienna in connection with the Klein–Freud split has often led to his getting the greater credit for the ideas they shared. For a discussion of the repression of these debates, see Zenia Odes Fliegel, "Feminine psychosexual development in Freudian theory: a historical reconstruction," *Psychoanalytic Quarterly*, 42 (1973), pp. 385–409 and "Women's development in analytic theory," in Judith L. Alpert (ed.), *Psychoanalysis and Women* (New York, Analytic Press, 1986), pp. 3–31. With little exception, psychoanalytic feminists, including myself, have ignored or criticized Horney as well. Recent work restores her rightful place in psychoanalytic feminist history. See Susan Quinn, *A Mind of Her Own: the life of Karen Horney* (New

York, Summit Books, 1987) and Marcia Westcott, *The Feminist Legacy of Karen Horney* (New Haven, Yale University Press, 1986).

5 Exceptions here are Dorothy Dinnerstein, *The Mermaid and the Minotaur* (New York, Harper & Row, 1976), and Elizabeth Abel, *Virginia Woolf and the Fictions of Psychoanalysis* (Chicago, University of Chicago Press, forthcoming), which traces the alternating Freudian and Kleinian subtexts in Woolf's writings.

6 I have been engaged since the early 1980s in an interview study concerning the experiences and impact of early women psychoanalysts (see chapter 10 for some description of this study and of my findings). This research suggests that the Kleinian debates, and Kleinian theory, were definitely genderized. As I note in chapter 10, a male member of the British "Independent" group (those British analysts who chose not to affiliate with either the Kleinians or the Anna Freud group during the reorganization of the British Psychoanalytic Society in the 1940s) referred to the Kleinian "phalanx of women in black." A Kleinian woman referred to herself as part of the "awful regiment of [Kleinian] women" who represented a theory about the all-powerful maternal breast. An Independent woman characterized the 1940s' "Controversial Discussions" between Kleinians and followers of Anna Freud as squabbles over who had the better mother. For discussion of the Kleinian controversies and debates, see Phyllis Grosskurth, *Melanie Klein: her world and her work* (New York, Knopf, 1986) and Hanna Segal, *Klein* (London, Collins, 1979).

7 Nancy Chodorow, *The Reproduction of Mothering: psychoanalysis and the sociology of gender* (Berkeley, University of California Press, 1978).

8 I use perceived here deliberately: if such mothers were truly *experienced as* powerless, their children would not care so much about these dynamics but simply ignore them. For further discussion of these issues, see Susan Contratto, "Father presence in women's psychological development," in Jerome Rabow, Gerald M. Platt, and Marion Goldman (eds), *Advances in Psychoanalytic Sociology* (Malabar, Fla., Krieger, 1986), pp. 138–57. My own discussions of the father's emotional role are found especially in *Reproduction*, chapter 7.

9 The unfortunate locution, "object," in object-relations theory seems to be a holdover from a psychoanalytic theory centered on drives, which have, in Freud's view, "objects" and "aims." In this model, the personhood of the object is not stressed, nor need the object be a person. Object-relations theorists tend to mean "other," although it can be argued that the term "self–other relations" might artificially inflate the wholeness and overemphasize the sociological reality of such psychic representations.

10 For example, Iris Young argues that the psychoanalytic, and any psychological or cultural, account focusses by necessity on gender difference, which is separate from male domination. Male domination in her view involves issues of power and is exclusively institutional, social structural, and material. It can be understood only within the purview of a social theory, and psychological and cultural accounts cannot contribute to our understanding of it. See "Is male gender identity the cause of male domination?" in Joyce Trebilcot (ed.), *Mothering: essays in feminist theory* (Totowa, N.J., Rowman & Allenheld, 1984),

pp. 129–46. Judith Lorber and Roger Gottlieb argue in a similar vein that a focus on psychoanalytic theory, even if this theory is centrally about gender and sexual inequality, is an entirely mistaken move away from a more correct socio-political–economic determinist analysis of gender phenomena, gender inequality, and even feelings about gender. See Lorber et al. "On *The Reproduction of Mothering*: a methodological debate," *Signs*, 6 (1981), pp. 482–514 and Gottlieb, "Mothering and the reproduction of power," *Socialist Review*, 77 (1984), pp. 93–119.

11 See, for example, Barbara Ehrenreich and Deirdre English, *For Her Own Good* (New York, Anchor Press, 1979); Barbara Easton [Epstein], "Feminism and the contemporary family," *Socialist Review*, 39 (1978), pp. 11–36; and Heidi Hartmann, "Capitalism, patriarchy and job segregation by sex," *Signs*, 1:3 pt 2 (1976), pp. 137–69.

12 Freud's case of "Dora," itself so transference- and countertransference-laden, seems to exhibit a gripping rawness about gender relations, domination, self, and sexuality that has made it the most excoriated and examined case in psychoanalytic history and a sort of urtext for feminist psychoanalytic critique. See for example Charles Bernheimer and Claire Kahane (eds), *In Dora's Case: Freud–hysteria–feminism* (New York, Columbia University Press, 1985).

13 My own reliance on object-relations theory was, as with many intellectual choices, a matter of accident as well as appropriate choice. Introduction to the work of Klein might have served the purpose of understanding the self as it is created through object relations, though clearly my analytic categories would have been very different as a result. My early feminist extreme wariness of biological explanations also probably kept me from seeing some of the strengths of the Kleinian contribution, couched as it is in the language of drive theory.

14 Margaret Mahler, "On the first three subphases of the separation–individuation process," in Peter Buckley (ed.), *Essential Papers on Object Relations* (New York, New York University Press, 1986), p. 223 and pp. 231–2.

15 This theoretical listing, I believe, comes from Mahler's Hungarian psychoanalytic roots and her early connections to Alice and Michael Balint, and through them, to Ferenczi. See, for example, Michael Balint, *The Basic Fault: therapeutic aspects of regression* (London, Tavistock, 1968), p. 74: "The ultimate aim of all libidinal striving is thus the preservation or restoration of the original harmony. . . This *unio mystica*, the re-establishment of the harmonious interpenetrating mix-up, between the individual and the most important parts of his environment, his love objects, is the desire of all humanity." Michael Balint's individuality and separateness, indicated in the independence and originality of his work and his seeming ability not to be absorbed into the feuds and debates of his colleagues, may have been taken for granted by him, and thus not in need of remark. He certainly describes both the fleeing from and clinging to objects: see *Thrills and Regressions* (New York, International Universities Press, 1959), but his work does not seem to see separateness as the same kind of basic goal as fusion.

Daniel N. Stern, *The Interpersonal World of the Infant* (New York, Basic Books, 1985), has demonstrated persuasively that Mahler's and other psychoanalysts' image of an infant who doesn't differentiate self and other is incorrect. Here, I am concerned with a feeling of self and with Mahler's imaging of an emotional preoccupation throughout life. In this context, whether or not this life course preoccupation reflects an actual early infantile state is not really at issue.

16 Hans Loewald, "Internalization, separation, mourning and the superego," 1962, in *Papers on Psychoanalysis* (New Haven, Yale University Press, 1980), p. 264. This was the first paper I read of Loewald's, in the early 1970s, and it was a powerful reminder that some psychoanalysts continued to adhere to the Freudian desire to interpret not only individual lives in the clinical situation but life in general.

17 Loewald, "The waning of the Oedipus complex," 1979, in *Papers on Psychoanalysis*, pp. 401–3.

18 Ibid., p. 394.

19 To my knowledge, the first article to make Loewald's work its explicit subject appeared only in 1988. See Arnold M. Cooper, "Our changing views of the therapeutic actions of psychoanalysis: comparing Strachey and Loewald," *The Psychoanalytic Quarterly*, 57 (1988), pp. 15–27. Like Cooper, I quote extensively from Loewald, because the power and profundity of his approach is found not just in the gist of what he says but in his precise literary usage.

20 My own impression is that these syncretistic qualities reflect the current state of American psychoanalysis. For perhaps the first time in the history of American psychoanalysis, synthetic and inclusionary theoretical tendencies seem to be more dominant than sectarian and exclusionary tendencies. In the journals, Winnicott is almost mainstream, non-self psychological writers occasionally discuss Kohut not in order to criticize him, and Kernberg, Loewald, and others draw from a variety of non-ego psychological sources like object-relations theory and Kleinian theory. Horney has been resuscitated in discussions of the psychology of women. One can only speculate about the relation of all this to the current decline in the profession – its fall from grace within psychiatry, its marginalized and minor relation to other psychotherapies, the continuing controversies about its founder – all perhaps leading to a somewhat defensive, even though welcome, reunification.

21 Loewald, "On the therapeutic action of psychoanalysis," 1960, in *Papers on Psychoanalysis*, p. 250.

22 Loewald, "Psychoanalysis as an art and the fantasy character of the psychoanalytic situation," 1975, in *Papers on Psychoanalysis*, pp. 362–3.

23 Loewald, "Waning," in *Papers on Psychoanalysis*, p. 402.

24 This issue, even as it challenges long-held psychoanalytic truth, also has particular import for psychoanalytic feminist theorizing. The recent infancy research reported by Stern, *The Interpersonal World*, suggests that the model of merged mother–child unity depicted by most object-relations feminists, as well as the imaginary mother–child relation that Lacanians think interrupted and destroyed by the intervention of the father, may not in fact characterize this earliest relationship. If we are originally in some sense separate from our mothers, as Stern argues, then we might ask, following Cooper (see n. 30 below), what childhood experiences lead women, more than men, to a "narrative construction" that merges self and other.

Provisionally, I would agree with Arnold Cooper's eclectic acceptance and rejection of the relation of past experience to present psychological life. Cooper ("Changes in psychoanalytic ideas," *Journal of the American Psychoanalytic Association*, 35 (1987), p. 83) argues that there are strong reasons for seeing psychoanalytic stories not as reconstructions but as constructions:

There is no other past than the one we construct, and there is no way of understanding the past except through its relation to the present.

Yet Cooper also claims (p. 84);

While a diachronic view may no longer suffice, it may also not be fully dispensable if our patients' histories are to maintain psychoanalytic coherence, rooted in bodily experience, and the loving, hating and terrifying affects accompanying the fantastic world of infantile psychic reality.

25 D.W. Winnicott, *Playing and Reality* (New York, Basic Books, 1971), pp. 79–85, also contrasts "being" as a female element with "doing" as a male element.

26 See Rosaldo's trenchant argument, which goes far beyond any critique I would make, that the entire *Woman, Culture and Society* paradigm, which she helped to create, with its emphasis on the importance of motherhood and the domestic–public split, is a reading of Western ideology and social organization into other societies. See Michelle Z. Rosaldo, "The use and abuse of anthropology: reflections on feminism and cross-cultural understanding," *Signs*, 5 (1980), pp. 389–417. My own strong emphasis during this early period on father-absence as a universal phenomenon may also owe partly to a brief field experience in Chiapas, Mexico, where Zinacanteco (Mayan) Indian men travelled many miles to the lowlands to harvest corn and stayed away for weeks at a time, as well as travelling from home to the ceremonial center. It is certainly the case in many non-Western cultures, as well as in some subcultures in our own society, that fathers and men have traditionally been around infants and children, and even caring for them, more than in the middle-class model that reached its apogee during the 1950s in the United States. For some discussion of this, see Carol B. Stack, *All Our Kin* (New York, Harper & Row, 1974); Diane K. Lewis, "A response to inequality: Black women, racism and sexism," *Signs*, 3 (1977), pp. 339–61, and Scott Coltrane, "Women's status and father participation in child care," *American Journal of Sociology*, 93 (1988), pp. 1060–95.

27 Adrienne Rich calls this need for closeness and feeling of identification with women the "lesbian continuum" ("Compulsory heterosexuality and lesbian existence," *Signs*, 5 (1980), pp. 631–60). Carroll Smith-Rosenberg's "The female world of love and ritual," *Signs*, 1 (1975), pp. 1–29, was certainly important during the period when this essay was published in arguing for "heterosexual" women's rootedness in a female world and in relations with women.

28 Juliet Mitchell, in *Woman's Estate* (New York, Pantheon, 1971), presages her later work when, in a largely negative and critical account of Freudian misogyny, she argues that feminists do need a science of the mind, and that psychoanalysis provides such a science.

29 See Susan Contratto Weisskopf, "Maternal guilt and mental health professionals: a reconfirming interaction," *Michigan Occasional Papers*, no. 5 (Ann

Arbor, University of Michigan Women's Studies Program, 1978); Susan (Contratto) Weisskopf, "Maternal sexuality and asexual motherhood," *Signs*, 5 (1980), pp. 766–82, and Contratto, "Mother: social sculptor and trustee of the faith," in Miriam Lewin (ed.), *In the Shadow of the Past: psychology portrays the sexes* (New York, Columbia University Press, 1984), pp. 226–251. I am especially grateful to Susan Contratto for allowing me to reprint our essay in this volume.

30 I agree here with Cooper's claim that psychoanalysis has empirical "anchoring points." As he contrasts "historical" and "modernist" models of transference, he writes ("Changes," pp. 83–4):

> psychoanalysis, like history but unlike fiction, does have anchoring points . . . evidences that events did occur. . . . These "facts" place a limit on the narratives and interpretations that may seriously be entertained. Psychoanalysis is anchored in its scientific base in developmental psychology and in the biology of attachment and affects. Biology confers regularities and limits on possible histories, and our constructions of the past must accord with this scientific knowledge. Constructions of childhood that are incompatible with what we know of developmental possibilities may open our eyes to new concepts of development, but more likely they alert us to maimed childhoods that have led our patients to unusual narrative constructions in the effort to maintain self-esteem and internal coherence.

Chapter 1 Being and Doing

1 The first section of this essay has been revised to incorporate the final published version of data on which I drew previously in unpublished form. I am grateful to Susan Contratto for first suggesting to me certain problems in male identity development which led me to the approach taken in this essay.

2 I am aware of many potential drawbacks in "cross-cultural" studies: their dubious reliability; in many cases, the relatively incomparable nature of much of the data used for cross-cultural comparisons, particularly those comparisons based on material from the Human Relations Area Files or other large-scale comparisons in which the original gathering of data was not under the control of the person using this data; the difficulty of rating cultures according to non-culturally defined variables; and the tenuous nature of causal explanations based on statistical correlation or comparison. Although it is beyond the scope of this essay to offer a specific criticism of such studies and beyond the scope of my abilities to evaluate statistical methods and results, I have attempted to avoid reliance on minute statistical differences for proof, and to attribute adequacy to explanations according to their logical and experiential plausibility, rather than their statistical reliability.

3 Margaret Mead, *Male and Female* (New York, William Morrow, 1949).

4 Herbert Barry III, Irvin L. Child, and Margaret K. Bacon, "Relation of child training to subsistence economy," *American Anthropologist*, 61 (1959), pp. 51–63.

5 Beatrice B. Whiting and John W. M. Whiting, *Children of Six Cultures: a psycho-cultural analysis* (Cambridge, Mass., Harvard University Press, 1975).

On cultural differences in children's behavior, see esp. pp. 70–135. I have called dependent–dominant behavior masculine, although it includes "seeking help," which could be seen in Western terms as feminine. Elsewhere, they differentiate dependent–dominant behavior from that which they call "intimate–dependent." This latter category of behavior seeks to include more of those forms of dependence – needy seeking of help rather than demanding help-seeking – that we culturally characterize as feminine. See also Whiting and Whiting, "Altruistic and egoistic behavior in six cultures," in Laura Nader and Thomas Maretzki (eds), *Cultural Illness and Health: essays in human adaptation* (Washington, D.C., American Anthropological Association, 1973). These researchers are measuring slightly different things. Barry, Child, and Bacon here and elsewhere are talking about *pressure toward* certain kinds of behavior in children, while the Whitings are talking about *observed* behavior.

6 George P. Murdock, "Comparative data on the division of labor by sex," *Social Forces*, 15 (1937), pp. 551–3, and Roy D'Andrade, "Sex differences and cultural institutions," in Eleanor M. Maccoby (ed.), *The Development of Sex Differences* (Stanford, Stanford University Press, 1966).

7 D'Andrade, "Sex differences," p. 176.

8 Herbert Barry III, Margaret K. Bacon, and Irvin L. Child, "A cross-cultural survey of some sex differences in socialization," *Journal of Abnormal Psychology*, 55 (1957), pp. 327–32.

9 This last claim is not stated explicitly but seems to be derivable from the data which they present on comparison within sexes for each type of society.

10 See *Children of Six Cultures*, pp. 136–51.

11 Zinacantan, a highland Mayan Indian community in Chiapas, Mexico in which I did field work, perfectly exemplifies this hypothetical description. Men's agricultural work is done in the lowlands, away from the community, and boys, depending on whether or not they are in school, do not work with their fathers until they are aged from nine to eleven. They perform a certain amount of "helping" work when they are young – fetching things, and so forth – but this is not seen as "real" work for them. They remain without real work training from their mothers, while their sisters as they grow up learn progressively how to tend fires, cook, and weave. As the boy's role in his house seems to become less and less relevant, and he is less and less able to fill his time meaningfully, he turns increasingly to antics to get attention from his all-too-busy mother and sisters.

12 See Barry, Bacon, and Child, "Cross-cultural survey."

13 Beatrice Whiting (personal communication) points to Six Cultures data that indicate that girl children stay closer to their mothers and receive more numerous and frequent commands than boys. She suggests that this is training specifically useful for child-rearing and household work, in which a woman has to expect to be interrupted irregularly in whatever tasks she is doing, and cannot detach herself from her surrounding situation nor try many new ways to work. This seems to relate to typical "feminine" intellectual characteristics – non-abstract thinking, field dependence, etc. – and also to be closer to the kind of training boys would get in economies where they are gradually trained and given specific work to do.

14 Barry, Child, and Bacon, "Relation of child training," p. 56.
15 On children's work, see Whiting and Whiting, *Children of Six Cultures*, pp. 82–113.
16 Barry, Bacon, and Child, "Cross-cultural survey," p. 330.
17 Ruth Benedict, "Continuities and discontinuities in cultural conditioning," in Margaret Mead and Martha Wolfenstein (eds), *Childhood in Contemporary Cultures* (Chicago, University of Chicago Press, 1955), p. 22.
18 Mead, *Male and Female*, p. 167.
19 Talcott Parsons, "Age and sex in the social structure of the United States," 1942, in *Essays in Sociological Theory* (New York, The Free Press, 1954), p. 90. I note here that the fact that these are "important aspects" does not necessarily mean that they are important in actual economic or social fact or in a society's, or the little girl's, evaluation of them. I discuss the implications of this fact for female development below.
20 Ibid.
21 Karen Horney, "The dread of women," *International Journal of Psycho-analysis*, 13 (1932), p. 359.
22 Mead, *Male and Female*, p. 167.
23 Ibid., p. 303.
24 Parsons, "Age and sex."
25 Mead, *Male and Female*, p. 295.
26 Simone de Beauvoir, *The Second Sex* (New York, Bantam Books, 1968), p. 278.
27 Mead, *Male and Female*, p. 298.
28 Horney, "Dread," p. 351.
29 Ibid.
30 Ibid., p. 357.
31 Ibid., p. 351.
32 Mead, *Male and Female*, p. 168.
33 Ibid.
34 Melford E. Spiro, *Children of the Kibbutz: a study in child training and personality* (New York, Schocken Books, 1965). The following interpretation was not made by Spiro, but seemed to me to explain fairly clearly many differences between men and women which Spiro did not seem to understand.
35 Spiro, *Children of the Kibbutz*, p. 291.
36 Ibid., p. 352.
37 Daniel G. Brown, "Sex-role preference in young children," *Psychological Monographs*, 70 (1956), pp. 1–19; "Masculinity–femininity development in children," *Journal of Consulting Psychology*, 21 (1957), pp. 197–202: "Sex role development in a changing culture," *Psychological Bulletin*, 55 (1958), pp. 232–42.
38 Brown, "Sex role development," pp. 237–8. See also Lawrence Kohlberg, "A cognitive-developmental analysis of children's sex role concepts and attitudes," in Maccoby (ed.), *Development of Sex Differences*.
39 Roger V. Burton and John W. M. Whiting, "The absent father and cross-sex identity," *Merrill-Palmer Quarterly of Behavior and Development*, 7 (1961), p. 91. Burton and Whiting define optative identity as "those statuses a person

wishes he could occupy but from which he is disbarred." The dynamics of matrilocality are not as clear as Burton and Whiting suggest. In most matrilocal societies, control or power rests in the hands of men, although these men are now "mother's brothers" or "mother's maternal uncles" rather than fathers and grandfathers. Because men may have to move back and forth between their marital residence and their lineage home, and because matrilineality, while male dominant, is generally less male dominant than patrilineality, women often have relatively more power than women in patrilineal, patrilocal situations. They also, from the point of view of the child, are more continuously present. Thus, while Burton and Whiting's findings seem empirically accurate, their assumption that matrilocality generates female control needs refinement. See, on matrilocality, David Schneider and Kathleen Gough (eds), *Matrilineal Kinship* (Berkeley, University of California Press, 1967).

40 Bruno Bettelheim, *Symbolic Wounds: puberty rites and the envious male* (New York, The Free Press, 1954), p. 45. Bettelheim does not restrict his interpretation to male initiation rites but claims that female initiation rites may equally be expressions of envy for the masculine role. He emphasizes male initiation and envy of the female because he feels that female envy of male sex functions – penis envy – has been overemphasized at the expense of the converse situation. According to Bettelheim, this is because "in any society, envy of the dominant sex is the more easily observed [and] more readily admitted, more openly expressed and more easily recognized" (p. 56). It is also true that female initiation rites are not nearly so widespread nor so complex as male rites. Bettelheim suggests, rightly, I think, that this is because women can express their jealousy of men openly in most societies, and it is considered only natural that they should be jealous ("the consensus is that it is desirable to be a man") whereas men's jealousy is not so admissible and "can be expressed only in ritual" (ibid.).

41 According to the account presented here, even in these societies, from the child's point of view, mothers have more control of resources and spend more time with children. Thus, boys would still have a harder time than girls in developing a masculine sex-role identity.

42 Burton and Whiting, "Absent father," p. 90.

43 Burton and Whiting, "Absent father," and Beatrice B. Whiting, "Sex identity conflict and physical violence: a comparative study," *American Anthropologist*, 67 (1965), pp. 123–40.

44 B. Whiting, "Sex identity conflict."

45 Philip Slater and Dori A. Slater, "Maternal ambivalence and narcissism: a cross-cultural study," *Merrill-Palmer Quarterly of Behavior and Development*, 11 (1965), p. 243. Both B. Whiting and Slater and Slater suggest that the personality structure of women in societies where husbands are absent or where the marriage relationship is distant may also be affected. Slater and Slater suggest that women may be resentful of their subordinate and isolated role in the society at large and compensate for this by exercising arbitrary and great power in the household, particularly over male children. The crux of this behavior is that it is not simply an expression of the mother's need to denigrate

sons in order to get back at older men for denigrating her, but that it expresses a need both to build up and to deflate sons, to push achievement and punish for success – thus, to ensure that a son's sense of self is dependent on his mother's arbitrary whim. B. Whiting suggests also that women raised in mother–child households and mothers in these households tend to be more assertive and dominant than women reared in nuclear households. This would combine with the actual fact of their sole power in the household and over children to create greater difficulty for boys to assert themselves or to feel capable of achieving a different male identity.

46 Mead, *Male and Female*, p. 303.
47 Ibid., p. 168.
48 de Beauvoir, *Second Sex*, p. 267.
49 Kohlberg, "Cognitive-developmental analysis," p. 162.
50 Slater and Slater, "Maternal ambivalence," pp. 249–50.
51 Kohlberg, "Cognitive-developmental analysis," p. 120. See also Kohlberg's immediately preceding discussion for other findings mentioned here. Further indication that these changes of preference do not reflect identity confusion but rather identity disenchantment is provided by the existence of parallel changes of preferences in disadvantaged racial groups. Kohlberg cites a study (Doris V. Springer, "Awareness of racial differences by preschool children in Hawaii," 1950) that shows that same-race preferences among Oriental children in Hawaii decline with age as do same-sex preferences in girls. In this case also, it seems inconceivable these children were becoming less sure of their racial identity as they grew older, just as it seems inconceivable that girls should become less sure of their female identity.
52 Ibid., p. 121.
53 Karen Horney, "The flight from womanhood: the masculinity complex in women, as viewed by men and by women," *International Journal of Psycho-analysis*, 7 (1926), pp. 337–8.
54 Ibid., p. 338.
55 de Beauvoir, *Second Sex*, p. 314.
56 Mead, *Male and Female*, p. 301.

Chapter 2 Family Structure and Feminine Personality

1 My understanding here of mother–daughter relationships and their effect on feminine psychology grows out of my participation, beginning in 1971, in the "mother–daughter group," a women's group that included some who were mothers and some mother–daughter pairs that discussed mother–daughter relationships in particular and family relationships in general. All the women in this group contributed to this understanding. An excellent dissertation by Marcia Millman ("Tragedy and exchange: metaphonic understandings of interpersonal relationships," Ph.D. dissertation, Brandeis University, 1972) first suggested to me the importance of boundary issues for women and became a major organizational focus for my subsequent work. Discussions with Nancy Jay, Michelle Rosaldo, Philip Slater, Barrie Thorne, Susan Contratto, and

Beatrice Whiting were central to the development of the ideas presented here. I am grateful to George Goethals, Edward Payne, and Mal Slavin for their comments and suggestions about earlier versions of this chapter.

2 Margaret Mead provides the most widely read and earliest argument for this viewpoint (cf. e.g. *Sex and Temperament in Three Primitive Societies* (New York, William Morrow, 1935) and *Male and Female* (New York, William Morrow, 1949)).

3 Unfortunately, the language that describes personality structure is itself embedded with value judgment. The implication in most studies is that it is always better to have firmer ego boundaries, that "ego strength" depends on the degree of individuation. David Gutmann, who recognizes the linguistic problem, even suggests that "so-called ego pathology may have adaptive implications for women" ("Women and the conception of ego strength," *Merrill-Palmer Quarterly of Behavior and Development*, 11 (1965), p. 231). The argument can be made that extremes in either direction are harmful. Complete lack of ego boundaries is clearly pathological, but so also, as critics of contemporary Western men point out (cf. e.g. David Bakan, *The Duality of Human Existence: isolation and communion in western man* (Boston, Beacon Press, 1966) and Philip Slater, *The Pursuit of Loneliness* (Boston, Beacon Press, 1970)) is individuation gone wild, what Bakan calls "agency unmitigated by communion," which he takes to characterize, among other things, both capitalism based on the Protestant ethic and aggressive masculinity. With some explicit exceptions that I will specify in context, I am using the concepts solely in the descriptive sense.

4 Philip Slater, in *The Glory of Hera: Greek mythology and the Greek family* (Boston, Beacon Press, 1968) provides one example of such an investigation. Robert Levine's work on psychoanalytic anthropology proposes a methodology that will enable social scientists to study personality development in this way: "The psychoanalytic studyc of lives in natural social settings," *Human Development*, 14 (1971), pp. 100–9.

5 See Chodorow, chapter 1, this volume; Sherry B. Ortner, "Is female to male as nature is to culture?" in Michelle Z. Rosaldo and Louise Lamphere (eds), *Woman, Culture and Society* (Stanford, Stanford University Press, 1974), pp. 67–87; and M. Z. Rosaldo, "Woman, culture and society: a theoretical overview," in Rosaldo and Lamphere (eds), *Woman, Culture and Society*, pp. 17–42.

6 I draw particularly on interpretations by object-relations theorists, e.g. W. R. D. Fairbairn, *An Object-Relations Theory of the Personality* (New York, Basic Books, 1952) and Harry Guntrip, *Personality Structure and Human Interaction* (New York, International Universities Press, 1961) and, with some similarity, by Talcott Parsons, *Social Structure and Personality* (New York, The Free Press, 1964) and Talcott Parsons and Robert F. Bales, *Family, Socialization and Interaction Process* (New York, The Free Press, 1955).

7 Melanie Klein and Joan Rivière, *Love, Hate and Reparation*, 1937 (New York, W. W. Norton, 1964).

8 Helene Deutsch, *The Psychology of Women* (New York, Grune & Stratton, 1944 & 1945), vol. 1, p. 205.

9 Leigh Minturn and John T. Hitchcock, "The Rajputs of Khalapur, India," in Beatrice B. Whiting (ed.), *Six Cultures: studies in child rearing* (New York, John Wiley and Sons, 1963); Edward B. Harper, "Fear and the status of women," *Southwestern Journal of Anthropology*, 25 (1969), pp. 81–95.

10 Robert Fliess, *Ego and Body Ego* (New York, International Universities Press, 1961).

11 John W. M. Whiting, "Sorcery, sin, and the superego: a cross-cultural study of some mechanisms of social control," in Clellan S. Ford (ed.), *Cross-Cultural Approaches: readings in comparative research*, 1959, (New Haven, Human Relations Area Files, 1967), pp. 147–68, and Whiting, Richard Kluckhohn, and Albert Anthony, "The function of male initiation rites at puberty," In Eleanor Maccoby, T. M. Newcomb, and E. L. Hartley (eds), *Readings in Social Psychology* (New York, Holt, Rinehart and Winston, 1958), pp. 359–70.

12 Slater, *Glory of Hera*.

13 On pre-Oedipal development, see, e.g., Ruth Mack Brunswick, "The pre-Oedipal phase of the libido development," 1940, in Robert Fliess (ed.), *The Psychoanalytic Reader* (New York, International Universities Press, 1948), pp. 231–53; Helene Deutsch, "Female homosexuality," 1932, in Fliess (ed.), *The Psychoanalytic Reader*, pp. 208–30 and Deutsch (ed.), *Psychology of Women*; Fliess, "Female and pre-Oedipal sexuality: a historical survey," in Fliess (ed.), *The Psychoanalytic Reader*, pp. 159–64; Sigmund Freud, "Female sexuality," 1931, *The Standard Edition of the Complete Psychological Works of Sigmund Freud*, ed. James Strachey (London, The Hogarth Press and the Institute of Psychoanalysis) (hereafter *SE*), vol. 21, pp. 223–43; Ernest Jones, "The early development of female sexuality," *International Journal of Psycho-Analysis*, 8 (1927), pp. 459–72; and Jeanne Lampl-de Groot, "The evolution of the Oedipus complex in women," 1927, in Fliess (ed.), *The Psychoanalytic Reader*, pp. 180–94.

14 See on this Lawrence Kohlberg, "A cognitive-developmental analysis of children's sex-role concepts and atittudes," in Eleanor M. Maccoby (ed.), *The Development of Sex Differences* (Stanford, Stanford University Press, 1966), pp. 82–173, and John Money and Anke Ehrhardt, *Man and Woman, Boy and Girl* (Baltimore, Johns Hopkins University Press, 1972).

15 The important distinction between "positioral" and "personal" identification comes from Philip Slater, "Toward a dualistic theory of identification," *Merrill-Palmer Quarterly of Behavior and Development*, 7 (1961), pp. 113–26, and Robert F. Winch, *Identification and Its Familial Determinants* (New York, Bobbs-Merrill, 1962).

16 Alexander Mitscherlich, *Society without the Father* (New York, Schocken Books, 1970).

17 On these processes see Roger V. Burton and John W. M. Whiting, "The absent father and cross-sex identity," *Merrill-Palmer Quarterly of Behavior and Development*, 7 (1961), pp. 85–95, and Slater, *Glory of Hera*. The processes by which individual personal experiences and psychological factors contribute to or are translated into social and cultural facts, and, more generally, the circularity of explanations in terms of socialization, are clearly very complicated. A discussion of these issues, however, is not within the scope of this chapter.

18 The question of the universality of the Oedipus complex as Freud describes it is beyond the scope of this chapter. Bakan points out that in the original Oedipus myth it was the father who first tried to kill his son, and that the theme of paternal infanticide is central to the entire Old Testament. He suggests that for a variety of reasons, fathers probably have more hostile and aggressive fantasies and feelings about their children (sons). See Bakan, *Duality of Human Existence*, and *Disease, Pain and Sacrifice* (Boston, Beacon Press, 1968). This more general account, along with a variety of psychological and anthropological data, convinces me that we must take seriously the notion that members of both generations may have conflicts over the inevitable replacement of the elder generation by the younger, and that children probably feel both guilt and (rightly) some helplessness in this situation.

19 These views, I believe, warrant the criticism that has been directed at them. Although the issue of penis envy in women is not central to this chapter, it is central to Freud's theory of female development. Therefore I think it worth while to mention three accounts that avoid Freud's ideological mistakes while allowing that his clinical observations of penis envy might be correct.

Thompson suggests that penis envy is a symbolic expression of women's culturally devalued and underprivileged position in our patriarchal society: that possession of a penis symbolizes the possession of power and privilege (see Clara M. Thompson, "Penis envy," 1943, in *On Women* (New York, Signet, 1964), pp. 73–8). Bettelheim suggests that members of either sex envy the sexual functions of the other, and that women are more likely to express this envy overtly, because, since men are culturally superior, such envy is considered "natural" (Bruno Bettelheim, *Symbolic Wounds: puberty rites and the envious male* (New York, The Free Press, 1954)). Alice Balint does not rely on the fact of men's cultural superiority, but suggests that a little girl develops penis envy when she realizes that her mother loves people with penises, i.e. her father, and thinks that possession of a penis will help her in her rivalry for her mother's attentions (Balint, *The Early Years of Life: a psychoanalytic study* (New York, Basic Books, 1954)).

20 In addition to references in n. 13, see David Freedman, "On women who hate their husbands," 1961, in Hendrik M. Ruitenbeek (ed.), *Psychoanalysis and Female Sexuality* (New Haven, College and University Press, 1966), pp. 221–37.

21 Deutsch, *Psychology of Women*, vol. 1, p. 205.

22 Guntrip, *Personality Structure*, p. 378.

23 Philippe Ariès, *Centuries of Childhood* (New York, Vintage, 1960).

24 Robert Jay, *Javanese Villagers: social relations in rural Modjukuto* (Cambridge, Mass., Harvard University Press, 1969).

25 Herbert Barry III, Margaret K. Bacon, and Irvin L. Child, "A cross-cultural survey of some sex differences in socialization," *Journal of Abnormal Psychology*, 55 (1957), pp. 327–32.

26 Bakan, *Duality of Human Existence*, p. 15.

27 See Gutmann, "Women and the conception of ego strength." Gutmann points out that all these qualities are supposed to indicate lack of adequate ego strength, and suggests that we ought to evaluate ego strength in terms of the

specific demands of different people's (e.g. women's as opposed to men's) daily lives. Bakan goes even further and suggests that modern male ego qualities are a pathological extreme. Neither account is completely adequate. Gutmann does not consider the possibility (for which we have good evidence) that the everyday demands of an autocentric milieu are unreasonable: although women's ego qualities may be "functional" for their participation in these milieux, they do not necessarily contribute to the psychological strength of the women themselves. Bakan, in his (legitimate) preoccupation with the lack of connection and compulsive independence that characterizes Western masculine success, fails to recognize the equally clear danger (which, I will suggest, is more likely to affect women) of communion unmitigated by agency – of personality and behavior with no sense of autonomous control or independence at all.

I think this is part of a more general social-scientific mistake, growing out of the tendency to equate social structure and society with male social organization and activities within a society. This is exemplified, for instance, in Erikson's idealistic conception of maternal qualities in women (Erik H. Erikson, "Womanhood and the inner space," in Robert J. Lifton (ed.), *The Woman in America* (Boston, Houghton Mifflin, 1964)) and, less obviously, in the contrast between Durkheim's extensive treatment of "anomic" suicide and his relegation of "fatalistic" suicide to a single note. See Emile Durkheim, *Suicide*, 1897, (New York, The Free Press, 1951).

28 Rae Carlson, "Sex differences in ego functioning: exploratory studies of agency and communion," *Journal of Consulting and Clinical Psychology*, 37 (1969), p. 270.

29 Rosalie Cohen, "Conceptual styles, culture conflict, and nonverbal tests of intelligence," *American Anthropologist*, 71 (1969), pp. 828–56.

30 Ibid., p. 836.

31 Meredith Tax, *Woman and her Mind: the story of daily life* (Somerville, The New England Free Press, 1970), p. 2, italics mine.

32 Slater, "Toward a dualistic theory."

33 See n. 3 for Gutmann's claim.

34 For an overview discussion on matrifocality, see Nancy Tanner, "Matrifocality in Indonesia and Africa and among Black Americans," in Rosaldo and Lamphere (eds), *Woman, Culture and Society*, pp. 129–56. Tanner pointed me to several ethnographies that I consider below.

35 Michael Young and Peter Willmott, *Family and Kinship in East London* (London, Penguin, 1966), p. 64.

36 Hildred Geertz, *The Javanese Family: a study of kinship and socialization* (New York, The Free Press, 1961) and Jay, *Javanese Villagers*.

37 Jay, *Javanese Villagers*, p. 103.

38 James T. Siegel, *The Rope of God* (Berkeley, University of California Press, 1969), p. 177.

39 See on this in addition to Young and Willmott, Mirra Komarovsky, *Blue-Collar Marriage* (New York, Vintage, 1967).

40 Guntrip, *Personality Structure*, p. 291.

41 Ibid., p. 293; my italics.

42 Grete Bibring, "On the 'passing of the Oedipus complex' in a matriarchal family setting," in Rudolph M. Loewenstein (ed.), *Drives, Affects and Behavior: essays in honor of Marie Bonaparte* (New York, International Universities Press, 1953), p. 281.

43 On this, see Slater, *Pursuit of Loneliness.*

44 See, e.g. Deutsch, *Psychology of Women, passim*; Erikson, "Womanhood," p. 162; Klein and Rivière, *Love, Hate and Reparation*, p. 18; Parsons, *Social Structure and Personality, passim*; and Parsons and Bales, *Family, Socialization, passim.* Their argument derives from the universal fact that a child must outgrow her or his primary identification with and total dependence upon the mother. The present chapter argues that the value implications of this dichotomy grow out of the particular circumstances of our society and its devaluation of relational qualities. Allied to this is the suggestion that it does not need to be, and often is not, relationship to the father that breaks the early maternal relationship.

45 Personal communication from Fatima Mernissi, based on her experience growing up in Morocco and her sociological fieldwork there. See her *Beyond the Veil: male–female dynamics in a Muslim society* (New York, Schocken Books, 1975).

Chapter 3 Oedipal Asymmetries and Heterosexual Knots

1 I am grateful for the helpful comments of Barbara Epstein and Lillian Rubin on an earlier draft of this chapter.

2 "'Civilized' sexual morality and modern nervousness," 1908, *The Standard Edition of the Complete Psychological Works of Sigmund Freud*, ed. James Strachey (London, The Hogarth Press and the Institute of Psychoanalysis), (hereafter *SE*), vol. 9, p. 198.

3 "A special type of choice of object made by men (contributions to the psychology of love I)," 1910, *SE*, vol. 11, pp. 163–75.

4 Freud, "'Civilized' sexual morality," p. 195. Durkheim's almost contemporaneous observation in *Suicide* (1897) that marriage raises the suicide rates of women must be seen as comment on the same institution, I think.

5 Gayle Rubin, "The traffic in women: notes on the 'political economy' of sex," in Rayna Reiter (ed.), *Toward an Anthropology of Women* (New York, Monthly Review Press, 1975), pp. 157–210. Her argument that marriage based on the exchange of women and the rule of obligatory heterosexuality is basic to male dominance is of course of central concern to me, though it is not analytically relevant to my argument here. At least in the case of the exchange of women, it is also to my mind problematic for an understanding of male dominance in the current historical period.

Analytically parallel to the Marxist view that a mode of production consists in the technology and social organization through which a society appropriates and transforms nature for purposes of human consumption, and transforms the experience of human needs to require further changes, a society's sex/gender system, according to Rubin, is "a set of arrangements by which the biological

raw material of human sex and procreation is shaped by human, social
intervention and satisfied in a conventional manner. . . The realm of human
sex, gender, and procreation has been subjected to, and changed by, relentless
social activity for millennia. Sex as we know it – gender identity, sexual desire
and fantasy, concepts of childhood – is itself a social product" (pp. 165–6).
This formulation includes the way in which biological sex becomes cultural
gender, the sexual division of labor, the social relations for the production of
gender and of sexual worlds, and the rules and regulations of sexual object
choice. Kinship systems, suggests Rubin, are "observable and empirical forms
of sex/gender systems" and "are made up of, and reproduce, concrete forms of
socially organized sexuality" (p. 169). Though Rubin's ostensible focus is on
the whole panoply of sex/gender arrangements, in fact her focus is upon the
domain of marriage and the creation of married and marriageable individuals.
She does not raise for analytic scrutiny the organization of parenting,
procreation, and babies. Though the substance of this paper was planned and
written, and its argument formulated, before I read Rubin, I am certainly
indebted to her for the force, and hopefully the persuasiveness, with
which I am able to point to heterosexuality as a central feature of sex/gender
systems.

6 These organizational rules, appropriately, are reflected in feminine personality,
   which, Johnson argues, consists in two components – the heterosexual and the
   maternal – created developmentally through different experiences and relationships. See Miriam Johnson, "Fathers, mothers, and sex-typing," *Sociological
   Inquiry*, 45 (1975), pp. 15–26.

7 This process also creates women ready to mother. For the purposes of this
   chapter I cut into the cycle in a different place and starting from the social fact
   of women's mothering.

8 See, e.g., Peter L. Berger and Hansfried Kellner, "Marriage and the
   construction of reality," in Rose L. Coser (ed.), *The Family*, 2nd edn (New
   York, St Martin's Press, 1974), pp. 157–74; Talcott Parsons and Robert Bales,
   Family, Socialization and Interaction Process (New York, The Free Press, 1955);
   Eli Zaretsky, "Capitalism, the family and personal life," *Socialist Revolution*
   nos 13–14 (1973), pp. 69–125 and 15 (1973), pp. 19–70.

9 Though some implications of this account probably hold in many other
   societies and other family structures, the specifics of these implications must be
   worked out before I would claim its universality. I am not arguing here, then,
   that Freud solves the universal Lévi-Straussian exchange problem (nor do I
   think it universal in the first place) as do Rubin and Mitchell (see Rubin,
   "Traffic," and Juliet Mitchell, *Psychoanalysis and Feminism* (New York,
   Pantheon, 1974). As several critics of Mitchell have pointed out, there is a
   fundamental discontinuity between Freud and Lévi-Strauss concerning the
   dyadic location of important incest taboos, the reasons for exogamy, and the
   question of which men exchange which women; see Elsa First, "Review of
   Juliet Mitchell, *Psychoanalysis and Feminism*," *New York Times*, May 19, 1974;
   Miriam Johnson, "Review of Juliet Mitchell, *Psychoanalysis and Feminism*,"
   Contemporary Sociology, 4 (1975), pp. 489–91; Elizabeth Long, "Review of
   Juliet Mitchell, *Psychoanalysis and Feminism*," *Telos*, 20 (1974), pp. 183–9; and

Sherry Ortner, "Oedipal father, mother's brother, and the penis: a review of Juliet Mitchell's *Psychoanalysis and Feminism,*" *Feminist Studies*, 2 (1975), pp. 167–82.

10 Superego formation is another primary outcome, but not relevant to my account here.

11 According to the account, a girl must also transfer her erotism from clitoris to vagina, and her erotic mode from active to passive. Regarding the former, it has been shown that there is no physiological basis for a hypothesis of two kinds of feminine orgasm (see William H. Masters and Virginia Johnson, *Human Sexual Response* (Boston, Little Brown, 1966)). Regarding the latter, there are huge definitional and conceptual problems with the psychoanalytic notion of activity–passivity. Once we remove (legitimately, I think) the instinctual component of these distinctions, the way they are experienced psychologically becomes derivative from the larger issue of heterosexual relationship itself.

I have reflected recently on the puzzling psychoanalytic claim concerning the child's original bisexuality. Though people may theoretically or potentially be "constitutionally bisexual" (whatever that means), it seems clear that empirically, in the situation where women mother, it is much more correct to speak of primary gynosexuality, or matrisexuality, in children of both genders.

12 Johnson, "Fathers, mothers, and sex-typing."

13 Alexander Mitscherlich, *Society without the Father* (New York, Schocken Books, 1970).

14 Freud, "Female sexuality," 1931, *SE*, vol. 21, p. 229.

15 Ruth Mack Brunswick, "The pre-Oedipal phase of the libido development," 1940, in Robert Fliess (ed.), *The Psychoanalytic Reader* (New York, International Universities Press, 1948), p. 238.

16 Helene Deutsch, *The Psychology of Women* (New York, Grune & Stratton, 1944 & 1945), vol. 1, p. 32.

17 Brunswick, "The pre-Oedipal phase," pp. 250–1.

18 See also David Freedman, "On women who hate their husbands," 1961, in Hendrik M. Ruitenbeck (ed.), *Psychoanalysis and Female Sexuality* (New Haven, College and University Press, 1966), for an excellent clinical account of this.

19 R. D. Laing, "The family and the 'family'," in *The Politics of the Family* (New York, Vintage, 1971), pp. 3–19.

20 Alice Balint, "Love for the mother and mother love," 1939, in Michael Balint (ed.), *Primary Love and Psycho-Analytic Technique* (New York, Liveright, 1965), pp. 91–108.

21 Janine Chasseguet-Smirgel, "Feminine guilt and the Oedipus complex," in Chasseguet-Smirgel (ed.), *Female Sexuality* (Ann Arbor, The University of Michigan Press, 1971), pp. 94–134; Bela Grunberger, "Outline for a study of narcissism in female sexuality," in Chasseguet-Smirgel (ed.), *Female Sexuality*, pp. 68–83.

22 I have discussed elsewhere the way in which the fact that a mother is real and a father fantasied affects the nature of processes of masculine and feminine identification and role assumption, focussing especially on the difficulties of masculine identification in the context of a boy's fantasied and abstracted relationship to his father (see chapters 1 and 2, this volume).

23 Jeanne Lampl-de Groot, "The evolution of the Oedipus complex in women," 1927, in Fliess (ed.), *The Psychoanalytic Reader*, pp. 180–94, and Freud, "Female sexuality."

24 Philip Slater, *The Glory of Hera: Greek mythology and the Greek family* (Boston, Beacon Press, 1968), and John W. M. Whiting, Richard Kluckhohn, and Albert Anthony, "The function of male initiation rites at puberty," in Eleanor Maccoby, T. M. Newcomb, and E. L. Hartley (eds), *Readings in Social Psychology* (New York, Holt, Rinehart and Winston, 1958), pp. 359–70.

25 Bibring here seems to be talking about middle-class and professional households. It seems to me that the same would hold for working-class fathers away from home much of the time because of work, spending recreational time in the company of men, and where the emotional division of the sexes and the sexual division of spheres is ideologically more pronounced than in the supposedly egalitarian middle and upper-middle classes. See Grete Bibring, "On the 'passing of the Oedipus complex' in a matriarchal family setting," in Rudolph M. Loewenstein (ed.), *Drives, Affects and Behavior: essays in honor of Marie Bonaparte* (New York, International Universities Press, 1953), p. 281.

26 Freud, *New Introductory Lectures on Psychoanalysis*, 1933, *SE*, vol. 22, p. 129.

27 According to Deutsch and Blos, the content and development of pubertal relationships confirm and reproduce this. See Deutsch, *Psychology of Women* and Peter Blos, "Pre-Oedipal factors in the etiology of female delinquency," *Psychoanalytic Study of the Child*, 14 (1957), pp. 113–21; *On Adolescence* (New York, The Free Press, 1962).

28 Deutsch, *Psychology of Women*, vol. 1, p. 205.

29 This claim comes from my own reading in the ethnographic literature and is confirmed by anthropologist Michelle Z. Rosaldo (personal cummunication).

30 See Martha Baum, "Love, marriage and the division of labor," *Sociological Inquiry*, 41 (1971), pp. 107–17; Arlie Russell Hochschild, *The Managed Heart: commercialization of human feeling* (Berkeley, University of California Press, 1983); Charles J. Hill, Zick Rubin, and Letitia A. Peplau, "Breakups before marriage: the end of 103 affairs," *Journal of Social Issues*, 32 (1976), pp. 147–68; William M. Kephart, "Some correlates of romantic love," *Journal of Marriage and the Family*, 29 (1967), pp. 470–4.

   Rhea Wilson pointed out (personal communication) that even in the nineteenth century men of most classes were dependent on their wives for the production of many essentials of life which were still home produced rather than produced for and therefore purchasable in the market.

31 George Goethals, "Symbiosis and the life cycle," *British Journal of Medical Psychology*, 46 (1973), p. 96.

32 Z. Rubin, "Loving and leaving," unpublished manuscript, 1975. See also Hill, Rubin, and Peplau, "Breakups before marriage."

33 Jessie Bernard, *The Future of Marriage* (New York, Bantam, 1972).

34 For clinical discussion of this, see Chasseguet-Smirgel, "Feminine guilt," and Grunberger "Outline for a study;" for sociological confirmation, see Kephart, "Some correlates."

35 Alan Booth ("Sex and social participation," *American Sociological Review*, 37 (1972), pp. 183–93) reports that women's friendships in our society are

affectively richer than men's. Mirra Komarovsky ("Patterns of self-disclosure of male undergraduates," *Journal of Marriage and the Family*, 36 (1974), pp. 677–86) found that men students confided more in a special woman friend and that they maintained a front of strength with men. Moreover, these men felt at a disadvantage *vis-à-vis* their woman confidante, because she tended to have a number of other persons in whom she could confide.

36 See, for cross-cultural confirmation, most ethnographies and also Michelle Z. Rosaldo and Louise Lamphere (eds), *Woman, Culture and Society* (Stanford, Stanford University Press, 1974). For contemporary society, see Booth, "Sex and social participation;" Elizabeth Bott, *Family and Social Network: roles, norms and external relationships in ordinary urban families* (London, Tavistock, 1957); Herbert Gans, *The Levittowners*, (New York, Pantheon, 1967); Mirra Komarovsky, *Blue-Collar Marriage* (New York, Vintage, 1967); Carol B. Stack, *All Our Kin* (New York, Harper & Row, 1974); and Michael Young and Peter Willmott, *Family and Kinship in East London* (London, Penguin, 1966).

37 Freud, *New Introductory Lectures*, p. 134. See also Michael Balint, "Eros and Aphrodite," 1936 in *Primary Love and Psycho-Analytic Technique*, pp. 59–73; Brunswick, "The pre-Oedipal phase;" Deutsch, *Psychology of Women*; Chasseguet-Smirgel, "Feminine guilt;" and Grunberger, "Outline for a study."

Chapter 4 The Fantasy of the Perfect Mother

1 We are enormously indebted to Linda Gordon, Arlie Hochschild, Sara Ruddick, Judith Stacey, Catharine Stimpson, and Barrie Thorne for their very careful reading of an earlier version of this essay. We also benefited greatly from discussions with Sherry Ortner and Norma Wikler. Although these people did not always agree with our positions, their ideas aided our ongoing explorations of the issues we examine. NIMH Training Grant MH 15 122–03 provided support for Susan Contratto during the writing of the essay.

2 The authors we discuss are all white and (broadly) professional/middle class. Thus they do not necessarily represent the whole feminist spectrum. We are focussing on certain dominant themes in several major feminist analyses of motherhood, but do not claim to discuss all aspects of these works nor all feminist writing on motherhood. Although we are often critical of the work we discuss, we have also learned from and been moved by some of this writing.

3 Nancy Friday, *My Mother/My Self* (New York, Dell, 1977).

4 Ibid., p. 105.

5 Ibid., pp. 133, 145.

6 Ibid., pp. 147, 157.

7 Ibid., p. 83.

8 Judith Arcana, *Our Mothers' Daughters* (Berkeley, Shameless Hussy Press, 1979).

9 Dorothy Dinnerstein, *The Mermaid and the Minotaur* (New York, Harper & Row, 1976).

10 Ibid., pp. 83, 85.

11 Ibid., p. 28.

12 Ibid., pp. 161, 164.

13 Ibid., p. 81.

14 Ibid., p. 253. Nancy Chodorow's *The Reproduction of Mothering: psychoanalysis and the sociology of gender* (Berkeley, University of California Press, 1978) has some important similarities with Dinnerstein's argument. Both books focus on the psychological meanings and consequences of women's mothering, and both argue that male and female parenting is essential for social change. Further, both take the stand that the conflicts typically found in relationships between adult men and women in our culture are grounded in the fact that both sexes are mothered by women. We are not considering Chodorow's argument here because we believe it is significantly different in ways that make it not relevant to our argument. Although Chodorow argues that women's mothering is perhaps the central feature in the reproduction of gender inequality, she also specifies the outcome of mothering in a way that leaves some autonomy to other aspects of cultural and social life. She does not take the extremist, portentous position of Dinnerstein and, in fact, has been criticized unfavorably on that score. As part of our argument holds that extremism in the analysis of mothering hurts feminist understanding and politics, we are more comfortable with this less apocalyptic approach.

15 Friday, *My Mother/My Self*, pp. 69, 113.

16 Arcana, *Our Mothers' Daughters*, p. 37.

17 Jane Flax, "The conflict between nurturance and autonomy in mother–daughter relationships and within feminism," *Feminist Studies*, 2 (1978), pp. 171–89.

18 Ibid., p. 175.

19 Adrienne Rich, *Of Woman Born* (New York, W. W. Norton, 1976); Alice S. Rossi, "Maternalism, sexuality and the new feminism," in Joseph Zubin and John Money (eds), *Contemporary Sexual Behavior* (Baltimore, John Hopkins University Press, 1973); Rossi, "A biosocial perspective on parenting," *Daedalus*, 106, no. 2 (1977), pp. 1–31; and Rossi, "Considering 'A biosocial perspective on parenting': reply by Alice Rossi," *Signs*, 4 (1979), pp. 712–17. Rich has been lauded and idealized by many feminists, whereas Rossi, also a feminist, has been criticized for making anti-feminist arguments. Rossi's work, put forth in several articles, is not nearly as theoretically complete or comprehensive as Rich's, but we cite them together because their accounts are remarkably similar in their fundamentals. Both decry the patriarchal alienation of women from their maternal bodies and mothering experiences; both link motherhood and sexuality (see below); both advocate compensatory training for men even while suggesting that women's maternal nature is in some way unique.

20 Rich, *Of Woman Born*, p. 292.

21 Shulamith Firestone, *The Dialectic of Sex* (New York, Morrow, 1970).

22 "Special Issue: Toward a feminist theory of motherhood" *Feminist Studies*, 2 (1978).

23 Rachel Blau DuPlessis, "Washing Blood," *Feminist Studies*, 2 (1978), pp. 1–12.

24 Kate Millett, *The Basement: meditations on a human sacrifice* (New York, Simon and Schuster, 1979).

25 Jane Lazarre, *The Mother Knot* (New York, Dell, 1976).

26 Phyllis Chesler's recent *With Child: a diary of motherhood* (New York, Crowell, 1979) echoes many of these themes in a more straightforward autobiographical manner.

27 Ruth H. Bloch, "American feminine ideals in transition: the rise of the moral mother, 1785–1815," *Feminist Studies*, 2 (1978), pp. 100–26.

28 See, for instance, Dinnerstein, *Mermaid and the Minotaur*; Norman O. Brown, *Life against Death* (New York, Vintage, 1959); and Lloyd de Mause (ed.), *The History of Childhood* (New York, Psychohistory Press, 1974).

29 David Levy, *Maternal Overprotection* (New York, Columbia University Press, 1943); Philip Wylie, *Generation of Vipers* (New York, Farrar, Rinehart, 1942); Erik Erikson, *Childhood and Society* (New York, W. W. Norton, 1950); Theodore Lidz, Stephen Fleck, and Alice R. Cornelison, *Schizophrenia and the Family* (New York, International Universities Press, 1965); Joseph C. Rheingold, *The Fear of Being a Woman: a theory of maternal destructiveness* (New York, Grune & Stratton, 1964); Philip E. Slater, *The Pursuit of Loneliness* (Boston, Beacon Press, 1970); Philip E. Slater, *Earthwalk* (New York, Doubleday 1974); and Christopher Lasch, *Haven in a Heartless World: the family besieged* (New York, Basic Books, 1977), p. 153.

30 For a more extended discussion of the issue of maternal blame in the psychological literature, see Susan Contratto Weisskopf, "Maternal guilt and mental health professionals: a reconfirming interaction," *Michigan Occasional Papers*, no. 5 (Ann Arbor, University of Michigan Women's Studies Program, 1978).

31 Selma Fraiberg, *Every Child's Birthright: in defense of mothering* (New York, Basic Books, 1977).

32 Benjamin Spock, *The Pocket Book of Baby and Child Care* (New York, Pocket, 1945, 1946, 1957, 1968); and D. W. Winnicott, *The Child, the Family, and the Outside World* (New York, Penguin, 1964).

33 Fraiberg, *Every Child's Birthright*; and T. Berry Brazelton, *Infants and Mothers: differences in development* (New York, Delacorte, 1969).

34 Frank Caplan, *The First Twelve Months of Life* (New York, Bantam, 1971); and Penelope Leach, *Your Baby and Child from Birth to Age Five* (New York, Knopf, 1978).

35 We are assuming in this argument that infants are at a stage of cognitive and ego development where they use concrete categories that are grossly affectively laden. With maturity, these categories become more elaborated, complicated, and subtle. See Jean Piaget, *The Construction of Reality in the Child* (New York, Basic Books, 1954); Piaget, *The Language and Thought of the Child* (New York, Humanities, 1959); W. R. D. Fairbairn, *An Object-Relations Theory of the Personality* (New York, Basic Books, 1952); Otto Kernberg, *Borderline Conditions and Pathological Narcissism* (New York, Jason Aronson, 1975); and Kernberg, *Object-Relations Theory and Clinical Psychoanalysis* (New York, Jason Aronson, 1976).

36 Rich, *Of Woman Born*, p. 4.

37 Rich's passionate, wide-ranging work has been the inspiration for much subsequent feminist writing on motherhood (see Sara Ruddick, "Maternal thinking," in Barrie Thorne (ed.), with Marilyn Yalom, *Rethinking the Family: some feminist questions* (New York, Longman, 1981), pp. 76–94; and "Special Issue: Mothers and daughters," *Frontiers* 3 (1978)). We also see her work as a magnificent contribution. In some ways we feel that in criticizing it and expecting it to be even more perfect, we are reproducing the fantasy of the perfect mother. Nevertheless, we continue to think that it is problematic to look to the uniqueness and potential of women's maternal bodies and relationships, however broadly defined, for the perfectibility of women and society, and we are critical of theories of motherhood that begin from notions of need, as we suggest later in this essay.

38 Helene Deutsch, *The Psychology of Women*, vols 1 and 2 (New York: Grune & Stratton, 1944 & 1945).

39 Therese Benedek, untitled "Discussion of Sherfey's paper on female sexuality," *Journal of the American Psychoanalytic Association*, 3 (1968), pp. 424–48; and Benedek, "On the psychobiology of gender identity," *Annual of Psychoanalysis*, 4 (New York, International Universities Press, 1976), pp. 117–62.

40 See Susan (Contratto) Weisskopf, "Maternal sexuality and asexual mother-hood," *Signs*, 5 (1980), pp. 766–82, for a more detailed discussion of these issues. We suspect that infantile fantasies are also part of the root of notions of asexual motherhood.

41 Jessica Benjamin has suggested that we make this ideological and political work sound too easy. We do not mean to minimize the psychological processes involved in genuinely overcoming extreme feelings about mothers and mothering, the difficult struggle and growth involved in giving up infantile idealization and rage and learning to tolerate ambivalence. This process, Benjamin suggests, is something like forgiving and mourning one's should-be-perfect mother and one's should-have-been-perfect childhood. Our point here is that even if this difficult psychological work has not been accomplished, another struggle must go on: that against allowing these feelings to become the basis of theory or politics.

As we have argued, this lack of mediation or self-censorship, this putting forth of fantasy as final truth, is certainly not unique to feminist writing on motherhood. Writing and thinking about motherhood across the spectrum is rife with unexamined assumptions about maternal perfection, overwhelming rage, and so forth. We stress here that such thinking is particularly problematic for feminists.

42 Psychoanalytic object-relations theory stresses the relational affective develop-ment we have in mind. For feminist uses of this tradition, see Jessica Benjamin, "The end of internalization: Adorno's social psychology," *Telos*, 32 (1977), pp. 42–64; Benjamin, "Authority and the family revisited: or, a world without fathers?," *New German Critique*, 13 (1978), pp. 35–57; Chodorow, *Reproduc-tion of Mothering*; and Evelyn Fox Keller, "Gender and Science," *Psycho-analysis and Contemporary Thought*, 1 (1978), pp. 409–33. Cognitive develop-mental psychology in the Piagetian tradition gives the child agency in making something of its environment and an interest in development and change. For a

feminist use of this tradition, see Carol Gilligan, "In a different voice: women's conceptions of the self and of morality," *Harvard Educational Review*, 47 (1977), pp. 481–517; Gilligan, "Woman's place in man's life cycle," *Harvard Educational Review*, 49 (1979), pp. 431–46.

Chapter 5 Gender, Relation, and Difference

1 I am very grateful to Susan Contratto, Michelle Z. Rosaldo, Jessica Benjamin, and Sara Ruddick for criticisms and comments on an earlier version of this essay.

The epigraph at its head is from *The Elementary Structures of Kinship*, quoted in Adrienne Rich, *On Lies, Secrets and Silence* (New York: W. W. Norton, 1979), p. 84.

2 See, for example, Alice Jardine, "Prelude: the future of difference," and Josette Féral, "The powers of difference," both in Hester Eisenstein and Alice Jardine (eds), *The Future of Difference* (Boston, G. K. Hall, 1980); "Women's exile: interview with Luce Irigaray," *Ideology and Consciousness*, 1 (1977), pp. 57–76; and Monique Plaza, " 'Phallomorphic power' and the 'psychology of woman'," *Ideology and Consciousness*, 4 (1978), pp. 4–36.

3 The work of Margaret S. Mahler, *On Human Symbiosis and the Vicissitudes of Individuation* (New York: International Universities Press, 1968), is paradigmatic. For a more extended discussion of the earliest development of the self along lines suggested here, see Nancy Chodorow, *The Reproduction of Mothering: psychoanalysis and the sociology of gender* (Berkeley: University of California Press, 1978), chs 4 and 5.

4 Ernest G. Schachtel, "The development of focal attention and the emergence of reality," 1954, in *Metamorphosis* (New York, Basic Books, 1959), provides the best discussion I know of this process.

5 D. W. Winnicott, "The theory of the parent–infant relationship," 1960, in *The Maturational Processes and the Facilitating Environment* (New York, International Universities Press, 1965), p. 45.

6 Alice Balint, "Love for the mother and mother love," 1939, in Michael Balint (ed.), *Primary Love and Psycho-Analytic Technique* (New York, Liveright, 1965), p. 97.

7 The new feminist/feminine blame-the-mother literature is one contemporary manifestation of failure in such a task (see esp. Nancy Friday, *My Mother/My Self* (New York, Dell Publishing, 1977)). See on this chapter 4, this volume. Of course, this is not to ignore or pass over the fact that men have been past-masters of such perceptions of women.

8 In what follows, I am drawing particularly on the work of D. W. Winnicott and Michael Balint. See Winnicott, *The Maturational Processes*, and *Playing and Reality* (New York, Basic Books, 1971); and Balint, *Primary Love*, and *The Basic Fault: therapeutic aspects of regression* (London, Tavistock, 1968). See also W. R. D. Fairbairn, *An Object-Relations Theory of the Personality* (New York, Basic Books, 1952), and Hans Loewald, "Internalization, separation,

mourning, and the superego," *Psychoanalytic Quarterly*, 31 (1962), pp. 483–504.

9 See Winnicott, "The capacity to be alone," 1958, in *The Maturational Processes*.

10 My interpretation here of differentiation, the self, and the goals of psychic life contrasts with the traditional Freudian view, which stresses ego and superego autonomy. For an excellent discussion of questions of ego autonomy and psychic structure, see Jessica Benjamin, "The end of internalization: Adorno's social psychology," *Telos*, 32 (1977), pp. 42–64.

11 See Sigmund Freud, "The dissolution of the Oedipus complex," 1924, *The Standard Edition of the Complete Psychological Works of Sigmund Freud*, ed. James Strachey (London: The Hogarth Press and the Institute of Psychoanalysis) (hereafter *SE*), vol. 19, pp. 172–9; "Some psychical consequences of the anatomical distinction between the sexes," 1925, *SE*, vol. 19, pp. 243–58; and "Femininity," 1933, in *New Introductory Lectures on Psychoanalysis*, *SE*, vol. 22, pp. 112–35.

12 See Roy Schafer, "Problems in Freud's psychology of women," *Journal of the American Psychoanalytic Association*, 22 (1974), pp. 459–85.

13 See Robert Stoller, "Facts and fancies: an examination of Freud's concept of bisexuality," in Jean Strouse (ed.), *Women and Analysis* (New York, Grossman Publishers, 1974); and other Stoller writings.

14 For reviews of the social psychological literature on this point, see Miriam Johnson, "Sex role learning in the nuclear family," in *Child Development*, 34 (1963), pp. 319–34; Johnson, "Fathers, mothers and sex-typing," *Sociological Inquiry*, 45 (1975), pp. 15–26; and Eleanor Maccoby and Carol Jacklin, *The Psychology of Sex Differences* (Stanford, Stanford University Press, 1974).

15 For further discussion, see Chodorow, *Reproduction of Mothering*, ch. 5.

16 Johnson, "Fathers, mothers and sex typing," makes this suggestion, and suggests further that the father's masculinity introduces gender difference.

17 See Juliet Mitchell, *Psychoanalysis and Feminism* (New York, Pantheon, 1974).

18 See Barrie Thorne, "Gender . . . how is it best conceptualized?" (Paper presented at the Annual Meeting of the American Sociological Association, San Francisco, August 1978.)

19 For a discussion of these general cultural preoccupations and their psychological origins, see Evelyn Fox Keller, "Gender and science," *Psychoanalysis and Contemporary Thought*, 1 (1978), pp. 409–33.

Chapter 6 Beyond Drive Theory

1 This chapter is dedicated to the memory of Michelle Zimbalist Rosaldo. I am grateful to Norman O. Brown for prompt, extensive, and helpful comments on an earlier version. I would also like to thank Jessica Benjamin, Margaret Cerullo, G. William Domhoff, Martin Jay, Donald Levine, Peter Lyman, Sherry Ortner, and Robert Wallerstein for comments, David Plotke for editorial and critical assistance, and the students in my "Psychoanalytic Theory and Society" seminars at the University of California, Santa Cruz. I have written this chapter with the support of a Summer Stipend from the

National Endowment for the Humanities, a sabbatical leave from the University of California, Santa Cruz, a Fellowship at the Center for Advanced Study in the Behavioral Sciences, where financial support was also provided by grants from the National Institutes of Mental Health, 5–T32–MH14581– 05, and The Spencer Foundation, and the hospitality of the Institute of Personality Assessment and Research, University of California, Berkeley.

2 Robert S. Wallerstein, "Reflections," in Edward D. Joseph and Daniel Widlocher (eds), *The Identity of the Psychoanalyst* (New York, International Universities Press, 1983), pp. 265–76.

3 My discussion concentrates on these two books (hereafter *EAC* and *LAD*). I also discuss Brown's *Love's Body* (*LB*), which Brown considers a "continuation" of *LAD*, but which differs fundamentally from it, both in its basic argument and (for my purposes) in its much less systematic reliance on psychoanalytic theory, and I mention Marcuse's other Freudian writings. See Norman O. Brown, *Life Against Death* (New York, Vintage, 1959) and *Love's Body* (New York, Vintage, 1966); Herbert Marcuse, *Eros and Civilization*, 1955 (New York, Vintage, 1962) and *Five Lectures* (Boston, Beacon Press, 1970). By the late drive theory, I mean the metapsychology of life and death that Freud articulates in *Beyond the Pleasure Principle*, 1920, *The Standard Edition of the Complete Psychological Works of Sigmund Freud*, ed. James Strachey (London: The Hogarth Press and the Institute of Psychoanalysis) (hereafter *SE*), vol. 18, pp. 7–64. It must be recognized that in insisting on this metapsychology, Brown and Marcuse differ from many "orthodox" analysts, who are sceptical or rejecting of Freud's claim for a death instinct.

4 Michel Foucault, *The History of Sexuality* (New York, Pantheon, 1978), offers a different criticism of what he calls the "repression hypothesis" which will not concern us here.

5 I take as my programme here Jane Flax's claim that "feminists should analyze the epistemology of all bodies of knowledge which claim to be emancipatory including psychoanalysis and Marxism": "Political philosophy and the patriarchal unconscious," in Sandra Harding and Merrill B. Hintikka (eds), *Discovering Reality: feminist perspectives on epistemology, metaphysics, methodology, and the philosophy of science* (Dordrecht, Reidel, 1983), p. 270.

6 Marcuse and Brown debate the issue of the separate ego, or "I" in an exchange about Brown's radical vision of union in *Love's Body*. See "Love mystified: a critique of Norman O. Brown" and "A reply to Herbert Marcuse," in Marcuse, *Negations* (Boston, Beacon Press, 1968), pp. 227–47.

7 *Civilization and Its Discontents*, 1930, *SE*, vol. 21, pp. 59–145.

8 Before examining Marcuse's and Brown's theories, I note that an opposing strand of critical psychoanalytic social theory also begins from the drive-repression dynamic. If Marcuse's and Brown's positions represent a radical libertarian position on the drive question, we might think of the other strand as a conservative superego morality position. See e.g., Lionel Trilling, *Freud and the Crisis of Our Culture* (Boston, Beacon Press, 1955), and *Sincerity and Authenticity* (Cambridge, Mass., Harvard University Press, 1971, 1972); Russell Jacoby, *Social Amnesia* (Boston, Beacon Press, 1975); Christopher Lasch, *Haven in a Heartless World: the family besieged* (New York, Basic

Books, 1977) and *The Culture of Narcissism* (New York, W. W. Norton, 1979); Max Horkheimer, "Authority and the family," in *Critical Theory* (New York, Herder & Herder, 1936); Horkheimer, "Authoritarianism and the family today," in Ruth Nanda Anshen (ed.), *The Family* (New York, Harper, 1949), pp. 359–69; Frankfurt Institute for Social Research, *Aspects of Sociology* (Boston, Beacon Press, 1972); Alexander Mitscherlich, *Society Without the Father* (New York, Schocken Books, 1970); Philip Rieff, *Freud: the mind of the moralist* (New York, Anchor, 1961), and *The Triumph of the Therapeutic* (New York, Harper & Row, 1966); and Marcuse, *Five Lectures*.

These writers agree with Brown and Marcuse that the drive theory forms the core of psychoanalysis and demonstrates that we cannot be totally culturally determined, and they condemn those "revisionists" who stress cultural influences or the compatibility of the instincts and culture. Even as they argue for the drive theory, however, they do not view drive repression as the root of human unhappiness, as Freud, Marcuse, and Brown would hold. Rather, our contemporary psychological crisis, helping to sustain social crisis, originates in the decline of those psychic agencies that institute repression: the superego, with its rigorous adherence to internally sustained standards of conduct and moral norms; and the autonomous ego with its clear identifications and goals and a consistently followed ego ideal. Thus, even as they hold that drives form our best hope against social domination, these theorists wish to resurrect the very agencies that repress the drives, to reinstitute a strong superego, a strong autonomous ego, and a return to earlier forms of instinctual control rather than the direct manipulation of drives or uncontrolled drive expression we now have.

A full critique of these accounts is beyond the scope of this essay. Briefly, they share with Brown and Marcuse a number of problems: simplistic, non-clinical readings of psychoanalysis (Mitscherlich is an exception, Lasch a partial exception here), of psychological development and psychic life, and fundamentally asocial social theories, theories that can only imagine, as the solution to direct domination, a return to intrapsychic repression and the creation of a superego and autonomous ego which, although initially internalizing parental rules and prohibitions, henceforth operate solely from within, without consideration of social demands or context; they do not allow intersubjectivity. In addition, these theories often display a peculiar blindness to some forms of domination and denial, particularly the dominations of gender and the denial of the mother. For a discussion of these problems, see Jessica Benjamin, "The end of internalization: Adorno's social psychology," *Telos*, 32 (1977), pp. 42–64, "Authority and the family revisited: or, a world without fathers?", *New German Critique*, 13 (1978), pp. 35–57, and "The Oedipal riddle: authority, autonomy, and the new narcissism," in John Diggins and Mark Kamm (eds), *The Problem of Authority in America* (Philadelphia, Temple University Press, 1981); Jane Flax, "Critical theory as a vocation," *Politics and Society*, 8:2 (1978), pp. 201–23; Stephanie Engel, "Femininity as tragedy: re-examining the 'new narcissism,'" *Socialist Review*, 53 (1980), pp. 77–104; and Mark Poster, "Review of Lasch, *Haven*," *Telos*, 35 (1978), pp. 226–30.

Martin Jay suggests that *EAC* is a response not only to Fromm's revisionism but also to Horkheimer and Adorno's wish to turn Freud into a "prophet of gloom": *The Dialectical Imagination* (Boston, Little Brown, 1973), p. 106. In this context we can see the two adjacent and incompatible chapters in *Five Lectures*, where he puts forth the *EAC* argument and the Horkheimer argument, never remarking on their incompatibility, as Marcuse's attempt to prevent a theoretical break with his two colleagues.

9 This general approach has reappeared recently in Lacanian psychoanalytic social theory. With his claim that entry into the "symbolic" constitutes the alienated individual, Lacan has been taken to imply that the "imaginary" is somehow truer (if unavoidably given up in the process of development) and thus to echo this idealization of the id: Jacques Lacan, *Ecrits* (New York, W. W. Norton, 1977). Gilles DeLeuze and Felix Guattari argue for a refusal to "Oedipize" and a reclaiming of the primitive wishes of the pre-ego, almost pre-"imaginary" "it" – a "politics of schizophrenia" that will be the final, irrefutable challenge to capitalism: *Anti-Oedipus: capitalism and schizophrenia* (New York, Viking, 1977). Luce Irigaray and other French Freudian feminists claim that women's writing is and should be formless, lacking in logic and exhibiting pre-Oedipal, "hysterical" consciousness that denies and refutes Oedipal phallogocentrism: "When our lips speak together," *Signs*, 6 (1981); "And the one doesn't stir without the other," *Signs*, 7 (1983); and "The sex which is not one," in Elaine Marks and Isabelle de Courtivron (eds), *New French Feminisms* (New York, Schocken Books, 1980). For a lucid discussion of these theories, see Sherry Turkle, *Psychoanalytic Politics* (New York, Basic Books, 1978). The present essay does not directly treat Lacan and his followers, but I believe that many aspects of my critique of the drive-repression perspective apply to these theorists as well.

10 Brown in fact also relies in *LAD* on the cultural writings of Roheim and in *LB* moves to an increasing reliance on Kleinian theory. These shifts reflect and create contradictions in his work.

11 *LAD*, p. 153.

12 Ibid., p. 57.

13 *EAC*, p. 17. Marcuse makes the same claim in *Five Lectures*. Richard King, *The Party of Eros: radical social thought and the realm of freedom* (Chapel Hill, The University of North Carolina Press, 1972), also discusses this aspect of *EAC*.

14 *LAD*, p. xii.

15 Ibid., p. 98.

16 Marcuse's argument here follows the Frankfurt School tradition. For a discussion of Frankfurt criticism of Fromm and revisionism, see Jay, *Dialectical Imagination*.

17 *EAC*, p. 227.

18 Ibid., p. 16.

19 Ibid., p. 184.

20 Ibid., p. 32.

21 Ibid., p. 182.

22 *LAD*, p. 156.

23 Perhaps as a result, Brown is much more attuned than Marcuse to the complexities of Freud's developmental and clinical accounts, to changes in the anxiety theory, and to post-Freudian writers.

24 On this, see Yiannis Gabriel, *Freud and society* (London and Boston, Routledge and Kegan Paul, 1983), and King, *The Party of Eros*.

25 *LAD*, p. 27.

26 Ibid., p. 308.

27 Ibid., p. 176.

28 *EAC*, p. 184.

29 Ibid., p. 185.

30 Ibid., pp. 185–6.

31 Ibid., p. 186.

32 Ibid., p. 155.

33 Ibid., p. 186.

34 Ibid., p. 189.

35 *LAD*, p. 30.

36 *EAC*, p. 190.

37 *LAD*, p. 11, and pp. 307–22.

38 *EAC*, p. 190.

39 Ibid., p. 156. See also Marcuse, *The Aesthetic Dimension* (Boston, Beacon Press, 1978).

40 *EAC*, p. 157.

41 Ibid., p. 158.

42 Ibid., p. 170.

43 *LAD*, pp. 65–6.

44 Ibid., p. 63.

45 Ibid., p. 66.

46 Ibid., p. 62.

47 *EAC*, p. 154.

48 Ibid., p. 153.

49 Ibid.

50 Ibid.

51 Ibid., pp. 153–4.

52 *LAD*, p. 42.

53 Ibid., p. 44.

54 Ibid., p. 45.

55 Ibid.

56 Ibid.

57 Ibid., p. 46.

58 Ibid., p. 47.

59 Ibid., p. 49.

60 Ibid., pp. 49–50.

61 *LB*, p. 149.

62 Ibid., p. 148.

63 Ibid., p. 87.

64 Ibid., p. 49.

65 Ibid., p. 84.

66 Marcuse, *Negations*, p. 236.
67 *LAD*, p. 40.
68 *EAC*, p. 113.
69 Ibid., p. 182.
70 Ibid., pp. 186–7.
71 Ibid., p. 191.
72 Ibid., p. 189.
73 Ibid., p. 194.
74 Ibid., pp. 191–3. Flax, "Critical theory," points to both the individualist view of labor in Frankfurt theory and the problems in Marcuse's reliance on an individualist instinct theory rather than a more relationally based view of primary process.
75 *EAC*, p. 177.
76 Benjamin, "The end of internalization" and "Authority," makes similar arguments concerning Horkheimer's and Adorno's social psychologies.
77 *LB*, p. 80.
78 Ibid., p. 141.
79 Ibid., pp. 253–4.
80 Martin Jay (personal communication) suggests, I think plausibly, that Victor Turner's conception of "communitas" is close to a social version of "limitless narcissism": Turner, *The Ritual Process* (Ithaca, Cornell University Press, 1977); Norman O. Brown has pointed out (personal communication) that he and Marcuse are caught not only in the tensions of Freudianism but also in the tensions between collectivist and anarchist tendencies within Marxism. Communitas, which develops, according to Turner, in the liminal space created by ritual, dissolves the social structuring of statuses and roles in favor of global, unstructured, spontaneous, immediate relations among historically specific, idiosyncratic individuals who are at the same time homogeneous rather than systematically or structurally unequal. Boundaries dissolve, as the only social boundary recognized is that coterminous with humanity itself. Communitas also includes a sense of innovative play and symbolically generative creativity. Its imagery is that of harmony, mutuality, universal justice, and peace rather than of hierarchy and instrumental use of the other. Turner argues that communitas must be transitional or temporary. Communitas itself, as it continues, develops a structure and patterns of institutionalized relationship through its very repetitions; moreover, human continuity requires organization and mobilization to produce life's necessities, an organization and mobilization that include the facing of difficulties, decision-making, the deferment of desire and gratification, and so forth. Turner argues that communitas and structure must alternate. In what follows I suggest specifically that Marcuse and Brown can adhere to a communitas-like model precisely through relying on a psychoanalytic account in which it is assumed that life's necessities will be met by an other who then does not have the freedom to participate spontaneously in communitas, and, more generally, that the mutuality of communitas and a psychoanalysis of drive gratification and limitless narcissism are contradictory.
81 Any utopian vision by necessity must include a much wider range of

possibilities in choice of sexual- and love-object than we now have. I am critical not of the homosexuality, but of the narcissism and instrumental view of the other that I believe inheres in this account, and the implied devaluation and denial of women in Marcuse's idealization of Orpheus.

82 *LAD*, pp. 105–6.

83 *EAC*, p. 6.

84 Ibid., p. 7.

85 *LAD*, p. xiii.

86 This focus contrasts noticeably with the rest of Marcuse's work, which stresses and centers on the Hegelian subject. In *EAC*, the instincts are all and the subject virtually disappears. Such a focus also undercuts Marcuse's general call for rationally based collective regulation of people's lives.

87 LAD, p. 99, my italics.

88 See ibid., pp. 109–15.

89 Ibid., p. 114.

90 Ibid.

91 Ibid., p. 115, my italics.

92 *LB*, pp. 146–7. Quotation "There is a continual . . ." is taken by Brown from Kleinian psychoanalyst Roger Money-Kyrle; "we are members" from Joan Rivière.

93 *EAC*, p. 7.

94 Jay, *Dialectical Imagination*, p. 112, discusses this convergence of Marcuse and Fromm.

95 A dynamic tension, or "contradiction," that Marcuse otherwise claims pervasive in social life.

96 And the repressive de-sublimation examined in *One-Dimensional Man* (Boston, Beacon Press, 1964).

97 *EAC*, p. 14.

98 Ibid., p. 177.

99 Ibid., p. 9.

100 Ibid., p. 88. This analysis, following Horkheimer, takes up only two pages in *EAC*, though Marcuse amplifies his commitment to the view in *Five Lectures* and *One-Dimensional Man*. See n. 8.

101 *LAD*, p. 96.

102 Flax, "Critical theory," p. 219, suggests that "the lack of development of an adequate notion of intersubjectivity" is found throughout critical theory, a criticism that Habermas has tried to meet.

103 See Freud, "On narcissism: an introduction," 1914, *SE*, vol. 14, pp. 69–102.

104 See Alice Balint, "Love for the mother and mother-love", 1939, in Michael Balint (ed.), *Primary Love and Psycho-Analytic Technique* (New York, Liveright, 1965); Margaret S. Mahler, Fred Pine, and Anni Bergman, *The Psychological Birth of the Human Infant* (New York, Basic Books, 1975); Chodorow, *The Reproduction of Mothering: psychoanalysis and the sociology of gender* (Berkeley, University of California Press, 1978), and chapter 5, this volume; and Benjamin, "Oedipal riddle."

105 *EAC*, p. 135.

106 I do not claim here to present a general criticism of narcissism in society, but

to show that the reliance on drive theory and on the notion of childhood authenticity generates an idealization of narcissism as a principle of social organization. This point about Brown and Marcuse is also made in Don S. Browning, *Generative Man: psychoanalytic perspectives* (Philadelphia, The Westminster Press, 1973), p. 67.

107 See Alice Balint, "Love for the mother;" and Ernest G. Schachtel, "The development of focal attention and the emergence of reality," 1954, in *Metamorphosis* (New York, Basic Books, 1959).

108 *EAC*, p. 186.

109 Ibid., p. 135. The role of memory plays a more complex role in Marcuse's work and in Frankfurt theory more generally than that which I discuss here. See, on this, Jacoby, *Social Amnesia*; and Martin Jay, "Anamnestic totalization: reflections on Marcuse's theory of remembrance," *Theory and Society*, 11 (1982), pp. 1–15. Even in *EAC*, memory is called upon to remind us not only of what can be but also what, regrettably, has been.

110 *LAD*, p. 60.

111 Ibid., p. 57.

112 Ibid., pp. 66–7.

113 Ibid., p. 67.

114 On this, see W. R. D. Fairbairn, *An Object-Relations Theory of the Personality* (New York, Basic Books, 1952), especially "A revised psychopathology of the psychoses and psychoneuroses," 1941, pp. 28–58; and Edith Jacobson, *The Self and the Object World* (New York, International Universities Press, 1964).

115 *LAD*, p. 45.

116 *EAC*, p. 185.

117 See Roy Schafer, "Problems in Freud's psychology of women," *Journal of the American Psychoanalytic Association*, 22 (1974), pp. 459–85.

118 Michael Balint, "On genital love," 1947, in *Primary Love*, p. 115. Alice Balint, "Love for the mother," considers this the progression from "naive egoism" to altruistic love.

119 See Sara Ruddick, "Maternal thinking," in Barrie Thorne (ed.), with Marilyn Yalom, *Rethinking the Family: some feminist questions* (New York, Longman, 1981). I should point out that Marcuse and Brown are hardly unique. Although psychoanalysis concerns child development in the family, the issue of parenting from the parental side is completely absent in Freud and almost non-existent in psychoanalytic writing since. However, most psychoanalytic writing is not actively hostile to parental concerns.

120 *LAD*, pp. 107–8.

121 *LB*, p. 54.

122 In "Political philosophy," Flax makes a related argument to those I make here and below, showing the influence of male childhood experience in relation to the mother on certain dominant political philosophies. Evelyn Fox Keller makes a similar argument concerning "normal science" in *Reflections on Gender and Science* (New Haven, Yale University Press, 1985). Nancy Hartsock, "The feminist standpoint: developing the ground for a specifically feminist historical materialism," in Harding and Hintikka (eds), *Discovering Reality*, discusses "abstract masculinity" as a product of male development.

This might also apply to Brown's and Marcuse's preference for drive theory –
a universalistic, non-concrete, non-specific, and non-historically based view of
human functioning – over a clinically based object-relations perspective. See
also Flax, "Psychoanalysis as deconstruction and myth: on gender, narcissism
and modernity's discontents," in Günter H. Lenz and Kurt Shell (eds), *Crisis
of Modernity* (Boulder, Col., Westview Press, 1986).

123 *EAC*, p. 155.

124 Ibid., p. 146.

125 Ibid.

126 As Michael Balint points out in "Eros and Aphrodite," 1936, in *Primary Love*,
the focus on Eros as sexual goal has gender- and generationally related mythic
origins in which female love is both adult and genital: "Eros issues out of
Chaos as a child and never becomes an adult, while Aphrodite was never a
child but, according to the myth, rose from the sea as an adult woman"
(p. 64).

127 Jessica Benjamin, "Rational violence and erotic domination," in Hester
Eisenstein and Alice Jardine (eds), *The Future of Difference* (Boston, G. K.
Hall, 1980), provides an extended argument that the dynamics of the desire to
deny dependence while maintaining connection lead to sexual domination.
Thus even as we may wish to move beyond the defensive separateness and
autonomy of the traditional Oedipal resolution, we must be wary of visions of
pre-Oedipal relatedness that leave no room for the differentiated subject or
self or that see union, relatedness, and connection as always mutual and an
expression of Eros. Evelyn Fox Keller, "Feminism and science," *Signs*, 7
(1982), pp. 589–602, also warns of the necessity for a delicate balance between
"pre-Oedipal" identification and empathy between subject and object and
letting a vision of a psychic or cognitive state that precedes the subject–object
split collapse into pure subjectivity.

128 *LAD*, p. 122.

129 Ibid.

130 Ibid., p. 123.

131 Ibid., p. 122.

132 Ibid., p. 125.

133 Ibid., p. 126. This claim anticipates later feminist writing, including my own.
Dorothy Dinnerstein, *The Mermaid and the Minotaur* (New York, Harper &
Row, 1976), makes such a claim the starting-place of her argument, and in
fact draws heavily on a reinterpretation of Brown. Brown here is confusingly
inconsistent. As I indicate above, he says elsewhere (*LAD*, pp. 113–14) that
the family maintains the child in a situation of prolonged helplessness,
creating psychic trauma and anxiety. Here, by contrast, he claims that such
dependence is given by nature.

134 *LB*, p. 36.

135 Ibid., pp. 49–50. Brown here makes explicit that which is implicit in all
claims for "limitless narcissism." Marcuse writes, "primary narcissism . . .
engulfs the 'environment'" (*EAC*, p. 153), passing over who the "environment" is.

136 *LB*, p. 49, my italics. As Schorske puts it, "Norman O. Brown in *Love's Body*

opens a radically new understanding of community identification as mother substitution." See Carl Schorske, *Fin de Siècle Vienna* (New York, Vintage, 1980), p. 159.

137 This is also true of Marcuse's talk, "Socialist feminism," where he attempts to bring women into the argument of *Eros and Civilization*. Here he discusses women, but in the form of an idealized woman who can serve as a symbol of male liberation, as much as serving as an agent of her own.

138 *Negations*, p. 237.

139 *LAD*, p. 292.

140 As Gabriel points out, in *Freud and society*, the problem of the death drives as a threat to social cohesion does not arise in the same way for Brown, since he does not presume that death is in essence a force toward destruction but a part of the natural alternation of life. It is only as it is distorted through its denial that it becomes a destructive force.

141 My account of Freud's drive and object-relational conceptions draws on Harry Guntrip, *Personality Structure and Human Interaction* (New York, International Universities Press, 1961), and Harry Guntrip, *Psychoanalytic Theory, Therapy, and the Self* (New York, Basic Books, 1971).

142 For a more extended discussion of this issue, see George Klein, "Two theories or one?" *Bulletin of the Menninger Clinic*, 37:1 (1973), pp. 102–32.

143 Freud, "Inhibitions, symptoms and anxiety," 1926, *SE*, vol. 20, pp. 77–174.

144 See Freud, *The Ego and the Id*, 1923, *SE*, vol. 19, pp. 3–59; "The dissolution of the Oedipus complex," 1924, *SE*, vol. 19, pp. 172–9; *Civilization and Its Discontents*, and *New Introductory Lectures on Psychoanalysis*, 1933, *SE*, vol. 22, esp. Lecture 31, pp. 57–80.

145 In this respect the conservative superego theorists move more fully beyond biological factors and drive theory than do Marcuse and Brown, since their stress upon superego formation and the development of ego autonomy in relation to the father involves social-relational factors. Yet while the conservative superego theorists do discuss relationships, their emphasis on conformity and the elimination of the individual likewise implies that people can exist without active psychological functioning. See n. 8.

146 See Freud, "On narcissism," and "Mourning and melancholia," 1917, *SE*, vol. 14, pp. 239–58.

147 Brown both extols primary narcissism and the oceanic feeling and cites Rivière (*LB*, p. 147), who implies the coexistence of a complex developed sense of individuation and interconnectedness, rather than simple primary merging. Marcuse alternates between "limitless narcissism" and "refusal to separate from the libidinous object," and a more clearly individualistic drive gratification and aesthetic stance. Though he mentions mature libidinal relations he never indicates what these might consist in or how they might develop.

148 Beyond the one Rivière quotation cited above (see full quote p. 158, this volume), the thrust of his work, as exemplified in his later exchange about it with Marcuse, argues for the illusory nature of all individuality and all separations, and suggests that he does not really accept the differentiation or individuation that is intrinsic to relatedness and mutual introjections.

149 I refer broadly to British object-relations theorists Balint, Fairbairn, Guntrip, and Winnicott. See M. Balint, *Primary Love; The Basic Fault: therapeutic aspects of regression* (London, Tavistock, 1968); Fairbairn, *An Object-Relations Theory*; Guntrip, *Personality Structure; Psychoanalytic Theory*; and *Schizoid Phenomena, Object-Relations and the Self* (New York, International Universities Press, 1969); and D. W. Winnicott, *Collected Papers: from paediatrics to psychoanalysis* (London, Tavistock, 1958), *The Maturational Processes and the Facilitating Environment* (New York, International Universities Press, 1965), and *Playing and Reality* (New York, Basic Books, 1971). See also Jay Greenberg and Stephen Mitchell, *Object Relations in Psychoanalytic Theory* (Cambridge, Mass., Harvard University Press, 1983). I have also been influenced by Jacobson's conceptions of the structuralization of drives (in *The Self and the Object World*), by Loewald's conception of the creation of internality and externality, in "Internalization, separation, mourning, and the superego," *Psychoanalytic Quarterly*, 31 (1962), pp. 483–504, by George Klein's arguments for the clinical basis of psychoanalytic theory in *Psychoanalytic Theory* (New York, International Universities Press, 1976), and by Roy Schafer's emphasis on the agency of psychological activity, in *A New Language for Psychoanalysis* (New Haven, Yale University Press, 1976).

150 In this schema, Fromm, Roheim, and Parsons are transitional figures. Parsons explicitly puts forth an object-relational perspective, but his is really a theory of role relationships and unidirectional internalization. He loses the psychodynamic – conflict, resistance, the transformation of experiences – as a separate level. Fromm and Roheim conceptualize the object-relational and social, but Fromm asserts human sociality in an idealized, unsubstantiated way, and Roheim remains too tied to the drive theory and to the mother as object. See, e.g., Erich Fromm, *Escape from Freedom* (New York, Avon, 1941); "The human implications of instinctivistic 'radicalism'," in *Dissent*, 2:4 (1955), pp. 342–9, and *The Crisis of Psychoanalysis* (Greenwich, Fawcett, 1970); Geza Roheim, *The Origin and Function of Culture* (New York, Nervous and Mental Disease Monographs 69, 1943); Talcott Parsons, *Social Structure and Personality* (New York, The Free Press, 1964).

I do not mean here to argue that psychoanalytic theory (of any sort) can form the only or exclusive basis for a critical social psychology. Within the critical theory tradition, for instance, Habermas turns to Mead and to Kohlbergian notions of moral development to develop an interactive psychological component of social theory, and Meadian concepts certainly underpin Parsons' theory. These theories are more cognitive and conscious – the concept of communicative rationality is a case in point – than that which concerns me here, though they certainly also point out the need for a social psychological component to social theory. My discussion here is limited to the psychoanalytic question of how unconscious processes and structures enter social life.

151 Jacobson, *The Self and the Object World*. Jacobson was part of a group of left-wing psychoanalysts: see Russell Jacoby, *The Repression of Psychoanalysis* (New York, Basic Books, 1983). Her theory, in which drives are fundamentally shaped by an active actor in a social world, may be a product of her Marxist

origins. See also Fairbairn, "Revised psychopathology" in his *An Object-Relations Theory*. Brown's account of development is very much of a piece with Fairbairn, but he implies that people could develop without drive organization and transformation.

152 Insofar as we want to consider her an object-relations theorist, since she has provided the most extensive, original account of the construction of an inner object world, Klein is an exception. Kleinian theory certainly argues for the insistence and pervasiveness of given (particularly aggressive) drives.

153 For an argument for Kleinian object-relations theory as a basis for a liberatory psychoanalytic social theory, see Michael Rustin, "A socialist consideration of Kleinian psychoanalysis," *New Left Review*, 131 (1982), pp. 71–96. See also Benjamin, "The end of internalization," "Authority," and "Oedipal riddle," and Flax, "Critical theory," and "Political philosophy."

154 This is Fairbairn's phrase.

155 Most object-relations theorists still take the point of view of the child, with mother as object. Only a few (mainly women) psychoanalysts and feminist theorists have taken seriously the problem of the subjectivity of the mother.

156 *Playing and Reality*, p. 13.

157 A few writers have begun to explore the implications of Winnicott's notions for a theory of culture and creativity. On scientific practice and scientific creativity, see Keller, *Reflections*; on religion, see Mary Ellen Ross and Cheryl Lynn Ross, "Mothers, infants, and the psychoanalytic study of ritual," *Signs*, 9 (1983), pp. 26–39; on art, see Peter Fuller, "Art and biology," *New Left Review*, 132 (1982), pp. 83–96.

Chapter 7　Toward a Relational Individualism

1 I am indebted to Ann Swidler and Abby Wolfson for very helpful responses to an earlier version of this paper and to Peter Lyman for general conversations about these issues. The argument in this paper is part of a larger project formulated in various ways over the past several years by Jessica Benjamin, Jane Flax, Evelyn Fox Keller, and myself. I have benefited from discussion and correspondence with all of them as well as from reading their work. Sherry Ortner first suggested to me the formulation "relational individualism."

2 Sigmund Freud, *Introductory lectures on psycho-analysis*, 1915–16, *The Standard Edition of the Complete Psychological Works of Sigmund Freud*, ed. James Strachey (London, The Hogarth Press and the Institute of Psychoanalysis), (hereafter *SE*), vol. 16, p. 285.

3 See Michel Foucault, *The History of Sexuality*, I (New York, Pantheon, 1978), and Fred Weinstein and Gerald M. Platt, *The Wish To Be Free* (Berkeley, University of California Press, 1969).

4 Sigmund Freud, "Dissection of the psychical personality," in *New Introductory Lectures in Psychoanalysis*, 1933, *SE*, vol. 22, p. 80.

5 The polarity I discuss is found in personality psychology as well as within psychoanalytic theory. See Avril Thorne, "Disposition as interpersonal constraint," (Ph.D. dissertation, University of California, Berkeley, 1983). But for a very different argument, for individualism in personality psychology, see

Gordon Allport, *Personality: a psychological interpretation* (New York, H. Holt & Co., 1937), who argues in his opening paragraphs not against a more relational conception of personality but against the scientific psychological attempt to cut up the self into nomothetically derived aspects that can be studied across persons without regard to their situatedness in the makeup of the whole person.

6 Sigmund Freud, "Some psychical consequences of the anatomical distinction between the sexes," 1925, *SE*, vol. 19, p. 257.

7 Kohut is somewhat paradoxical in terms of the antinomy I am trying to develop here. On the one hand, he is seen as an object-relations theorist par excellence, who locates disorders of the self squarely in early failures of the mirroring and idealizing relationship to mother and father. He is contrasted (and contrasts himself) with the classical theorists in his focus on the self and the self's disorders, as opposed to the classical concern with conflict. Yet on the other hand, his goals for the self – ambitions and ideals mediated by skills and talents – could not be more individualist. In his version, the object-relations route is to lead to individual fulfillment of individual goals. Where Freud, Hartmann, and others assume that harmonizing internal conflict will somehow harmonize relations with the external world, Kohut seeks to harmonize external relations to enable internal resolution. See his *Analysis of the Self* (New York, International Universities Press, 1971) and *Restoration of the Self* (New York, International Universities Press, 1977).

8 "On narcissism: an introduction," 1914, *SE*, vol. 14, p. 85. Freud in this essay still makes object-relatedness residual. Thus he assumes that libido proceeds onto the object as a spillover from narcissism: "What makes it necessary at all for our mental life to pass on beyond the limits of narcissism and to attach the libido to objects? The answer which would follow from our line of thought would once more be that this necessity arises when the cathexis of the ego with libido exceeds a certain amount." And although he notes the *two* original love-objects of the infant (mother and self), he and his followers go on as if primary narcissism precedes any object-directedness and is the exclusive original state of the infant.

9 See Carol Gilligan, *In a Different Voice: psychological theory and women's development* (Cambridge, Mass., Harvard University Press, 1982), and "Remapping the moral domain: new images of the self in relationship," in Thomas Heller, Morton Sosna, and David Wellbery (eds), *Reconstructing Individualism* (Stanford, Stanford University Press, 1986), pp. 237–52.

10 See Michael Balint (ed.), *Primary Love and Psycho-Analytic Technique* (New York, Liveright, 1965), and *The Basic Fault: therapeutic aspects of regression* (London, Tavistock, 1968); W. R. D. Fairbairn, *An Object-Relations Theory of the Personality* (New York, Basic Books, 1952); Harry Guntrip, *Personality Structure and Human Interaction* (New York, International Universities Press, 1961), and *Schizoid Phenomena, Object-Relations and the Self* (New York, International Universities Press, 1969); Edith Jacobson, *The Self and the Object World* (New York, International Universities Press, 1964); Margaret S. Mahler, Fred Pine, and Anni Bergman, *The Psychological Birth of the Human Infant* (New York, Basic Books, 1975); and D. W. Winnicott, *Collected Papers: from*

paediatrics to psychoanalysis (London, Tavistock, 1958), *The Maturational Processes and the Facilitating Environment* (New York, International Universities Press, 1965), and *Playing and Reality* (New York, Basic Books, 1971).

11 Recent infancy research claims that the infant's cognitive sense of separateness is innate, rather than developed in the manner described by Mahler and others. Such a revision of our understanding of the infant's mental capacities does not undermine the understanding of the affective and object-relational components of sense of separateness and relatedness that I discuss here. See Daniel N. Stern, "The Early Development of Schemas of Self, Other, and 'Self with Other'," in Joseph D. Lichtenberg and Samuel Kaplan, eds., *Reflections on Self Psychology* (Hillsdale, N.J., Analytic Press, 1983).

12 On the primary creation of internality and externality, see Hans Loewald, "Internalization, separation, mourning and the superego," 1962, in his *Papers on Psychoanalysis* (New Haven, Yale University Press, 1980), and Jacobson, *The Self and the Object World*.

13 In the course of this development, what were originally unstructured and unorganized drive potentials come to be differentiated into aggressive and libidinal components, given affective meaning and organized by attachment to aspects of the inner world. See Jacobson, *The Self and the Object World*.

14 Sigmund Freud, "Outline of psychoanalysis," 1940, *SE*, vol. 23, p. 206.

15 Joan Rivière, "The unconscious phantasy of an inner world reflected in examples from literature," in Melanie Klein, Paula Heimann, and R. E. Money-Kyrle (eds), *New Directions in Psychoanalysis* (New York, Basic Books, 1955), pp. 358–9. This essay and quotation came to my attention in Norman O. Brown, *Love's Body* (New York, Vintage, 1966).

16 Ibid., p. 347.

17 Sigmund Freud, *The Ego and the Id*, 1923, *SE*, vol. 19, p. 29.

18 See Roy Schafer, "Narrative in the psychoanalytic situation," *Critical Inquiry*, 7 (1980), pp. 29–53.

19 As we know from Freud and others, this is hardly the stance that Freud himself took. He took walks with patients, talked to their relatives, gave and got cigars, and in the case of Dora was quite happy to attempt to browbeat her into submitting to his definition of the intrapsychic and interpersonal situation. Yet officially his interpretive stance was closer to the classic model of interpretation of resistances. In addition, as I mention below, he felt that countertransference signified inadequacy on the part of the analyst. See on this Samuel Lipton, "The advantages of Freud's technique as shown in his analysis of the Rat Man," *International Journal of Psycho-Analysis*, 58 (1977), pp. 255–73.

20 See Elizabeth R. Zetzel, "Therapeutic alliance in the analysis of a case of hysteria," in her *The Capacity for Emotional Growth* (New York, International Universities Press, 1970), and other papers in that volume; and Ralph Greenson, *Technique and Practice of Psychoanalysis* (New York, International Universities Press, 1967).

21 For the most fully formulated account of this position, see Charles Brenner, *Psychoanalytic Technique and Psychic Conflict* (New York, International Universities Press, 1976). For a lively account of the debate, see Janet Malcolm, *The Impossible Profession* (New York, Vintage, 1980).

22 See M. Balint, *Primary Love* and *The Basic Fault*; Kohut, *Analysis of the Self* and *Restoration of the Self*; Frieda Fromm-Reichman, *Principles of Intensive Psychotherapy* (Chicago, University of Chicago Press, 1950); Margaret Little, *Transference Neurosis and Transference Psychosis* (New York, Jason Aronson, 1981); Leo Stone, *The Psychoanalytic Situation* (New York, International Universities Press, 1961); Harold Searles, *Countertransference and Related Subjects* (New York, International Universities Press, 1979); and D. W. Winnicott, *The Maturational Processes* and *The Piggle* (New York, International Universities Press, 1977).

23 Elizabeth R. Zetzel, "Current concepts of transference," *International Journal of Psycho-Analysis*, 37 (1956), p. 374. A discussion of gender in the creation of psychoanalytic theory is beyond the scope of this essay. I note, however, that women analysts were particularly central to focussing psychoanalytic interest on the importance of countertransference. See Fromm-Reichman, *Principles*; Annie Reich, "On counter-transference," *International Journal of Psycho-Analysis*, 32 (1951), pp. 25–31; Lucia Tower, "Countertransference," *Journal of the American Psychoanalytic Association*, 4 (1956), pp. 224–55; Margaret Little, "Counter-transference and the patient's response to it," *International Journal of Psycho-Analysis*, 32 (1951), pp. 32–40; Paula Heimann, "On counter-transference," *International Journal of Psycho-Analysis*, 31 (1950), pp. 81–4; and Mabel Blake Cohen, "Counter-transference and anxiety," *Psychiatry*, 15 (1952), pp. 501–39. I noticed this while reading Peter Loewenberg, "Subjectivity and empathy as guides to counseling," unpublished paper.

24 See Josef Breuer and Sigmund Freud, *Studies on Hysteria*, 1893–95, *SE*, vol. 2; and Sigmund Freud, *The Interpretation of Dreams*, 1900–1901, *SE*, vols. 4 and 5. See also Nellie Louise Buckley, "Women psychoanalysts and the theory of femininity: a study of Karen Horney, Helene Deutsch, and Marie Bonaparte" (Ph.D. dissertation, University of California, Los Angeles, 1982), part of which has been published as Nellie L. Thompson, "Helene Deutsch: a life in theory," *The Psychoanalytic Quarterly*, 56 (1987), pp. 317–53, who suggests that the dominant psychologies of women emerged from their own life histories, if not their own self-analyses.

25 See the introduction to Harold Searles, *Collected Papers on Schizophrenia and Related Subjects* (New York, International Universities Press, 1965); and Little, *Transference Neurosis*.

Chapter 8 Feminism, Femininity, and Freud

1 See, e.g., Jessica Benjamin, "The end of internalization: Adorno's social psychology," *Telos*, 32 (1977); "Authority and the family revisited, or a world without fathers?," *New German Critique*, 13 (1978); "Rational violence and erotic domination," in Hester Eistenstein and Alice Jardine (eds), *The Future of Difference* (Boston, G. K. Hall, 1980); and "The Oedipal riddle: authority, autonomy, and the new narcissism," in John Diggins and Mark Kamm, *The Problem of Authority in America* (Philadelphia, Temple University Press, 1981);

Dorothy Dinnerstein, *The Mermaid and the Minotaur* (New York, Harper & Row, 1976); Jane Flax, "The conflict between nurturance and autonomy in mother–daughter relationships and within feminism," *Feminist Studies*, 4 (1978), pp. 171–89; "Critical theory as a vocation," *Politics and Society*, 8:2 (1978); "Political philosophy and the patriarchal unconscious," in Sandra Harding and Merrill B. Hintikka (eds), *Discovering Reality: feminist perspectives on epistemology, metaphysics, methodology, and the philosophy of science* (Dordrecht, Reidel, 1983); and "Psychoanalysis as deconstruction and myth: on gender, narcissism and modernity's discontents," in Günter H. Lenz and Kurt Shell (eds), *Crisis of Modernity* (Boulder, Col., Westview Press, 1986); "Mother–daughter relationships: psychodynamics, politics and philosophy," in Eisenstein and Jardine (eds), *The Future of Difference*; Miriam Johnson, "Fathers, mothers, and sex typing," *Sociological Inquiry*, 45 (1975); "Heterosexuality, male dominance and the father image," *Sociological Inquiry*, 51 (1981), and "Locating male dominance," in Jerome Rabow, Gerald M. Platt and Marion Goldman (eds), *Advances in Psychoanalytic Sociology* (Malabar, Fla., Krieger, 1987); Evelyn Fox Keller, *Reflections on Gender and Science* (New Haven, Yale University Press, 1985); Juliet Mitchell, *Psychoanalysis and Feminism* (New York, Pantheon, 1974); and Gayle Rubin, "The traffic in women: notes on the 'political economy' of sex," in Rayna Reiter (ed.), *Toward an Anthropology of Women* (New York, Monthly Review Press, 1975).

2 This stance, I think, is still quite prevalent. See, for instance, Pauline Bart's review of Nancy Chodorow, *The Reproduction of Mothering: psychoanalysis and the sociology of gender* (Berkeley, University of California Press, 1978), in Joyce Trebilcot (ed.), *Mothering: essays in feminist theory* (Totowa, N.J., Rowman & Allenheld, 1983).

3 Jean Baker Miller, *Toward a New Psychology of Women* (Boston, Beacon Press, 1976), and Miller (ed.), *Psychoanalysis and Women* (New York, Penguin, 1973).

4 See, for instance, Harold P. Blum (ed.), *Female Psychology* (New York, International Universities Press, 1977), and Herman Roiphe and Eleanor Galenson, *Infantile Origins of Sexual Identity* (New York, International Universities Press, 1981).

5 See Betty Friedan, *The Feminine Mystique* (New York, Dell, 1963), and Weisstein, "Kinder, Kuche, Kirche: Psychology Constructs the Female" (Somerville, New England Free Press, 1968).

6 Sociologists are in the middle here. Traditional sociology would agree with the feminist that gender is social and not psychological, or if it is psychological, a social learning perspective explains it. A feminist sociologist would also be critical of Freud's misogyny. But a traditional sociologist would also take the psychoanalytic methodological position in favor of value-free theory and method, against the feminist sociologist who would argue for a "sociology for women," and that traditional science is male-biased like psychoanalysis.

7 Freud, "Femininity," 1933, in *New Introductory Lectures on Psychoanalysis, The Standard Edition of the Complete Psychological Works of Sigmund Freud*, ed. James Strachey (London: The Hogarth Press and the Institute of Psychoanalysis) (hereafter *SE*), vol. 22, pp. 112–35.

8 See "On narcissism: an introduction," 1914, *SE*, vol. 14, pp. 69–102.

9 Ruth Mack Brunswick, "The pre-Oedipal phase of the libido development," in Robert Fliess (ed.), *The Psychoanalytic Reader* (New York, International Universities Press, 1940), pp. 231–53.

10 Bibring, "On the 'passing of the Oedipus complex' in a matriarchal family setting," in Rudolph M. Loewenstein (ed.), *Drives, Affects and Behavior: essays in honor of Marie Bonaparte* (New York, International Universities Press, 1953), pp. 278–84; Karen Horney, "The dread of women," *International Journal of Psycho-Analysis*, 13 (1932), pp. 348–60.

11 Freud, "'Civilized' sexual morality and modern nervousness," 1908, *SE*, vol. 9, pp. 179–204.

12 Freud, *Studies on Hysteria*, 1893–5, *SE*, vol. 2.

13 The following discussion is taken from Chodorow, *The Reproduction of Mothering*, ch. 9.

14 "Some psychical consequences of the anatomical distinction between the sexes," *SE*, vol. 19, 1925, p. 257.

15 *New Introductory Lectures*, *SE*, vol. 22, p. 132, and "Some psychical consequences," p. 253.

16 "Femininity," p. 131.

17 I am indebted in this discussion to Roy Schafer, "Problems in Freud's psychology of women," *Journal of the American Psychoanalytic Association*, 22:3 (1974), pp. 459–85.

18 See Schafer, "Problems in Freud's psychology," and Rubin, "Traffic in women."

19 See Johnson, "Locating male dominance."

20 "The dissolution of the Oedipus complex," 1924, *SE*, vol. 19, p. 178.

21 "Some psychical consequences," p. 258.

22 "Femininity," pp. 116–17.

Chapter 9 Psychoanalytic Feminism and the Psychoanalytic

1 Earlier versions of this chapter were written for presentation at a Stanford University Conference, "Theoretical Perspectives on Sexual Difference," February 1987, and at the Chicago Institute for Psychoanalysis Symposium, "Contemporary Women and Psychoanalysis: Critical Questions Reconsidered," May, 1987. I am grateful for comments from Elizabeth Abel, Daniel Greenson, Lisby Mayer, Barrie Thorne, and Abby Wolfson.

2 My labels here do not do justice to the complexities of these protagonists' identities. Some who have contributed prominently to the mainstream psychoanalytic literature about women and femininity would certainly label themselves as feminist – as critical of and wishing to change the gendered and sexual status quo and the situation of women in the psychoanalytic profession. Some whom I consider to have contributed primarily to psychoanalytic feminism – Jessica Benjamin, Jane Flax, and myself among object-relations feminists, Jean Baker Miller and her colleagues among interpersonal feminists and Juliet Mitchell among Lacanian feminists – are practicing analysts or therapists. I discuss another in-between group, feminist psychoanalysts, in n. 6 below.

3 Freud, *New Introductory Lectures*, 1933, *The Standard Edition of the Complete*

Psychological Works of Sigmund Freud, ed. James Strachey (London, The Hogarth Press and the Institute of Psychoanalysis), (hereafter *SE*), vol. 22, p. 116.

4 I discuss these issues in "Feminism, femininity, and Freud" (chapter 8, this volume).

5 Freud, *New Introductory Lectures*, p. 118.

6 My account of dominant trends in the psychoanalytic psychology of gender draws from what we might call mainstream Freudian journals. I do not consider here those whom I call feminist psychoanalysts, who do have the potential, as possibly do psychoanalytic feminists who are clinicians, to bridge the psychoanalytic and psychoanalytic feminist approaches that I discuss. Prominent feminist psychoanalysts include Carol Nadelson, Malkah Notman, and Ethel Person. These writers have led the feminist challenge from within psychoanalysis, focussing not only on deficiencies in psychoanalytic theory but also on the role and treatment of women in society. Perhaps as a result of their explicit feminism, they are rarely published in the mainstream orthodox journals. At the same time, their writing, like that of most psychoanalysts, does not seem to be much read by the academic psychoanalytic feminists whom I discuss. I am not yet clear how to characterize feminist psychoanalysis as an autonomous theoretical contribution, as these writings seem rather to substantiate and clinically specify and elaborate dominant psychoanalytic feminist positions. Both classical analysts who write about femininity and psychoanalytic feminists tend to write more from a developmental perspective, whereas Nadelson and Notman and their collaborators, and to a lesser extent Person, write more from a clinical perspective about adult women's issues.

Nadelson and Notman, whom I would place in terms of my discussion of psychoanalytic feminism closest to the feminist interpersonal school, as they have collaborated frequently with Jean Baker Miller and are extensively critical of male-dominant culture, have written on, among other topics, aggression, rape, and the female life cycle. See, e.g., Miller, Nadelson, Notman, and Joan Zilbach, "Aggression in women: a reexamination," in Sheila Klebanow (ed.), *Changing Concepts in Psychoanalysis* (New York, Gardner Press, 1981); Nadelson, Notman, Miller, and Zilbach, "Aggression in women: conceptual issues and clinical implications," in Notman and Nadelson (eds), *The Woman Patient*, vol. 3, *Aggression, Adaptations, and Psychotherapy* (New York, Plenum Press, 1982); Nadelson, Notman and Elaine (Hilberman) Carmen, "The rape victim and the rape experience," in W. Curran (ed.), *Modern Forensic Psychiatry and Psychology* (Philadelphia, F. A. Davis, 1986); Nadelson and Notman, "Rape," in Z. Defries, R. Friedman, and R. Corn (eds), *Sexuality: new perspectives* (Westport, Greenwood Press, 1985); Nadelson and Notman, "Psychoanalytic considerations of the response to rape," *International Review of Psycho-Analysis*, 6 (1979), pp. 97–103; and several articles on marriage, work, motherhood, reproduction, and menopause, in Nadelson and Notman (eds), *The Woman Patient*, vol. 2, *Concepts of Femininity and the Life Cycle* (New York, Plenum Press, 1982).

Person, whom I locate more as an object-relations feminist psychoanalyst, has written on, among other topics, gender identity, male and female sexuality and love, women and work, and bias in psychoanalytic theory and theories of the psychoanalytic process. Like object-relations feminists, Person is more likely than Nadelson and Notman to discuss development and to focus on male and female psychology as a conceptually and empirically interrelated whole. See, e.g., "Sexuality as a mainstay of identity," *Signs*, 5 (1980), pp. 605–30; "Women working: fears of failure, deviance and success," *Journal of the American Academy of Psychoanalysis*, 10 (1982), pp. 67–84; "The influence of values in psychoanalysis: the case of female psychology," in *Psychiatry Update: The American Psychiatric Association Annual Review*, vol. II (Washington, D.C., American Psychiatric Press, 1983), pp. 36–50; "The erotic transference in women and men: difference and consequences," *Journal of the American Academy of Psychoanalysis*, 13 (1985), pp. 159–80; "Working mothers: impact on the self, the couple and the children," in Tony Bernay and Dorothy W. Cantor (eds), *The Psychology of Today's Woman: new psychoanalytic visions* (Hillsdale, N.J., Analytic Press, 1986); *Dreams of Love and Fateful Encounters: the power of romantic passion* (New York, W. W. Norton, 1988); and Ethel S. Person and Lionel Ovesey, "Psychoanalytic theories of gender identity," *Journal of the American Academy of Psychoanalysis*, 11 (1983), pp. 203–26.

These feminist psychoanalysts have been joined in recent years by a series of writers published in such anthologies as Bernay and Cantor (eds), *Psychology*; Judith L. Alpert (ed.), *Psychoanalysis and Women: contemporary reappraisals* (Hillsdale, N.J., Analytic Press, 1986); and Martha Kirkpatrick (ed.), *Women's Sexual Development: explorations of inner space* (New York, Plenum Press, 1980); and Kirkpatrick (ed.), *Women's Sexual Experience: explorations of the dark continent* (New York, Plenum Press, 1981).

7 See Herman Roiphe and Eleanor Galenson, *Infantile Origins of Sexual Identity* (New York, International Universities Press, 1981), and many papers.

8 Janine Chasseguet-Smirgel, "The consideration of some blind spots in the exploration of the dark continent," *International Journal of Psycho-Analysis*, 57 (1976), p. 281.

9 See, for example, Judith Kestenberg, "Outside and inside, male and female," *Journal of the American Psychoanalytic Association*, 16:3 (1968), pp. 457–520; "The inner-genital phase," in D. Mendel (ed.), *Early Feminine Development: contemporary psychoanalytic views* (New York, Spectrum, 1980); "Maternity and paternity in the developmental context," *Psychiatric Clinics of North America*, 3:1 (1980), pp. 61–79, and other writings.

10 James Kleeman, "Freud's views on early female sexuality in the light of direct child observation," *Journal of the American Psychoanalytic Association*, 24:5 (1976), pp. 3–28; and Harriet Lerner, "Parental mislabeling of female genitals as a determinant of penis envy and learning inhibitions in women," *Journal of the American Psychoanalytic Association*, 24:5 (1976), pp. 269–84. Some analysts might argue that labelling was really not relevant, that the issue of genital schematization was an internal issue and not an external one, and that internal factors determine how a child of a particular age can and will understand his or her body (see, for example, Freud's arguments about the cloacal theory and theory of anal birth). Both Kestenberg and Anita Bell, "The significance of scrotal sac and testicles for the prepuberty male," *Psychoanalytic Quarterly*

(1965), pp. 182–206, make the point that parents (and psychoanalysts) don't do so well with the male genitalia either, in this case letting the more external, phallic term, penis, stand for parts of the genitalia that seem to have more inner functions and aspects (we might also point out the psychoanalytic phallicization of castration, which in fact means removal of the testes, not the penis). To cite a more everyday example of the results of lack of specific genital labelling: a boy of three and a half years telling his mother, as he noticed his urethral opening, that he had a splinter in his penis that was always there and didn't need to be removed because it didn't hurt.

11 Elizabeth Lloyd Mayer, " 'Everybody must be just like me': observations on female castration anxiety," *International Journal of Psycho-Analysis*, 66 (1985), pp. 331–47.

12 See, for example, Mayer, " 'Everybody' "; Shahla Chehrazi, "Female psychology: a review," *Journal of the American Psychoanalytic Association*, 34 (1986), pp. 141–62; and Phyllis Tyson, "A developmental line of gender identity, gender role, and choice of love object," *Journal of the American Psychoanalytic Association*, 30 (1982), pp. 61–86.

13 Kleeman, "Freud's views," and Robert Stoller, "A contribution to the study of gender identity," *International Journal of Psycho-Analysis*, 45 (1964), pp. 220–6; "The sense of maleness," *Psychoanalytic Quarterly*, 34 (1965), pp. 207–18; "The sense of femaleness," *Psychoanalytic Quarterly*, 37 (1968), pp. 42–5; "Primary femininity," *Journal of the American Psychoanalytic Association*, 24:5 (1976), pp. 59–78, and other writings.

14 For another example that stresses the role of object relations, see Virginia L. Clower, "Theoretical implications in current views of masturbation in latency girls," *Journal of the American Psychoanalytic Association*, 24:5 (1976), pp. 109–25.

15 Freud, "Female sexuality," 1931, *SE*, vol. 21, pp. 223–43.

16 See Eva P. Lester, "The female analyst and the erotized transference," *International Journal of Psycho-Analysis*, 66 (1985), pp. 283–93; Marianne Goldberger and Dorothy Evans, "On transference manifestations in male patients with female analysts," *International Journal of Psycho-Analysis*, 66 (1985), pp. 295–309; Laila Karme, "The analysis of a male patient by a female analyst: the problem of the negative Oedipal transference," *International Journal of Psycho-Analysis*, 60 (1979), pp. 253–61; and Phyllis Tyson, "The gender of the analyst," *Psychoanalytic Study of the Child*, 35 (1980), pp. 321–38. I distinguish debate here from an extensive resurgence in clinical writing on many women's issues – aggression, work inhibitions, later life cycle transitions (see references in n. 6, as well as Adrienne Applegarth, "Some observations on work inhibitions in women," *Journal of the American Psychoanalytic Association*, 24:5 (supplement), (1976), pp. 251–68. I focus on cross-gender transference because the issue has been so much cast as a debate and because of the profound importance for psychoanalytic theory and practice since its inception of any implicit or explicit claim that women cannot fully analyze men.

17 Phyllis Tyson, "The female analyst and the male analysand," paper presented at the San Francisco Psychoanalytic Institute, February, 1986, and David L. Raphling and Judith F. Chused, "Transference across gender lines," *Journal of*

the American Psychoanalytic Association, 36 (1988), pp. 77–104. This article, notably, dilutes the explicitly feminist issues raised by the original formulation of the problem by turning the specific asymmetric issue of men's response to powerful women into a generalized concern with any cross-gender transference.

18 Elizabeth Lloyd Mayer, discussion of Tyson, February, 1986. See also Raphling and Chused, "Transference."

19 Person, "The erotic transference in women and men."

20 Lacanians sometimes call object-relations theorists Anglo-American theorists, in contrast to themselves as "French" theorists. Both approaches in the first group would fall under the gynecentric theoretical rubric that Miriam Johnson distinguishes from phallocentric Lacanian theorists: see "The reproduction of male dominance," in Jerome Rabow, Gerald M. Platt, and Marion Goldman (eds), *Advances in Psychoanalytic Sociology* (Malabar, Fla., Krieger, 1986), and *Strong Mothers, Weak Wives* (Berkeley, University of California Press, 1988).

21 Galenson makes a related point about the relative lack of attention to the integration of ego psychoanalytic concepts about non-conflictual and autonomous spheres into psychoanalytic understandings of feminine development (Panel Reports of Scientific Proceedings, "Psychology of women," *Journal of the American Psychoanalytic Association*, 24 (1976), p. 159).

22 My views have been elaborated in *The Reproduction of Mothering* and in the essays in this volume. I first argued in Chodorow, "Family structure and feminine personality" (chapter 2, this volume) that "feminine personality comes to define itself in relation and connection to other people more than masculine personality. . . For boys and men, both individuation and dependency issues become tied up with the sense of masculinity. . . For girls and women, by contrast, issues of femininity, or feminine identity, are not problematic in the same way" (pp. 45–6).

23 Chodorow, *Reproduction*, p. 169.

24 Ibid., p. 209.

25 Ibid., p. 169.

26 Dorothy Dinnerstein, *The Mermaid and the Minotaur* (New York, Harper & Row, 1976). I stress differences in the way reactions to the mother are constituted in men and women more than Dinnerstein, but such distinctions are not necessary for our purposes here. My own understanding of these issues probably came first from Philip Slater; see *The Glory of Hera: Greek mythology and the Greek family* (Boston, Beacon Press, 1968).

27 See Jessica Benjamin, "The end of internalization: Adorno's social psychology," *Telos*, 32 (1977); "Authority and the family revisited, or a world without fathers?", *New German Critique*, 13 (1978); and *The Bonds of Love: psychoanalysis, feminism and the problem of domination* (New York, Pantheon, 1988); Jane Flax, "Critical theory as a vocation," *Politics and Society*, 8:2 (1978); "Political philosophy and the patriarchal unconscious," in Sandra Harding and Merrill B. Hintikka (eds), *Discovering Reality: feminist perspectives on epistemology, metaphysics, methodology, and the philosophy of science* (Dordrecht, Reidel, 1983); and *Thinking Fragments: psychoanalysis, feminism, and postmodernism in the contemporary west* (Berkeley, University of

California Press, forthcoming); and Evelyn Fox Keller, *Reflections on Gender and Science* (New Haven, Yale University Press, 1985). See also Isaac D. Balbus, *Marxism and Domination* (Princeton, Princeton University Press, 1982), and Nancy C. M. Hartsock, "The feminist standpoint: developing the grounds for a specifically feminist historical materialism," in Harding and Hintikka (eds), *Discovering Reality*.

28 See Elizabeth Abel (ed.), *Writing and Sexual Difference* (Chicago, The University of Chicago Press, 1980, 1981, 1982); and Abel, Hirsch, and Elizabeth Langland (eds), *The Voyage In: fictions of female development* (Hanover and London, University Press of New England, 1983); Kahn, "The hand that rocks the cradle: recent gender theories and their implications," in Shirley Nelson Garner, Claire Kahane and Madelon Sprengnether (eds), *The (M)other Tongue: essays in feminist psychoanalytic interpretation* (Ithaca, Cornell University Press, 1985), pp. 72–88; and Janet Adelman, "Born of woman: fantasies of maternal power in MacBeth," in Marjorie Garber (ed.), *Cannibals, Witches and Divorce: estranging the Renaissance*, Selected Papers from the English Institute, 1985 (Baltimore, Johns Hopkins University Press, 1987).

29 On the subjectivity of the mother, see Benjamin, "The end of internalization"; Chodorow and Contratto, "The fantasy of the perfect mother" (chapter 4, this volume); Chodorow, *Reproduction*, "Difference," (chapter 5, this volume), and "Beyond drive theory" (chapter 6, this volume), and Keller, *Reflections on Gender.*

30 Jean Baker Miller, *Toward a New Psychology of Women* (Boston, Beacon Press, 1976), and Carol Gilligan, *In a Different Voice* (Cambridge, Mass., Harvard University Press, 1982). See also Janet L. Surrey, "Self-in-relation: a theory of women's development" (1985); Judith V. Jordan, "Empathy and self boundaries" (1984); Miller, "The development of women's sense of self" (1984); all Work in Progress papers from the Stone Center for Developmental Services and Studies, Wellesley College, Wellesley, Mass., and other papers from the Stone Center. The firmly critical political stance and general critique of social inequality found in Miller's book and her later writings is not emphasized by her Stone Center colleagues, who stick more closely to psychological issues.

Miller and her colleagues are all practicing clinicians. Her book, however, is read by a non-clinical audience and grouped with Gilligan, and her theories have thus entered one part of the psychoanalytic feminist dialogue. The emphasis on women's relatedness found in Miller's work as well as my own, along with the work of Gilligan, have helped inspire a range of what are sometimes called femininist theories about women's special capacities and qualities: see, for instance, Sara Ruddick, "Maternal thinking," in Barrie Thorne (ed.), with Marilyn Yalom, *Rethinking the Family: some feminist questions* (New York, Longman, 1981); Mary Field Belenky, Blythe McVicker Clinchy, Nancy Rule Goldberger, and Jill Mattuck Tarule, *Women's Ways of Knowing* (New York, Basic Books, 1987); and Nel Noddings, *Caring: a feminine approach to ethics and moral education* (Berkeley, University of California Press, 1984).

31 See Miller, *Toward a New Psychology*; "The construction of anger in women

and men," Stone Center Working Paper (1983); "Women and power," *Social Policy*, 13:4 (1983), pp. 3–6; and co-authored papers cited in n. 6. See also Harriet Goldhor Lerner, *The Dance of Anger* (New York, Harper & Row, 1985).

32 See, e.g., Judith V. Jordan and Janet L. Surrey, "The self-in-relation: empathy and the mother–daughter relationship," in Bernay and Cantor (eds), *Psychology*, which reproduces much of the account in Chodorow, *Reproduction*.

33 See Chodorow, *Reproduction*; Jane Flax, "The conflict between nurturance and autonomy in mother–daughter relationships and within feminism," *Feminist Studies*, 4 (1978), pp. 171–89, and "Re-membering the selves: is the repressed gendered?" in *Women and Memory*, Special Issue of *Michigan Quarterly Review*, 26 (1987), pp. 92–110; and Jessica Benjamin, *Bonds of Love*, and "The alienation of desire: women's masochism and ideal love," in Alpert, *Psychoanalysis*. See also Susan Contratto, "Father presence in women's psychological development," in Rabow, Platt, and Goldman (eds), *Advances*; and Keller's discussion of "dynamic autonomy" in *Reflections*.

34 Paradigmatic Lacanian feminist statements can be found in Juliet Mitchell, *Psychoanalysis and Feminism* (New York, Pantheon, 1974) and *Women: the longest revolution* (New York, Pantheon, 1984); Mitchell and Jacqueline Rose, "Introductions," in Jacques Lacan, *Feminine Sexuality* (New York, W. W. Norton, 1982); and Jane Gallop, *The Daughter's Seduction* (Ithaca, Cornell University Press, 1982). Lacanian feminist literary criticism can be found in Garner, Kahane, and Sprengnether (eds), *The (M)other Tongue*, and in an extensive literature by Gallop, Shoshana Felman, Toril Moi, Naomi Schor, and others. To my knowledge, Lacanian feminists do not discuss the work of the Miller group. Mitchell, now a psychoanalyst, engages directly with other psychoanalysts. Her 1974 book, a founding Lacanian feminist statement, tried, via a somewhat Lacanian reading, to rescue Freud from his feminist detractors, his psychoanalytic critics and supporters, and in some sense from himself. Her recent writing sticks more closely to Lacan, and her critical polemic is directed less toward other feminists (except as they use psychoanalytic theories she doesn't like) and more toward primary femininity, Kleinian and object-relations theories – theories that argue, against the Lacanian and Freudian stress on the Oedipal father, for the importance of pre-Oedipal mother–child experience. The more literary proponents of Lacanian theory tend to engage with Lacan and Freud among psychoanalysts, with postmodernist French critics like Derrida, and otherwise with object-relations psychoanalytic feminists.

35 Against a reading of Lacan which singles out woman as the lack, or the Other, we find a French feminist anti-Lacanian revolt. In another version of the argument for primary femininity and for a genital awareness that does not hinge on perception and acceptance of unequal genital difference, Luce Irigaray, Hélène Cixous, and others reject male discourse and argue for women's reappropriation of their own unconscious, their body and their genital configuration, for women's being in themselves rather than being a lack in the male psyche. This being in themselves expresses the self-enclosed female genitalia, the "two lips speaking together" (Irigaray, "When our lips speak

together", ch. 11 of *This Sex Which is Not One* (Ithaca, Cornell University Press, 1985), in which a woman secures herself to herself or in relation to other like-constructed women.

This argument is both about body experience and about alternate forms of linguistic construction in women – about "women's language" and "writing the body," and it pays less attention to female development than to an elaborate working out of female experience. It is, arguably, gynecentric and valorizes feminine qualities, but it pays less attention to the centrality of relations among women and the mother–daughter relationship than the object-relations account. Indeed, accounts of the mother–daughter relationship tend to retain Lacanian and traditional psychoanalytic views that mothers and mother-attachment are traps, depicting mothers who constrain, compete, and destroy. In this view, it is not from her mother that a girl attains her femininity or selfhood, but seemingly from herself, insofar as she rejects her mother. See Hester Eisenstein and Alice Jardine (eds), *The Future of Difference* (Boston, G. K. Hall, 1980), Part II, "Contemporary feminist thought in France: translating difference," and Elaine Marks and Isabelle de Courtivron, *New French Feminisms* (New York, Schocken Books, 1981).

36 See Johnson, "Reproduction," and *Strong Mothers*, and Gayle Rubin, "The traffic in women," in Rayna Reiter (ed.), *Toward an Anthropology of Women* (New York, Monthly Review Press, 1975). Johnson argues, against the Lacanians, that the Oedipus complex and Oedipal transition institute male dominance and sexism, not gender difference *per se*, and that the father installs a male dominance that inheres in the normal husband–wife relationship. She radically transforms the traditional psychoanalytic position that suggests that the boy doesn't have to change objects and the girl does, arguing that the boy's generational change of object, from powerless and subordinate to powerful and dominant *vis-à-vis* women, is as absolute as the girl's gendered object change from mother to father.

37 Johnson ("Reproduction," and *Strong Mothers*), whose own work might be called patricentric, rather than phallocentric, makes this point more concretely, arguing that the gynecentric perspective obscures the father's critical role in emphasizing and constituting gender difference and gender domination in the family. The mother, she claims, represents and institutes a common humanity in both sexes. Her own empirical research shows that the father, by his actual behavior and not simply as a symbol of culture and the phallus, creates sexuality and gender-typed behavior in both son and daughter.

38 The causes and future of such fragmentation can be interpreted in two ways. For some Lacanian psychoanalytic feminists it is a product of a phallocentric culture that can be transformed. For those whose reading of Lacan comes more via postmodernism and Derrida, where language dissolves identity and fixed difference, it is an inevitable product of culture in itself. In fact, another ground for the Lacanian critique of object-relations feminists and of post-Freudian analysts is that these accounts all speak of the self or identity (including gender identity) as if these can exist in any kind of wholeness or potential wholeness. The Lacanian subject, by contrast, can never be whole or have the humanistic fiction called self.

39 I cannot engage here in a sociology of psychoanalytic epistemology, but, briefly, I would suspect that many non-Lacanian French psychoanalysts would also be more comfortable with anti-empiricist claims, as would Latin Americans influenced by Lacanian ideas. In general, European analysts, even if they are critical of Lacanian theory and practice, are not as likely as Americans to identify themselves as medically trained scientists, or even to be medically trained. They are thus probably more comfortable with theory in itself, where clinical experience illustrates but does not need to confirm or prove scientific claims.

40 I have mentioned Stoller, Kleeman, and Clower as exceptions here. Stoller claims:

> As a description of human childhood development, Freud's observations on zonal phases have been confirmed and can be so any time with biologically normal children. However, no studies have been published that confirm the implications drawn from the observations. It has not yet been shown that any class of neurosis, including perversion, or psychosis is caused by a disruption of the sensual experiences of the mouth, defecatory or urinary systems, or phallus. . . (There is, however, much evidence that disturbed *object relations* during these phases cause psychopathology.) (Robert Stoller, *Perversion: the erotic form of hatred* (New York, Pantheon, 1975) pp. 32–3).

Another interesting exception is some recent work on perversions. Robert Stolorow and F. Lachman, "Sexual fantasy and perverse activity," in *Psychoanalysis of Developmental Arrests* (New York, International Universities Press, 1980), pp. 144–70, argue that there is a relationship between sexual fantasies and the structuralization of self and object representations and that perversions are compensations for faulty self–other boundaries; and Milton Jucovy, "Transvestism: with special reference to pre-Oedipal factors," in Toksoz B. Karasu and Charles W. Socarides (eds), *On Sexuality* (New York, International Universities Press, 1979), pp. 223–41, relates transvestism to disorders of self and identity and to separation anxiety as much as castration anxiety. See also Stoller, *Presentations of Gender* (New Haven, Yale University Press, 1985) and *Observing the Erotic Imagination* (New Haven, Yale University Press, 1985); and Charles Socarides, "A unitary theory of sexual perversions," in Karasu and Socarides (eds), *On Sexuality*.

41 This example is inspired by talks given back to back at "Women and Psychoanalysis: Today and Yesterday," a Symposium celebrating the 50th Anniversary of the Boston Psychoanalytic Society, February 1984, one by Galenson and the other by Miller, Nadelson, Notman, and Zilbach.

42 These points are discussed in Keller, "Is sex to gender as nature is to science?", *Hypatia*, 2 (1987), pp. 37–49, and in Jane Flax, "Postmodernism and Gender Relations in Feminist Theory," *Signs*, 12 (1987), pp. 621–43.

43 In fact, the Freudian theory of the development of sexual orientation was not very persuasive, even if the Horney–Jones postulate of innate heterosexuality was also inadequate. And whereas psychoanalysts have done interesting work explaining the development of particular sexualities – those that are neither statistically nor culturally dominant – they have not systematically revised or done research toward understanding sexual development in general, and in particular the development of "normal" heterosexuality. My impression is that

in spite of Freud, most psychoanalytic accounts assume that there is some biological force that predisposes most people, in interaction with early family experience, toward heterosexuality. Tyson, "A developmental line," hinges the girl's turn to the father on her identification with her mother, which seems not to speak to the independence and insistence of sexual desire which psychoanalysis also describes. Further, I think that many psychoanalysts who have been reflecting on female psychology would not hold to Freud's penis–baby equation as the dominant motivation for motherhood in women. They would hold to unspecified biological assumptions about maternal instinct, to psychosexual claims of the sort that we find in Kestenberg's inner-genital phase or in Klein's intensive focus on internal objects and their meanings, and to theories about the girl's identification with or reparation toward her mother.

44 At the same time, as psychoanalytic feminism has become so fashionable that it warrants treatment in a *New Yorker* article (see Janet Malcolm, "Reflections: J'appelle un chat un chat," April 20, 1987), one begins to think that perhaps an individual psychoanalyst working with troubled patients may be doing more to change gendered lives than the psychoanalytic feminist and her elegant interpretation of texts.

45 For discussion of this reluctance, see Nadelson and Notman, n. 6, and Judith Herman, *Father–Daughter Incest* (Cambridge, Mass., Harvard University Press, 1981).

46 Stoller, *Perversion*, p. 26.

47 On gender-salience, see Jane Atkinson, "Anthropology" review essay, *Signs*, 8 (1982), pp. 236–58. See also recent psychological work in gender schema theory, e.g., Sandra Lipsitz Bem, "Gender schema theory: a cognitive account of sex typing," *Psychological Review*, 88 (1981), pp. 354–64. I am indebted for these points about gender-salience not only to feminist theory but also to many women of the second generation of psychoanalysts (see chapter 10, this volume).

Chapter 10 Seventies Questions for Thirties Women

1 This chapter was first written as a paper for presentation at the 1984 Meetings of the American Sociological Association. Research upon which it is based was supported by the Russell Sage Foundation and the National Endowment for the Humanities. I am grateful to Alida Brill, who was associated with the Russell Sage Foundation, for general encouragement and support, to Avril Thorne for helping to shape my thinking about the research and for continuing discussions about feminist methodology, and to Rose Laub Coser, Annette Lawson, Shulamit Reinharz, Judith Stacey, Barrie Thorne, and Norma Wikler for comments and suggestions. I also acknowledge support from the Center for Advanced Study in the Behavioral Sciences, the University of California, Santa Cruz, and the Institute of Personality Assessment and Research, University of California, Berkeley.

2 Dorothy Smith, "A sociology for women," in Julia Sherman and Evelyn T. Beck (eds), *The Prism of Sex* (Madison, The University of Wisconsin Press,

1977), p. 135. See also Shulamit Reinharz, *On Becoming a Social Scientist: from survey research and participant observation to experiential analysis* (New Brunswick, N.J. Transaction Books, 1984), and "Experiential analysis: a contribution to feminist research," in Gloria Bowles and Renate Duelli Klein (eds), *Theories of Women's Studies* (London, Routledge & Kegan Paul, 1983), pp. 162–91; Susan Krieger, *The Mirror Dance* (Philadelphia, Temple University Press, 1983), and "Beyond 'subjectivity': use of the self in social science," *Qualitative Sociology*, 8 (1985), pp. 309–24; Maria Mies, "Towards a methodology for feminist research," in Bowles and Duelli Klein (eds), *Theories*, pp. 117–39; Sandra Harding (ed.), *Feminism and Methodology* (Bloomington, Indiana University Press, 1987); and Helen Roberts (ed.), *Doing Feminist Research* (London, Routledge & Kegan Paul, 1981). For early programmatic statements on feminist sociology, see Marcia Millman and Rosabeth Kanter (eds), *Another Voice: feminist perspectives on social life and social science* (New York, Anchor, 1975). Such methods do not originate with a feminist sociology for women but in reflexive, interpretive, and critical sociology more generally, and much of this literature situates itself explicitly in the traditions of Schutz, Garfinkel, Glaser and Strauss, Lukacs and Mannheim. It also reflects, and is reflected in, feminist writings in other fields: see, for instance, Sandra Harding and Merrill B. Hintikka (eds), *Discovering Reality: feminist perspectives on epistemology, metaphysics, methodology, and philosophy of science* (Dordrecht, Reidel, 1983), and Evelyn Fox Keller, *Reflections on Gender and Science* (New Haven, Yale University Press, 1985).

3 The question of imposing contemporary feminist standards on women of other eras has been discussed and debated extensively by feminist historians. My own research is somewhat different, in that my research subjects, whose consciousness was formed in another era and by another political and professional culture, have in fact lived through the era of second-wave feminism and have incorporated and reacted to this feminism. For related discussion, see Carol Ascher, Louise DeSalvo, and Sara Ruddick (eds), *Between Women: biographers, novelists, critics, teachers and artists write about their work on women* (Boston, Beacon Press, 1984).

4 Lurking in my unconscious was probably a romanticized image of the reproduction of professional mothering.

5 For insightful discussion of the felt threat of differences among women, see Jane Flax, "The conflict between nurturance and autonomy in mother–daughter relationships and within feminism," *Feminist Studies*, 4 (1978), pp. 171–91; Krieger, *Mirror*; Valerie Miner and Helen Longino (eds), *Competition* (New York, The Feminist Press, 1987); Ascher, DeSalvo, and Ruddick, *Between Women*, and Hester Eisenstein and Alice Jardine (eds), *The Future of Difference* (Boston, G. K. Hall, 1980). Arlene Kaplan Daniels, "Self-deception and self-discovery in fieldwork," *Qualitative Sociology*, 6 (1983), pp. 195–214, makes a related point concerning the relations between the field researcher and her informants.

6 For an early suggestion that we pay attention to situations of gender-salience, see Barrie Thorne, "Gender . . . how is it best conceptualized?", paper presented to the 1978 Meetings of the American Sociological Association;

excerpted in Laurel Richardson and Verta Taylor (eds), *Feminist Frontiers* (Reading, Mass., Addison-Wesley, 1983), pp. 61–3.

7 Evidence for these claims about women's acceptance in the field is beyond the scope of this chapter. Briefly, I note that for most of the period since 1925 in England, participation has ranged between 30 percent and 50 percent, and at its current low is still over 25 percent. In Europe since 1930 it has ranged between 25 percent and 35 percent. In the United States, participation has been lowest, peaking during the 1940s and early 1950s at around 28 percent and declining since. However, when American analysts were asked recently to name the most important practitioners in their field over the past fifty years in the United States, three of the top seven were women: see Lewis Coser, *Refugee Scholars in America* (New Haven, Yale University Press, 1984), pp. 42–54; and women have been appointed to the prestigious status of training analyst in favorable disproportion to their numbers. See on this Chodorow "Varieties of leadership among early women psychoanalysts," in Leah Dickstein and Carol Nadelson (eds), *Women Physicians in Leadership Roles* (Washington, D.C., American Psychiatric Association Monograph, 1986). See also Chodorow, "Psychoanalysis and its early women practitioners," unpublished paper in English; published as "Der Beitrag der Frauen zur Psychoanalytischen Bewegung und Theorie," *Psyche*, 41 (1987) and in an earlier version as "Histoire et vie des premières femmes psychanalystes," *Psychotherapies*, 6 (1986).

8 During the early 1980s, I talked, in formally scheduled, very open-ended, interviews throughout the United States, in Great Britain, and in the Netherlands, to eighty people. Forty-four of these were women psychoanalysts trained in the 1920s through mid-1940s, the oldest born in 1894, the youngest in 1918, and most born between about 1900 and 1910. Eighteen were men of the same generations. Interviewees of these early generations have been members of the American, British or International Psychoanalytic Associations – in the United States, this means "Freudian" analysts; in England, Freudian, Kleinian, and "Independent." They have been lay and medical, and were born, trained, and have practiced – in a variety of combinations of mobility characteristic of their analytic generation – in the United States, England, Austria, Germany, Hungary, Czechoslovakia, the Netherlands, and elsewhere. About two-thirds of the women (and all the men) had married, and about one-half had children. Ten interviewees were sons, daughters, and one a granddaughter of early women psychoanalysts, eight of whom are themselves practicing analysts or therapists. Six were analysts of the next generations (for the most part in their fifties and trained around the mid-1950s) who had had close relationships with particular early women psychoanalysts or were particularly knowledgeable about the history of psychoanalysis. Two, finally, were women married to men of the early generation, and who participated in the interviews with their husbands. In addition, I have treated the research somewhat ethnographically, talking informally over the years with a number of other people – historians, analysts, relatives of early women analysts, staff of various analytic institutes, and so forth.

Since I began this research, there has emerged a veritable industry of biographies, autobiographies, or studies of early women psychoanalysts: Paul Roazen, *Helene Deutsch* (New York, Anchor, 1985); Marcia Westcott, *The Feminist Legacy of Karen Horney* (New Haven, Yale University Press, 1986); Susan Quinn, *A Mind of Her Own: The Life of Karen Horney* (New York, Summit Books, 1987); Perry Meisel and Walter Kendrick (eds), *Bloomsbury/ Freud: the letters of James and Alix Strachey 1924–1925* (New York, Basic Books, 1985); Celia Bertin, *Marie Bonaparte* (New York, Harcourt Brace Jovanovich, 1982); Phyllis Grosskurth, *Melanie Klein: her world and her work* (New York, Knopf, 1986); Muriel Gardiner, *Code Name "Mary": memoirs of an American woman in the Austrian underground* (New Haven, Yale University Press, 1983); Beulah Parker, *The Evolution of a Psychiatrist: memoirs of a woman doctor* (New Haven, Yale University Press, 1987); Aldo Carotenuto, *A Secret Symmetry: Sabina Spielrein between Jung and Freud* (New York, Pantheon, 1982); Raymond Dyer, *Her Father's Daughter: the work of Anna Freud* (New York, Jason Aronson, 1983); Uwe Henrik Peters, *Anna Freud: a life dedicated to children* (New York, Schocken Books, 1985); and Elizabeth Young-Breuhl, *Anna Freud: a biography* (New York, Summit Books, 1988). Paul E. Stepansky (ed.), *The Memoirs of Margaret S. Mahler* (New York, The Free Press, 1988), draws in part on my interview with Mahler.

9 Gender in the analytic situation has been a subject of interest since women first entered the field. Study of the transference toward women played a central role in the development of the psychology of femininity (see Freud, "Female sexuality," 1931, *The Standard Edition of the Complete Psychological Works of Sigmund Freud*, ed. James Strachey (London, The Hogarth Press and the Institute of Psychoanalysis), (hereafter *SE*), vol. 21, pp. 223–43). It has been in recent times a subject of lively debate; see, for example, Rebecca Goz, "Women patients and women therapists: some issues that come up in psychotherapy," *International Journal of Psychoanalytic Psychotherapy*, 2 (1973), pp. 298–319; Laila Karme, "The analysis of a male patient by a female analyst: the problem of the negative Oedipal transference," *International Journal of Psycho-Analysis*, 60 (1979), pp. 253–61; Phyllis Tyson, "The gender of the analyst," *Psychoanalytic Study of the Child*, 35 (1980), pp. 321–38; Ethel Person, "The erotic transference in women and men: differences and consequences," *Journal of the American Academy of Psychoanalysis*, 13 (1985), pp. 159–80.

10 See, for example, Judith Kestenberg, "Outside and inside, male and female," *Journal of the American Psychoanalytic Association*, 16:3 (1968), pp. 457–520: "The inner-genital phase," in D. Mendel (ed.), *Early Feminine Development: contemporary psychoanalytic views* (New York, Spectrum, 1980); "Maternity and paternity in the developmental context," *Psychiatric Clinics of North America*, 3:1 (1980), pp. 61–79; and other writings; Melanie Klein, "Early stages of the Oedipus conflict," in *Love, Guilt and Reparation*, 1928 (New York, Delta, 1975), and other writings; and Marie Langer, *Maternidad y Sexo: estudio psicoanalitico* (Buenos Aires, 1952).

11 We can remind ourselves here of Freud's claim, in his 1925 essay, "Some psychical consequences of the anatomical distinction between the sexes": "We must not allow ourselves to be deflected from such conclusions [about women's

inferior character traits] by the denials of the feminists, who are anxious to force us to regard the two sexes as completely equal in position and worth" (*SE*, vol. 19, p. 258).

12 There are of course major exceptions to this claim. Horney not only profoundly criticized Freud's theory of femininity; she did so by appealing to her own experience: "I, as a woman, ask in amazement, and what about motherhood?" ("The flight from womanhood," in *Feminine Psychology*, 1926 (New York, W. W. Norton, 1967), p. 60).

13 As other studies have shown, participation in a rebel movement, even if this movement may be sexually traditional or even sexist, can provide ways for women to change roles and transform their lives. Wini Breines, in "A review essay: Sara Evans' *Personal Politics*," *Feminist Studies*, 5 (1979), pp. 495–506, points out that this may be particularly true if the movement's practice draws on women's traditional strengths, and such seems to be the case for psychoanalysis, which requires listening, understanding, empathy, intuition, etc. I also pointed out above that for many of the early women psychoanalysts, psychoanalysis provided a theory that emphasized, rather than denied, women's sexuality and sexual desires.

14 Gender differences are of course mentioned in Freud's *Three Essays on the Theory of Sexuality* and in his other discussions of the Oedipus and castration complexes, but one can read these and simply accept their claims. Meisel and Kendrick (eds), *Bloomsbury/Freud*, provide one first-hand account of reactions to the theory of femininity. One gets a sense of irreverence and amusement on the part of the Stracheys and those around them, a playful attitude toward sexual theory and little sense that it must be seriously challenged (see, e.g., p. 152, Alix's discussion of Klein's theory of the female Oedipus complex and the girl's fear of castration: "Tho' many are puzzled as to how this threat can affect the little girl, who has nowt to castrate." Or, James to Alix, p. 196, about a meeting of the British Psychoanalytic Society "devoted exclusively to a question raised by Bryan upon whether some kind of excitation of the clitoris was not after all essential before a female could have an orgasm. . . The discussion was rather heated; but went round & round. And the extraordinary thing was that no one seemed to know what an orgasm was. Mrs Rivière asserted flatly that there was a vaginal orgasm & a clitoris orgasm. . . But the gentlemen of the party seemed not to agree with this.")

15 Zenia Odes Fliegel, "Half a century later: current status of Freud's controversial views on women," *Psychoanalytic Review*, 69 (1982), pp. 7–27.

16 Karen Horney, it must be remembered, held a biological theory of natural femininity, although her biological theory disagreed with Freud's, and although her early writings were also sensitive to cultural discrimination against women and to the unconscious childhood components in the Freudian views of women. See Horney, *Feminine Psychology*.

17 For further discussion of the issue of equal treatment, see Chodorow, "Varieties of leadership," and for a later generation of analysts, Eleanor Schuker, "Creative productivity in women analysts," *Journal of the American Academy of Psychoanalysis*, 13 (1985), pp. 51–75. For at least one example of a contemporary male attitude to some early women analysts, see Meisel and

Kendrick (eds), *Bloomsbury/Freud*, in which James repeatedly disparages as a group the women child analysts in London.

18 Freud, *New Introductory Lectures*, 1933, *SE*, vol. 22, p. 135.

19 Judith S. Kestenberg, "The three faces of femininity," *Psychoanalytic Review*, 67 (1980), pp. 313–35.

20 Still, both mothers and non-mothers did not accept what they saw as women having children and then virtually never parenting. In this context they expressed concern about how the demanding professions of today prevent women from taking pleasure in their children, because they have no time to spend with them. And they particularly faulted the organization of training and practice in their own specialties, medicine and psychiatry. These fields argue for the importance of extensive maternal care, but, by refusing part-time options and leaves, make it impossible for women residents and interns to mother.

21 In Vienna, where being a governess was a respectable women's profession, some younger analysts in training and nursery school teachers studying with Anna Freud took care of more established analysts' children.

22 See also Helene Deutsch, *Confrontations with Myself* (New York, W. W. Norton, 1973), who describes leaving her son with his father in Vienna for several months while she pursued analysis and further training in Berlin, and, for a related instance, see Meisel and Kendrick (eds), *Bloomsbury/Freud*, in which Alix Strachey reiterates the necessity of remaining apart from James for the sake of her personal analysis. I emphasize that I use these examples not to criticize the early women analysts for inadequate mothering or for maternal deprivation on a daily or long-term basis. My point is to stress the contrast between their behavior and sense of appropriate maternal care and subsequent psychoanalytically derived views that every child needs full-time maternal care for the first several years. I also point out that mothers expressed conflict about cases of longer separation, and that some of these were thought necessary because of refugee status and the stress of emigration.

23 Kay Trimberger, "Women in the old and new left: the evolution of a politics of personal life," *Feminist Studies*, 5 (1979), pp. 432–50, has suggested that the crucial differentiating feature between old left and new left feminist politics concerns the latter's assertion that the personal is political, and that domestic, rather than just public, structures of gender inequality and differentiation must be challenged and transformed. Barbara Epstein, "Feminism and the contemporary family," *Socialist Review*, 8 (1978), pp. 11–39, and Ellen DuBois, "The radicalism of the woman suffrage movement: notes toward the reconstruction of nineteenth-century feminism," *Feminist Studies*, 3 (1975), pp. 63–71, argue that nineteenth-century feminists ignored or opposed attempts to challenge domestic inequality and difference as they focussed on change in the public arena.

24 Readers who have commented on this chapter have been extremely puzzled by this claim that my interviewees did not think of the theoretical as personal, as they have assumed, not unreasonably, that the process of psychoanalysis is mainly about re-rendering the personal via psychoanalytic theory. I cannot speak directly for my interviewees on this point, but my sense in general is that

analysts think of the analytic process mainly in process terms: in terms of uncovering resistances, and making the unconscious conscious. It is not a question of matching up psychological contents with a theory of expected psychological contents. I would also say that today as well, the culture of psychoanalysis maintains a firm separation between practitioner and patient. In discussions, examples are never given in terms of the self, but only of patients: one has a "personal analysis," but one applies the theory to those one treats.

25 See also Brenda Webster, "Helene Deutsch: a new look," *Signs*, 10 (1985), pp. 553–71, who argues that the evidence we have from Helene Deutsch's published case accounts indicates that, rather than imposing her theories about women's biologically inevitable passivity, masochism, and narcissism on women patients, Deutsch worked hard to overcome these qualities both in these patients and in herself.

26 See Cynthia Epstein, *Woman's Place: options and limits in professional careers* (Berkeley, University of California Press, 1970), and Sherry Ortner, "The founding of the first Sherpa nunnery, and the problem of 'women' as an analytic category," in Vivian Petraka and Louise A. Tilly (eds), *Feminist Re-Visions: what has been and might be* (Ann Arbor, University of Michigan Women's Studies Program, 1983).

27 Schuker, "Creative productivity," suggests that women of the current generation may be very much influenced by expectations about appropriate feminine behavior and feminine role norms, and that traditional and conformist gender-role pressures on them may well be greater than on women in other fields. My own observations support this.

28 Jane Atkinson, "Anthropology" review essay, *Signs*, 8 (1982), p. 257. See also Cynthia Epstein, "Ideal roles and real roles, or the fallacy of the misplaced dichotomy," *Research in Social Stratification and Mobility*, 4 (1985), pp. 29–51.

29 For the strongest statement of this position, see Michelle Z. Rosaldo, "The use and abuse of anthropology: reflections on feminism and cross-cultural understanding," *Signs*, 5 (1980), pp. 389–417. See also Ortner, "Founding of the first Sherpa nunnery," and Ortner and Harriet Whitehead (eds), *Sexual Meanings: the cultural construction of gender and sexuality* (Cambridge, Cambridge University Press, 1981).

Index

Abel, Elizabeth, 220, 263
Adelman, Janet, 263
age and differences in gender
  personality, 25–6
agency
  repression and, 132–5
  sense of, in development of self,
  106–7
agency/communion opposition, 56
aggression, 186
  Freud on, 146
  in mother–child relationship, 85–6,
  92, 93–4
  see also assertive behavior;
  authoritarian–aggressive behavior
"all-powerful mother" in feminist
  writing, 80–2
Allport, Gordon, 254
Alpert, Judith L., 219
analysts, see psychoanalysts
Anshen, Ruth Nanda, 244
Anthony, Albert, 230, 236
Applegarth, Adrienne, 261
Arcana, Judith, 81, 95
Ariès, Philippe, 54
art
  Brown on, 121–2, 127, 137
  Marcuse on, 121–2
Ascher, Carol, 268
assertive behavior
  learning of, 29–30

see also aggression; authoritarian–
  aggressive behavior
Atjeh, 61, 62
Atkinson, Jane, 216, 267, 273
authoritarian–aggressive behavior, 24,
  28; see also aggression; assertive
  behavior

Bacon, Margaret, 24, 25, 26, 27
Bakan, David, 56, 229, 231, 232
Balbus, Isaac, 263
Bales, Robert, 234
Balint, Alice, 71, 104, 148, 221, 231,
  248, 249
Balint, Michael, 148, 157, 221, 241,
  249, 250, 252, 256
Barry, Herbert, 24, 25, 26, 27, 55
Bart, Pauline, 257
Basement, The (Millett), 86
Baum, Martha, 236
Beauvoir, Simone de, 33, 41
Beck, Evelyn T., 267
Belenky, Mary Field, 263
Bell, Anita, 260
Bem, Sanra Lipsitz, 267
Benedek, Therese, 91
Benedict, Ruth, 226
Benjamin, Jessica, 186, 240, 242, 244,
  248, 250, 253, 256, 262, 263, 264
Berger, Peter L., 234
Bergman, Annie, 254

Chiang's son, Chiang Ching Kuo (Jiang Jing Gwo), in power, much as the Koxinga family had done centuries before. There was no effective democratic opposition. Contacts with Mainland China were forbidden under penalty of imprisonment. The currency exchange rate stood at approximately NT$40 to U.S.$1.

However, the decade ended with a Taiwanese-born Kuomintang legislator, Lee Teng Hui (Li Deng Hwei), in power as president. Martial law was lifted. History books painting a negative picture of the Kuomintang appeared on the black market and then gradually as tacitly approved publications. These included translations of Sterling Seagraves' Chiang Kai Shek roast, *The Soong Dynasty*. Opposition members of the National Assembly from various grass roots parties could regularly be seen coming to blows (real fists!) with other members of the Legislative Council (*Yuan*). Open discussion of the *Er Er Ba* incident took place and the government apologized for its role. Legal contacts with Mainland China began, just in time to allow many of the ageing *Wai Sheng Ren* (who had come to Taiwan so many decades ago) to see once more their homeland and the families they had left behind. In addition, the New Taiwan Dollar stood at NT$25 to U.S.$1, a dramatic 60-percent increase.

The challenges of Taiwan in the 1990s are to reconcile its past with its future. Under 35 years of martial law, all kinds of things were allowed or ignored by the government, so long as the population was politically quiet. The urban environment grew without implemented planning. Pollution, both from transport and industry, renders much of the landscape an eyesore and the atmosphere a lung- burner. Corruption, though less rampant than in decades past, is still present. However, as the opposition becomes increasingly effective and begins to focus on present issues more than past wrongs, they will undoubtedly hammer out a plan for the nation.

The government is now much less sensitive about discussion of Mainland China events, politics, and relations, and the Taiwanese people discuss the future in all conceivable forums, from talk shows to coffee shop chats. A direct dial phone service is now allowed between China and Taiwan, and discussions are underway to improve the mail service. However, there are still no direct flights, unless you count the one-way 'direct flights' that are frequently highjacked from China to Taiwan. Highjackers, especially mutineer jet fighters from the Mainland China Airforce, used to be welcomed in Taiwan, being given vast sums of gold, a house, a commission in the Taiwan Airforce and even an arranged marriage! Now such activities are considered an embarrassing reminder of the discrepancy between the lives of the Taiwanese and their Mainland brethren. There is also a growing problem with illegal Mainland Chinese workers being smuggled into Taiwan and working for low wages. Many Taiwanese feel these people have contributed to the deterioration of local law and order. Given these facts, you can guess that everyday people's opinions about the relations between Mainland China and Taiwan will be varied. Before you enter into the fray and express your own views, it is best to get to understand the situation completely, as well as the politics of the person with whom you are talking. Even an educated opinion from a long-term resident can be misconstrued as imperialistically patronizing or unsympathetic. In discussions of politics, foreigners would do best to just listen and ask questions.

In conclusion, Taiwan is still a part of China which is not a part of China. It is still a freewheeling and exciting place to live and do business in. It still makes for a culturally rich experience. And, in many places and in many ways, it is still the *Ilha Formosa*!

–Chapter Two–

TOUCHDOWN TAIWAN

Historically, most visitors to Taiwan arrived by sea. Keelung in the north and Kaohsiung in the south are still visited by cruise ships and there is a regular ferry service from Okinawa to Keelung. But it is far more common for modern visitors to arrive by air. Taiwan can be reached with direct flights from most Asian capitals, as well as from New York, Los Angeles, San Francisco, Minneapolis, Seattle, Portland, Schiphol, Frankfurt, Johannesburg, and Zurich. Taiwan has two international carriers: China Airlines was established by the government (not to be confused with the Civil Aviation Administration of China, which is the airline of Mainland China) and EVA Air was more recently set up by the formidable Evergreen Shipping Group. Sadly, neither airline can boast a service to rival some of its other Asian competitors.

There are presently two international points of entry by air: Chiang Kai Shek Memorial International Airport in Taoyuan, about 45 minutes (traffic permitting) southwest of Taipei, and Kaohsiung International Airport at the southwestern tip of the island.

VISAS

For arrival from most countries, including the United States, you must have a valid visa in your passport before setting foot in Taiwan. Because of its unusual diplomatic status, most countries do not have Taiwan Republic of China consulates or embassies. Instead, Taiwan maintains special correspondence offices in many countries which effectively, but not officially, serve the same purpose as a consulate. In the United States, for example, it is called The Coordination Council for North American Affairs. Applications for a visa can be made by post or in person. If you are applying in person, allow a minimum of two working days for it to be processed, although the time varies from office to office.

Short-Term Visits

If you are going to Taiwan only once as a visitor and plan to stay no longer than six months, apply for a 60-day visitor visa. It is valid for a 60-day stay but can then be extended twice at police headquarters in Taiwan. If you plan to visit Taiwan more than once on your travels, make sure to request a multiple entry visitor visa. It will be easier to obtain a multiple entry visa if your Taiwan business contact sends you a letter or fax requesting you to come to Taiwan on business. With a visitor visa, you are allowed to study, tour, or engage in business, but not obtain employment without authorization, which is not easy to obtain.